THE GRANITE FARM LETTERS

THE Granite Farm LETTERS

The Civil War Correspondence of Edgeworth & Sallie Bird

Edited by John Rozier

Foreword by Theodore Rosengarten

THE UNIVERSITY OF GEORGIA PRESS
Athens and London

Paperback edition, 2012

Athens, Georgia 30602
www.ugapress.org

Designed by Warren Chappell
Set in 11 on 14 Fairfield by the Composing Room of Michigan

Printed digitally in the United States of America

The Library of Congress has cataloged the hardcover edition of this book as follows:

Bird, Edgeworth, 1825–1867.
The Granite farm letters : the Civil War correspondence of Edgeworth & Sallie Bird / edited by John Rozier ; foreword by Theodore Rosengarten.
xxxvi, 330 p., 9 p. of plates ; 25 cm.
Bibliography: p. [301]–307.
Includes index.
ISBN 0-8203-1042-5 (alk. paper)
1. Byrd family—Correspondence. 2. Baxter family—Correspondence. 3. Plantation owners—Georgia—Correspondence. 4. United States—History—Civil War, 1861–1865—Personal narratives, Confederate. 5. Georgia—History—Civil War, 1861–1865—Personal narratives. I. Rozier, John. II. Bird, Sallie, 1828–1910.
E487 .G76 1988
973.7'82—dc19 88-13978

Paperback ISBN-13: 978-0-8203-4108-8
ISBN-10: 0-8203-4108-8

British Library Cataloging-in-Publication Data available

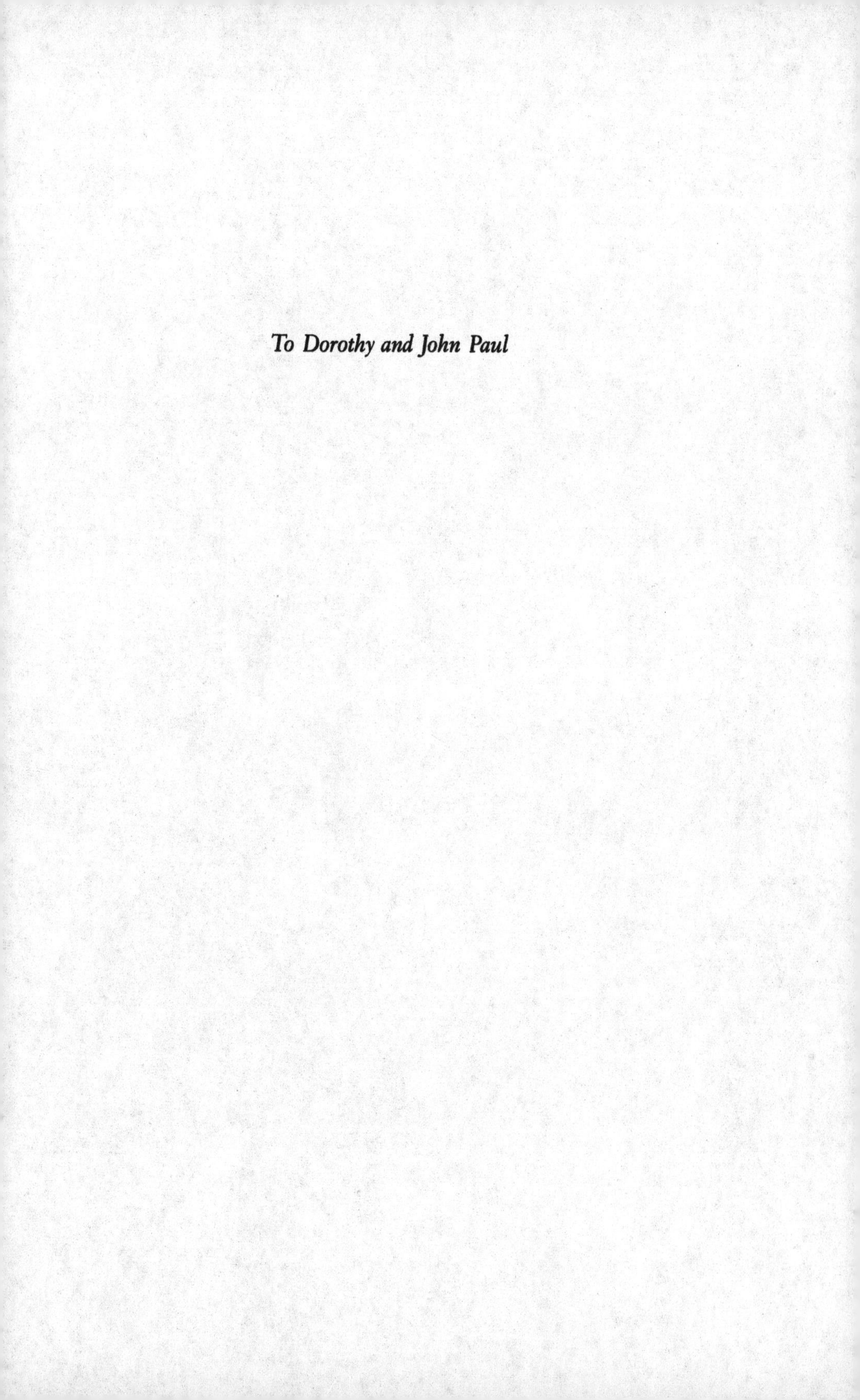

To Dorothy and John Paul

CONTENTS

FOREWORD

The great British historian Arnold J. Toynbee once remarked that had he grown up in the American South he would have known that *history* was something that "had happened to my people in my part of the world." He would have known that history was not something that happened only in faraway cities and countries, but in his own town, on his own farm, to his mother and father and their parents before them. Of course, there are histories of extraordinary times, like the era of the Civil War, and histories of private lives spent walking behind a mule and plow. In the more incisive records of the past, such as these wonderful *Granite Farm Letters*, we feel the keen points of intersection between what are commonly thought of as historical events and the mundane occurrences that pass for normal life.

Thus, Edgeworth Bird goes off to war and fights in Virginia in the shadow "of our glorious Stonewall," helps bury his friends at Gettysburg (from where he retreats without knowing who has won), and survives intact the burning hell of the Wilderness. His mind runs, however, on his family and plantation back home in Middle Georgia. He gives little space in his letters to his experiences under fire, though what he does say about his part in the fighting is frank and moving. His war news consists chiefly of rumors from other fronts, broad assertions about the tide of the conflict, hopeful forecasts that the reader knows are impossible, and reports on the deaths of his Georgia neighbors.

He reserves his sharpest focus for the goings-on at home. Far from trivializing his letters, these details of everyday life in the midst of war have a humanizing effect. When Edgeworth advises his wife Sallie how "to deliver" her flower garden from "the depredations of the rabbits," or instructs her with microscopic precision where to stack the cotton harvest, he defies the distance between Virginia and Georgia, and overwhelms the prospect of death with the substance of life. His attention to the price of peach brandy and to the exact measurement of logs for a new carriage house are the very expressions of his tenacity for living.

The source of this vitality is love: Edgeworth's love for his wife and his children, their love for each other and for him. *The Granite Farm Letters* tell a love story quite unlike anything else in the literature of the period. Perhaps the most remarkable aspect of the story is the tender age and emotional maturity of young Sallie, called Saida. The Birds' daughter is twelve years old in 1861, their son Wilson, eleven, at the start of the wartime correspondence. More than half the family letters here are addressed to Saida. "Love me always as I do you," Edgeworth beseeches his daughter. "I tell you what, my darling Papa," she writes shortly after he leaves for camp, "I begin to long for one sight of your face very much."

Edgeworth and Sallie take turns writing to Saida, recommending books for her to read and explaining why women should cultivate their intellectual gifts—a strikingly progressive idea for the era. Sallie leaves Granite Farm several times during the war when she goes to visit Edgeworth in camp. "I think it would kill me if my dear Edge were to suffer unaided and away from my tender love," she writes her daughter from Virginia. Young Saida must have the maturity and strength to hear not only her father's accounts of sickness and carnage, but her mother's testimonials of love for him—love not necessarily diverted from Saida, but in muted competition with her own. "I see your Father every day," Sallie writes Saida on a visit to Edgeworth early in the war, "and his Captain is so good. He lets him stay with me at night, so far, and all the men seem willing and glad to have him with me."

These intimacies come as a revelation, at a time when contemporary histories of the Old South emphasize the alienation of planters from their wives. The idea that sexual restraint, apart from efforts at having children, typified behavior inside the plantation Big House, will have to be reexamined.

The charm and power of *The Granite Farm Letters* owe as much to the beauty of their language as to their sentiments and ideas. The Birds and their friends were avid readers; they prized good conversations. The war turned the Birds into writers, and the more they wrote to each other the better writers they became. A high standard of composition was itself a theme of the letters. Sallie wrote Saida that Edgeworth had praised "very warmly" a recent letter from the girl. "Said it was a sweet, affectionate, well-written letter." Edgeworth, veiling his feelings in a fatherly tone, praised Saida's letters directly, noting "with increased pleasure your improvement in penmanship and style." She was growing up quickly, becoming the woman he wanted her to become.

Given their intelligence and education, their motives for writing, and the time they had to devote to the task, it may not be surprising that Sallie and Saida achieved a very high level of English. Edgeworth had less time to write, yet his prose is the most distinguished of the three.

Writing letters occupied Edgeworth's time out from fighting and camp duties. In the moments he found to write, he gathered up the threads of his personality and contrasted his individuality with the regiment and army that absorbed him into a gray mass. Clearly one of his major pleasures was to write instructions, verging on orders, to his wife, and through her to his overseer, at Granite Farm. When he told them which sheep to cull from the herd or ordered them to sell a recalcitrant slave he was saying to everyone, himself included: This is my world. Here is life as I know it and arrange it.

It was the life of a planter and slavemaster. Giving orders gave Edgeworth a purpose and a place. He was trained to do it; his concepts of justice and fairness were bound up with the Negro system of labor and the white system of command. He belonged to the wealthy class of planter families in Hancock County, Georgia, who owned more than forty slaves. The population of the county was two-thirds black, and the economy was based on cotton. Granite Farm was a cotton plantation, and a profitable and efficient one. The people who lived there produced large quantities of a staple crop for market and many of the goods that they used every day. John Rozier, editor of *The Granite Farm Letters,* describes the plantation as "a largely self-supporting community. At Granite Farm there were shoemakers, candle makers, soap makers, basket weavers, carpenters, persons with skills of all types." As the heads of this operation, Edgeworth and Sallie Bird "shared responsibility for running what amounted to a small village and factory." It could also be called a small kingdom, whose rewards were more than monetary. Their status gave the Birds access to the schools and households of the Southern elite. They were cousins of Eva Barrien Eve, second wife of Charles Colcock Jones, Jr., the Savannah lawyer and historian whose family's letters were published in Robert Manson Myers' *The Children of Pride*, hands down the most impressive family correspondence in American literature. The Birds had famous neighbors and kinfolk; they knew the leading agricultural thinkers and political figures of the day. Though these people are scarcely mentioned in *The Granite Farm Letters*, the influence of the social milieu is deeply felt in the tone and opinions of the Birds.

Apparently they had no second thoughts about slavery. They called their slaves "servants," who were to be looked after with an attitude of noblesse oblige. They never mention the threat of physical force that maintained the social order. The Birds believed in a society divided into castes—permanent divisions based on race *and* class. Thus, Saida has to be taught with whom she may sympathize, and what kind of people make suitable friends. It is "absolutely necessary" to Sallie that her son Wilson dress "according to station."

In this vision of life, Negroes, like horses, were born to work. Edgeworth took along his body servant to wait on him in the army. The image of an orderly camp laid out with rows of officers' tents in front and servants' tents in the rear seemed to confirm his feeling that God was blessing the Southern cause. He avowed that planters were the true friends of their slaves, that the Yankees wanted only to use the blacks as cannon fodder to put down the Southern rebellion. To shore up the loyalty of "our black people" at Granite Farm, he instructed his wife to stock an abundance of food. Sallie was not convinced that slavery would survive the war, no matter who won. Edgeworth tried to reassure her that if the rebellion succeeded, slavery "is established for centuries."

In this and other dreams he was disillusioned. He tried, for example, to put the best face on the fall of Atlanta. "All will yet be well," he comforted his wife. "Every advance is peril to Sherman; our head men will yet devise a plan to crush him." Very seldom would he allow himself to see the dark side of things. The Yankees' growing superiority in weaponry and their strategy of waging total war—shooting milk cows that belonged to civilians, for instance—began to shake his faith. More disturbing was the thought that the South might lose from lack of support. "There are so many within our circle who have never raised a finger in defense of home and family," he complained to Sallie, in a rare, endearing burst of anger.

Sallie and Saida Bird kept Edgeworth's letters and valued them above all things. The story of this defender of the old regime, this optimistic, cheerful man and the family he loved, has been brilliantly shaped by John Rozier. Rozier happens to be a native of Hancock County. The Bird letters, as he has edited them, are unfailingly appealing. They stimulate our imagination, inform us about hidden sides of life, and carry us, in fresh and spontaneous language, on adventures of love and war during the pivotal crisis in American history.

THEODORE ROSENGARTEN

ACKNOWLEDGMENTS

I OWE a tremendous debt to the staff of the Special Collections Department, University of Georgia Libraries, for their help, and to Dorothy Evans Rozier, my wife, who spent many hours there helping me decipher the faded letters of the Baxter-Bird-Smith family papers. It is hard to read the letters in that place without becoming part of the lives of Sallie and Edgeworth Bird. Sallie grew up nearby; many times the young couple walked paths visible from the library windows. Thomas E. Camden, head of the department, kindly gave me permission to use the collection. Larry Gulley and others of the staff were most helpful to me.

John M. Sheftall of Atlanta generously supplied photographs from his collection. Karen Orchard of the University of Georgia Press was an invaluable source of encouragement. Edward Weldon and his staff at the Georgia State Archives helped over a period of many months. The late Richard B. Harwell of Washington, Georgia, an authority on the South, gave sage advice. G. L. Dickens of Milledgeville provided descriptions and a sketch of the house at Granite Farm. Mrs. Ann Harris Marbury of Sparta was particularly helpful in letting me read and use her Harris family collection of nineteenth-century letters. I am grateful, too, to Miss Sarah F. Little of Sparta for use of the memoirs of Judge Frank L. Little; to the Department of Cultural Resources, Division of Archives and History, Raleigh, North Carolina; to the Texas State Library at Austin; to R. M. Willingham of Washington, Georgia, and to the late Miss Freda Lemon of New York City for preserving the Bird letters after the death of Edgeworth Smith.

I am indebted also to the Southern Historical Collection at the University of North Carolina for use of items from the papers of Samuel H. Wiley and Benjamin C. Yancey; to the Manuscripts Department of the Baker Library at Harvard Business School for Dun Reports; to Forrest Shivers, Hancock County historian; to Louis Rozier of Sparta; to Dr. Judson C. Ward and Mrs. Kent Leslie of Emory University; to the New York Public Library; to James Helminski, manuscripts processor at the Georgetown University Library; also to the Augusta-Richmond County Library; the Georgia Historical Society; the Military Archives Division of the National Archives; the Virginia State Library; Mrs. A. N. Bowers, Jr., of Athens, Georgia; Mrs. Frank A. Hollowbush of Savannah; Mrs. B. D. Aycock, reference librarian, Union Theological Seminary; Mrs. Merita Rozier, formerly at the Georgia State Archives; Mrs. Cynthia McClelland, archives assistant, Seeley G. Mudd Manuscript Library of Princeton University; the Library of Congress; John C. Edwards, university archivist, University of Georgia; the Eufaula Heritage Association, Eufaula, Alabama; the Enoch Pratt Free Library, Baltimore; Smythe Newsome of the *Wilkes Press*, Washington, Georgia, for permission to use material from the *History of Hancock County;* the South Carolina Department of Archives and History, and George Appel of Sandersville, Georgia, for information about the Shoals and the Bird foundries.

In the many months of checking names, tracking down people and places of the nineteenth century, the resourceful staff at Emory University's Robert W. Woodruff Library were a tremendous boon. Dr. Linda Matthews, head of Special Collections, and Mrs. Virginia Cain were always helpful, as were members of the reference staff, many of whom were called on over a period of several years.

And last, because he began work when the rest of us thought we had finished the task, Charles East of Baton Rouge, Louisiana, whose sharp editorial eye made me step lively.

To all of these and many more, I say thanks.

JOHN ROZIER

INTRODUCTION

SOME OF life's most interesting moments come by serendipity. The purest form of serendipity led me to the letters of Edgeworth and Sallie Bird at the University of Georgia. I was looking for something else and learned about them, little knowing that the writers and their children, Saida and Wilson, would become treasured friends over the years as my wife and I transcribed their words.

The letters, part of a larger collection of nearly four hundred family letters going back to the early 1800s, did not introduce the central characters until 1844, when Edgeworth Bird, then nineteen and a senior at Georgetown College (now Georgetown University) in Washington, wrote his mother in Hancock County, Georgia, urging that she and his father come to his impending graduation. An 1847 letter to Sallie Baxter in Athens, Georgia, from her Uncle Leroy Wiley in New York presented her for the first time and noted her plans to marry. Leroy Wiley, as diplomatic as he was rich (worth two million dollars, Dun's said), did not mention Edgeworth Bird by name. "You are aware the gentleman of your choice does not come within the range of my acquaintance," wrote Sallie's uncle. "The character of his family is unexceptionable, and having all confidence in your own discrimination and excellent judgment, I yield my approbation if it was your intention to ask it." The marriage took place the following year.

Letters between Edgeworth and Sallie Bird in the 1850s revealed the travels, social customs, favorite books and plays, and the entertainments of the Southern planter class. They told of the children, Sallie (Saida), born in December 1848, and Wilson (Bud), born in January 1850. The correspondence of the 1850s was fascinating in its details, but it was the Civil War (when Edgeworth Bird left Granite Farm to fight in Virginia) that turned the Bird family into increasingly more polished writers, and it was the Civil War that I finally decided upon as the starting point of this volume. This central core of letters, more than a hundred, beginning with the war and ending with the death of Edgeworth Bird in January 1867, unfolded the life of a planter family in wartime.

The letters are distinguished by the quality of the writing and the varied aspects of wartime life they covered. Sallie Bird's travels to the front in Virginia, her work in the hospitals of Richmond, and her observations of the fashions and social life of the times added a new dimension to her reporting from the plantation. Edgeworth Bird carefully observed the war throughout the Virginia campaigns to Gettysburg, Chickamauga, and beyond to the closing days. His description of the Confederate army moving north into Pennsylvania on the way to Gettysburg, for example, is almost novelistic in its sense of drama: "I told you of how beautiful and highly cultivated the country was, the splendid grass, clover and wheat fields; of how methodically we tramped them down along the turnpikes and grazed cattle and horses on them. From thence we passed on, changing our course towards Gettysburg. There we found the enemy posted in a terribly secure position. Now, I know, we should not have attacked him there on high hills and mountains, but we did so."

In another letter, written the following year, he tells his wife that "Early's main force has not crossed the Potomac yet, but his cavalry has taken a little turn. Pennsylvania has burning homesteads and desolate wives. The beautiful town of Chambersburg is a black, charred mass. There is retribution at last."

Even in the most difficult times Edgeworth Bird's letters reflected his basic sense of hope and optimism. As late as September 1864 he was writing Sallie not to be downhearted, "All will yet be well. . . . God will yet bless our cause." But there were moments when he faltered, and news of Sherman's march across Georgia inevitably took its toll. By then Sallie had come to Richmond to be with him, and in a letter written in late November 1864 he told Saida, "Mama is very much depressed, but bears it more bravely than you would imagine. . . . She can hold up under a great deal here, but would scarcely be able to witness the destruction of the place on which she has so liberally lavished both care and affection."

The letters do considerably more than report a war, they give a revealing view of the intimate life of a Southern planter family, breaking stereotypes about the relationship between planter couples and the way they brought up their children. The involvement of the Birds' daughter in the correspondence and the remarkable love displayed between Saida and her parents adds texture to the story as it unrolls. There are occasional glimpses, too, into the relations between these humane slaveowners and the slaves who made their way of life possible.

Toward the end Edgeworth and Sallie Bird view Georgia from Richmond as Sherman makes his devastating march, endangering Granite Farm where Mary Baxter, Sallie Bird's mother, describes the scene. Another view of the collapse comes from Saida as she flees Savannah.

The death of Edgeworth Bird removed one of the principal characters from the stage and brought a logical end to the story. Fewer than a third of the total collection of letters were eventually used, but they included all of the letters written during the Civil War period with the exception of one or two that had aged beyond deciphering.

Mary Baxter, widowed by the death of Thomas W. Baxter in the 1840s, became a principal figure in the family correspondence. Of Sallie Bird's six brothers, only two were major characters in the Civil War letters. Her youngest brother, Richard Baxter, then still living in his mother's home in Athens after graduating from the University of Georgia, wrote the initial wartime letter in the collection. Another of her younger brothers, John Springs Baxter, a physician in Macon, Georgia, also wrote from Virginia.

Although hundreds of relatives, friends, and acquaintances appear in the wartime correspondence, the letters for the most part are from Edgeworth and Sallie Bird and their daughter Saida, with an occasional letter from their son Wilson. Sallie Bird treasured her husband's letters, saving them from the days of his travels in the 1850s and on through the war. Since Edgeworth Bird was away in the war, his wife's letters to him unfortunately were not equally well kept. Her letters home from Virginia when she went there to join her husband in 1862 and again in 1864 were kept and treasured by Saida, and somehow the children's letters to their father were saved.

During the period of the Civil War correspondence, Hancock County was the focal point of the Bird family. Both Sallie Baxter and Edgeworth Bird had paternal grandfathers who, after fighting in the Revolutionary War, migrated south to frontier Georgia with thousands of other settlers from the older colonies. Sallie Baxter's parents grew up in Hancock County, eventually moving some sixty miles north to Athens, where the University of Georgia (then Franklin College) was struggling to bring learning to a rough new country. Sallie's girlhood was spent there. Edgeworth Bird's parents moved from Virginia in their early years and lived most of their adult lives in Hancock County.

The Baxters and the Birds came down to fresh new Georgia lands just being wrested away from the Indians. Many of the settlers around them were poor, uneducated, sometimes drunken backwoodsmen. The new lands in Piedmont Georgia were a long way from urban outposts such as Savannah and Charleston. However, change came rapidly with the invention of the cotton gin. By the 1820s, when Sallie Baxter and Edgeworth Bird were born, Middle Georgia had become the largest cotton-producing area in the world. Wealthy planters were replacing their crude cabins with comfortable, sometimes elegant homes. At Mt. Zion, a center for Presbyterians, the Wileys and Baxters helped build a church and an academy that became famous across the South.

The thousands of frontiersmen and small farmers who had flooded into Hancock County after the Revolution pushed on westward as more Indian lands were opened up. Large planters acquired their lands they left behind; by 1810 yeoman country had changed to planter country. Never after that time did antebellum Hancock County have more free citizens than slaves. The new planter elite controlled Middle Georgia and subsequently the state. They and their kin ran the cotton country stretching from Virginia to Texas.

As Steven M. Stowe noted in *Intimacy and Power in the Old South*, "The push and pull of Jacksonian America notwithstanding, the southern elite drew satisfaction from the hierarchy of all values and habits."

The Birds were very much aware of their place in the social order. When Sallie Bird took her young son Wilson with her to Virginia to be near her husband she wrote her daughter of her wish to have a new suit made for the boy. In the anonymous crowds of wartime Richmond she felt it was "absolutely necessary to dress according to station." Later in the letters, when the Birds' daughter Saida admired a fellow student at the Academy of the Visitation who was not of good family background, Sallie replied that Saida must be kind and polite to her but that intimacy was out of the question. "It is very sad, when you speak in such warm terms of her, but caste is absolutely necessary in society."

Sallie Bird grew up in Athens, where the struggling university was attracting some of the state's most notable families. Wealthy planters built columned mansions in the town, creating a community that John Muir, the naturalist, found to be the most attractive in the South when he came through on his journeys after the Civil War. Sallie was educated in the academies there, learning languages, music, literature, and the fundamentals of mathematics and English grammar. Society was stimulating and cosmopolitan for a town on the edge of Georgia's Cherokee Indian country. Athens appears frequently in the letters. It was the home of Sallie Bird's mother until her death. The Baxter home was a place of refuge for the Birds and their children in time of trouble.

The hub of Hancock County and of the county's planter society was Sparta, twenty-four miles to the east of Milledgeville, Georgia's antebellum capital. If Sparta was not Savannah, it was at least an unusual rural community, inhabited by people who wrote and read books, traveled widely, had extensive libraries and handsome homes. A few years after its founding in 1795, the town had a newspaper, a subscription library, and a female academy that boasted of possessing thirteen pianos.

Twelve miles east of Sparta was the Aviary, the original Bird family home built by Edgeworth Bird's grandfather, Colonel William Bird, Jr., who was the son and namesake of Pennsylvania's great ironmaster. After fighting in the Revolution, Colonel Bird moved to Alexandria, Virginia, where he took as his second wife Catherine Dalton, daughter of John Dalton, Revolutionary patriot and friend of George Washington. Colonel Bird's son Wilson (Edgeworth's father) was born in Alexandria.

In the 1790s Colonel Bird migrated to the Shoals of the Ogeechee, the river boundary between Hancock and Warren counties; he established mills there, including what may have been Georgia's first ironworks. The Bird home attracted numerous visitors including old Alexandria friends, the Caseys. Edgeworth Bird's mother, Frances Pamela Casey, was well acquainted with Alexandria society and with the Daltons and Birds; she and her brothers were the children of Dr. John Casey of Maryland and grew up nearby.

Perhaps the most interesting of Edgeworth Bird's cousins were the Yanceys, William Lowndes and Benjamin, children of his Aunt Caroline and her first husband, Benjamin Cudworth Yancey. After his death she married Nathan S. Beman, who had come from Middlebury College, Vermont, to Mt. Zion in Hancock County to run the new academy that he soon made famous. Beman eventually returned North to become a leading abolitionist. His stepson William Lowndes Yancey became a prominent spokesman for secession.

In his early years Edgeworth Bird lived with his parents in a handsome house in Sparta that is still standing. Young Edgeworth attended academies in Sparta and at thirteen enrolled as a preparatory student at Georgetown College, where he graduated in 1844 with an A.B. degree. Edgeworth loved Georgetown with a passion that never left him. His love for the school included love for the languages he had learned there, particularly Latin, and the books he had read there. He was Jeffersonian in his interests, which ranged from the gardens, fields, and stock of his plantation to the architecture of his house and on to politics, billiards, and foxhunting.

In the antebellum years the Birds lived near Dr. William Terrell, a leader in the Whig party of the state, a major planter and politician who created at the University of Georgia the first liberally endowed professorship of agriculture in the United States. Dr. Terrell's daughter Lucy was a lifelong friend of the Birds. Linton Stephens, brother of Alexander Stephens, who became vice-president of the Confederacy, lived only a short distance away. David Dickson, Georgia's premier planter, operated a plantation not far from Granite Farm, where Sallie and Edgeworth Bird spent their married lives. Richard Malcolm Johnston, well-known author and teacher of his time, was among their Hancock County friends. During the war years Johnston ran a school for boys at Rockby, not far from Granite Farm.

Other friends and acquaintances of the Birds included Robert Toombs, the former United States senator who served briefly in the Confederate cabinet as secretary of state; Alexander H. Stephens, vice-president of the Confederacy; John LeConte, scientist and educator who helped to develop the University of California into an outstanding university; Joseph LeConte, brother of John and a scientist and philosopher who became recognized as one of America's foremost intellectuals; and the Semmes family, among them Admiral Raphael Semmes.

The family ties of the Birds and Baxters extended across the South in every direction. Judge Eli H. Baxter, Sallie Bird's uncle, operated Cornucopia plantation near Mt. Zion and like David Dickson and other Georgia planters began to amass quantities of land in Texas where he became an important figure. In addition to the Yanceys in Alabama and Georgia, the Springs and Cunningham families in South Carolina were among Sallie and Edgeworth Bird's numerous kinsmen. Charles C. Jones, Jr., of Savannah, lawyer and historian whose family letters were the basis of *The Children of Pride*, married Edgeworth Bird's cousin Eva Berrien Eve, introducing another group of powerful and interesting connections.

The center of the young Bird family was always Granite Farm. It lay four miles east of Sparta on the road to the Shoals of the Ogeechee. The house at Granite Farm started out as a modest cottage and was never very elaborate, although Hancock historian Elizabeth Wiley Smith wrote that it was "one of the most beautiful in the county."

Miss Edith Guill, whose grandfather bought Granite Farm in 1884, described it as a large one-story dwelling with a huge attic. Wings had been added over the years. A square widow's walk on the roof provided a view for miles in every direction. The main part of the house consisted of four large rooms with a big center hall. A wide veranda enclosed this portion; the windows went to the floor, and when raised functioned as doors. One added wing included a master bedroom and a sitting room; another provided a large dining room and a serving pantry. As was the custom, the kitchen was separated from the house. A spring house nearby kept milk, butter, and fruits chilled. Granite Farm survived Sherman's destructive march in the late fall of 1864 but succumbed to fire in the 1920s.

By 1860 Hancock County, despite its relatively poor soil, had become a leader in the old cotton belt, "a modern mecca," as one visitor described it. Disturbed by eroded red hills and desolate farms, the county's leaders in 1837 established the Hancock Planters Club, the first successful planters club in the Georgia cotton belt. A small number of determined and enlightened men brought a change in farming methods that won attention throughout the region. In 1855 the Savannah *Journal and Courier* reported that "no county in Georgia can produce more intelligence and refinement than Hancock, and its agricultural skill and energy are preeminent." A visitor from South Carolina in 1860 commented on its thriving appearance, the variety of small local manufacturing establishments and the availability of more labor-saving machinery and better plows than any community in the South. Other visitors mentioned the mansions, the beautiful orchards, and the well-tended gardens.

The prosperity of the community rested on slavery. In 1860 two-thirds of the 12,000 inhabitants of Hancock County were slaves; fifty families owned more than forty slaves each, and six Hancock planters owned more than a hundred each. The Birds, father and son, between them owned forty-five. These large planters were for the most part enlightened, well-educated, and humane by the standard of the times. The planters sought self-sufficiency by raising food and grain for themselves, their slaves, and their animals. In addition, large sums of money came from the production of cotton, the cash crop which paid for fine libraries, college educations, and extensive travel.

Both Sallie and Edgeworth Bird had received good educations and their letters reflect the value they placed on disciplined minds. As Stowe pointed out in *Intimacy and Power in the Old South*, nineteenth-century letter writers, North and South, followed certain rituals. Letters were in fact an important ritual in Victorian marriages themselves. Edgeworth Bird held his wife to a high standard of letter writing. The only times he showed annoyance with Sallie were when her letters were infrequent, too short, or too hurriedly written. He once wrote her, "There is such an appearance of hurry about your letters. Surely you can find a quiet time occasionally and, darling, *surely* sometimes you feel as if you *loved* to write to me. Precious don't write that day you are so engaged or fatigued."

The Birds' interests and concerns expressed in their letters often centered on the education of their children, particularly their daughter Saida. Sallie Bird taught both of the children at home during their early years. As she grew older, Saida attended Lucy Cobb Institute in Athens and later, to the great joy of her father, the Academy of the Visitation in Washington. At times Wilson, or Bud as he was called, went to school in Athens, finally preparing for college at Richard Malcolm Johnston's school at Rockby.

Edgeworth Bird was particularly concerned about Saida. "A boy can go through life with ordinary help," he wrote his wife, "but for a woman to do her part well, she must have early training and advantages." In August 1864 Edgeworth Bird wrote Saida from Richmond to discuss her schooling at Lucy Cobb Institute. He insisted, he said, on a thorough knowledge of Latin and French. "I would have you neglect nothing, my child, that will contribute to giving you a vigorous and cultivated mind."

On another occasion he told his daughter that "an enlightened, well polished mind, well regulated and stored with useful knowledge, is the greatest blessing you could prepare for yourself." Her mother was more down-to-earth in her instructions. "*Obey strictly* your Grandma who has your interest *always* at heart," she wrote.

Many of the letters from both parents were devoted to education and instruction. Sallie wrote her daughter, "You can make a grand letter writer, I think, if you will practice it. But to do that, you must *read, read, read,* closely, indefatigably. . . . *Study, study*, oh my little one, study. An uncultivated woman is so unlovely."

When Saida went to the Academy of the Visitation after the war, her father regularly sent encouragement and advice. A Roman Catholic himself, he was delighted to have his daughter taught by the Catholic nuns. When Saida was in Savannah with her Catholic cousin Eva Berrien Jones, he wrote her, "I am very willing, my daughter, for Cousin Eva to make you a good Catholic. I feel my loneliness in that regard, tho' I have the most perfect assurance that my faith is right." His children had been brought up as Presbyterians by their mother, a source of underlying tension between husband and wife. Despite the strong bond between them, his deferral to her in the matter of the children's religious upbringing created a "chasm"—Edgeworth's word for it—that would remain to his death.

The Birds showed intense interest in the proper rearing of their children. They poured out advice on everything from what novels to read to how to sit in rockers (young ladies should avoid them). They were companions as well as teachers; Sallie Bird took Wilson with her on the first of her two stays in Virginia. At Granite Farm she taught both Saida and Wilson who, in addition, learned the arts of animal husbandry and fox-hunting from his father.

Jane Turner Censer, in her study *North Carolina Planters and Their Children, 1800–1860*, found patterns remarkably similar to those in the Bird family and similar to those among the elite in the North. The North Carolina families were, like the Birds, strongly child-centered. Contrary to some earlier scholarly findings, Censer found the Southern elite, at least in North Carolina, to be "fond, anxious parents" who sought "to shape their children's characters and to cultivate the youngsters' self-reliance and self-discipline." The parents that Censer studied "wished to be friends and confidants as well as figures of authority to their children." She could have written no more apt description of the attitudes of Edgeworth and Sallie Bird.

The concern for their children extended to their sexuality. Edgeworth Bird was anxious about his daughter as she began to mature. In August 1863 he wrote his wife, "I share with you a great anxiety on her entering the outer court of the temple of love. There are a thousand perils for the young and inexperienced of which they dream not, and it would indeed be culpable of a parent not to give such teaching as they may." Most often the parents directed their concerns to Saida, but occasionally the son was the object of their thoughts. "So far, he is a pretty good boy,"

Edgeworth wrote. "Knows how to groom colts and may one day be a pretty good horse jockey. This is all very well, a very excellent addition to a gentleman's education, but t'would indeed be sad were this all. No, let other aspirations now seize his mind."

Edgeworth and Sallie Bird did not fit any of the stereotypes about love in the Victorian marriage, nor those about planter families in this respect. Their correspondence was astonishingly frank and their love not only romantic but also openly and candidly physical. When Edgeworth Bird came home on leave early in 1864, Sallie Bird wrote Saida, "Oh, daughter, how happy I am to be in your precious Father's arms once more. . . . He is so good, so sweet, so beloved, and making me *so full of repose!* Oh, how I have sighed for *that!* My darling precious Edge! He is *so* happy himself."

Christmas 1861 Sallie gave Saida an ornament made of her hair, a typically Victorian thing to do. With it she wrote a message, "God grant that as this is the first, so it may be the last Christmas we shall spend away from him who is nominally and really the head of our home, the chief of our hearts. May Heaven bless him this day, with richest favors of its grace."

Sallie's image of her husband as the patriarchal head of her home extended in practice to a large family including distant cousins. The Birds were outstanding examples of the Southern planter's devotion to family. Stowe viewed such devotion as a celebration of the hierarchical values of love, authority, and moral belief. There was an element of selfishness and possessiveness in the love, with a hint that it could be stifling. Sallie Bird once wrote Saida, "And how much are you going to love me? I can never be satisfied with any but an eager, heartfelt love—such as I know my children do give me. And, ah, what does *not* a child owe a mother?"

Distant cousins felt obligations to each other. Edgeworth's two sisters died in infancy and he grew up an only child. Nonetheless, his mother's relatives were close. Philoclea Casey Eve and her daughter Eva Berrien Jones were frequent visitors to Granite Farm. Saida Bird felt free to stay with the Jones cousins in Savannah when she needed a place of refuge during the war. Eva Jones tutored her and took her to her mother's crowded home in Augusta when Savannah fell to Sherman. The Benjamin Yanceys several times welcomed Saida and Wilson into their Athens home when the tides of war made it necessary.

Toward the end of the war, in January 1865, Sallie Bird wrote her daughter, by that time with the Yanceys, "It is a very great pleasure to your Father and me to feel that you are never cast among strangers, but always among loving and kind relatives." Sallie's mother, Mary Baxter, opened her home to children, grandchildren, and their friends, often for extended stays of many months.

The elaborate extended family system with all of its obligations was made easier by the life of the plantation. The plantation was more than a farm; it was a largely self-supporting community. At Granite Farm there were shoemakers, candle makers, soap makers, basket weavers, carpenters, persons with skills of all types. Edgeworth and Sallie Bird shared the responsibility for running what amounted to a small village and a factory. In addition to teaching her children at home, Sallie Bird saw to the gardens, tended the sick, supervised the household servants, cut out garments for the servants as the seasons changed, sewed for her own household, and performed myriad other tasks.

During the war the burdens of the plantation mistress became even heavier. Edgeworth Bird wrote his daughter that her mother "has many trials and burdens at home; the care of a plantation is a new onus and not properly belonging to her department, but under necessity she assumes it bravely, and right ably and skillfully does she direct." Family friends like John DeWitt—and sometimes Wilson Bird, Edgeworth's father—were around to give advice, but it was Sallie's task to see that the farming continued smoothly. She negotiated with George Rhodes, the overseer, and tried to follow her husband's frequent instructions by mail. The marriage of Edgeworth and Sallie Bird was a partnership in every sense of the word.

With all of his intellectual interests and his knowledge of banks and railroad stocks, Edgeworth Bird was at heart a farmer. In the summer of 1864 he wrote Sallie from Virginia, "Were I only at home, I know we'd have a greater abundance on the plantation, for it has always been a very peculiar business and one that I love and, of course, I could conduct it more successfully." He went on to advise how to stop the cholera in the hogs and to get the sheep in good condition for the winter. "Make all the syrup you can," he urged, "and let us keep an abundance on hand to feed the negroes. Continue to plant such vegetables, after rain, as do well later in the season. Save all the peas you possibly can, and if we have rain, we'll do very well."

Early in the war Edgeworth Bird, away in Virginia, advised Sallie to "take pains to gain the affection of the negroes. You can attach them to you and govern them through their hearts better than any overseer can through fear." Slavery touched everything in the life of Hancock County, particularly the life of a planter. It even touched the life of a planter's son away at college. In an early letter (1844) Edgeworth Bird wrote his mother he was going to make his graduating speech at Georgetown on Daniel O'Connell, the Irish leader then fighting to repeal the union between Ireland and Britain. "I will have to defend the position he has taken with regard to American slavery," he said, "which I expect would not prove very agreeable to some of our Georgia slaveholders were they present. But in such a case, his position can be defended without advocating his principles."

Frances Casey Bird was quick to reply. "If your friend O'Connell, whom you intend to eulogize, could see how much care we take of our Slaves and how well they are treated, he would not have been so severe on slavery; our slaves are a thousand times better off than the poorer class of his countrymen." She complimented her son for choosing "a fine theme for a display of eloquence," but added, "You should have it clearly understood that you do not advocate his *Anti-Slavery Principles*. How can you as the son of a *Southern Slave Holding Planter* defend his proposition in that respect? You may have Southern hearers and . . . *you, yourself*, at some period not far distant, will own such property. Unless you have become an *abolitionist* and intend to free them you cannot consistantly defend him."

Always a humane and kindly master, Edgeworth Bird exemplified the highest type of slave owner; nonetheless he became a strong defender of the institution. When Georgia chose delegates to the state secession convention in January 1861 he ran as a secessionist and was defeated by a cooperationist ticket led by Linton Stephens. More Georgians voted for cooperationists than secessionists, yet 208 delegates voted for secession and only 89 against. Richard Malcolm Johnston, one of Edgeworth Bird's closest friends, had a strong sense of foreboding and refused to take part in the celebrations in Athens where he was teaching when Georgia seceded.

Many friends of the Birds were old-time Whigs, conservatives who feared the disruption of the union which their grandfathers had created. They led Hancock County into voting for Bell, a Unionist, in the 1860 presidential election, rather than for the Southern Democrat John C. Breckinridge. (Breckinridge was the candidate of Edgeworth Bird's cousin William Lowndes Yancey, who broke up the 1860 Democratic convention in Charleston and split the party.) Then they and the planter counties surrounding them in Middle Georgia voted with the cooperationists and against immediate secession. The vote brought about a rare alliance of wealthy planters with independent small farmers of the North Georgia hill country and the South Georgia wiregrass lands where there were few slaves. The planters of coastal Georgia and the residents of the larger cities such as Savannah voted to secede. Alarmed by Lincoln's election, Howell and Thomas R. R. Cobb of Athens abandoned their pro-Union positions and helped lead Athens and the state into secession.

Edgeworth and Sallie Bird accepted slavery as a fact of life, like water and air. They did not use the word "slave" in their letters, instead referring to their slaves as "the servants." The Birds viewed their slaves as part of the plantation family, sending greetings to individual ones and sometimes addressing all with a "howdy to the servants."

Apparently Edgeworth Bird continued to be a staunch supporter of slavery. In August 1863, after the Southern defeat at Gettysburg, he wrote Sallie, "Your conclusions about slavery are not a sure thing. I think it entirely dependent on the results of the rebellion. If we come out with flying colours, it is established for centuries."

It is intriguing to speculate on what Sallie Bird had said in her letter to him—one of her letters that did not survive. What conclusions about slavery had she reached? We must also wonder whether she went along with her husband in his seeming defense of the institution, or whether she held a different view. If there was a division of opinion on the subject, it never surfaces in these letters. As to slavery, the master of Granite Farm proved to be a poor prophet.

The Baxter-Bird-Smith Family Papers, as they are now called, did not come into the collections of the University of Georgia Libraries until 1982. I learned of their existence earlier while working on another book. When the letters were finally acquired and cataloged, I went to Athens to inspect them and began the five-year task of transcribing the correspondence and identifying the many persons mentioned. The letters had been saved by Sallie Bird after she left Georgia to make her home in Baltimore; they had been passed down to her daughter Saida, and finally to Saida's only son, Edgeworth Smith, who entrusted them to the care of a friend, Freda Lemon.

My original intention was to begin this collection with the 1844 exchange of letters between Edgeworth Bird and his mother and to include the letter that Sallie's Uncle Leroy Wiley wrote her before her marriage, as well as the letters Edgeworth wrote Sallie from Washington, New York, and Louisville in the 1850s. However, I eventually decided that the coming of the war in 1861 was a more logical starting point. I would have preferred that the first letter had been written by Edgeworth Bird, but Richard Baxter's letter to his sister on the eve of his departure for Virginia seemed to be, chronologically, the correct note to introduce the war.

As the story reveals itself, there are moments when we wish that more of the Bird correspondence, especially more of the letters that Sallie Bird wrote to her husband, had survived. We can only be grateful that we have as much as we have. Given the times in which the letters were written, the richness of the collection seems nothing short of amazing.

All of the letters brought together here except five are from the Baxter-Bird-Smith Family Papers. Those five were included because I felt for one reason or another they complemented the letters written by the Birds and the Baxters. Three were written by Sallie Bird herself—one of these to Sarah Yancey and the other two to Elizabeth Harris. I have also included a letter from Edgeworth Bird's friend Samuel H. Wiley, who served with him in Virginia, and one from Cornelia Ann Soullard that gives us a glimpse of wartime Savannah. As I have already mentioned, all but one or two of the family letters from 1861 to the death of Edgeworth Bird in 1867 were included.

In editing these letters I made no attempt to speak for Sallie or Edgeworth Bird or for their children. They speak too eloquently for themselves. I came to know them, to suffer with them and rejoice with them. In transcribing the letters I did introduce commas and sometimes periods in the interest of clarity and readability, and I took the liberty of paragraphing. Occasionally I deleted formulaic phrases or phrases (and in some cases sentences) that were repetitious; in every instance the deletion has been noted by an ellipsis. Otherwise the letters appear as they were written. I made no effort to correct spelling or grammar.

Brackets were used to indicate where words or sentences were illegible or pages were missing. In the notes, where the state is omitted in reference to places the reader may assume the location is Georgia except for major cities or where the context makes the location obvious.

Much of the appeal the letters had for me is that they unfolded the story of a single Georgia family during the most extraordinary times in their history, and that through their letters Edgeworth and Sallie Bird and their children were able to reveal themselves to me—something, I should add, that is not true of all, perhaps not even many, such collections. The fact that the center of their world was Hancock County, the county in which I grew up, and that many of the families mentioned were families I had some association with, made them especially interesting to me.

It is of course the war that gives these letters much of their significance. In one sense this book is the narrative of a planter family's progress from optimism to despair and defeat and on to the uncertain new world that lay ahead of them. Moreover, the letters are important not only as wartime letters but as the family correspondence they are, and for what we see of that family from a number of perspectives. They are the letters of parents writing to children and of children writing to parents, and also letters written by or to grandparents. They are letters that reveal a great deal about family relationships of this particular class in this particular place and at this particular time—the plantation South of the 1860s. They upset notions that we may have had about what such relationships were; what the concerns and values of the planter elite were; what they expected of their children; what they brought to their marriages; about how they—and perhaps by inference we—might respond, given these circumstances.

The letters would not be as engaging as they are, nor as useful to scholars as they surely must be, had Sallie Bird remained at Granite Farm. Her two visits to Virginia to be near her husband, first in 1862 and again in 1864–65, give the correspondence another aspect, and, indeed made it possible for her to write the letters to her children and her mother and others.

As I have already suggested, the fact of the Birds' kinship with or association with prominent figures of the period such as William Lowndes Yancey, Robert Toombs, and Alexander H. Stephens and his brother Linton adds to the significance of the letters. Edgeworth and Sallie Bird's relationships with such persons were casual and intimate.

But beyond this, and perhaps most importantly, the writers command our attention with distinctive prose and intense feeling. "How complete a void your absence makes in my heart," Edgeworth once wrote Sallie. "There's no Georgia or anything where you are not."

The Birds and the Baxters

Edgeworth Bird
(William Edgeworth Bird, b. 1825)

his wife

Sallie Bird
(Sarah C. J. Baxter, b. 1828)

their children

Sallie (Saida) Bird
(Sarah Baxter Bird, b. 1848)

Wilson (Bud) Bird
(Wilson Dalton Bird, b. 1850,
later Wilson Edgeworth Bird)

Mary Pamela (Leila) Bird
(1853–1857)

Edgeworth Bird's father

Wilson Bird
(James Wilson Bird, b. 1787,
m. Frances Pamela Casey, 1791–1855)

Sallie Bird's mother

Mary Baxter
(Mary Wiley, b. 1798,
m. Thomas W. Baxter, 1787–1844)

Edgeworth Bird had two sisters who died in infancy

Sallie Bird's brothers and sisters

Andrew Baxter, b. 1820 (m. Martha Williams)
Mary Baxter, b. 1822 (m. John J. Gresham)
Thomas Baxter, b. 1825 (m. Ellen Scott)
John Springs Baxter, b. 1833 (m. Caroline Tracy)
Eli Leroy (Link) Baxter, b. 1834 (m. Mary Burton)
Edwin Gilmer Baxter, b. 1838 (m. Julia Hardwick)
Richard Bolling Baxter, b. 1840 (m. 1st Kate Rucker, 2nd Mrs. Leila Mabbet)

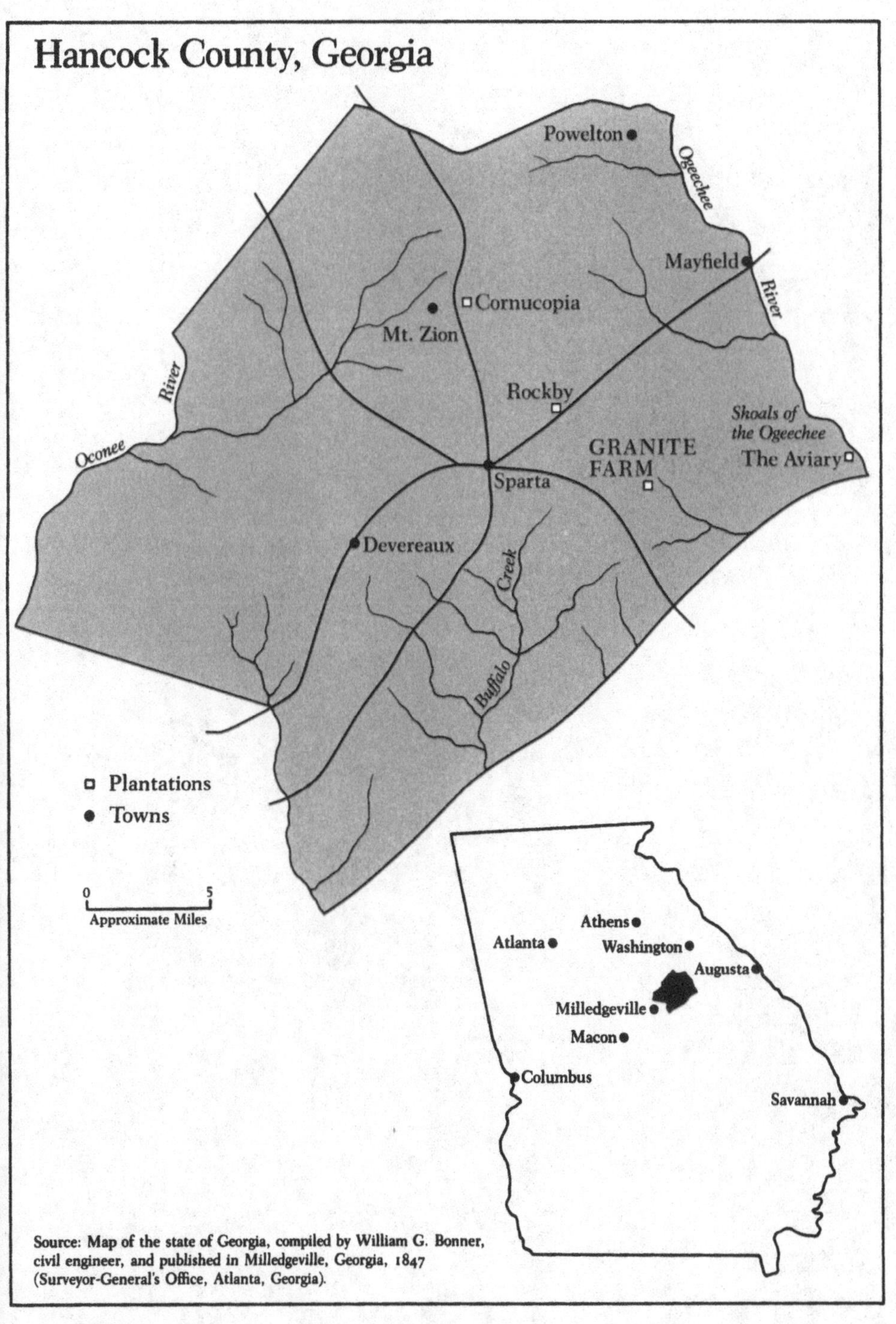

Source: Map of the state of Georgia, compiled by William G. Bonner, civil engineer, and published in Milledgeville, Georgia, 1847 (Surveyor-General's Office, Atlanta, Georgia).

ONE

Off to War

"I have talked for the South,
and now I am going to fight for her."

RICHARD BAXTER

THE 1850s had been a prosperous time in the cotton country, but there were dark shadows as attacks on slavery became increasingly bitter. John Brown's raid at Harpers Ferry in October 1859, followed by the election of Abraham Lincoln as president the next year, frightened and angered many Southerners.

Edgeworth Bird was among those who felt it was time to leave the Union. When Governor Joseph E. Brown called for a convention to meet in January 1861 to decide Georgia's course, Bird ran with two other Hancock County planters as avowed secessionists. However, the county's conservative old-line Whigs were not ready to separate from the Union their grandfathers had created, and Bird's secessionist ticket was defeated.

But the passions building up were too great to be contained. The secessionists won at the convention; Georgia left the Union. The secession of the Southern states was quickly followed by the Montgomery convention to establish the Confederacy, the election of Jefferson Davis as provisional president, the firing on Fort Sumter 12 April, and Lincoln's call for troops 15 April. The war had started. By mid-July Edgeworth Bird was off with the Hancock Volunteers to Atlanta and on to fight in the Virginia campaigns.

Richard Baxter to Sallie Bird

Athens, 22 May 1861

Dear Sister,

Mother arrived home safely yesterday morning. She wrote to you today. There is no news here, in fact there are no people here. Athens is indeed deserted.[1] I merely write to bid you all good bye. I shall leave here Saturday for Virginia to join the "Athens Guards."[2] I have received a letter from them wishing me to join and it was the very thing I wished. I have talked for the South, and now I am going to fight for her.

Tell Mr. Bird[3] that, ere long, I hope to shake hands with him on the soil of the "Old Dominion." Of this fact rest assured, dear Sister, that I will never disgrace the family and I will never disgrace my state. No stain shall ever mar the beauty of her escutcheon through me. I dread the parting from Mother. Oh, I know it will be hard to part with her for perhaps the last time. It is terrible to think of leaving you all, but I am not afraid to go. With a firm reliance upon God, who will ever be on the side of right, I am willing to cast myself into the gap and dare to "Nobly stem tyrannic pride or nobly die a second glorious part that my country may be free."

If war should commence, I must share the fortunes of war. If then, after a battle, you should see my name among those who "sleep the sleep that knows no waking," shed one tear for the memory of him who, with all his faults, with all his roughness, still loved you like a brother. Kiss all the children for me and tell them, should I return, I will tell them some *wonderful tales* of a soldier's life.[4]

I will write to you from Virginia sometimes. And now I close, bidding you all an affectionate farewell. Yours truly, R. B. Baxter

P.S. I must thank you for the butter and the wine. The former, I still say, as I always did, is the best, by far, I ever tasted. Mother sends love to all. RBB

1. Athens, a town of four thousand inhabitants in 1860, provided all northeast Georgia with freight and mail. Rail and telegraph lines linked it to the main line of the Georgia Railroad at Union Point. Three volunteer fire companies, a police force with an elected marshal, and three military companies served the town, which had forty stores, two banks, a building and loan association, three insurance companies, and three cotton factories. Athens was the home of the University of Georgia, then called Franklin College. Kenneth Coleman, *Confederate Athens* (Athens, Ga., 1967), 2–6.

2. The Athens Guards (Company K, Third Georgia) left for Virginia 29 April 1861. Organized in 1854, they were a special favorite, marching on ceremonial occasions in blue coats with red trim, white trousers, and red and white plumes. When they left for war, the Oconee Cavalry, Hope Fire Company, and a large crowd of citizens accompanied them, waving hats and handkerchiefs and cheering loudly. The railroad cars were decorated with flowers. John F. Stegeman, *These Men She Gave: Civil War Diary of Athens, Georgia* (Athens, Ga., 1964), 25.

3. Edgeworth Bird, Sallie's husband.

4. Richard Baxter, Sallie Bird's youngest brother, had graduated from the University of Georgia the year before. After being wounded at Sharpsburg, Md., Baxter was transferred to Edgeworth Bird's company. Captured in January 1864, he marched out in the last squad to leave Rock Island, Ill., prison in 1865. He married Kate Rucker of Athens that year, and for a time lived at Granite Farm, later moving to Sparta, where his home still stood in 1988. Elizabeth Wiley Smith, *The History of Hancock County, Ga.*, 2 vols. (Washington, Ga., 1974), 2:70–71.

Sallie Bird to Sallie (Saida) Bird

Atlanta, Thursday, July 1861

My dear Sallie,

I received your sweet letter this morning, and be assured, dear child, it gave us great pleasure. Your father and I, with another person *very* dear to you and to us all, read the letter together. Guess who that was? Why, your dear Grandma.[1] She came up Tuesday night and was here this morning at the reading of your letter. Her dear kind heart could not permit papa to go away without seeing him, and bidding him goodbye. Besides, she wanted to comfort me in my great trial.

She left this morning for Macon. She felt that being so near to your dear Uncle John,[2] she must go on to see him and express our sympathy in his awful bereavement. I have read a letter which gives many particulars of your dear Aunt Carrie's illness and death. She was resigned to God's will; declared that she loved her savior and was willing to trust all to him. She regretted that she had not publicly shown her love for him by joining the church. But I will tell you all when I return.

I see your Father every day and his Captain is so good. He lets him stay with me at night, so far, and all the men seem willing and glad to have him with me. I trust, darling, I shall bear this bitter sorrow better for being with him this long. He is so dear, so good, so true, that it will be indeed a desolate home without him, but let us pray, night and day, to our Heavenly Father to shield and bless him, to hold him in the hollow of his hand, to restore him to us in unbroken health. He praised your letter very warmly. Said it was a sweet, affectionate, well-written letter, and shewed him what a warm heart his dear little daughter had. His eyes filled with tears when he read it.

We, your Cousin Sarah,[3] Grandma, and I, went to the camp yesterday afternoon. My visit gave me pleasure. They all looked so cheerful, so contented. They cheered me when I went around their tents. Your Father is very much beloved by the men, I find. Dear Cousin Sam[4] was well and looked well. His heart seemed very full when we first met him, but he soon became cheerful and talked with us. Mother wanted to see him, and I too, so we got one of his men to call him. They pointed him out to us, down at a branch washing his hands, or a handkerchief. He came up and Mother had a talk with him.

Mother and I, you may be sure, have wept many bitter tears for our own beloved Carrie. She was a woman of rare loveliness, of great intellect, and exquisite refinement. I trust, dear child, you will never forget her. Cherish and love her memory. Be earnest in your endeavor to imitate her. She was so gentle, so pure, so lovely, that my heart aches and bleeds at the remembrance that so much of beauty and loveliness has gone down to the grave. But we shall see her again, if we live as one ought.

I hope Aunt Eliza[5] is improving. Your letter was very satisfactory, daughter. You told us many things we wanted to hear. I thank your Cousin Sallie[6] for her kind care of you. I felt perfectly easy on that score. They all deeply regret and deplore that I did not bring you, but we thought it best not to bring you both. Wilson's[7] hair has been cut very short this morning by the barber. He is delighted. I have been out this morning. We carried your Grandma to the depot and then I went to get medicines for Papa, to take him, and gloves, etc., etc.

Tom Latimer[8] is elected captain of the Confederate Guards; John Culver,[9] 1st Lieut.; Mark Latimer,[10] 2d, and Dan Connel,[11] 3d. I see a great many acquaintances here. Mrs. Maxwell[12] is at Mrs. Gardiner's.[13] Mrs. Haygood's[14] little baby is dead. Poor little thing. I found it could not live the day we came up. I told Cousin Sam of my seeing you all after he left. He will write his letters by me to Sallie. Col. Thomas[15] is making his regiment a speech this morning. Linton Stephens[16] is Lieut. Col. and Capt. McIntosh[17] is major; Dr. Alfriend,[18] surgeon.

I met Mrs. Burt[19] of Mt. Zion on the street this morning. Cousin Ben's[20] company will be off in about two weeks. I saw Terrell Crawford[21] this morning. The regiment he is in rendezvous at Decatur, 7 miles below here. He is captain of his company. He tells me Col. Cantey's[22] Regt. in which Edgar Dawson[23] is major will soon be ordered off, he thinks. Dear Lucie's[24] trial will then come. Your dear Father sends you his love and a hundred kisses. Says he loves his little daughter a hundred fold more than he can tell, that he will pray God to bless her and make her a good child. He says I must tell you to remember your promise to him.

The mess of which Cousin Sam is a member think the world of him. They say he is so handy and helps them along so much, is *such* a clean fellow. Wilbur Little[25] is a very fine fellow. He messes with Cousin S.[26] He is just as merry as a cricket. Ben Alfriend[27] is suffering with a boil. I sent him some plaster to take with him and use. Your Grandma will be back in time to go down the road with me after Papa leaves. I don't know when that will be, but in a very few days. It is a hard effort to control myself, but it was best that I came. I feel better for it; so does your Father.

Wilson and Hamilton[28] are very happy together. Mary Lou[29] is a dear, sweet little girl. She has a Cousin Anne Harris with her. They both wish for you. Caro[30] sends you many loving messages and often wishes for you. They are all just as kind to me as they can possibly be, and I love Cousin Sarah very much. She, too, is in distress, for Cousin Ben's turn to go will soon come. I want you to kiss Birdie and Bessie for me, and your Cousin Mary's[31] dear little baby. Give a great deal of love to all, especially to Sallie,[32] who is taking, I know, such kind care of my little daughter. Cousin Sam is as well as he can be. I am going to see them again this afternoon. Goodbye, my dear child. I hope you pray for us every night. Try to love God and to *believe* that he will answer your prayers for your dear Father. God bless you, your devoted Mother S. C. Bird.

1. Mary Wiley Baxter of Athens.

2. John Springs Baxter, a Macon physician and Sallie Bird's brother. His wife Carrie (Caroline Tracy) had recently died, leaving an infant son named Tracy. A few months after this letter was written, Dr. Baxter enlisted as a private in Company B, Second Battalion, Georgia Infantry. He was appointed assistant surgeon 2 May 1862, was later made surgeon of the Forty-sixth Regiment, and served through the war, surrendering at Greensboro, N.C., 26 April 1865.

3. Sarah Hamilton Yancey, wife of Benjamin C. Yancey. Yancey's mother was Edgeworth Bird's aunt. Augustus Longstreet Hull, *Annals of Athens, Georgia, 1801–1901* (Athens, Ga., 1906), 453, 483.

4. Cousin Sam was Samuel Harris Wiley of Hancock County, often mentioned in Edgeworth Bird's letters. Wiley joined Company E, Fifteenth Regiment (Hancock Volunteers), 15 July 1861, and served throughout the war. He kept a diary briefly, noting that the Hancock Volunteers left Sparta July 15, arriving in Atlanta July 16 where they put up tents and arranged messes. The next day they elected officers: T. W. Thomas, colonel; Linton Stephens, lieutenant colonel; W. McIntosh, major; [Atticus] Haygood, chaplain; and E. W. Alfriend, surgeon. On Sunday, July 21, they struck their tents and left for Lynchburg, Va., by rail, not reaching there until the following Friday. There they first heard of the Confederate victory at the Battle of Manassas and saw four Yankee prisoners. Their regiment was mustered into the services of the Confederate States 1 August. Samuel H. Wiley Papers, Southern Historical Col-

lection, Library of the University of North Carolina at Chapel Hill.

5. Eliza DeWitt Wiley, wife of Edwin Wiley and mother of Samuel H. Wiley and Elizabeth Wiley Harris. Born in Connecticut, Eliza Wiley lies in the Mt. Zion Cemetery among the New Englanders who brought learning to the Georgia frontier.

6. Cousin Sallie was Sarah Elizabeth Carnes, the wife of Samuel H. Wiley.

7. Wilson (Bud) Bird, Saida's brother.

8. Thomas H. Latimer, elected captain, Company K, Fifteenth Regiment, 15 July 1861, resigned 1 Nov. 1861. Lillian Henderson, comp., *Roster of the Confederate Soldiers of Georgia, 1861–65*, 6 vols. (Atlanta, 1955–62), 2:473.

9. John Culver, son of Hardy C. Culver, founder of the Hancock County village of Culverton. Thomas H. Latimer resigned as captain, and Culver was promoted to that position, serving in Virginia and Maryland campaigns until 1863, when ill health forced him to resign. After recovery, he reentered the army as special escort to Major General G. W. Smith. After Reconstruction he served in the Georgia House and Senate, and was chairman of the Hancock County Board of Revenues, 1876–1905. Smith, *History of Hancock County,* 2:21.

10. Mark Latimer was elected captain when John Culver resigned. Severely wounded at the Battle of Chickamauga in September 1863, he was retired until March 1865, when he was assigned to duty with Lieutenant Colonel Wallace, inspector of Georgia's Fourth Congressional District. "No soldier was more gallant than he," Ivy Duggan wrote in the Sparta *Times and Planter.* "When I was sick, scarcely able to walk, Mark Latimer carried my gun for me." Ivy Duggan Papers, Special Collections, Robert W. Woodruff Library, Emory University.

11. Dan Connel, listed in the *Georgia Roster,* 2:473, as Daniel Connell, Jr. Connel was elected second lieutenant 20 July 1862, first lieutenant 11 May 1863, and captain 17 Nov. 1864. He surrendered at Appomattox 9 April 1865 while commanding his company. Ivy Duggan wrote: "The soldiers say 'Old Dan is always there.' He was never at the hospital and came home only twice during the war, when wounded and when his father died." Ivy Duggan Papers, Emory University.

12. Possibly Sarah Maxwell, wife of J. E. Maxwell, Athens planter.

13. Mrs. Gardiner is not identified.

14. Mrs. Haygood, the wife of Atticus G. Haygood, who later became president of Emory College and a Methodist bishop. The Haygoods lost their infant son Paul shortly before Sallie Bird's letter. Haygood was en route to Virginia as chaplain of the Fifteenth Georgia Regiment. The regimental colonel, Judge Thomas W. Thomas, was a man "of powerful intellect but uncultured and without religious inclination." Nonetheless, he gave Haygood the chance to preach to "three thousand of the best men in Georgia" by assembling them on a hot Sunday afternoon under the oaks at Manassas Junction. The sermon made Haygood famous; he was twenty-two at the time. Elam Franklin Dempsey, *Atticus Green Haygood* (Nashville, Tenn., 1939), 76–77. Harold W. Mann, *Atticus*

Greene Haygood: Methodist Bishop, Editor and Educator (Athens, Ga., 1965), 34, 38, 40, 45, 49.

15. Thomas W. Thomas, colonel, Fifteenth Regiment, Georgia Voluntary Infantry, 15 July 1861; resigned, disability, 26 March 1862. *Georgia Roster,* 2:408. Mary Ann Cobb wrote from Athens to Howell Cobb, December 1861, "What is the cause of Judge Thomas and Mr. Linton Stephens coming home? Disaffection toward the president?" Kenneth Coleman, *Athens, 1861–65,* 33.

16. Linton Hodges Stephens, half brother of Alexander H. Stephens, vice-president of the Confederacy. A lawyer, Linton Stephens served in the Georgia House and Senate and was the youngest man to sit on the Supreme Court of Georgia when appointed in 1859. He and Alexander Stephens unsuccessfully worked against immediate secession at the Georgia convention in 1861. Despite his opposition to secession, he helped raise a company of volunteers and went with them to Virginia, but soon returned home because of ill health. He represented Hancock County in the Georgia House for the rest of the war. Kenneth Coleman and Charles Stephen Gurr, eds., *Dictionary of Georgia Biography,* 2 vols. (Athens, Ga., 1983), 2:925–26.

17. William M. McIntosh became a major 15 July 1861. Elected lieutenant colonel 21 Dec. 1861 and colonel 29 March 1862, he was killed at Garnett's Farm, Va., 27 June 1862. *Georgia Roster,* 2:408.

18. Dr. Edward W. Alfriend was appointed surgeon 15 July 1861 and resigned for disability in May or July 1862. *Georgia Roster,* 2:409.

19. Henry L. Burt was a physician in Hancock County, according to the 1860 census. His wife was a music teacher.

20. Benjamin C. Yancey was a major in Cobb's Legion, later the Ninth Georgia Cavalry.

21. Captain Joel Terrell Crawford was a nephew of Mrs. William Terrell of Sparta. He was wounded at Cold Harbor, Va., 27 June 1862, and died of pneumonia in December of that year. *Georgia Roster,* 2:301.

22. Possibly Colonel James Cantey of the Fifteenth Alabama Infantry, who was promoted to brigadier general following his victory at Cross Keys, Va., 8 June 1862.

23. Edgar Gilmer Dawson of Columbus, Ga., who married Lucy Terrell of Sparta. Dawson later organized an artillery company named for Dr. William Terrell, his father-in-law.

24. Lucy Terrell Dawson.

25. Jacob Wilbur Fisk Little, recently graduated from Auburn, came to Sparta to join Company E, Fifteenth Georgia Regiment, with his brother Frank. He later served in the Twentieth Georgia in a company commanded by his brother Ransom, with whom he walked home to Georgia from Appomattox. From the papers of Judge Franklin Lightfoot Little, collection of Miss Sarah F. Little, Sparta, Ga.

26. Samuel H. Wiley.

27. Benjamin A. Alfriend enlisted in Company E, Fifteenth Georgia Regiment, 15 July 1861. See *History of Hancock County,* 1:136.

28. Hamilton Yancey, son of Benjamin C. Yancey and his second wife, Sarah Hamilton.

29. Mary Lou Yancey, daughter of Benjamin C. Yancey and Sarah Hamilton.

30. Caro was Caroline Bird Yancey, the daughter of Benjamin Yancey and his first wife, Laura M. Hines.

31. Mary Carnes Wiley, wife of William Wiley, who was listed as a schoolmaster, age twenty-three, in the 1850 census. Their children were Eliza DeWitt, James Jones, Mary Julia, and Hallie. Birdie and Bessie were Sarah Bird and Mary Elizabeth, daughters of Samuel H. and Sarah Carnes Wiley.

32. Sarah Carnes Wiley.

Sallie (Saida) Bird to Edgeworth Bird

Sparta, 4 August 1861

My dear, dear Papa,

I wrote you a long letter last week by Mr. Alfriend,[1] and, as I have a good chance again, I thought I would write you again by Mr. Henry Culver[2] and make it a little longer than my first letter. Grandpa[3] spent last Thursday with us; he rode over the corn with Mr. Edwards[4] and they both thought it was fine. Mr. Edwards thinks it is the finest crop you ever had. Did you know that Uncle Richard's regiment (the 3rd) had been ordered to Manassas?[5] I tell you of it because I thought you might not know it, and, so you might hunt Uncle Richard up when he gets there. We had a nice rain at Granite Farm yesterday evening and one in the morning. It is raining just enough now at Grandpa's[6] to make the rain run in the gutters.

Yesterday was the barbacue and the negroes seemed to enjoy it finely and ate with a *real* good will. I wish you could have been there, my darling Papa. I forgot in my last letter to tell you what Uncle John sent me by Mamma; it was a beautiful little perfume casket, and had been Dear Aunt Carrie's[7] and she used it every day, which made me value it all the more. Cousin Sallie[8] is here and is going home with us tomorrow evening. Mrs. Whitehead[9] staid with us last week. Bud and I study our lessons all the time, when any body comes to see Mamma. Mr. Smith[10] preached here this morning and is preaching again this evening, but it rained so we could not go. Mamma received your letter from Manassas this morning, dear Papa.

Tomorrow there is a meeting at Mrs. Turner's[11] for the purpose of rolling bandages for the Soldiers. Mama and Cousin Sallie are going if nothing prevents. Mama has cut a good many things out of the papers to send you and among them is a peice that I send you, a letter to the *Louisville Journal* in poetry. I tell you what it is—smart—as you will see when you read it. Robert Wiley[12] was right sick last night; indeed, we had to send for the doctor. The doctor is here now, and he says he is better this morning, but *don't tell* Cousin Sam as it might make him uneasy about nothing.

It looks very gloomy this morning, and I fear that it will rain this evening so that we can't get home.

Mamma gave your address to Mr. Whitehead[13] yesterday and he says that he is going to write to you in a few days and so does Dr. Will Alfriend,[14] I believe. Lieut. Henry Culver is here now on a visit to Mamma and Cousin Sallie; they are talking of you and Cousin Sammy and he is going to say goodbye now, for I don't expect that we will see him again. Auntie and Minnie and the boys have gone to Athens.[15] How I do wish I was there, and I hope I will be soon. Don't Mamma write you nice long letters? I wish I could get such. I hope I will get a *little* letter, anyhow, from you before long, dear Papa.

Mrs. Morrell[16] has not got home yet, though she is expected home every day from Atlanta. Now, my darling Papa, I have written you a right long letter for me, and, as you see, my hand is getting a little tired and I will bring my letter to a close and I do wish you would write me a *little* letter. Jule Alfriend[17] got a letter from her father. Tell Sam[18] howdy for me, and his wife says she is going to write to him. All send their love to you, and for me, dearest Papa, I do not know what to say. I think of you every hour in the day. I wish I could go on with Mr. Culver to see you, but I must close now and with much love to all. I'm more than ever your affectionate little daughter. Sallie

P.S. As Cousin Sallie has just received Cousin Sam's letter, you can tell him of it.

1. Benjamin A. Alfriend, a member of Edgeworth Bird's company.

2. Henry Harris Culver, second lieutenant 15 July 1861, Company E, Fifteenth

Georgia Regiment; elected first lieutenant 13 May 1862. Culver was wounded in the right shoulder and permanently disabled at Second Manassas, 30 Aug. 1862, and resigned because of disability 7 Sept. 1863. *Georgia Roster,* 2:442.

3. Wilson Bird (1787–1868).

4. James B. Edwards, sixty at the time of the 1860 census.

5. Richard Baxter's company went to Portsmouth, Va., rather than to Manassas.

6. The Bird home in Sparta at the southwest corner of Broad and Rabun streets.

7. Mrs. John Baxter of Macon, who had recently died.

8. Mrs. Samuel H. Wiley.

9. Julia Burnet Whitehead, daughter of James H. Burnet and Sarah C. Tucker and wife of Charles E. Whitehead. Myers, *Children of Pride,* 1727–28. She grew up in the Burnet home on Rabun Street (also called Maiden Lane) in Sparta, later the home of Sallie Bird's brother, Richard Baxter. See Mrs. Terrell Moore, "The Baxter-Wiley House," Sparta *Ishmaelite,* 8 Aug. 1963.

10. R. C. Smith, Presbyterian minister.

11. Mrs. Thomas Mickleberry Turner was born Sarah Rawls Clayton at Sylvan Hill, Hancock County. Her husband was a planter. She lived most of her married life in Sparta at the Sayre-Turner-Shivers house on the southeast corner of Rabun and Broad streets opposite the home of Wilson Bird. The handsome house still stood in 1988. See National Society of Colonial Dames, *Early Georgia Portraits* (Athens, Ga., 1975), 233; Mrs. Terrell Moore, "The Sayre, Turner, Shivers House," Sparta *Ishmaelite,* 21 March 1963.

12. Robert Wiley, son of Samuel H. Wiley and Sarah Carnes Wiley. He later became a beloved family physician in Hancock County.

13. Charles E. Whitehead, son of Dr. James Whitehead and Ruth Berrien of Burke County, Ga., lived in Baker County prior to the Civil War; he was in the insurance business in Atlanta after the war. In 1878 he returned to Sparta, where he died. *Children of Pride,* 1727–28.

14. Dr. William H. Alfriend, one of three Alfriend brothers who were physicians in Hancock County, and the father of another, Dudley Alfriend. Smith, *History of Hancock County,* 2:60.

15. Mrs. John J. Gresham of Macon and her children. Mary Gresham was Sallie Baxter Bird's sister.

16. Mrs. Morrell is unidentified.

17. Jule Alfriend was the daughter of Dr. Edward W. Alfriend, who was the surgeon with Edgeworth Bird's company.

18. Edgeworth Bird's body servant.

Wilson (Bud) Bird to Edgeworth Bird

Sparta, 5 August 1861

My dear Papa,

The evening that you left us Mrs. Morrell came to see Mamma and staid till night, and said that you asked her to come. Grandpa went down to Granite Farm while we were in Atlanta. The crop is fine and the corn especially. The coons have commenced eating it considerably on the low ground. Mr. Minton and Henry[1] went hunting and killed four coons. Edith has got a calf. I have not seen it but Eliza says it is a very nice one.

Emma's colt is getting *finer* every day and as for my colt, she gets *finer, prettier* and *gentler* every day. All the stock is coming on finely. The young roan bull of Mr. Tom Hunt[2] is the prettiest creature I ever saw, well formed in every way. Mr. Edwards has staid with us ever since [illegible] went home. Grandpa has been riding Brownie ever since the Princess went away, and he says that he likes him better than he ever did before.

Mr. Edwards goes home with us every night and comes to town in the morning. Yesterday Mr. Edwards went down to see Mr. David Dickson[3] and says he is suffering for rain very much. We are beginning to want rain ourselves, but it is cloudy now, and I think it will rain today or tomorrow. We have had elegant watermellons, and I think, if it would rain, they would be splendid for a month to come because the vines are covered with young ones.

We came up this morning to the Society and are going back this evening, and Mr. Edwards is going back with us. Araminter[4] is here and she says that Cousin Edge Eve[5] is gone to the war and is a lieutenant in the Company that he is in. Mr. and Mrs. Whitehead went down to our house Thursday evening and came up Saturday evening. The 3rd Ga. regt. has been ordered to Manasas, and I hope that you will see Uncle Richard and Cousin George Hayes.[6] We had the barbacue last Saturday and a great many of Grandpa's hands were down there. Cousin Sally Wiley is going home with us this evening and is going to stay till next Sunday. Tell Jimmy Alfriend[7] that I have not had a chance to tell Miss Betty Brown what he said in Atlanta, but I will as soon as I have a chance. Tell Cousin Sam that Eddy and Bob send him their love. I am your ever loving and kind son,

Wilson D. Bird[8]

1. William Minton, the overseer, was listed as a farm laborer in the 1860 census. Henry was a slave at Granite Farm.

2. Thomas Mitchell Hunt, son of James Hunt. Smith, *History of Hancock County,* 2:91.

3. David Dickson, called "the prince of farmers," was a neighbor of Edgeworth

Bird. Dickson owned fifteen thousand acres of land in Hancock and Washington counties. He devised a scientific system of crop rotation and developed his own fertilizer for cotton. See *Dictionary of Georgia Biography,* 1:258–59.

4. Araminter is unidentified.

5. Francis Edgeworth Eve, grandson of Edgeworth Bird's uncle John Casey, had a temporary lieutenancy in the Fourth North Carolina Regiment at the time. Myers, *Children of Pride,* 764, 1123, 1281. Many years later his kinsman described him as "a dashing trooper, born soldier and sabreur." Charles Edgeworth Jones, *Georgia in the War: 1861–65* (Augusta, Ga., 1909), 46.

6. George E. Hayes, son of Sallie Bird's aunt Sarah Ann Hayes, left Athens for Virginia 29 April 1861 as an ensign with the Athens Guards. Hull, *Annals of Athens,* 226–28.

7. James W. Alfriend, son of Dr. Hamlin Alfriend. *History of Hancock County,* 2:60. He was a sergeant with Company E (Hancock Volunteers), Fifteenth Georgia Regiment. *Georgia Roster,* 2:448.

8. Edgeworth Bird has written at the top of his son's letter, "Bud's efforts are tremendous but Eddie and Bob being with him, he don't write very well. My darling, I love you so dearly." Wilson was born in 1850.

Edgeworth Bird to Sallie (Saida) Bird

Camp Walker [Va.], 19 August 1861

I wrote and mailed today a letter for Mama and another for Grandpa, My dear little daughter, and now comes your turn. You asked for just a "little letter" and you shall have it, tho' somewhat longer than your emphasis called for. Three or four days elapsed without my writing Mama, a very unusual thing nowadays, and I hasten to supply the deficiency by sending home two today and this to you tomorrow.

I was suddenly detailed as officer of the guard to supply the place of a sick man, and its duties, being very fatiguing from loss of sleep, unfitted me for anything but sleep. I have received from you two very nice letters, and one wee little fellow from Bud. I gave Bud's letter to Jimmy Alfriend to read, and his reply on returning it was, "I tell you, Mr. Bird, he writes a mighty nice letter for a little fellow." He has written Wilson and will look anxiously for an answer. He must be sure and answer it. Tell him to take his time, and write nicely, and a good deal about Jimmy's sweethearts. And you, dear daughter, remember I always show both your letters to a half dozen gentlemen, and you both should take a great deal of care in composition and neat penmanship.

All the news I might send you is contained in the letters to Mama and grandpa and would be stale the third reading. Just while I am writing General Toombs[1] has arrived. He makes his headquarters at our camp and his tent will be pitched in 30 yards of our tent. So we shall breathe the atmosphere of distinguished men, and its being Brigade Headquarters will make our encampment quite a place of resort. Just here darkness came on and I stopped rite after supper. I perceive General Toombs has erected his tents about a hundred yards from us in the open field. He has four much larger than Mama saw us have in Atlanta, all placed in a row and a servants tent in the rear. They present a very nice appearance. The view from a neighboring hill is very beautiful. I wish my little daughter could stand with me and see it. One can see for many miles in every direction and, at one *coup d'oeuil,* no less than the encampments of sixteen Regiments. Think what a splendid view they present, how the white canvass glistens in the sunlight; and the white tents far away in the distance, dotting the green plain of pines, seem like great white swans on some far off water. But we've had no sun of late, nothing but rain, rain and slush. We've a good many sick from colds and measles in the regiment tho' few in our two companies.

Now for a word of advice. Do you love your Papa so far away from you? Will you and Wilson value his commendation if God spares him to come to you again? If so, then try and perform all your duties honestly and faithfully. Be *truthful,* never attempt deceit in *anything* or with *anybody.* Never neglect to say your prayers, and study your lessons well that you may never fret Mama, who makes so many sacrifices for you both. Obey your grandpa as you would me. Do these things, my little ones, and God will bless you both, as I do. Kiss Mama for me a hundred times, and Bud and grandpa. Bud shall have a letter soon. Remember me to Jule Alfriend and any of your little friends that care for it. Howdye to all the servants. Tell Allen[2] I think of him often, and how anxious he was to come with me. Sam[3] sends a heap of love to them and is in good health. Mama must write to me very often, bless her darling heart. Her letters are half my life nowadays and I must have them every day or so. So far I am in good health. Goodbye, my darling child. Remember, be pure in heart and truthful. Your affectionate Father, Wm. E. Bird

Postscript: Kindest regards to Mr. Edwards and love him for his kindness to you all. Bud must take good care of the colts and the nice Kentucky calves.

1. Robert Toombs (1810–1885), a former congressman and United States senator, served the Confederacy briefly as secretary of state, resigning to accept command of a brigade in the Army of Virginia in July 1861. Always in opposition to President Jefferson Davis's defensive strategy, Toombs resigned again in 1862 after his brigade fought well at Sharpsburg and he did not receive a promotion. He was opposed to Davis's policies on conscription and suspension of the writ of habeas corpus, joining Confederate Vice-President Alexander H. Stephens and Georgia's Governor Joseph E. Brown in attacks on Davis. *Dictionary of Georgia Biography,* 2:988–91.

2. Allen was one of the slaves at Granite Farm.

3. Sam, a family slave, accompanied Edgeworth Bird to the war as a body servant.

Sallie (Saida) Bird to Edgeworth Bird

Athens, 25 August 1861

My dearest, dearest Papa,

Here we are at last in dear old Athens, and without you for the first time since I can remember, and I tell you what, it makes us all feel rather bad to be up here without you. Then, we haven't even the pleasure of thinking we shall see your dear face when we go home but must always think of you as a soldier in Virginia, and, what is worse than all, in danger. Now I must tell you about our trip up here. The roads were so heavy that we did not get to Double Wells in time for the five o'clock train, and so we had to stay at that "delightful" place all night, and a nice time we had of it. We got up the next morning and took the three o'clock train to Union Point; there we got off and took the Athens branch, and after that we got on pretty well.

This morning I went to Sunday School and I intend going as long as I stay here. I am going to Mrs. Richardson's[1] class as Minnie is in it. Uncle John and his baby are still here and Tracy[2] is so sweet. When he wants to go anywhere he points out the way with his little finger, and laughs and crows so prettily when you tell him you are going to take him to Laura or Uncle John. I think he is very much like our dear Aunt Carrie indeed. I heard yesterday that Mr. Johnston was going to take charge of the Lucy Cobb Institute.[3] I do not know whether it is true or not, for, you know, he has changed his mind several times between staying or going back to Hancock.

Mrs. Dr. Jones,[4] Miss Mary Williams that was, came to see Mamma the other day and they both seemed so glad to see each other. Mamma says that Mrs. Jones cried when she met her. She says she is coming to see Mamma often. I tell you what, my darling Papa, I begin to long for one sight of your face very much, and I do hope that if Mamma ever goes on to see you that she will take me with her, for it would do me so much good to see you once more. Minnie and Alice[5] send their love to you, and they both say they are going to write to you, but I do not know whether they will as they are both lazy about writing, as bad as Wilson. Judy[6] sends her love to you and Sam. Tell him howdy for me. I must close now, and do not forget, my dearest Papa, that I am a hundred times more than ever, your affectionate little daughter, Sallie B. Bird

[Sallie's mother fills up the remaining space.]

Don't let an ambrotypist[7] come into your camp and go off without having your picture taken for me. My dearest *do* send it home by John Berry.[8] I am crazy for it. Can't you have it taken at Manassas? I should think there was a man in your country there who could take your picture for me. I do want it *so* much. Mary Jones (my old friend Mary Williams) came to see me yesterday. It was quite an agitating meeting to both of us. We had not met in eight years. We had both seen sorrow and wept many tears in that time. She seemed so glad to see me, that it refreshed my soul. And now, dearest, goodbye. I found this blank page on Sallie's sheet and could not let it go, so I've filled it up. Tell Cousin Sam I shall keep his letters always. I sent it to Sallie to read. I've given John the needlework I had finished, but I am going to make some more. If I don't get letters often, I'll get down sick, so take care, precious, write often to your own true loving Birdie

1. Mrs. Elizabeth B. Richardson, forty-five, is listed in the 1860 Athens census.

2. Tracy, the son of Dr. John Baxter, left motherless by the death of Carrie Tracy Baxter.

3. Lucy Cobb Institute, Athens school for girls established in 1858. Richard Malcolm Johnston had been teaching at Franklin College (the University of Georgia). The author and educator returned to Hancock County and opened a school for young men at Rockby, his plantation near Sparta.

4. Mary Williams, daughter of William Williams and Rebecca Harvey, married William Louis Jones. Hull, *Annals of Athens*, 477–78.

5. Alice, the daughter of Andrew Baxter, Sallie Bird's oldest brother, was a first cousin of young Sallie Bird. Minnie was the daughter of Mary Baxter Gresham.

6. Judy, a slave at Granite Farm, was the wife of Sam, Edgeworth Bird's body servant.

7. Ambrotypist, a photographer.

8. John Berry, Company E, Eighth Georgia Regiment, was discharged for wounds 2 August 1861. *Georgia Roster*, 6:948.

Edgeworth Bird to Sallie Bird in Athens

Camp Walker near Manassas [Va.] 2 September 1861

I think there have gone two or three letters to Sparta for you, Dearest Sal, tho' I can't exactly say, not knowing how many of my recent letters may have reached you. . . . I somewhat feared you would have some uneasiness as I mentioned that we all expected . . . we were about to make a forward movement. Indeed, within and during the last three days, we've had quite a "hurlybalew" (How'll that orthography answer?) or much ado about nothing. We had orders to cook rations for three days and be prepared to march at a moment's notice. Of course, we were soon ready.

The next morning the Brigade was reviewed, balance of day all quiet as ordinary. Next morning Brigade was again reviewed by Genl. Toombs in person. Immediately after dinner order was given to strike tents and load the wagons; there is a large four horse affair of this kind to each Company. We did so, and just as we were in readiness to leave, a reverse order came to unload wagons and pitch tents again. The boys were completely deceived, tho' I expected the march would scarcely be taken up for several good reasons, and that the true object was to ascertain how much plunder our wagons would carry.

We are still located at Camp Walker. But I must tell you about the Review. It was the handsomest sight I've yet seen. There are five regiments which constitute the Toombs Brigade, viz. 1st Georgia Regt. of Volunteers, 15th Geo. Rgt., Col. Semmes's[1] Rgt., Col. H. Cobb's[2] Rgt., and Col. Smith's[3] Regiment. The three first are the only ones present at this place and in the Review. We marched from our Camp to the field chosen, and found the other two drawn up in Line of Battle. We immediately took our position, dressing on the same line. Col. Paul Semmes seemed to be in command and issued all the orders. As soon as all was arranged, we were reviewed by Genl. Toombs who rode slowly over the front of our line, attended by his staff, and back gain by the rear. There were very many horsemen in the Field, the staff officers of the different Regiments, all dressed in uniform and galloping from point, bearing orders.

Then, darlie, there was one of the finest bands I ever listened to, to the music of which we did all our marching. From being reviewed in line, we were wheeled into column and marched about the field and immediately by Genl. Toombs and staff. To a looker on, it must have been a splendid spectacle.

Dearest, so far we've chatted of pleasant matters. I would not draw a faithful picture of my present life were I not to present both sides. We have a great deal of sickness amongst our men. A few days ago there were 300 on the morning report. Yesterday, about one hundred were sent to Georgia Hospital at Richmond, many of them obstinate fever cases, some measles and recovering, others just taken. Amongst the latter was Mark Latimer.[4] His father went with him. I do not think he'll be sick much. Tom, German and Ben Culver[5] were sent, the latter very ill. Dr. Alfriend[6] went with them, also Mr. Haygood.[7] I think we've been very fortunate, considering the number of the sick. There have been only two deaths among the whites and, night before last, two among the negroes. I am pained to say, one of them was Jeff Lawrence's[8] boy, Green, a severe loss to the pocket, but worse than that, he was much attached to his master and valued accordingly.

Like you in Georgia, we've had weeks of rain, and when not raining, ugly, damp days; and I believe from this springs most of our sickness. We're camped in a grove of trees, and I've no doubt vegetable decomposition goes on very rapidly. Then, darling, Jack Smith[9] has been lying close to death's door. I never saw anyone give way more completely to depression of mind before he left the camp. I rejoice to say that for two days there has been a decidedly favourable change, and I understand he'll certainly recover without any untoward change. Precious, my darlie, are you not grateful that your old fellow has not been taken down? Do you not feel recompensed for the numberless prayers you've offered up for him? Are you not encouraged to persevere in a simple reliance on a strength greater than our own and to feel assured that we will always receive what is properly asked for?

Levoisier[10] has just learned through a letter, received today by Frank Little,[11] from Mrs. Sasnett,[12] that his wife is no better. Mrs. S. says that she believes Mrs. L. is going into a decline. He is very much distressed about it and has asked me to go to Col. Thomas and see if there be a chance for him to get a furlough such length of time as the perilous condition of his wife's health may require. I fear myself there is much cause for fear from what you've written, and Frank's letters have more than confirmed it. She has not been able to write for some time. Henry Harris[13] has been writing but they have refrained from stating more than general sickness and confinement to bed. I am truly sorry for him, and under similar circumstances I would come to you *noleus voleus*, Genl. Johnston[14] or Genl. anybody else.

Again, how much cause for gratitude to that good Providence which has preserved my darlings, free from the ills and accidents the flesh is heir to. I've glanced back and remember with mounting thankfulness that not one word of ill news have I received from home; all in good health, all behaving well, fine crops, stock, etc. This has been the burden of your song and it has been echoed by others. I had a letter from

Mr. Minton. He spoke or rather wrote most encouragingly of everything. Said he had never seen better behaved or more easily managed negroes in his life. This is indeed cheering. I shall send this letter out south by Flavius Pearson.[15] He has obtained a discharge from the army and returns home tomorrow. He is a very delicate person; has not been on duty a half dozen days since he left Georgia. I send by him also a letter for Father and one for John DeWitt.[16] I learned he had returned to Sparta from Julian Ransome,[17] who dined with us a day or so since. He is trying to arrange to get up a battery of six or eight guns and be major of the concern.

I learn from our Adjutant West[18] that Edge Eve is in a N. Carolina Regt. and at present not far from us. West has seen him. He knows Eve well and Caro Yancey. Eli Baxter[19] was in camp two days ago, and tho' he sat talking with the boys for some time, I had only time to shake hands with him. Twas the day we struck our tents, and we had several long company rolls to make out. He understood it; is looking very well. Linton is much under the weather as the saying goes; has gone to Richmond with his brother[20] who has been near us for several weeks and occasionally in camp. You see, there are so many of our old friends among us it is half like being in Georgia, but not entirely, my precious Sal; there's no Georgia or anything where you are not.

Ah, old Birdie, in every letter I tell you of how necessary you are to me, how complete a void your absence makes in my heart. I never knew my complete dependence upon you till I lost your support. I have not yet realized fully my loss and will not unless I should be prostrated by illness. Then you are to me like a mother to an infant. But I've seen our poor fellows weak and languid on a bed of straw and blankets, many bearing every pain and discomfort without a murmur. In such an hour of trial, I doubt not that I should be given strength. But whenever I am seriously ill or wounded, should such a chance come along, you must assuredly come. But, dearie, I am looking ahead for troubles. I've no moping feeling about me that induces me anticipate any evil of that kind.

I think, a few days ago, our leaders rather anticipated a great battle from the orders and preparation. I do not believe there is any present prospect of it now, and if we have none within a month, there will not probably be one before spring. In the meantime, your ideas about peace may be realized. But who knows what a day may bring forth. Even now the fiat may have gone forth to bring about the clash of arms and the rough work of war. Yes, I have a message for Mrs. Hunter.[21] Give her my love, and say that here amid camps and armies, I recall with a perfect pleasure her unvarying kindness to me since we knew each other—to continue to evince that kindness to you and ours and I'll love her still better. Give my brotherly love to Sister Mary and say I hope she'll find time to write me. She has so much more time than I have, I know she'll not count letters on me. Is the Squire[22] with you? My kindest regards to him, and from him I certainly look to have a long dissertation. My love to Tom, dear [illegible] Minnie[23] and kisses to them all; and very many to my dear little daughter for her nice letter and to Bud for the one that's coming. Why don't he answer Jimmy Alfriend's? Kind remembrance to Mr. and Mrs. Hull.[24] Kiss your dear Mother for me. I have such a calm, quieting feeling that you all are in safe hands with her. I wish I could throw my arms around you all and give you a great big squeeze. I suppose John has left. I see Richard's Regiment is ordered to N. Carolina. Darley, dear, dear wife, I kiss you a thousand times. As I hold you to my heart, which so longs for the reality, continue to write often, and to love always your own true Edge

[The following notes were added between the lines, a habit of the time which makes deciphering difficult.]

Dearest, have you received any letter from me asking you to send me a warm, grey suit of clothes? Pantaloons, with blue cord on the leg, and coat with the stripe on shoulder with one small cross bar for a 1st Lieut. And besides, send another pair of pants, either grey or blue, for every day use, all of it with the blue cord. Still, I wish it nice. I can't stand this stuff the factories turn out. It don't suit me, nor I it. If you haven't my measure, I think Bloomfield[25] has. Find somebody about 5 ft. 9-1/2 inches high and weighing 155 pounds and take their measure.

Dear, dear Sal, haven't I filled my sheet? I'll write you again in a few days, if only I can learn you're real glad to get my letters. These clothes must be sent by private opportunity. A box of any description costs terribly. It seems to me there might be from Athens a private opportunity to Richmond and the person inquire at the Georgia Hospital for some member of Comp. E, 15 Geo. Regt. who'll find a chance, or, in a last resort, deliver to Alec Stephens, if he be there, tho' I believe I wouldn't do that. Goodbye again, my old precious. I love you the best of all on earth. No one else can ever love you half so well. Your own Edge

Wilbur Little has just passed by and sends his kind regards. Sam[26] had a letter from Sallie today. He gave it to me to read. Speaks of your loaning her [illegible] and buggy. I'm glad you did it.

Dear old fellow, I hate to close but haven't time to undertake another paper. Sam[27] sends love to Judy. He is our only dependence now. Charlie is with Captain Smith. If he should be taken, we'd be afoot. I've been to see Col. T about Levoisier's furlough; have carried an application from him to Gen'l Toombs. Thomas was very kind and made a strong application. Toombs promised me to do his best. It is only for thirty days.

1. Colonel Paul Jones Semmes, appointed brigadier general the following March. Wounded at Gettysburg, he died 9 July 1863. *Georgia Roster,* 1:373. From Wilkes County, Ga., Semmes was one of three Confederate brigadier generals educated at the Beman School at Mt. Zion, Hancock County. Smith, *History of Hancock County,* 2:143.

2. Howell Cobb (1815–1868), Athens lawyer, politician, and planter, served as secretary of the treasury in the Buchanan administration. After Lincoln's election, Cobb returned to Georgia and led the fight to take the state out of the Union. President of the provisional Confederate Congress when war broke out, he raised a regiment and fought in Virginia, returning to Georgia in September 1863. Cobb commanded state and Confederate reserve forces until the end of the war. *Dictionary of Georgia Biography,* 1:202–3.

3. William Duncan Smith, colonel, Twentieth Georgia Infantry Regiment, 14 July 1861, later brigadier general, died at Charleston, S.C., 4 Oct. 1862. Jones, *Georgia in the War,* 94.

4. Mark Latimer, second lieutenant, Company K, Fifteenth Georgia Regiment; elected first lieutenant, 1 Nov. 1861, captain, 11 May 1863; retired to invalid corps, November 1864. *Georgia Roster,* 2:473. Latimer was the son of John Latimer, listed in the 1850 Hancock County census as age forty-three with a son, Mark, age thirteen.

5. Thomas H., German P., and Ben C. Culver were all sons of Hardy Culver of Culverton, Hancock County. See Smith, *History of Hancock County,* 1:x, 140.

6. Dr. Edward W. Alfriend, the regimental surgeon.

7. Atticus Greene Haygood was a chaplain with the Fifteenth Regiment from 15 July to 13 Nov. 1861 when he resigned. Methodist Bishop George F. Pierce had brought the brilliant young graduate of Emory College to the bishop's home church in Sparta, which explains his service with a Hancock County company. Haygood later achieved fame as a president of Emory, a leader in reconciliation efforts after the Civil War, and a Methodist bishop.

8. Jeff Lawrence may be James Jackson Lawrence of the Pierce Guards, Hancock County volunteers, who chose the name of Methodist Bishop George F. Pierce. *History of Hancock County,* 1:139. J. J. Lawrence, twenty-eight, appears in the 1860 census as a planter.

9. Captain Theophilus Jackson Smith survived twenty more years, and despite rising to the rank of lieutenant colonel was known as Captain Jack until his death. His beautiful home, Glen Mary, still stood south of Sparta on the Linton road in 1988. Glen Mary was sold in 1869 to General Ethan Allen Hitchcock, grandson of the Revolutionary hero Ethan Allen. Mrs. Terrell Moore, "Glen Mary," Sparta *Ishmaelite,* 17 June 1965. See *Georgia Roster,* 2:442, for Theophilus J. Smith.

10. The *Georgia Roster* 2:442 lists Lavoiscia L. Lamar as junior second lieutenant with the Hancock Volunteers (Company E). Smith's *History of Hancock County,* 1:136, 2:84, spells the first name Lavoisieur and identifies his wife as Louise Harris, daughter of Benjamin Tarpley Harris. Clara Harris, Louise's sister, married David Dickson, the planter.

11. Frank L. Little, an 1858 Emory College graduate, began the practice of law with Sparta attorney Charles W. DuBose in the fall of 1860. The law partnership may have resulted from Little's speech at Sparta's Fourth of July ceremonies that year at "the splendid county fair grounds" where five military companies gathered. After the war Little was one of the attorneys involved in six years of litigation over the estate of the planter David Dickson, who left large sums to his mulatto descendants. His memoirs are in the possession of his granddaughter, Miss Sarah F. Little of Sparta. See *Georgia Roster,* 2:446. Also see Mrs. Terrell Moore, "The Judge Little House," Sparta *Ishmaelite,* 14 March 1963.

12. Mrs. Richard Sasnett, the former Mary Ann Harris, was Frank Little's mother-in-law. Her husband's father was Joseph Richard Sasnett, the first Hancock planter to produce more than one hundred bales of cotton, known thereafter as "the cotton king."

13. Henry Harris, son of Benjamin T. Harris and brother of Mrs. Lavoisier Lamar.

14. Confederate General Joseph Eggleston Johnston (1807–1891) had just been promoted to rank fourth among Confederate generals following his leadership at the Battle of First Manassas (Bull Run).

15. Flavius Pearson. The *Georgia Roster,* 2:448, lists Flavius J. Pierson [*sic*] as a private in Company E, Fifteenth Georgia Regiment. Shortly before the war Pearson eloped with Ella, the youngest daughter of

Captain Theophilus Jackson Smith. Mrs. Terrell Moore, "Glen Mary," Sparta *Ishmaelite,* 17 June 1965.

16. John DeWitt, Sparta businessman and kinsman of the Wileys.

17. Possibly Benjamin J. Ransone, private, Company M, Thirty-eighth Regiment, 15 Nov. 1861; transferred to Captain Hanleiter's Company, Georgia Light Artillery, 10 June 1862. *Georgia Roster,* 4:238.

18. A. A. West, adjutant, Fifteenth Regiment, 15 July 1861; resigned 3 Sept. 1861. *Georgia Roster,* 2:408.

19. Eli Baxter, son of Judge Eli Baxter of Hancock County and Cherokee County, Texas. Baxter served as a colonel in the Twenty-eighth Texas Cavalry. Claud Estes, *List of Field Officers, Regiments and Battalions in the Confederate States Army, 1861–65* (Macon, Ga., 1912), 10.

20. Linton Stephens and his brother Alexander Stephens.

21. Hull mentions two Mrs. Hunters in *Annals of Athens:* Mrs. B. T. Hunter (p. 380) and Sarah Golding, who married Captain N. W. Hunter in 1846 (p. 483).

22. John Gresham, husband of Sallie Bird's sister Mary.

23. Tom and Minnie were children of John and Mary Gresham.

24. Dr. and Mrs. Henry Hull, prominent citizens of Athens.

25. R. L. Bloomfield, Athens merchant and manufacturer.

26. Samuel H. Wiley.

27. Edgeworth Bird's body servant.

Sallie (Saida) Bird to Edgeworth Bird

Athens, 20 September 1861

My dear, dear Papa,

I am ashamed that I should let so long a time pass without having written to you, but I hope you will excuse it, as it is the first time, and I hope will be the last that I have neglected you, and having made my apology, I will commence my letter. Bud and Nat Linton[1] have gone to spend the day with the Rucker[2] boys, and I hope he will have a nice time. There was a concert here Wednesday night. I went to it and enjoyed myself finely. Miss Helen Pardee[3] played at it, and I think she did it very nicely and prettily. I wish you could have seen and heard it. I thought of you very often while it was going on.

I went with Cousin Teadee,[4] and Alice[5] went with Mamma in Mrs. Richardson's carriage. Mamma expects to go home pretty soon. I am very sorry, for the time has passed away so pleasantly and quickly, that I feel as if I had only been here a week or two. I wish you were here to go home with us. You don't know how happy I would be if you were. Mrs. Richardson talks about going down with us. I hope she will.

Mamma went to Dr. Linton's[6] to tea last night and went to ride in the evening with Mrs. Henry Hull, and then staid with her until time to go to Dr. Linton's. I will stop now, for I must learn my Sunday School lesson, and besides, the breakfast bell has rung, and so I must finish after breakfast. We have had a most delicious breakfast, but I will not give you the bill of fare, for I know it would make you real hungry for that, or some other nice thing. Alice is writing to some of the folks at home now. She says that it is as hard for her to write as it is for Bud, and is always asking me what she shall say, as she doesn't know.

Tracy is so sweet. Papa, he will come to me from every body except Grandma, Uncle John or Laura,[7] and yesterday he came to me from Uncle John. I felt so proud when he did it, you may be sure. Uncle John expects to go home next Friday, and Mamma says that she is going as far as Union Point with him. Mamma wrote to you yesterday, and if you hear the same things in my letter that you heard in Mamma's you will know how to excuse it, for Mamma always tells you everything that is tellable. Bud is writing to Cousin Leroy,[8] and says tell Jimmy Alfriend that he will write to him as soon as he gets home and can say something that will interest him.

How is Cousin Sammy? How I wish I could see him. Give my love to him and tell him I am going to write him when I get home. I am so glad to hear that Captain Smith is better, and Sam, too. I hope they are both well and up by this time. I have written to Grandpa since I came here, and I hope I will receive an answer before I leave, for he said he would write to me when he got my letter. It has been quite cool up here for the last two mornings, especially today, and we have fire's this morning.

Grandma, Alice, and myself sleep in the room over the Parlor, and Mamma in the room over the dining room, and, I tell you what, we have nice time's. We moved there after Aunty left because Mamma could not sleep for the noise in the backyard. I did not finish my letter yesterday, and so I am doing it today.

I went to Sunday School this morning, but my teacher, Mrs. Richardson, was sick and did not come, so I said my lesson to Miss Lucy Thomas.[9] I like her very well, but not as well as I do Mrs. Richardson. Anne Richardson has been quite sick for six or seven weeks with neuralgia. I am so sorry for her. One of the reasons that Mrs. Richardson is going down to Hancock is to let Dr. Burt[10] see Anne, and see if he can't do something for her, for none of the doctors up here do her any good. Today Grandma sent her some of her nice dinner and I know she enjoyed it, for nobody can help eating Grandma's dinners. Cousin Teadee's health is a great deal better, she say's. She came down Friday and spent the day with us and we had a heap of fun.

When I go home I intend writing to Dr. Alfriend because he was so kind to write to you. Have you written to Dud[11] yet, Papa? I am going to write to Cousin Sam Wiley, too, for he writes such nice letters, and I hope I will get one of them. You know he wrote to Mamma. Bud is reading *The Young Voyagers*, one of Mayne Reid's[12] books. He like's it very much, he say's. I believe I will read it when he gets through with it. Mamma is writing to Uncle Richard now. We have not heard from him in some time. Grandma says she don't know what to make of him.

In the Third Regiment there have been four men detailed out of every company to man a battery and Uncle Richard and Mr. Bob Dougherty[13] are two of those detailed out of the "Athens Guards." I hope Uncle Richard will be an officer, though we can't tell anything about that. Last Tuesday was Tracy's birthday. He was just one year old. I don't believe there ever was as much fuss made over one baby as we made over Tracy on his birthday. Uncle John say's that I must tell you that Bud has gone under the house to *corrupt* a sitting *duck*. Every body but me are at the fig tree; how I wish you could be there, too. I know [you] would enjoy yourself. But I must close now. Grandma, Uncle John and Bud send love to you. Give my love to all your friends, and believe me to be, your affectionate little daughter, Sallie

1. Nat Linton, the son of Dr. John S. Linton of Athens.

2. Jep and Tinny (T. W.) Rucker, sons of Tinsley White Rucker and grandsons of Joseph Rucker. *Dictionary of Georgia Biography,* 2:856–57; 1860 census, Clarke County.

3. Helen Pardee played for Miss

Sawyer, who sang "Sicilian Night." Kenneth Coleman, *Athens, 1861–65*, p. 24.

4. Teadee was probably Sarah C. Hayes, daughter of Sarah Ann Hayes of Athens. Sarah Ann Hayes was the sister of Mary Wiley Baxter.

5. Alice was the daughter of Andrew Baxter, Sallie's oldest brother.

6. Dr. John S. Linton, a medical graduate, built the first paper mill in Georgia, organized the Athens Foundry, enlarged the Athens Factory, took contracts to build railroads, and owned large plantations and many slaves. Hull, *Annals of Athens*, 394–95, 481, 484.

7. Laura was a servant in the Athens home of Mrs. Mary Baxter.

8. Leroy Wiley Gresham of Macon, son of John and Mary Gresham. He was twelve at the time of the 1860 census.

9. Lucy Thomas, daughter of Stevens Thomas, Athens banker.

10. Henry and Moody Burt were physicians in Hancock County.

11. Dudley Alfriend, son of Dr. William H. Alfriend of Sparta. He also became a physician. Smith, *History of Hancock County*, 2:60. Dudley, a private with the Hancock Volunteers, later was elected first lieutenant. He surrendered at Appomattox. *Georgia Roster*, 2:443.

12. Thomas Mayne Reid (1818–1883), British novelist, produced adventure stories based on his experiences in America. The novels had titles like *Scalp Hunters*, *White Chief*, and *The Rifle Rangers*.

13. Robert Dougherty of the Athens Guards. *Georgia Roster*, 1:535.

Edgeworth Bird to Sallie Bird

Camp Pine Creek, near Fairfax Courthouse, Va.
22 September 1861

This is Sabbath evening, my dearest, most precious of Birdie's. Around me, instead of the deep, hushed quiet of the Lord's eve, I hear the merry, boisterous laugh of hundreds, the swelling, noisy hum of the camp. All along the wide street of some eighty feet, between the officers tents and those of the men, are large *rail* fires, and around each of these, groups of men are collected, sitting, standing, stooping in various attitudes—and the quiet buzz of conversation, the merry joke or pealing laugh goes on as descriptive of the character of each. Henry C.[1] and myself are seated at the camp table telegraphing thoughts of love to those we love.

Last evening the mail man brought me a letter, and *two* two days before, from my heart's home. Oh! darling, shall I again say how sweet and consoling, or have you learned the oft-told tale by heart? You ask in your last if it was not quite a love letter for an old Benedict to receive. Who'll write us love letters, dearie, if we do not to each other? And who has a warmer, more glowing love than we, whose ardent feelings thirteen years may have mellowed, but has lessened neither depth or intensity? Keep up the chain then, Precious. Our hearts alone may see their rich glow of love, our hearts alone imbibe their genial warmth. I have thought of you a great deal today, and talked of you, too.

After dinner, Henry C. and myself started out of camp on a strolling tour. Away off in the woods we sat down neath the shade of a friendly oak to chat away the hours in converse about various topics—and you can be well assured, home folks were prominent. After awhile, Henry fell asleep, and I read over your last two letters, and glanced through them again and again. For a long time, my thoughts were entirely with you. I strolled with you along our home haunts, around the flower and vegetable garden, to the spring, and [to the] cotton lots where, of late, we walked so often. Dearie, wherever you were, whatever you were doing, my spirit was with you. . . .

After awhile . . . we strolled on, chancing around for incidents. We presently came on one in view of a large white house. That didn't particularly strike us, as they are generally deserted, but some large straw stacks in the rear did, and we put out for them. Straw for the tent is a great desideratum for the soldier, and our dirt floors happen to be particularly nude. . . . Presently the loud boom of a cannon . . . burst upon our ears. One after another, in solemn cadence, they moaned through the air, as if grieving for the misery and destruction man's folly compelled them to scatter.

We hurried towards home (Bah, only think of that word as applied by us to a camp), not knowing what orders might [be] sent, or how soon we be called to double quick it up to Munson's Hill.[2] The firing continued some time after we reached camp; have heard nothing from it as yet. Earlier in the day all our spades were sent for to throw up entrenchments somewhere in front, so it may be there's a row going on.

It was rumoured that our people intended to dislodge the enemy from some house they were fortifying. I sent off a letter after we came in to Messrs. Turner and Harris[3] in relation to ourselves—clothing, etc. The guns were banging away while I wrote. While on the subject of strolls, I may as well mention another we took yesterday. It was ordered, after morning drill, that the balance of the day should be devoted by the men to washing their clothes, themselves, etc. Henry and I, after dinner, started off to hunt a good bathing place. After steering over country, passing a few farm houses, a sick camp, or so, a great many fine views from high hill tops, and sundry well opened chinkapin bushes, we found ourselves by a clear, cool branch, some 3 miles from camp. Stripping to the natural man, we plunged in, and, by dint of soap and violent manipulation, we became as new creatures. Washed of our camp dirt and clad in clean garments, we sat us down "in clover"; partook of some teacakes from Hancock we had provided, imbibed a little rye juice from a flask accidentally found in a pocket, lit our meerschaums, and laid away our bodies that our souls might have a holiday for a trip to fairyland. . . .

Before we dreamed of it, so comfortably were we lolling and puffing away, the rain was upon us. . . . Through rain and slush we tramped it to camp, forgetful that we had turned out pleasure seeking and thoroughly impressed with the belief that we were two flaming lights on the altar of patriotism, breasting the storm and fatiguing forced march for our country's good. . . .

You might imagine . . . that my spirit was free and joyous, . . . but our present life is a very serious reality. My responsibilities are rather heavy, and the more so for not being bargained for. . . . As you well know, I have no confidence in myself. I ask of *Him* what I need, and have faith to believe I shall *receive* what I *ask* for. I think I told you Mr. Hardy Culver had been with us. He has gone, and left a blank as such a Hancock man must leave. His boys are doing well.[4]

T'is just midnight and I thought myself alone, awake, but have just been interrupted by Wilbur Little, who stepped in with some nice brandy and sugar and water to offer me a treat. He had it by a rare chance; was determined I should taste it. We drank to you, to the Confederacy, and pretty women generally. The latter suited Wilbur. He sends kindest regards. Sam is lying near me. He has been moved up. The fever is broken; [he] is, I think, in safe condition. I am so thankful to a kind Providence.

Sam Wiley is quite well; joins me in love. We have our chats now and then. There are none of your friends sick. Harris Sasnet[5] is in feeble health. Will go to Richmond. We've lost one man, a nice fellow, Wm. B. Moran—poor, poor fellow—I wrote you of it, did I not?[6] Many thanks to your dear, dear mother and kisses innumerable. I need the blanket. There isn't one in this country. Love and kisses to the children. I sent your letters home directed to Father for you, and you must put them away for me. Kiss your mother and Alice. Howdy to the servants.

Darling, good night, a world of love to you. What can I say? You're in my heart and soul. You are loved more than woman ever was. I direct this to Athens, but I believe you will be in Sparta. I'll direct my next to Sparta. Henry Culver sends thanks for your mention of him. Go and see Mrs. C when you get home. Always speak of her. First Georgia Regulars have gone to Munson's Hill on picket duty. Tell Mrs. Hill[7] we will be back in a few days. Their tents are near us. We'll go soon. Darling of my soul, goodnight. Your *own, own, own* heart's love, Edge

1. Henry Harris Culver, second lieutenant, Hancock Volunteers.

2. The Confederates evacuated Munson's Hill 28 and 29 September after a brief affair at Vanderburgh's House. There had been an earlier skirmish 31 August at the hill located near Alexandria, Va. E. B. and Barbara Long, *The Civil War Day by Day* (Garden City, N.Y., 1977), 113, 122.

3. Thomas Mickleberry Turner and Benjamin T. Harris were leading planters in Hancock County.

4. Culver had six sons in the Confederate army.

5. Henry Harris Sasnett, private, Hancock Volunteers. *Georgia Roster,* 2:448. Sasnett came from Auburn (then East Alabama Male College), where he was a student and his uncle William J. Sasnett was president, to join the Hancock Volunteers with his brother, William Pembroke Sasnett, and his brother-in-law, Frank L. Little. He came home from Virginia because of illness, later joining the Terrell Artillery at Savannah. Papers of Judge Franklin Lightfoot Little in the possession of Miss Sarah F. Little, Sparta, Ga.

6. Moran, the first Hancock County soldier to die, succumbed to pneumonia.

7. Her husband, Captain A. A. Frank-

lin Hill, had been called by the Georgia Regulars. Hill, former navy physician, lawyer, and *Banner* editor, was a favorite citizen of Athens. He had earlier organized the Troup Artillery Company. Stegeman, *These Men She Gave*, 24.

Edgeworth Bird to Sallie Bird

Camp Pine Creek near Fairfax, Va.
25 September 1861

Some three days ago I was up quite late writing you, my precious, dearest wife, and now I am doing so after dinner, and while the regiment is out on battalion drill. The nights here are quite cool and chilly now, and I am inclined to believe those late sittings are not the best way to promote one's health. Our present camp is a better location than the first, a finer spring of water never bubbled than we have close and convenient, but the days are very warm and nights very cool, and tho' all came well to this camp, we have a considerable sick list already.

Occasionally a few are returned from Richmond, but they come in slowly. About 20 or 30 came up today, and I learn from them that our Company has lost another man, J. R. McWhorter,[1] a son of old Eli McWhorter living below us and near Davy Dickson. We left him at Camp Walker, and while there he received a box from home of good things, and sent me up a bottle of delightful catsup. He was sent off to Richmond at the final breaking up of that camp. I did not believe he had looked his last upon his company.

John Layfield[2] of Latimer's Company died at Camp Walker, just before its breakup. Mirabeau Boyer[3] is in Richmond and, they report, very low. His father is with him. Harris Sasnet is in low health; I fear taking typhoid fever. He has done very little duty since we came here, and today we are trying to procure him a discharge. His constitution has always been very feeble, and the exposure and duties of camp life are more than it will bear. Levoisier[4] now receives letters from his wife, and has written to Richmond to have his resignation withdrawn; has heard nothing from it as yet.

Well, my precious old Darling, what shall I tell you in the shape of news? There is none here that would interest. I told in my last of strolls in the country and hearing the cannon boom away in the distance. We have heard of nothing to infer a battle has been fought, or little, and now see no prospect of one. I hear through Madame Rumour that genl Johnston is blamed as bringing us all up here to no purpose, and against that he certainly intends fighting before long. Others say he will be obliged to bring about a battle to keep himself from being blamed. Again I heard that he and Toombs had some words, and that Toombs charged around him considerably; that Johnston hadn't much to say for fear of Toomb's influence in the Congress which is supreme and etc. etc. etc. Now, darley, I hardly know what Toombs was charging about, and simply allowed some of the chat I heard to day run off the pen.

The Regulars first went to Munson's Hill to do picket duty; then Semmes's Regt to relieve them, and the Regulars should have been back yesterday, but have not yet arrived. It is said we are to go on Friday, and remain some five or six days. It will be our first trip away from our tents, and, during that time, with the starry heavens above us and old mother earth underneath. We are to take all weather as it chances. They will not allow a tent to be stretched up there. The two forces are in sight of each other, and the white tents would present too shining a mark, and maybe tempt them to try us at long shot. I'm told it's a dirty place on that hill; it has been occupied by so many different regiments. It is said that the orders to those who may be in occupation at the time of an attack are to hold it for four hours against all odds, and they will be fully supported by that time.

Captains Oscar Dawson[5] and Tom Ryan[6] of the 8th Georgia (which has been camped within a hundred yards of us, now moved three miles up) came over and gave us their experiences up there. The firing of the pickets at each other had been pretty well stopped. It several times happened that they would wave white handkerchiefs to each other, and meet half way out and talk. Ryan, Dawson and someone else went out on invitation by a wave of handkerchiefs and had a long talk with five or six yankee's; had quite a pleasant chat about matters in general and some about the war. When they parted, our men told them, while shaking hands, they'd be glad to see them at Manassas again—at which they winced, but didn't kick up.

Dawson said something about outflanking them at Manassas. The reply was, "Outflank, hell, why sir, our battle line was twenty miles long." And they acknowledged their retreat to have been shameful. I honestly believe, as I've written before, that Providence gave us that battle. It inspired the hearts of our boys and they fought with unparalelled valour; but, more than that, it struck the hearts of our enemies with fear, and put upon them a panic as unnecessary as it was effectual to give us the victory. I pray that it may do so again.

Dearest, I shall direct this to Sparta. This is the 25th. It will be mailed tomorrow and get off next and be in Sparta by the third or fourth of October. From what you wrote I am sure you'll all, and Mother Baxter, too, be safely stowed away in cozy Granite Farm. Oh! How I love to imagine you all there. It is so easy for my mind to picture you at any hour of the day. With your mother with you, I know you'll be happy. That is, dearest, as happy as you can be with me away. Precious, I know I am necessary to you. I feel that I form a portion in you that if taken away could not be replaced. Every letter you send me breathes it in every line and my *heart* tells me of its truth, you precious darling of my soul. I hope to hear that Linton has given you a good dividend. You are soon to have one from the G.R. road.[7] I hope Mr. DeWitt will be able to make some collections, and from these sources, you will be able to prepare against a rainy day.

We will make a large crop of corn and have a considerable surplus. As soon as possible after corn is hard enough, gather the corn in the cornfields and fill the new crib to the very top, as we did last year, and then Yancey's crib, and you'll know you have an abundance. You can put the balance in the big crib and sell it for *cash* as you may be able. What goes in Yancey's crib had better be shucked on what may be to sell, for the cows will need a great many shucks for winter. Then the hogs must be got into those lower fields very early, so as to eat the peas, and let them [the fields] be ready for sowing down in oats and wheat. You'll find the cotton will be very open and ahead, but this time tell Mr. Minton to quit it, and gather that corn as soon as *it is dry enough*. The hogs will be fine by it [the peas], and it will save corn in feeding them. Let Mr. M keep the cotton closely ginned and packed up. If the mules show any tender foot from ginning, let them be shod in front immediately. I hardly think it would be best to send our cotton to Savannah immediately. You must talk with Father and others and learn what will be best.

I have received Mr. Edwards'[8] letter and one from John and Mr. Lane.[9] Shall answer them when I can. My kindest regards to Mr. E and John. You must take Mr. Edwards in and treat him as one of the family. Do be careful, Darley, and don't let him see you lose your temper with Richard or Dinah.[10] Ain't I naughty to suppose such a thing? My love and kisses to your mother. Oh, I know you and she'll be happy there. You can plan and execute just as you please. Kiss again and again my dear Sallie and Bud. I shall have to add another half sheet to say several things.

[Note added at top of page.] Dearest, light of my life, goodbye. I reserved this corner to tell you how entirely I am yours and how I feel you are mine. Good night, dearest darling, Your own Edge.

Sam W is writing by me. He is just called off to roll call; will return and finish. My love to Cousin Sallie and all the Wileys and Cousin Lizzie and Jimmy Harris.

1. J. R. McWhorter, private, Company E, Fifteenth Georgia Regiment (Hancock Volunteers). *Georgia Roster,* 2:448.

2. John Layfield was a member of Company K, Fifteenth Georgia Regiment. Smith, *History of Hancock County,* 1:141. Not listed in *Georgia Roster.*

3. Mirabeau Boyer, private, Company E, Fifteenth Georgia Regiment. *Georgia Roster,* 2:448.

4. Lavoisieur Lamar.

5. George Oscar Dawson, captain 15 May 1861, Greene County Volunteers; major 16 December 1862, Eighth Georgia Regiment. *Georgia Roster,* 1:913, 980.

6. T. D. Lawrence Ryan, Company G, Eighth Georgia Regiment (Pulaski County Volunteers); captain 16 May 1861; resigned 11 Feb. 1863; resignation accepted 20 March 1863. *Georgia Roster,* 1:193.

7. Linton was Dr. John S. Linton, who managed several Athens enterprises in which the Baxters owned stock. G.R. was the Georgia Railroad.

8. James B. Edwards.

9. John DeWitt and Andrew Jackson

Lane. Lane had a large plantation at Granite Hill, not far from Rockby, home of Richard Malcolm Johnston.

10. Richard and Dinah were slaves at Granite Farm.

Sallie (Saida) Bird to Edgeworth Bird

Granite Farm, November 1861

Mon Cher Papa,

Je vous ecris une petite lettre Francaise que je recoive une reponse et la mets dans la lettre de Mamma, que vous voyerez que j'ai fait des progres. Mamma est ecrivant une lettre a vous. Monsieur Minton va tuer la vielle vache Patsey ce soir, mais nous vous n'avons pas ici cher Papa pour la deplouer, comme vous deplorait la vielle Red Moon l'annee passee. Elle is si gros avec beaucoup de difficulte.

Chere Grand Mere porte mieux aujourdui et elle se promenait dans le jardin des fleures un peu de temps. J'ai ecrit une lettre a ma cousine Minnie hier au soir et j'ai fait Mll. Lucy, ma poupon, ecrit a sa poupon Anne. Madame Alfriend est alle a Virginia voir son fils Jimmie qui est malade. J'ai entendu dire qu'il se porte mieux a present et elle etait tres triste qu'elle ne le connait pas aucune faire. Bud, avec Candice, Dinah, et Rachel ont ete deterre les pommes du terre. Mamma se porte bien et "Bud" aussi. Je me porte bien, cher Papa, et je sais que vous serez bien aise de l'entendu il est tres difficile pour moi a ecrire en Francaise et j'espere que vous m'excuserez si je fais des fautes. Adieu, mignon Papa. Je vous aime de tout mon coeur.

Votre petite fille bien affectieuse,
Sallie[1]

1. Little Sallie, age twelve, wrote to show her father the progress she was making in French. The news from Granite Farm was rustic. Mr. Minton, the overseer, was going to kill the old cow Patsey. Grandmother Baxter had arrived from Athens and enjoyed a walk in the flower garden. Sallie had made her doll, Mademoiselle Lucy, write to her cousin Minnie Gresham's doll, Anne. Mrs. Alfriend was

going to Virginia to visit her son Jimmy who was sick. Sallie's brother Bud had helped the servants Dinah, Candice, and Rachel dig potatoes. Edgeworth Bird returned the letter to his wife with the comment, "Pretty good for our little daughter, isn't it?"

Dr. John Baxter to Sallie Bird

Norfolk, [Va.] 10 November 1861

My dear Sister,

Your smart letter, so full of loving words and kindly sympathy, was received yesterday, and, as I read it in my tent surrounded by others, I could not prevent the tears, hard as I struggled, from rising and almost running over. I pulled my cap down over my eyes and read on—for I dislike for others to be witness of my emotions who cannot understand, and, if understanding, cannot enter into nor appreciate. My feelings are more easily stirred than in former days, and I am really fearful I am becoming too tenderhearted in these fearsome times of war and peril. But it does seem as if I loved Mother far better than ever before, and when you write about her it moves me deeply.

And, secondly, your letter conveyed the sad news of the death of her, who was for years your nearest, dearest friend, and upon whom I looked with a brother's fondness, and a remembrance of whose many virtues and excellencies I shall always fondly cherish. Next to you and Mother she stood, and if there was nothing else, the letter full of friendly advice and consolation which she recently sent me, written, as she said, upon a bed of pain and suffering, would have won and closely drawn her to me. I feel deeply for Dr. Robinson[1] in his affliction, for there is no loss like his and mine, and if you have not already written, so speak for me. I have felt much inclined to write to him, and feel so now, but you can tell him better.

This is the Sabbath and the tenth November. Do you remember the date? Tis a double anniversary for me. Twas on the 10th of November we were married and on the 10th of the month my darling died. How different it was on the same day of the month three, two and one year ago. Three years ago I felt as if my life had just begun in reality, and everything was so bright, so joyous and happy. Now, all is gloom and darkness, and I feel as if the best part of my life were gone. My sky has been darkened by a black cloud which overshadows all, and my feelings are those of an old man. I should not feel so, nor give way to such despondency. My dear friend, Miss Lizzie,[2] warned me against this very fault. There is one ray which pierces the gloom, one bright, small spot to relieve the blackness, that is my doubly precious, smart and darling Tracy, left behind. How I do love him, he only knows. And I trust that he and I may be spared to each other, that to me he may be a companion and a solace, and may he find in me a proper guardian and protector.

I cannot fill the place of his mother, no one can, but I must do my duty toward him and be to him a double parent. My dear sister, you must pardon my writing in such a sad strain, but to you, Mother and my Tracy, I feel that I can talk and that you'll be patient listeners. . . .

I promised her [Mother] before leaving Macon that I would go to see Richard,[3] but explained my failing to do so in my last letter. She has heard from Richard, so have I, and about his well doing we were both satisfied. Still, I should have been very glad to see him. You would scarcely be interested in hearing about camp life and incidents connected with so small a force as a Battalion after reading the same, so ably depicted by Mr. Bird, surrounded by an immense multitude. . . . We are about one mile and a half from Norfolk in what was formerly a splendid clover field, but now in a state of utter ruin. It is a part of a dairy farm, and just beyond a marsh, on one side of our encampment, there is another clover field in which some very fine cows may be seen grazing. The owner of the farm estimates the damages to his property at a very high figure.

The people farm very much like the Yankees, and get much more out of the land than we farther South. Very near us is the camp of a Virginia Artillery Company. We can witness their drilling from our tents. All around us within a few miles soldiers are encamped. Yesterday I went down to the beach opposite Fortress Monroe and Rip-Raps. With a good glass one could see the fortifications and their surroundings distinctly, and it certainly is a very strong place and would cost thousands of lives to storm it successfully.

I visited the old camp at Sorrell's Point, a sand battery thrown up to protect Norfolk. The entrenched camp, about three miles from Norfolk, is *untakable* with a proper force behind the entrenchments. Our winter quarters are rapidly going up, and in three or four weeks we will occupy. We, that is the Battalion, are in hopes we will be ordered to the coast of S. Carolina or Georgia. The enemy ousted us with their great fleet, but this success, so far, does not pay for what they lost by shipwreck. Genl. Lee,[4] in whom I have great confidence, has taken charge of the Department of S.C., Geo. and Florida. He, Gen'l Lee, outgeneraled the Enemy in W. Virginia, and put a check to his advance. The North now acknowledges that their campaign in that region has been a failure. We must now thrash them on the Potomac under McClellan,[5] and their backbone will be broken. Tell Mother I am arrayed in the drawers and shirt she made me in Athens, and for the needle case I am now prepared to thank you, for its value appears now in all its glory. Those who have seen it say it is the "clean thing," the most complete of its kind. I am glad Bud is satisfied with Genl. Beauregard.[6] Love to Mr. B in your next letter. Much love to Mother.

yr. Brother Jno. S. Baxter

Finding my letter was too late for the mail, I will add a few lines more. . . . My mess will be a very select one, and in which a place has been kept for some time for me. The members perhaps you would like to know. I'll give their names: Col. Speer,[7] who is the patriarch of the mess, his son and brother, Sam Hunter,[8] Carl Branham,[9] Charley Wiley,[10] Dr. Van Geisen,[11] DeGraffenreid,[12] and Sewell[13] and myself—four lawyers, one dentist, one doctor. Four are members of the Church, and all a fine set of fellows to associate with.

We heard firing in the direction of Ft. Monroe, and the booming of these big guns could be heard frequently after the reception of their glorious "!" victory on the South Carolina coast. Yesterday, I had my first experience in camp cooking. Our cook had permission to be absent, and we had to provide for ourselves, or go to bed supperless. I cooked the meat and made the coffee; and my success was loudly applauded, and it was unanimously agreed that I could take excellent care of myself through a campaign.

Yesterday, I washed myself thoroughly in cold water in the open air, and as I stood in a state of nudity on the bank of the marsh, which rises and falls with the tide, I thought of Richard washing in the little room adjoining the billiard *saloon* at Granite Farm. I am now drilling every day and tomorrow will be my first experience in standing guard. I think I will make a pretty fair soldier and believe the life of camp will suit me admirably, and I hope to put some flesh on my bones. The hardships I feel physically able to undergo as well as any man of my weight, as Sam Wiley would say. You have seen an account of our victory at Belmont. Port Royal is a black speck on the horizon, but we must not expect to conquer every time.

Yet, I feel perfectly sure [we] will defeat them on the Potomac when the trial comes, if McClellan should ever be willing to test the matter. The Carolina success does not amount to much. But that miserable Union bridge burning fellow should be dealt with according to the forms observed by one Judge Lynch. Every suspected man should be attended to at once. Next Sunday Tracy will be fourteen months old. I think Papa will write him a letter. I wish I could see him just a little while. Tell Mother the woollen jacket she gave me will be the thing for these cold, biting, wintry blasts, though up to this date the weather has been very pleasant. Very much like our Nov. at home.

The men are urging me to attend the sick in the two companies from Macon. Say I must do it; they want no one else. But I persistently refuse except to give advice occasionally. I attended to a poor fellow in the guard tent, put there for drunkenness and threatened with the horrors, for which he was very grateful. Give my love to Mother again and again, and kiss her frequently and at all odd times. Tell her I think of her and her loving kindness and tender interest always. Love to Mr. Bird, children, and for yourself you have the love of your brother.

Jno. S. Baxter

1. Possibly Dr. P. Gervais Robinson with the First South Carolina (McCreary's Brigade).

2. Elizabeth Wiley Harris of Hancock County.

3. Richard Baxter.

4. Confederate General Robert E. Lee (1807–1870) declined Lincoln's offer of command of the Federal forces in the field and returned to his home in Virginia, although he opposed both slavery and secession. His efforts in western Virginia in 1861 were not successful, despite John Baxter's assessment. He returned to Richmond and was sent to organize the coast defenses of the Carolinas at the time of this letter.

5. Union General George B. McClellan (1826–1885) won fame early in the war for seizing territory in western Virginia, assuring the creation of the Union state of West Virginia. After the Union disaster at Manassas (Bull Run), Lincoln called on him to organize the defenses of Washington. McClellan organized the Army of the Potomac and planned the Peninsula campaign aimed at taking Richmond.

6. Pierre Gustave Toutant Beauregard (1818–1893) was enjoying an excellent reputation following the victory at Manassas, where he was second in command of the Confederate forces. He earlier commanded the Confederates who fired on Fort Sumter.

7. H. A. Speer of the Twenty-eighth North Carolina Infantry is the only colonel by that name in the *List of Field Officers*, 117. Alexander M. Speer, a friend of John Baxter, was a private in Company B, Second Battalion, and became a major later. *Georgia Roster*, 4:924. Baxter was also a private in Company B. He did not become an assistant surgeon until the following May. *Georgia Roster*, 6:784.

8. Samuel Hunter was a private in Company B (Macon Volunteers). He became captain and assistant quartermaster 18 November 1861. *Georgia Roster*, 6:771.

9. Joel and Junius W. Branham were members of Company B, Second Battalion, at this time. *Georgia Roster*, 6:785.

10. Charles M. Wiley, a first sergeant, was commissioned adjutant of the Forty-fourth Regiment of Georgia Infantry in April 1862. *Georgia Roster*, 6:783.

11. Uriah Van Geisen, twenty-seven, is listed in the Bibb County, Ga., 1860 census as a dentist. The name does not appear in the *Georgia Roster*.

12. Francis H. DeGraffenried, major, Fourth Georgia Infantry. *List of Field Officers*, 36. DeGraffenried was a junior second lieutenant, Company E (Albany Guards), Fourth Regiment, at the time of this letter. *Georgia Roster*, 6:792.

13. J. Wesley Sewell, private, Company B, Second Battalion. Sewell died in Richmond 3 Feb. 1863. *Georgia Roster*, 6:792.

Edgeworth Bird to Sallie Bird

Camp Centreville, 19 November 1861

Dearest Darling, yesterday came your dearest, sweetest of letters. . . . Your description of the beauty and attraction of our home was fine . . . never was I so able to appreciate the rich bloom of your roses, their freshness now in such beautiful contrast to the "sear and yellow leaf" of autumn.

Darlie, shall I complete the antithesis and draw you a picture of my present home? In a scrubby pine thicket of the Old Dominion I dwell. The dwarfed produce of an impoverished soil stretch forth around me. . . . Dark curling smoke from a hundred blazing log heaps wraps the white tents in a happy shroud, through which your humble servant and other grim visaged individuals stalk and flit around, coughing and sneezing and weeping big tear drops. . . . The horrid smoke is one of our greatest trials; it is the mosquito and sand fly of camp life. . . .

At dark this evening we got orders to prepare three days rations and go out on picket tomorrow for that length of time. So, in violation of your orders, I am writing late at night. . . . I have been to the bottom of the box and many of us have discussed its contents. The pickles were very fine and so acceptable. We've been having them on our mess table every day. Haven't as yet sampled the hams; shall probably take one out on picket with us. Of the ginger snaps, I can only wish we had ten bushels. From your only sending one bottle of whiskey, Henry[1] thinks that you are afraid to trust me with much of the article. But we are doing very well, having just received a keg from Richmond.

Darlie, I can't say where we are to go into winter quarters. We are just now in a blessed state of uncertainty. We, that is our brigade, has been the extreme left wing of the Army of the Potomac, and under the command of a Genl Smith. Today I learn we have been changed and are now under Genl. Kirby Smith[2] and belong to the Reserve, hence we may soon change our location and be moved again.

It has been for some time rumoured that Gov. Brown[3] has called for our Brigade to go to Georgia. I have entirely refrained from alluding to it to you, thinking it might raise hopes that if indulged would lead to a disappointment. Since you spoke of it yourself, I will say I have no hope of it. That is, it has always been rumours, and I have never heard it from any reliable source. It does seem that we are needed now at Savannah, but I presume our chiefs know best.

My dearest darling, amid the deluge of bad news you've of late been accustomed to hear of friends in the army, I have another to mention. Captain Lafayette Lamar[4] is no more. . . . He died at Warrenton [Va.] and had the intense consolation of having his wife with him. He is regretted by all, for we had no nicer man among us. His company is now without a commissioned officer of its own, the rest being absent from sickness, and one resigned from ill health. It is now under command of Lieut. John Tilly,[5] your old acquaintance, who has been assigned to that duty. Tilly and I are great friends. He's as solid as a meat block and perfectly reliable. He is full of dry wit, and many is the joke we get up on each other and others.

I thank you, dearest, for your advice about cultivating the social traits. Your views are correct. You know me so well that you can readily imagine how slowly I formed acquaintances or unbosomed myself to these strangers. But I am progressing. None are strangers to me now, and my relations are pleasant with all the officers. My relation to Col. T[6] has been particularly so, and he has always treated me with uniform courtesy and kindness. I can never conscientiously join in the hue and cry after him. His faults have always been of the tongue, from hasty words. None have ever accused him of unjust acts or undue severity.

Darlie, you must continue to tell me of how the horses progress in your esteem and affection. Do inquire into the matter of how the [Hancock County] Confederate Guards came to have no shirts, or rather so few sent them. We had in our box some 135 of those blue cotton ones. Mrs. Fraley[7] wrote Henry there were probably enough to give two to a man which was what they required. I think the Confederates did not receive a dozen in their boxes.

Dearie, I paid today fifty cents for a package of envelopes. Send me three or four bunches, like the one that encloses this letter, by Captain Smith or any [other] opportunity. Captain S[8] wrote me of your visit; spoke most kindly of you and your Lucie. I hope he may soon be here with us. I am gratified to hear Sam[9] is so true to me and to his Regiment. I miss him *very* much, and should be a *great deal* more comfortable, could I have his services. No one washes or cooks like Sam here. Indeed, I do without many comforts I should have, were he here to call on. If he is entirely well, I should like to have him come on with Captain Smith. Read what I say to Father. I've just sent him a long letter. Give him my best love. Kiss Sallie and Bud and your dear good mother, with oceans of love. Remember me to Mr. and Mrs. Minton. Howdye and kind wishes to all our servants.

Added notes: Henry C and Sammy[10] are both well. Verily I have written tonight "cunente calamo" and neglected many things I wished to say. Be very quiet in your inquiries about the shirts. It will be easy to get in a muss about it, and I wish you ever to keep clear of the like o' that. Remember me kindly to Sam. Tell John how pleased I am to hear so well of him. Darlie, good night, you dear, sweet, precious darling. Love me and pray for me, and believe me always your own. Edge

1. Henry H. Culver.

2. Edmund Kirby Smith became a Confederate brigadier general in June 1861 and was wounded at First Manassas. The month before this letter was written he was promoted to major general, and subsequently he became a full general. In the last years of the war he was in charge of Confederate troops west of the Mississippi.

3. Joseph E. Brown (1821–1894), Georgia's wartime governor, did not call Edgeworth Bird's men home, but he frequently contested authority with Confederate President Jefferson Davis. "Georgia was his world; he had difficulty seeing beyond her borders," as one biographer put it. *Dictionary of Georgia Biography,* 1:119–21.

4. LaFayette Lamar, captain, Lamar Confederates (Lincoln County), died at Warrenton, Va., 17 Nov. 1861. *Georgia Roster,* 2:454.

5. John M. Tilley, a first lieutenant in the Stephens Home Guards (Taliaferro County, Ga.), was killed at Garnett's Farm, Va., 27 June 1862. *Georgia Roster,* 2:435. When Tilley, then thirty-five, left his home near Crawfordville to go to war he wrote his wife: "If I fall or die, don't grieve over me. . . . You interposed no selfish objections to your husband doing his duty and I would, were I a woman, vastly prefer to be a true man's widow than some men's wives." Tilley Papers, Georgia State Archives.

6. Colonel Thomas W. Thomas.

7. Martha Massey married William Fraley in 1843. Smith, *History of Hancock County,* 1:179. Fraley was listed as a planter in the 1860 census.

8. Theophilus Jackson Smith.

9. Edgeworth Bird's body servant.

10. Henry H. Culver and Samuel H. Wiley.

Edgeworth Bird to Sallie Bird

On Picket, 21 November 1861

Dear, dearest Sal,

You will not abuse me for calling you Sal or anything else nowadays, will you darling, so there is a loving epithet connected with it? Dr. Will Alfriend[1] arrived among us yesterday evening and, as seems fated with our Hancock friends, found us out on picket duty. . . . I am seated at the foot of a tree pencilling you a few lines for the Dr. to take to you. . . . Our present picket post, like our last one, is not at all pleasant. We are encamped in a low flat woodland, and the country round bears no marks of the improvements we sometimes find. The morning we came out was rainy and cloudy and promised either rain or snow, but it has cleared off beautifully.

It is quite cool, but shall have a bright moon to enliven us on post tonight. I learn Mrs. Skrine[2] is in Richmond with Mrs. A.[3] Her husband is there quite sick, but I hope not in a dangerous condition. Death continues now and then to lift his merciless finger among us. I told you of the much lamented death of Captain Lamar. Now another of the "Volunteers" has gone to his long home, a fine bright boy of seventeen summers. Joe Rushin,[4] a son of Mr. James Rushin who lives near Jack Smith on Buffalo. He had been sick and shaking from chills and fever, and then his bowels were attacked, and while he was on picket last he was sent off to Charlottesville. His brother-in-law, Fayette Cumming,[5] went off sick at the same time and was with him when he died. We only heard of it last evening. I learn he has been permitted to take his body home. This makes four taken from our company by death, and there have been some sixteen discharged, several absent on furlough.

Please say to Wm. Sasnett[6] I have received Dr. Pendleton's[7] certificate and his application for an extension of his furlough and will attend to it as soon as I return to camp. He, of course, understands I can do nothing until then. Dr. Alfriend is now absent in Richmond to meet his wife. He tells me that Mrs. Dawson is with her husband there. I believe he met her at the hospital.

Darling, when the war is over, if it be God's will, I'll meet you in our own sweet home, tho' there is a chance for that good, good time to come sooner. When the campaign is over, and we go regularly into winter quarters, and Captain Smith returns, Henry[8] and I will come home on furlough, if it be possible. There will be thousands of applications, but I haven't been exceeding three or four days off duty and, I think, shall deserve the favour. I am glad your cotton is turning out well. Sixty bags from 80 acres will be a credible yield. Have it placed as I suggested on the far and lower side of the screw on thick logs and covered well with boards. I mean what cannot stay under the screw; put no bags in the seed room. Tell Mr. Minton to reserve as many seed oats as he thinks will be necessary.

Darling, I know your own ideas about such things are very proper, but still I'll say a word of warning. Don't ask the highest prices for anything in these straightened times. We should all assist each other, as we best can. There is no strait for corn yet, and I would not sell until it is worth 1.00 per bushel. Mr. E[9] can dispose of oats, if you have them to spare, at the market price. I think the advice given you about pork was good. Still retain a surplus. We cannot see into our own supply another year, and if that be promising, it will sell readily. Such things as we have to sell are necessaries and *will* and should command cash. You have no other chance for money for our family. I am now down to a five and shall have to retain the $90 now due me which I shall get in a few days, but I'll send you a lift occasionally.

Darling, remember Father needs pork; supply him if he wishes it. Offer it to him yourself. And the good Mother, too, is to be supplied in whatever she wants that we have.

Darling, from what Alfriend says, I [illegible] somebody's been troubling the hogs. Never mind it, old fellow, don't let it trouble you. Who'll mind petty trials in these times? Take pains to gain the affection of the negroes. You can attach them to you and govern them through their hearts better than any overseer can through fear. Remember me to them all, to Arthur, John, Lewis, old Aunt Sallie; regards intended to all. I can't write all their names, but I have them all in mind. Tell Zeph I'm a pretty good hand to sew on buttons since Sam has quit me. I miss the youngster greatly; ask him when he thinks his furlough will expire.

Best love to Father and your mother, the good "old folks at home" who'll advise you and take care of you. A hundred kisses to dear Sallie and Bud.

Jimmy Alfriend is going home, I believe. Bud must open a correspondence with Dud. He's a fine fellow and smart, too. His address is E. D. Alfriend. Darling, goodbye; the sun shines brightly and cheerily on me at the foot of this old post, and I take it as a harbinger of good to our cause and [to those] whom I love. The Dr. tells me Mr. E. has bagged a grey [fox?] but could tell me nothing about [it]. My love to Mr. E and I hope he'll give me an account of it and bag a half dozen more. Good bye again, my own precious wife. Let us pray for each other.

Your own Edge

1. Dr. William H. Alfriend.

2. Eugene A. Skrine, private, Company E (Hancock Volunteers), died of disease June 1863. *Georgia Roster,* 2:447.

3. Mrs. William H. Alfriend.

4. Listed as J. G. Rushion [*sic*], *Georgia Roster,* 2:448. Ivy Duggan wrote that he died of typhoid fever at Delevan Hospital, Charlottesville, Va., 13 Nov. 1861, when "but a boy." Duggan Papers, Emory University.

5. F. D. Cumming, private in the Macon Guards, was killed at Second Manassas 30 August 1862. *Georgia Roster,* 1:937.

6. William Pembroke Sasnett, first corporal, later fourth sergeant, Company E, died of heart disease 30 Dec. 1864. *Georgia Roster,* 2:442.

7. Dr. Edmund M. Pendleton, a Sparta physician, wrote one of the first college texts on agriculture. He was interested in the health of the black population, studying the diseases to which they seemed susceptible. James C. Bonner, *A History of Georgia Agriculture, 1732–1860* (Athens, Ga., 1964), 111–14.

8. Henry H. Culver.

9. James B. Edwards.

Sallie (Saida) Bird to Edgeworth Bird

Sparta, 15 December 1861

Dear, dear darling Papa,

As I have not written to you in some time, I thought I would sit down and write you a good long letter and beg you to forget the long time which has intervened since I wrote you last. Grandpa and Mamma are talking about the Yankees and the war. Grandpa[1] is as warm as ever on the latter subject and is, as we all are, delighted at the prospect of your getting a furlough, dear Papa.

Grandma[2] has been gone now nearly two weeks and has not yet returned. We are looking every day for a letter saying when she will return. I tell you what, Papa, we miss her more than you would think, especially Mamma, who was in better spirits after Grandma came. I must go to supper now.

After supper—I have made some sleeping caps for you and some of your men. I expect Mamma has described them to you. I have made one for you, Lieut. Culver, Mr. John Mullaly,[3] Mr. Frank and Wilber Little. I don't know Mr. Wilber, but I am going to send him one because you like him, and I have one also for Cousin Sammy, and one more that I do not know who I shall give to. Mr. Eugene Burnet[4] leaves for Yorktown in the morning. He has been home on furlough, but he saw in the paper the other day that Genl. Magruder[5] had revoked all the furloughs of the men who were absent from Yorktown at that time.

I saw Mr. Frank Mullaly[6] and his bride today; they are here on a visit to Mrs. Ponce.[7] He preached in our church today, and a splendid sermon it was. Mrs. Mullaly is, I think, *very* pretty. She is about Mamma's size and has dark hair and beautiful dark eyes. I think Mr. Mullaly is very handsome and much like his Brother John. Don't you think so? He is not as handsome as Mr. John is, because he has not as pretty brown eyes. How is Cousin Sammy? I hope he is better and able to be once more among you.[8] I wish he would write to me if he has time. Mr. Smith[9] the preacher staid with us at Granite Farm last night and came up this morning with us; he is now at Mrs. Terrell's. I have begun to have stys again and had two on one eye at the same time, while I was at Cousin Sallie's[10] this week. I now have one coming, which I am trying to keep off by bathing it with camphor water, and I think it helps them. I will stop now, for my eyes "are a snapping." I will stop for tonight, so bonsoir, dear Papa.

I hope, dear Papa, you will excuse the writing on this page, for I was very sleepy when I wrote it and will try and make up for it by writing the rest of my letter more slowly and carefully. Mamma is writing to you now, and so I will try and finish this, so that it can go in hers. Mamma is going to see Mrs. Mullaly this morning. I am going to carry some flowers to the church yard this morning. The roses are blooming here like they do in Spring; the Malmaison bush is covered with flowers and buds and some of them are beautiful. Mr. Latimer, who was discharged out of your company,[11] came to see Mamma Saturday. I did not see him, as I was in the house helping Nancy[12] to put up the winter curtains in the parlor. Oh, Papa! You don't know how sweet the parlor looks. I wish you could see it. Mrs. McKinley of Athens[13] is here on a visit to Mrs. Terrell and Mrs. Harris.[14] I saw her at church yesterday.

Mamma received a short letter from you yesterday. It was the shortest one she ever got. I must close now for Mamma wishes to send her letter off. Give my love to all of your friends, especially to Cousin Sam and believe me to be,

Your affectionate and loving little daughter,
Sallie

1. Wilson Bird of Sparta.

2. Mary Wiley Baxter of Athens.

3. John T. Mullaly was second sergeant with the Hancock Volunteers, later becoming lieutenant and then captain in March 1863. *Georgia Roster,* 2:442. Ivy Duggan wrote that he was almost mortally wounded at Cold Harbor in 1864 and that he possessed "all the traits of a polished gentleman and a gallant officer." Duggan Papers, Emory University.

4. Eugene Paul Burnet, a brother of Sallie Bird's friend Julia Burnet Whitehead, was third sergeant in the Sydney Brown Infantry (Company A, Sixth Georgia Regiment) at the time of this letter. He was appointed captain and inspector general of Colquitt's Brigade in 1864 and was elected major in January 1865. He surrendered at Greensboro, N.C., 26 April 1865. *Georgia Roster,* 1:751.

5. John Bankhead Magruder became a major general in the Confederate army in October 1861. He was getting ready for the moves that in the spring of 1862 successfully delayed McClellan's Peninsula campaign. Magruder failed to follow up with his superior force, however, and was transferred to Texas. Jon L. Wakelyn, ed., *Biographical Dictionary of the Confederacy,* (Westport, Conn., 1977), 305–6.

6. Francis P. Mullaly was at one time pastor of the Sparta Presbyterian Church. Smith, *History of Hancock County,* 1:40.

7. The only Ponces listed in the 1860 Hancock County census are Dimos Ponce, seventy-seven, planter, and Dimos, nineteen, presumably his grandson.

8. Samuel Wiley wrote in his diary that on 19 Nov. 1861 he was taken sick in camp with chilly sensations and fever. He was lodged in the hospital in Richmond.

Samuel H. Wiley Papers, Southern Historical Collection, Library of the University of North Carolina at Chapel Hill.

9. The Rev. R. C. Smith, Presbyterian minister and former professor at Oglethorpe College. See James Stacy, *A History of the Presbyterian Church in Georgia* (Atlanta, 1912), 144.

10. Sallie Wiley (Mrs. Samuel H. Wiley).

11. Thomas H. Latimer, captain, Company K, Fifteenth Regiment, resigned 1 Nov. 1861. *Georgia Roster,* 2:473.

12. Nancy was a servant at Granite Farm.

13. The 1860 census of Clarke County (Athens) listed Antoinette McKinley, forty-six, in the household of T. W. Rucker, planter.

14. There were several Mrs. Harrises. Saida would have called Mrs. James Harris "Cousin Lizzie."

Sallie Bird to Sallie (Saida) Bird

Granite Farm, 25 December 1861

I give you, my dear child, an ornament made of my hair. I trust and believe you will appreciate it, and show that you do by keeping it always. May God bless you and save you is my daily prayer.

In the long continued absence of your beloved Father and the agony of mind which I endure, being separated from him who is dearer than life itself to me, you have it in your power, my dear child, to do much towards softening that pain. You can, by a ready cheerful obedience, and an earnest desire to do your duty, whatever that duty may be, go far towards helping me bear the cruel trial of the absence of your precious Father. You may learn lessons of self-denial and self-control which will influence nobly your character hereafter. God grant that as this is the first, so it may be the last Christmas we shall spend away from him who is nominally and really the head of our home, the chief of our hearts. May Heaven bless him this day, with richest favor of its grace. He *can* enable us to bear our burdens.

With many prayers and wishes for your present and future happiness and usefulness, I remain your devoted Mother, Sallie Bird

Edgeworth Bird to Sallie Bird

[Virginia] 10 January 1862

I looked for a letter from you today with certainty, dear Darlie, but it didn't come. . . . I sent a letter by John Stafford[1] and another I wrote you in which I spoke of a young Crawford[2] sent home on sick furlough. I have heard from neither and I wonder sometimes whether all my letters go straight.

I've just finished dinner on toasted biscuit and fried sausage meat, only two dishes, but quite satisfying to the inner man. We find it quite difficult to have much variety in our bills of fare at this time and place. The fact is this country is about "grazed down." One comfort is we often have oysters, and Henry and I often live for days on nothing else. They are somewhat cheaper now, too. We get them for $2.25 a gallon. They are large fine ones, and I often wish I could send you a gallon or so in a letter. I so well know how the Granite Farm "mess" would enjoy them. You could coax Father down, too, a little oftener than he seems to visit you, if so tempting a bait could be offered him. I wrote him day before yesterday.

The time has nearly come for Capt. Smith[3] and his party to set out for the wars. As I sit here, I can well imagine the great trial it will be to them to leave home and friends. I have a feeling memory of how the heart sinks at the idea of looking possibly for the last time on the old familiar scenes, and how its very fibres are torn, when at last forced to say goodbye to those we love better than life. But most of these have tried it once, and Tom Beman[4] is the only [one] who has to run the gauntlet of farewell for the first time. Well, Precious, how do you like old war beaten Sammy's[5] phiz? I know you've had to look at it by this time; has he bared his bleeding bosom to you and shown where the ruthless vandals, impious invaders of his country's firesides, have driven in the gleaming steel?

No, Providence so far has shielded us from harm from friend or foe. Outwardly, you can take Sam as a sample of the balance of us. He has borne the same exposure of camp life and the march; has been smoked and frozen up and thawed and *bedeviled* after, pretty much the same style as the balance of us. Note the changes, or how much of the Same old Sam you find about his appearance, and prepare yourself accordingly to look upon your own Old Fellow. Inwardly, he is not a fair sample, for it may be that not all have maintained the mental equilibrium and the pure and spotless heart as well as good old Sammy. Were you all not taken greatly by surprise when you first heard of his arrival?

Doc Pierce,[6] too, is rejoicing his Sallie's heart. You, poor old Birdie, are still balanced on the toe of expectancy and know not the day or the hour when the absent mate may flutter in at the homestead. Truth to say, he does not know himself. About the twentieth I'll put in an application. If it shares the same fate as those recently put in, it will still be many days before I finally get off. It has now been eight or ten days since Col. M,[7] Forbes,[8] and others applied. As they say here, "the mill doesn't grind." The drought of a Yankee advance is upon it. The cold spell has passed by and we are now in the midst of a thaw. I don't know if we haven't hopped from the frying pan into the fire. Step out of your tent and in any direction you are up to your ankle in red mud. During the cold spell the ground had frozen to the depth of some five or six inches, and now as it thaws all this is a perfect loblolly. And my recollection of this country is the freeze and the thaw generally succeed each other all winter. It is seldom that after a thaw there is a dry spell long enough for the earth to dry and become pleasant under foot. So you see our discomforts.

We've four cabins up, daubed and raftered; two of them are canvass-roofed and inhabited. We began today putting up two small cabins for the officers; of course, we still occupy our tent. The ground on which we sleep is as wet as can well be, but if we have a bed of leaves and on this spread your oil cloth, then with three blankets under me and six over, I rest pretty well. But I believe I've enlightened you on the subject of our dormitory before. I've never felt camp life so dull as now. So many are absent. Military duties are all laid aside, morning and evening roll call being the only vestige left of it. We have nothing before us but dull, prosy work, and that of a very uninteresting character, such as notching logs, piling one upon another and daubing them with dirt. Isn't that an intellectual pastime?

Dear precious old fellow, I pine for you more than ever in these dull times; the idea of having only thirty days furlough is a sort of nightmare to me. I feel as if once seated in the dear house at Granite Farm, with you in my arms and the dear children around me, I would be willing never to look upon the sky or the stars for a twelvemonth to come. Oh, would that this unhappy war could end in our liberty and deliverance, and we could be united in love, never again to be separated.

I believe the war will not last long. They've given up Mason and Slidell,[9] but steeped in infamy, they've still another case to dispose of; they've appeased England and gained her contempt. England's interest unerringly points to an issue with them, and it will surely come. Let us adhere closely to our policy. Let us keep our cotton and let not a single bag go, except in exchange for necessary articles. Were our little mite exposed to the Yankee's, I would wish you, yourself, to apply the torch.

I hope Mr. Whitehead may finally conclude to settle in Sparta. I learn the railroad is let out beyond Sparta and will be completed to Macon. It will then be as accessible a point as any. Why don't he secure the Wynn[10] place on the hill? He will then have a little farm around him to raise provisions, and his wife [will] be near her relatives and friends. I presume our own Railroad friends will be again located in Sparta.

Darlie, dearest, give my love to your Mother, reassure her of my gratitude and love for her kindness to me and mine. Kiss the little folks; tell them to be good and studious. Now is their harvest time of knowledge. I owe them both a little letter and must try and send them. Best love to Father. I've just written him. Love to Mr. Edwards, and John and Cosby when you see them, and Linton.[11] I hope Judge T[12] is better. Please remember me to Mrs. Terrell, Whitehead, Connell,[13] and all friends. I have heard that Dawson[14] with his artillery have been ordered back to Georgia on the coast somewhere. If Mrs. D be with you, give her my kindest love. My own darling, goodbye. Love me and pray for me, as I do you, and believe me, always your own Edge

1. John Stafford was a private in Company E (Hancock Volunteers) at the time. *Georgia Roster,* 2:447.

2. Captain Joel Terrell Crawford of Early County, Ga.

3. Captain Theophilus Jackson Smith.

4. Thomas S. Beman, son of Carlisle Beman, the Mt. Zion educator, and nephew of Nathan Beman, the abolitionist, was a private in Company E, Fifteenth Regiment. He was killed at the Battle of Second Manassas, 30 Aug. 1862. *Georgia Roster,* 2:443.

5. Samuel H. Wiley.

6. Lovick Pierce, Jr., private in the Hancock Volunteers, later appointed adjutant, was wounded at Gettysburg. He was among those who surrendered at Appomattox. *Georgia Roster,* 2:446. Lovick, son of Methodist Bishop George Foster Pierce, bore the name of his clergyman grandfather, but was always called "Doc." When he was severely wounded at Gettysburg, Bishop Pierce went to Virginia and brought him home, nursing him back to health. George G. Smith, *The Life and Times of George F. Pierce* (Sparta, Ga., 1888).

7. Colonel William M. McIntosh, Fifteenth Regiment staff, had just been elected lieutenant colonel at the time of this letter. He became a colonel in March 1862 and was killed at Garnett's Farm, Va., three months later. *Georgia Roster,* 2:408.

8. H. W. Forbes was captain and assistant quartermaster of the Fifteenth Regiment. He was assigned as assistant to the brigade quartermaster, Benning's Brigade, Army of Northern Virginia, 15 Sept. 1864, and was paroled 20 May 1865 at Augusta, Ga. *Georgia Roster,* 2:409. Forbes died in Sparta in 1866. Ivy Duggan Papers, Emory University.

9. James Murray Mason and John Slidell, Confederate commissioners en route to Europe on the British merchant ship *Trent,* were removed by the U.S. warship *San Jacinto* and imprisoned 8 Nov. 1861. They were released to avert war with Britain.

10. The Wynn place (later the home of Colonel Henry A. Clinch) was a large, columned house standing on a high hill at the entrance to Sparta from Greensboro. It was burned during racial disturbances in 1974.

11. James B. Edwards, John DeWitt, Linton Stephens. Cosby not identified.

12. Judge James Thomas of Sparta.

13. Dr. Alva Connel[l] of Hancock County, who married Jane Baxter, daughter of Judge Eli H. Baxter.

14. In September 1861 Edgar Dawson organized a battery at Columbus, Ga., named for his father-in-law, Dr. William Terrell. Composed of men from Hancock and Muscogee counties, it principally served in the Georgia coastal area. Smith, *History of Hancock County,* 1:138.

Sallie (Saida) Bird to Edgeworth Bird

Granite Farm, 11 January 1862[1]

My dear darling Papa,

As Captain Smith will leave for Centreville tomorrow, I thought I would sit down and write you a long letter by him and tell you everything I can think of. Bud is writing to you now, too, and I should not be surprised if we both told you the same thing. Mamma received a sweet, long letter from you last night. I don't know how Mamma would get along, even as well as she does, without you, if it was not for your sweet letters you write so often to her. I received a letter from Cousin Teadee the other day. Grandma had one from Aunt Sarah Ann[2] in which she says that Dr. Mell, whose wife has been dead for only five months, has married his sister-in-law, a Miss Cooper,[3] and old Dr. Henderson who is, you know, the Episcopal preacher in Athens, is going to marry an heiress from Savannah. Her name is Miss Scriven;[4] she is a sister to the man that married Miss Addy Moore.

The other day, Captain and Mrs. Smith and Dr. and Mrs. Alfriend spent the day with Mamma. The Doctor told Mamma she ought to shake hands with me forty times, because I do it so much like you. I think Captain Smith looks very well indeed, and so does Dr. Alfriend. Mamma says she wants to go to town this evening to see Capt. Smith off and give him some things for you. There are a good many going with him, and Mr. Lamar is among them.

Mr. and Mrs. Campbell[5] are going to live in Milledgeville and Mr. Gardner[6] is coming to Sparta. I am sorry Mrs. Campbell is going away so far, for I think she is so sweet. Mamma wrote a long letter to you yesterday and is now writing to you again. Grandma received a long letter from Uncle Andrew yesterday with a short one from Alice in it; you know she has gone back to Texas.

Mamma is very uneasy about her meat. She fears that this warm weather will hurt it, but Mr. Edwards says that the weather that we have had will not hurt it at all, but she fears it will. Ginny, one of Mama's cows, has got a nice little calf; great news ain't it? Dr. and Mrs.

Alfriend went out to see Cousin Sammy the other day and found him in bed. Dr. Alfriend says he had some fever. Mamma says she is going to see him the first day she can. What do you think, Papa, Eddie and Bob[7] took him to be? Why, one thought he was a peddler, and the other thought he was an organ-grinder. I know I'll know you, Papa.

Mamma has had Aunt Melinda[8] making candles for the last two or three days. She has made 15 dozen and is just half done. Ain't that a heap for Mamma? Mr. Culver has just sent Yancy over to get his colt. Nancy says he don't look fat and sleek like he did when he was here. Bud has gone out to look at him now. Grandma says I must tell you that she thinks I say very good lessons; at least I try to, dear Papa.

All the negroes seem delighted at the prospect of your returning. They say they think it is time you were coming home. I went down to Aunt Sallie's[9] house yesterday evening, and she asked me all about you and, among other things, she asked me when you were coming home. I told her you would try to come when Captain Smith went back. Said she, "I wish he would make haste and go, for Mas Edge is better 'an any of them there, and yet he can't come home. I spec he will let all his company come before he will." Arthur[10] seems quite indignant every time any of your company come. Mr. Ben Alfriend and Mrs. William Hunt have just gone. They came down to see Mamma. I think Mr. Alfriend is going back to Virginia with Captain Smith, though I don't know.

I must bring my letter to a close now, dear Papa. I send you one cap without a name. You can give it to Capt. Smith, if he has not got one, but if he has, you can give it to anybody you please. Goodbye, give my love to all the soldiers. Once more goodbye and believe me to be

Your own little daughter, Sallie

1. Saida dated her letter 1861, but the context makes 1862 the obvious date.

2. Mary Wiley Baxter's sister, Sarah Ann Wiley, who married John R. Hayes of Thomasville, Ga. Cousin Teadee was probably her daughter Sarah.

3. Patrick Hues Mell became vice chancellor of the University of Georgia in 1860. The death of his wife, Lurene Howard Cooper, left eight motherless children. He then married Eliza Elizabeth Cooper and had eight children by her. After his son Benjamin was killed in the war in Virginia in October 1862, Mell en-

tered the war as colonel of a regiment of faculty and students he raised. The University of Georgia reopened in 1866 and he was made chancellor in 1878. *Dictionary of Georgia Biography,* 2:704–6.

4. The rector of Emmanuel Episcopal Church in Athens, the Rev. Matthew H. Henderson, married Ada Screven of Savannah in January of 1862. Coleman, *Confederate Athens,* 140–41.

5. Mr. and Mrs. Ned Campbell do not appear in the 1860 Georgia census. However, Edward F. Campbell, Jr., a civil engineer, age thirty, was living in the home of his father in Augusta at that time.

6. Not identified.

7. Eddie and Bob were children of Samuel H. Wiley, who was home on leave after a long spell of illness at the front.

8. Aunt Melinda, a slave at Granite Farm.

9. Aunt Sallie, a slave at Granite Farm.

10. Arthur, a slave at Granite Farm.

Edgeworth Bird to Sallie (Saida) Bird

Camp Georgia near Bull Run, 12 January 1862

Dear Daughter,

I have received from you at different times various letters which have remained unanswered, but have always been acknowledged in my letters to Mama. I have always fully appreciated the affectionate tone of your letters, my child, and have noted with increased pleasure your improvement in penmanship and style, and have not failed always to thank the good God who gave me so capable a daughter, and her so efficient and admirable a Mother.

Tho' you've never been to school from home a day in your life, yet you've had advantages that few are lucky enough to meet up with, and if Bud and yourself had failed to improve them, you would indeed be very censurable. The very best teacher, who has twenty or more pupils to instruct, could never have taken the same pains or been near so thorough as your dear Mama has been, and you both owe her *double* duty and love during life.

As the saying goes, you are just entering your "teens," young lady, and it behooves you to begin to prepare yourself in earnest to face the stern realities of life. Hitherto you have been as a little machine, entirely under the direction and control of another motive power. In a few short years your happiness, both in this life and the one to come, will depend upon your own sound judgement and good conduct. The day may come when you may have neither Mama or Papa to counsel you, and it is *now* time that you were fitting yourself to steer your own bark through life's troubled waters, relying upon the chart of your own good sense and virtue to direct you.

Learn always, be the consequence life or death, to speak the truth and to *love* the truth; to practice virtue and to *love* virtue. Truth and virtue are twin sisters, and if personified in heaven, would be seated there on golden thrones as queens. A young girl's heart and mind should be as pure and spotless as a field of snow. As a shower of muddy water would stain and deface the one, so do the gusts of Passion, Untruth, Deceit, defile and corrupt the other. Try then, daughter, to love and practice every virtue—to exercise a calm control over any evil prompting of your nature. Be cheerful, be lively, be jubilant if you will, but never let there be malice or ill nature in your mirth. Try never to be giddy; never let reason lose her sway. Be studious; Knowledge is power; store your mind with useful knowledge. Cultivate a literary taste and the light accomplishments if you wish; they sit gracefully on a woman, but lean not on them as a staff to make your way happily through life. Patience, Purity, Humility, a stern sense of duty—these will bear you up and o'er every wave of trouble, and hurl back every billow of misfortune that Satan's rage or a world's envy may cast at you.

My dear little daughter, I find I have produced more a lecture than a letter, and will speak of other things. I am quite well; only anxious to get home and take you and Bud and Mama and Grandma all in my arms, and Grand Pa, too. Won't I have a great armfull? Kiss Mama a thousand times for me, dear sweet Mama, and love and obey her well. Kingdoms of love to Bud and Grandma and to Grandpa and Mr. Edwards. Howdy to all the servants. Goodbye, daughter. Your own loving Papa, W. E. Bird

Cornelia Ann Soullard to Elizabeth Harris

Savannah, 21 February 1862[1]

My dear friend,

My many thanks for your long, interesting, and much valued letter. . . You begin to feel that you are growing old and ask if I do.[2] From many standpoints I do indeed. . . . When memory went back to childhood and retraced the incidents and events of my life . . . it seems to me I must have lived a hundred years, but as to my present feelings I don't know that I am sensible of any great change . . . I think when my eyesight begins to fail, of which I have always had a great horror, I shall most assuredly both feel and realize the fact. I have tried them shamefully and outrageously during the last year by reading at night fine newspaper print, but I cannot resist it in these exciting times. I must know everything that is going on.

I laugh very much at Mr. S.[3] who has been obliged in the last few weeks to resort to eyeglasses, and which he hasn't learned to use boldly. "It isn't necessary at all, oh, no! But this miserable *Richmond Dispatch* I cannot read by gaslight, it is printed so badly," and such like excuses which it always amuses me to hear in those who have to "come to it." I hope and trust I will be spared that yet awhile tho' I must make up my mind to be prepared for it if I live many years longer, I suppose.

Well, Lizzie, as you perceive, Savannah stands yet, tho' face to face with the enemy and all his legions, and here we all are anxiously waiting and expecting from day to day some demonstration on his part, either by land or water or both. . . . I hope sincerely we may be ready for him when he comes, but there are so many opinions about it. . . . One day I have my confidence pretty steady . . . and the next I feel desponding and I think it is impossible to continue against such power as they have with such limited forces and means as we have. . . . Especially in the last three days we have had so much to depress us in the terrible news of our great reverses, that it is on my part difficult sometimes to rally from a settled conviction that not only Savannah but our cause is destined to an overthrow.

I know it is wrong, for General Walker[4] (who took breakfast with us yesterday morning) says, "Oh, you ladies musn't despond and give up now. Why, it is that very pluck of theirs not to give up to the yankees, but fight it out, that's urged and cheered us on, and has from the beginning." So I began to think, if so much depended on us, we ought by all means to keep up a stout heart and not indulge in croaking or despondency. But yesterday's news from Tennessee could not but cast a deep gloom over the whole city, but I am satisfied it will cause and create a spirit of more determined and desperate resistance on our part.[5]

Several officers were here to breakfast (headquarters of the State forces being very near to us) and I could see that altho' they felt it very keenly they spoke with great spirit. "Why should we imagine such things should happen on Georgia soil? We are not Tennesseans but Georgians, and because they are defeated is no reason that we should be." It is cheering to hear them speak so, and God grant that their hearts and arms may be strengthened for the work before them. . . .

Last Friday was a fast day in behalf of the city, and we have Wednesday afternoon union prayer meetings; yesterday an exceedingly interesting one conducted by Dr. Axson.[6] . . . On Saturday the congregations in the city meet to engage in prayer for the success of the permanent government—between 11 and 12 o'clock, the hour in which the inaugural ceremonies are being performed in Richmond. A very good idea, if it were only carried out in every church in the Confederacy.

Mr. S has come home with good news from Tennessee. That is that it isn't so bad as first reached us. There is a vast difference between the loss of 15,000 and 2,500 men, the latter being the number given today. How strange it is that we can't have a direct and true account. We are so often kept in needless agony for days, and this week especially made to believe that even Nashville has surrendered. We hear also today that General Lee said last night he now considered Savannah well defended against any fleet they have now in our vicinity. . . . But then, when we consider how secure Roanoke Island, Fort Donelson, and other places were thought to be . . . my heart sinks.

And when, too, we see a whole regiment of troops (. . . in General Capers[7] brigade about ten miles from town) . . . on dress parade without a sign of a gun, and some other companies merely armed with pikes, we wonder how they are going to contend with such an enemy. There are, I believe, from 10,000 to 15,000 men in the vicinity and about half of them, those who are in the State service, . . . so green and many of them sickly looking, tallow-faced specimens of the piney woods and look as if they had scarcely spirit enough to fight a [illegible]. . . . I wonder if they wouldn't run at the first fire. I hope they will disappoint me, but I confess to many misgivings when I see of what material so many of our soldiers is composed, and so short a time to drill them. . . .

I see by this morning's papers that they are increasing their forces largely at Port Royal,[8] to act upon Savannah. Fort Pulaski[9] is about cut off entirely from communication with the city by gunboats which are stationed on the north side of the river in one of the cuts that leads round from Port Royal between the islands. . . . I wish they could all be blown sky-high. They have erected a battery over there somewhere on the Carolina side which, [together] with three or four boats, fire incessantly upon our boats that attempt to go to the fort. Altho' Commodore Tattnall[10] with his little fleet is as brave as a lion, it is not thought best to risk too much as the fort is well supplied and is now considered almost impregnable, but those who have friends there of course feel very badly.

Poor Mrs. Olmstead,[11] the wife of the colonel who is in command there (and who, by the way, was Florence Williams of Milledgeville) and who lives just opposite me, is just confined with her first child, all alone, and now not even able to hear from her husband. I feel very sorry for her. Mrs. Erwin,[12] too, who is now in Sparta is, I hear, so distressed that she is coming home which, however, will do no good. By the way, if you go to Sparta, I would like it if you would go to see her. You will like her very much. . . .

I don't expect now to go to Sparta for a long time to come. If there is a necessity, I shall send the children and servants, but I shall remain as long as possible, and then go up a little ways and drop down on the railroad somewhere within hearing distance. Sparta would be too far off when I have to leave my husband behind. We were guilty of a very foolish action not long since in sending the children away and then bringing them back. Mamie[13] went up to Sparta on a visit of a week, and the day she was to return was the very one on which the gunboats appeared in our river and fired upon ours. . . . I was down at the office all day witnessing the fight between our little fleet and theirs through a spy-glass . . . and I could not help feeling excited, seeing the bursting of the shells in the air and the smoke of the cannon. . . . We concluded to send Lilly and Rose[14] off that night to meet Mamie and go back in the carriage. . . . We were sorry for acting so hastily that we telegraphed for them to come back instead of going to Sparta. . . .

I am very glad to hear that your brother[15] has recovered but pained to learn that your father and mother are in such feeble health. Do give a great deal of love to them for me and Sallie and Mary, also, with my congratulations upon the new baby. Much love to all at the Villa, and tell Aunt Avis[16] I am going to answer her very precious little letter by Mamie very soon. She was much delighted with her short visit out there.

As to the butter, dear Lizzie, I am much obliged to you, but don't trouble to send it as I have quite a supply on hand sent me from Sparta. . . . Times are so uncertain I don't provide for the future, but live, as it were, from hand to mouth. With much love to Mr. Harris and hoping to hear from you very soon, I am, as ever, your attached friend, C.

1. This letter is from the collection of Mrs. Ann Harris Marbury, Sparta, Ga.

2. Cornelia Ann Smith, daughter of James Richard Smith of Mt. Zion and Sparta, married Edward A. Soullard, Jr., by this time a commission merchant in Savannah. The 1860 census gives her age as thirty-four.

3. Edward A. Soullard, Jr., grew up in the Powelton area of Hancock County near Mt. Zion and later moved to Savannah, where he became a very successful businessman. He was forty-seven at the time of the 1860 census.

4. William Henry Talbot Walker, brigadier general in the Confederate army, was trained at West Point and decorated for gallantry in the Mexican War. A native of Augusta, Ga., he served on the Georgia coast during the winter of 1861–62. He later commanded a division at Vicksburg and Chickamauga and was killed at Atlanta 22 July 1864. Myers, *Children of Pride*, 1711.

5. Fort Donelson had fallen 16 Dec. with the loss of 15,000 men.

6. Isaac Stockton Keith Axson became pastor of the Independent Presbyterian Church of Savannah in 1857 and spent the rest of his life in that city. His grand-

daughter, Ellen Louise Axson, was the first wife of President Woodrow Wilson. Her grandfather performed the wedding ceremony at the manse of his church. *Children of Pride*, 1456.

7. Francis Withers Capers was superintendent of the Georgia Military Institute at Marietta when the Civil War began. He and his cadets helped with drilling new recruits. In the winter of 1861 he was appointed brigadier general and commanded the Second Brigade, Georgia State Troops. He spent most of his life after the war teaching at the College of Charleston. *Children of Pride*, 1484–85.

8. Union forces had taken nearby Port Royal, S.C., the previous November.

9. "Almost impregnable" Fort Pulaski fell to Union assault in April.

10. Josiah Tattnall, of a distinguished Savannah family, resigned his captaincy after a long career in the U.S. Navy to fight for the Confederacy. He opposed a formidable fleet under Commodore Samuel Francis Du Pont at Port Royal with a few small gunboats and won praise for making do with very little. A few weeks after this letter he took charge of the naval defenses of Virginia with the ironclad *Virginia* (once the *Merrimac*) as his flagship. He was forced to burn the *Virginia* when Norfolk was evacuated, and returned to take charge of Savannah's naval defenses. *Children of Pride*, 1698.

11. Florence Williams, daughter of Peter J. Williams of Milledgeville, married Charles Hart Olmstead in 1859. Olmstead, a Savannah businessman, was colonel of the First (Olmstead's) Regiment, Georgia Infantry. He surrendered Fort Pulaski 11 April 1862 after a day and a half's fierce bombardment. Taken prisoner, he was exchanged after five months and fought until the end of the war, at which time he resumed his life as a Savannah businessman. *Children of Pride*, 1637.

12. Not identified.

13. Mamie, age eleven in the 1860 census, was the Soullards' daughter, a friend of little Sallie Bird.

14. Lilly was the Soullards' other daughter, who was eight at the time of the 1860 census. Rose, unidentified, was perhaps a servant.

15. Samuel H. Wiley.

16. Avis DeWitt Beman, wife of Carlisle P. Beman, the Mt. Zion educator, whose home was called The Villa.

TWO

Sallie Bird Goes to Virginia

"I've seen so many heart-rending scenes here, such awful agony, that I think it would kill me if my dear Edge were to suffer unaided and away from my tender love."

SALLIE BIRD

THE FIGHTING in Virginia quieted after the battle at Manassas (Bull Run). Sallie Bird took advantage of the opportunity to move as near her husband as she could, taking their young son with her and sending little Sallie to stay with her grandmother in Athens. Wilson (Bud) Bird was twelve, his sister thirteen.

Prodded by Lincoln, General George B. McClellan began his Peninsula campaign aimed at capturing Richmond, the Confederate capital. His forces took Yorktown in early May 1862 and reached the outskirts of Richmond at Seven Pines the last of that month. The city seemed to be within McClellan's grasp, but the final battles of the Peninsula campaign, ending at Malvern Hill, snatched the prize away. The threat to Richmond was removed altogether late in August by Lee's brilliant tactics at Second Manassas, where Edgeworth Bird was seriously wounded.

Sallie Bird to Sallie (Saida) Bird

Petersburg, Va., 2 March 1862

My dear, dear Sallie,

I wrote to your dear Grandma from Wilmington, and a hurried note from Double Wells. This time I write to you, and I hope you will receive my letter, and that it will give you as much pleasure as letters always do. My dear child, I must describe my present position to you. We travelled all night, from 2 o'clock yesterday until 8 this morning; left Wilmington at 2 and arrived here at breakfast. We are at Garrett's Hotel, an extremely nice, pleasant house; had for breakfast splendid hot rolls, oysters, beef steak, coffee, rich yellow butter, etc. I really enjoyed my breakfast highly and have had a very pleasant trip so far. The weather has been beautiful until today. It is now raining. Our breakfast over, we are in our rooms. I've taken a good bath, so have dearest Papa and Bud, and we are now sitting by a glowing coal fire, thinking and speaking of the dear ones at home.

Be sure, my precious child, you and your dear Grandma fill the first space in my heart, and I hope you are now both well and happy. The failure to connect at Wilmington, which I mentioned in my letter to Mother, causes us to spend the day here, instead of in Richmond. This morning, as we passed the train bound South, I saw George Jones[1] and had a little talk with him. He did not see Edge, as he was that moment engaged in talking with Louis Camak[2] on the same train, bound home on recruiting service. Louis C looks very well. George Jones not so well. Edge was so sorry he did not see Geo and Geo so sorry he did not see Edge. However, we shall probably meet at Manassas, as he is stationed there. I did not have time to ask how long he would be home. You know he is your Uncle Jones'[3] cousin.

Your Cousin Sam is very well, and I see him constantly. I secured him a good seat, all to himself, in the car last night, so that he could lie down and sleep. The cars are very crowded everywhere, but we've succeeded in getting good seats all the time. The seat we got for Cousin Sam was in the ladies car with us. He and I drank Birdie's[4] health yesterday. Dear, darling child, I often wish it could be so arranged that you were with us to see all the sights. Perhaps you may, one day. Bud says I must give you his love and say he will write to you as soon as he gets quiet, but that he cannot write as I do, *any*where. I found a pen and ink on the mantel peice, and I took the little drawer out of the table in the room and I am writing on that for a desk. The umbrella is safe so far, but the can of lard and basket with [illegible] was left in Augusta. Edge came to me in Augusta (at the depot) and asked me if I had a can of lard. I said *no* decidedly and I never knew until I left Augusta that Mother had sent one up by John.[5] Sam knew it but did not speak of it till the last moment in A[ugusta]; so Edge told Mr. Eve[6] to get them from the hotel where they were carried with the rest of the baggage and take them to his house.

I shall write to Cousin Philo[7] to sell the lard for me as long as it is in the city. I'll take the can home with me as I return. My dear Sallie, you need not send but two of the Irving books to me by Mr. Culver, *Goldsmith* and *The Alhambra.*[8] Have them carefully put up and ask Mr. C to please put them in his trunk. And I wish Wilson had a nice suit of clothes like the [illegible] or something of that sort. Ask your Grandma please to get his patterns out and have a suit made for him if possible to get the material. I find, already, that your Father was right. Up here, where we see thousands of soldiers and many little boys in uniform, we see how necessary it is to dress according to position. The cloth like Lieut. Reid's[9] uniform is the sort needed. It is absolutely necessary to dress according to station. I know there is no cloth in Augusta of the kind, nor in Sparta. It has to be trimmed and faced with light blue. If I possibly can, I'll get the material for a suit in Richmond and send it to Mother to have made. The only difficulty is that I may not have time.

Edge says today he is sorry I had the coarse suit made for Bud, but I'll make him wear it in bad weather and at the boarding house while we are there.

A number of fine bells are ringing for church; but for the rain we would all go. I would, and Papa, and Bud. Mrs. Smith[10] is a great traveller; she can get along just as well alone as with a score of gentlemen. We are travelling with a nice lady and gentleman from Vicksburg, Miss. They are bride and bridegroom. She was raised in Richmond and is going back there now to stay. Her husband is assistant surgeon in the 21st Mississippi Regt. I must tell you some good news we heard on the cars last night. The *Nashville*[11] has got in, on the N. Carolina coast, under the guns of Fort Macon. The *Ella Harley* got out of Charleston two nights ago with a rich cargo and the *Carolina*[12] left Wilmington and got out safely the other night with a $250,000 cargo. The *Nashville* brings in $2,000,000 in specie. Ask Grandma if all this isn't good news.

The rumor is, this morning, that an attack is expected at Manassas, but these rumors don't gain much belief. In North Carolina the people solidly condemned Col. Shaw[13] for his surrender and conduct at Roanoke Island. They say that every order given by Lt. Col. Trice was countermanded by Shaw. Although a North Carolinian, his state condemns Shaw bitterly. He is released on parole, but they are going to court martial him.

Give my love and a kiss to dear, sweet, precious Mother, in which Edge and Wilson join. Love to Aunt Sally, Nancy, Eliza, Judy, Rachel, Can and Dinah, and to all the other servants. We all speak of them very often. You must not show my letter to anyone but Grandma, but you can tell your Grandpa you've heard from us, safe and well so far. Love to Grandpa from all of us. We'll write to him when we reach Manassas. God bless you, my child, Your devoted Mother.

I directed the envelope, before I left home, to your Grandma. The light gray is too light for Bud. Edge says it ought to be very dark steel or iron gray, or else black trimmed with blue. Do get it made, dear Mother, to come on by Mr. Culver. If Grandma should cut any pants for Bud, tell her the pattern is all right except to make them *an inch* longer. Goodbye for the present, my dear child. Write often and direct just as you did to dear Papa until I tell you differently. Did I tell you that Janey Dickson was at the cars to meet me and that I had a sweet, short interview with her?

1. The only likely name in the lists is George H. Jones of Glascock County, a neighboring county to Hancock. Jones was a captain in Company B, Twenty-second Regiment, at the time. *Georgia Roster,* 4:162.

2. Louis Camak, whose grandfather was James Camak, a railroad official. Hull, *Annals of Athens,* 444.

3. James Hardwick Jones who married Sarah Wiley, Sallie Bird's great-aunt.

4. Samuel Wiley's daughter, Sarah Bird.

5. A slave at Granite Farm.

6. William Joseph Eve, who married Philoclea Edgeworth Casey, niece of Edgeworth Bird's mother.

7. Cousin Philo, Mrs. William Joseph Eve, was an important link in the family connections of Edgeworth Bird.

8. Washington Irving (1783–1859), best known as the creator of Rip van Winkle, wrote *The Alhambra: A Series of Tales and Sketches of the Moors and Spaniards* (1832) and the *Life of Oliver Goldsmith, with Selections from His Writings* (1849).

9. James M. Reid, first lieutenant, Sydney Brown infantry of Hancock County, was wounded at the Battle of Seven Pines in May 1862 and died the next month in Richmond. *Georgia Roster,* 1:751.

10. Mrs. Theophilus Jackson Smith, the former Mary Gonder. Her husband may have named his beautiful Glen Mary plantation house in Hancock County in her honor.

11. The *Nashville,* a Confederate raider, had been converted from a side-wheel steamer engaged in the coastal trade between New York and Charleston until seized by Confederate authorities. Returning from a successful trip to England, she evaded the blockading ships at Beaufort, N.C., "by a daring trick" and made it into the port 28 Feb. 1862. J. Thomas Scharf, *History of the Confederate States Navy* (Albany, N.Y., 1894), 795–96.

12. The *Carolina,* also called *Theodora, Gordon,* and finally *Nassau,* successfully ran the blockade out of Wilmington and Charleston until 28 May 1862, when she was captured and sent to New York as a prize of war. *Civil War Naval Chronology, 1861–1865* (Washington, D.C., 1961), 315.

13. Henry M. Shaw, colonel, Eighth North Carolina Infantry (state troops). *List of Field Officers,* 112. Shaw was captured at Roanoke Island 8 Feb. 1862 and paroled at Elizabeth City 21 Feb. He was exchanged at Aiken's Landing, James River, Va., 10 Nov. 1862, and was present and accounted for until killed at Batchelder's Creek, near New Bern, 1 Feb. 1864. Weymouth T. Jordan, Jr., comp., *North Carolina Troops, 1861–1865: A Roster, Vol. IV Infantry* (Raleigh, N.C., 1973), 521. Shaw was apparently never court-martialed.

Sallie Bird to Sallie (Saida) Bird

Gordonsville, Va., 10 March 1862

My dearest Sallie, I wrote to your dear Grandma two days since and now commence a letter to you. I am sure you'll be glad always to get a letter to add to your treasured packages in your desk, especially from Mamma, won't you? Well, darling, whether I write to you or Grandma, my heart is full of love to you both, and the only thing that mars my content is a desire to see you and her. . . . He [your Papa] says all his duties are pleasures now, since I am near him. . . . He speaks often and lovingly of his little daughter and says he feels perfectly easy about you, that you are in the best hands.

Our only care is to impress upon you, darling, the *command* that you are good, obedient, and grateful to my precious Mother, your dear, good, indulgent Grandmother. Tell her when you get to Athens to send you to school, if she thinks best upon inquiry to do so. I would be glad to have you improve every hour of your time. If you don't go to school, you must study faithfully and you can recite to Grandma and study French with Teadee. Dear darling, don't be idle and careless, for every hour is important to you now. Mrs. Smith sends her dear love to you. Mrs. McIntosh[1] says tell Grandma please, after you go to Athens, whenever you hear from me, let Mrs. Harris[2] know that she is well. Mrs. M is a very sweet woman, gentle, lovable, and kind.

Bud has written you one letter and says he will write to Grandma soon. His eyes are busy all the while, so many soldiers, such immense trains of ammunition and cannon, etc. We see both roads from our room, the Richmond and Manassas and the Charlottesville road. The sentinels are pacing up and down before every church door, the churches being filled with powder, cartridges, cannon balls, etc. Then they are now seizing private houses to use as officer's headquarters, etc. The people are in great trouble, but it is a military necessity. Troops are pouring in by carloads. The officers dress distinguishes them. Everybody likes your dear Papa. The ladies at Dr. Marstella's[3] all fell in love with him, they said.

Col. McIntosh is a delightful man. I like him extremely. He is very fine looking and very agreeable and warmly attached to your dear Papa. Mrs. McIntosh says he loves Edge dearly. He is so cheerful (the Col.) and has fine manners. . . .

We are boarding at Mrs. Smith's. The house we staid at last night or night before was an excellent one, but they could not let us stay. However, they've pressed an out-house on the lot for Genl Johnston's servants,[4] and I hope we won't be turned out from here, tho' all the residents are uneasy. But we'll manage, don't be uneasy about us. Mrs. Smith is captain of "our mess" and she don't mind anything, but is a splendid hand to fix and arrange. She don't mind trifles.

Write to me often, daughter. . . . I've not had a letter yet, but it is because they've moved the Regt. I shall get some soon, I know. I've written to your Cousin Sallie Wiley and I shall write soon to your Aunt Julia.[5] Kiss Grandma for me and give much love to all the servants. Tell Aunt Sally I'll answer her letter whenever she writes and she must write me a full account of all home affairs. Direct to Mrs. W. E. Bird, care of T. B. Jackson, Gordonsville, Va.[6] Tell Henry to take good care of all the stock. Sam is well and getting along finely. I have not seen him since we parted at the cars, the day we reached Manassas. God bless you, dear daughter. Never neglect your Bible or your prayers.

1. Mrs. McIntosh was the wife of Colonel William M. McIntosh, who was killed three months later at Garnett's Farm, Va.

2. Mrs. Young Harris or Mrs. Sampson Harris of Athens.

3. Not identified.

4. Confederate General Joseph E. Johnston.

5. Julia Richardson, the wife of Eli H. Baxter, Sallie's uncle.

6. Jackson was postmaster at Gordonsville.

Edgeworth Bird to Sallie Bird

Camp Toombs, near Culpepper Courthouse, 15 March 1862

Capt. Smith and myself both wrote the day before yesterday and he again yesterday. Today I write again to you, my dearest treasure, and thus by alternating you will all hear the oftener. The letter I sent you was a hurried affair, and I scarcely had time to give any incidents of the march. It was half past two o'clock before the Col[1] and I got to bed the night we left you all. Sammie's horse was very lame and we made slow haste; however, we managed to capture another steed before we left the "Pike" and carried him in triumph into camp. But by daylight he proved worthless, and the quartermaster turned him loose.

I mentioned that Company E was detailed as rear guard to the Brigade and that we had a "sweet, sad time." Our chief duty was to keep up stragglers, and towards the dewey eve these wearied gentry fell back in numbers. We'd come on them in squads of three or four lying by the road side, sore of foot and limb, and some quite ill, but under imperious orders we would have to hurry them on, and I assure you it was a very disagreeable duty.

Capt S[2] couldn't march on foot and was mounted on Col. Mac's spare horse and was scarcely with us. But he was doing noble duty for us by riding out to the farm houses and providing cakes, hardboiled eggs, etc. We had been ordered to provide three days rations, but they gave out in half the time, and a hungrier set of fellows you've never had the ill luck to meet up with. At night we raked up leaves, spread our blankets, and slept under heaven's canopy. The most of the march was in sight of the Blue Ridge mountains; away in the distance they lay in huge masses, wrapt in their bluish robes and, with the intervening scenery, formed a most enchanting picture. From every hill we had splendid views of them.

We passed the Warrenton springs, and being halted there a while, some of the boys filled their canteens with the white sulphur water, and horrid faces and nasal twitches most of them made at it. The buildings are splendid and large enough to accommodate fifteen hundred persons. They are a favorite resort in this portion of Virginia, but I fear their beauty has been sadly marred, for a regiment of cavalry has been quartered in them for some time, and they've been generally used as a hospital during the whole war.

Several little towns lay along the route, of little note. *Our* boys altogether stood the march remarkably well; none better, tho' the heavy knapsacks gave them jesse.[3] I suffered no inconvenience from it except weary pedestals. I learn that tomorrow we again take up the march, I presume to Gordonsville, tho' no one knows anything except General Johnston himself. But I have little doubt we go towards you, my own darling, and that will scatter flowers along the muddy path we tread tomorrow.

Your sweet "pencillings" were received this morning. Shannon[4] woke us up about 5 o'clock and gave the letter and the certain news that you were all comfortably housed at G[ordonsville]. I was glad you have Mrs. Dorsey[5] still with you, as it adds to the comfort of her position and pleasures you all mutually. Darlie, dearest, won't you talk with her a great deal?

Precious, I love you so entirely and devotedly and so desire and crave that there should be no shade between our souls. You ladies must be very wise and far seeing and shape your course accordingly. Keep as near us as you can. In three days after this my impression is we will be with you. You must be as economical as is proper for no [one] can say what may turn up, or what call may be made on one's resources. Darling, I would make me a bag of strong material with short strings to tie around my waist and wear it under my dress. In this, place all your money except what is required for present purposes. *Never* leave your money in your trunk whilst travelling. You can so easily lose the trunk. Capt. Smith and the Col. are both well and desire love and kindest regards to you all.

Birdie, I am seated under a waggon cover stretched over poles and it is raining disagreeably. It spatters on my paper, and that's why it is so blurred up. The rain will make our march very uncomfortable tomorrow. I expect Willy M[6] and Bud have a good time together, there are so many new sights to see. I hope they are good friends by now. Say to Mrs. Dorsey, I will, with pleasure, send news of her to Mr. D, if I can have the chance. I don't know what Brigade he is attached to. You ladies must have your bottles well filled with the staff of life, so as to enliven us when we come. This camp is as dry as a powder horn. This suggestion comes from Capt. Smith who is lying nearby. I believe the fellow would drink himself to death if he could get it.

Precious darling, give my love to all the ladies of your Regiment. When we write we'll form a Brigade. Kiss Bud goodbye, my own precious heart's love. I hope to see you in a few days. May God bless you and preserve you to your own Edge

1. Colonel William M. McIntosh.

2. Captain Theophilus Jackson Smith.

3. "Gave them jesse," a slang expression, meaning to thrash.

4. Peter J. Shannon of Company I, Fifteenth Regiment, had just been appointed adjutant. Elected a major in August 1862, he fought on until the surrender at Appomattox. *Georgia Roster,* 2:466.

5. Mrs. Dorsey was from Maryland. The two officers in the Maryland list by that name were Lieutenant Colonel Ed R. Dorsey, First Maryland Infantry, and Lieutenant Colonel Gustavus W. Dorsey, First Maryland Cavalry. *List of Field Officers,* 38.

6. Willy McIntosh, the son of Colonel William W. McIntosh.

Sallie Bird to Sallie (Saida) Bird

Gordonsville, Va., 15 March 1862

My dear, dear little daughter,

I've written you and dear Grandma so many letters since we parted, that if you've received them all, you have been fully aware of all our movements. You will be sorry to hear, I'm sure, that up to this day, more than three weeks since I left Georgia, I've not had one single letter from home. Of course, I understand how it is, for the falling back of the Army completely disarranges the mail, and after a while we hope to get a budget. . . .

We are still pleasantly situated at Mrs. Jackson's and hope to be able to retain our position. Mrs. McIntosh is one of the sweetest women that ever lived, so amiable, gentle, and good. I have been sleeping with her until a few nights ago when Mrs. J gave us another room with a bed. In that we put Mrs. McIntosh and Willie. Wilson and I sleep together, and Mrs. Smith and Mrs. Dorsey. Mrs. Dorsey is the "light and life" of our mess. Her fun and frolic are very cheering to any one of us who may be in a despondent mood. For my own self, I am ever cheerful. It is so sweet, darling, to be near your dear Father. to *feel* that I am, in some sense, in his presence and to realize that in two hours I could get to him.

Great excitement is felt here, and the movements of the Army of the Potomac are still a mystery. Nothing is known in Richmond and very little here. We only know they have fallen back, but we know no more. We know where Toombs' Brigade is, too. I've sent Papa a letter every day for four days. This morning Maj. Melton of S.C., a member of Gen'l Smith's staff,[1] left here and took letters for us. The mail still remains unorganized, tho' Mr. Jackson, postmaster here, tells me he thinks there will be a mail today. There has been no mail from the direction of Manassas since our forces fell back. So that you see, if I was in Georgia, I would suffer from hearing not a word. None of us have had letters, but we have had telegrams and hear that all are safe and well. . . .

Yesterday (Saturday) was a terrible day. It rained all day, a very cold rain, and the streets are again a perfect quagmire. Toombs' Brigade are encamped about a mile this side of Culpeper. I thought all day yesterday of the dear soldiers who've changed suddenly from winter quarters to cold tents again. May a good Lord preserve them from all harm. I believe if I were a man I would never lay down my arms in this glorious struggle, till the fiendish invader was driven back step-by-step from our soil. The wretched Yankees admit they were disastrously defeated in the Naval Battle at Hampton Roads.[2] My earnest desire is now that the noble *Virginia* may not lie by but push her triumphs until the blockade is broken and the Yankee fleets destroyed. We ought to have twenty *Virginias*. You know she was the *Merrimac*.

I want you to read the papers and keep up with the current events. And daughter, I hope you are not idle, but busily improving your time. I want you to study and to take music lessons in Athens, if you can get a good teacher. And I *do* hope you will industriously avail yourself of any means of improving your mind. Remember, I wish you to read no *book* or *novel* unless with the advice and consent of a judicious friend. You might poison your young mind by improper reading. And dearest child, be faithful to your Bible and your prayers. Papa says he feels so anxious to have you a *good* girl, honest, true, obedient, and affectionate. I pray that you may be all that our loving hearts desire for you. My precious Edge is perfectly well as I said before, and told me when I wrote always to send you and Grandma a kiss from him. He is very busy now.

I hope very soon to see Mr. Culver.[3] He is to pass through this place and we'll be on the lookout and get my things from him. I shall get, as I said before, a letter from Papa today. . . . I see a daily Richmond paper every day and hear the movements of the Army in that way, but you must never fail to tell me when you write, if any news has been received. I still direct to Sparta as I hope you are there yet, but I expect Mother wants to be getting home, and do give my love to all the servants. Tell Aunt Sally, Eliza, and Nancy that I hope to hear a good report from them of all things. Judy and Rachel were, of course, to go to the field when Mother leaves. Give my love to them.

Bud waits on me a good deal, and yet I almost wish he was with you and at school. Education is so important, and then he is, of course, an expense. But he enjoys everything, often wishing you were here. From twelve to twenty freight trains are running all the time. I saw 9 trains yesterday. I will write to Aunt Sally soon.

I hope Mother has started my garden for me. I don't care for peas, but other things. I often think of my dear flowers that I love so well—of the big oval, and the new walk, and Mother's little grass bank. I think it will do well as it will not have the afternoon sun in summer. Write to me every five days, daughter. One letter a week is not enough. When I have your Father's address, I'll send it so you can write to him, but our letters will answer for each other. Tomorrow I shall write to dear Lucie D.,[4] if nothing happens. I've written to your Aunty,[5] a long letter to Loy, to John, to Sallie Wiley, Julia W,[6] 8 letters to you and Mother, and one to Grandpa, besides the three other letters Wilson has written. I hope all go to hand safely. I mention it often because I fear some letters may be lost, and when you go to Athens give my love to Aunty and Teadee, and always to Mr. and Mrs. H. Hull. Goodbye, darling daughter. Kiss dear Grandma sweetly for me. Your devoted Mother.

1. Samuel W. Melton, South Carolina lawyer, served on the staff of Major General Gustavus W. Smith at the time of this letter. Later Melton was assigned to the

office of the adjutant and inspector general in Richmond.

2. The steam frigate *Merrimac* was sunk when Union forces evacuated Norfolk. The Confederates raised it and added armor plate and a cast-iron ram. The ship, renamed the *Virginia,* attacked Union ships blockading Hampton Roads on 8 March 1862, destroying several. The news raised Southern hopes and caused panic in the North, but the *Virginia* was not seaworthy. Her challenge was soon met by the Union armored ship *Monitor.* J. G. Randall and David Donald, *The Civil War and Reconstruction* (Lexington, Mass., 1969), 442–43.

3. Second Lieutenant Henry H. Culver.

4. Lucy Terrell Dawson.

5. Mary Baxter, wife of John J. Gresham of Macon.

6. Julia W was Julia Burnet Whitehead. Loy (Eli Leroy Baxter) and John were Sallie Bird's brothers.

Edgeworth Bird to Sallie Bird

Camp between Orange C.H. and Fredericksburg, 8 April 1862

We are in the midst of a terrible spell of weather, dearest of precious darlings. It was horrible yesterday and last night. We thought we would go to Fred'burg, but were halted some time here and then ordered to lay by until morning. I overtook the Regt. a few minutes after they left camp. We marched all night, till nearly four.

Last night we were ordered to be at Louisa C.H. tonight. It is 24 miles through the snow and mud. I don't believe half the Regt. can make it. Darling, I thought of you all my waking hours last night, and you were my first thought this morning.

We have thought and talked the matter over seriously and earnestly. Richmond is the point of attack. If we are successful in defending it and driving them back, all is right. If not, the panic and confusion incident to such a scene would, of course, be sufficient for us to desist. You should all not be there. Richmond is no place for you. The road below is threatened at Goldsboro. Under all circumstances, we have concluded this. We trust you to the good judgment of Mr. Newman.[1] We think you had better remain with him until you hear from us, unless your retreat by Gordonsville to Lynchburg and Charlotte is threatened. If all goes well, you can come to us when we write.

If not, and you should leave to go to Blandy's,[2] you can still come to us. If the Yankees begin to scout in this direction, of course you'll leave. Capt. D and the Col.[3] and I have agreed upon this. Dr. A is not with us at present. My precious, say for me to Mr. Newman that I cannot express my grateful feeling to him for his very great kindness to you and us all. I only hope I may be able to repay him some day. Present all these views to him about going by Lynchburg to Charlotte, where your Cousin is, in an emergency. The Col. and Jack are well. So am I, dearest, and my trust is in God to preserve us all to each other. And precious Birdie, I have a bright, cheerful hope about it. Won't you have it, too, my own Dearie? Kiss my little boy for me, and he must be obedient and good. Kind love to Mrs. M.[4] and most sincere regards to every member of Mrs. M.'s family. The Col. says he will write her from Louisa C.H. Goodbye, My *Blessing*, my own Sallie. Be cheerful. I'll send a line when I can.

Darlie, my precious, show yourself a little hero and patriot. Don't despair, but try to be a support to others.

Goodbye, your own Edge

1. James Stanley Newman of Orange, Va., later moved to Hancock County, Ga., where he taught at Richard Malcolm Johnston's school and eventually bought Rockby plantation. Mrs. Terrell Moore, "Rockby," Sparta *Ishmaelite*, 20 June 1963.

2. Julia Blandina Baxter, daughter of Eli H. Baxter and Julia Richardson of Cornucopia plantation. Blandie had married A. B. (Baxter) Springs of Springfield, Fort Mill, S.C., near Charlotte. Three years later, when he fled Richmond, President Jefferson Davis spent the night at the home of Colonel Springs on his way south. Davis got down on his knees and played a game of marbles with the two Springs boys, Eli, thirteen, and Johnny, eleven. Burke Davis, *The Long Surrender* (New York, 1985), 103.

3. Colonel William M. McIntosh and Captain Dudley McIver DuBose, who later became a brigadier general. *Georgia Roster*, 2:408.

4. Mrs. William M. McIntosh.

Sallie Bird to Sallie (Saida) Bird

Richmond, 21 April 1862

My dear little daughter,

I don't know whether I shall be able to finish my letter today, but at any rate I commence it. I do not write as often as I did, darling, because paper and envelopes are so high. . . . Envelopes are 50 cents a quire, paper $1.50 a quire. . . . Day before yesterday, I had a sweet letter from your dear Papa, the first I've had since he went to Yorktown. . . . Mrs. Smith has had a letter since, and so has Mrs. Alfriend. Mrs. McIntosh had not had a letter yet.

Your dear Father, my child, is now in great peril. I want you, night and day, to pray earnestly for him and beseech God, if it be his holy will, to spare his precious life to us. He is now often in less than a quarter of a mile of the Yankees. The shells come flying over their heads, but as yet "nobody is hurt" in the 15th. There were two of the Regulars killed and six men wounded the other day in Toombs Brigade. Our men were in the trenches when we last heard from them, and the enemy are shelling the camps all the time. Of course, you have heard of the fight there the other day in which the 16th Geo. and another Regt. were engaged, and our men repulsed the Yankees. Of course, too, you have read all the accounts at Corinth. The battle at Yorktown, almost every one seems to think, will come off very soon, and a bloody battle it will be.

Oh, my child, think of what life would be to me forever, if your precious Father should be killed! But if he is wounded, I am here to nurse him and take care of him. Pray then to our Heavenly Father for your beloved, your *good* Father. I cannot tell you how glad I am to be here, for I hear from Yorktown frequently. But I hear the mails from there are stopped, or at any rate, very irregular. All the last week there was only one mail to this city from the Peninsula.

I have had two visits from Willie Seymour,[1] two or three from Cousin Jule Curry,[2] many from Mr. Sims,[3] one from Mrs. Trippe,[4] and two from Margaret Nisbet.[5] Margaret is going to leave tomorrow to try to work her way into Washington. She and I had a pleasant promenade together the other day. She is a very agreeable woman. Yesterday we all went to the Catholic church. It was a great sight to Bud.

Charlotte [N.C.], 24 April. My dear Sallie, I was interrupted in my letter by a visit from Cousin Will[6] who insisted upon my leaving the city. He said I must come with him and his family, which I did, and am here now. I sent on a note to Mother by Col. Barrow[7] this morning, also the black trunk and key to it. Ask Mother, please to put up my furs for me, and woolen things, and take care of everything else. I sent home everything not absolutely necessary, for I feared I might be troubled, so now I have but one trunk, I am glad to say. I bought you a pretty muslin dress this morning. Muslin and everything else are scarce and high. I bought one for you and a dark one for myself, which will be all I buy in the dress line. I got a half or back bonnet in Richmond. The prices are awful. *Plain drawn* silk bonnets without a flower in them cost 17 and 18 dollars in R[ichmond]. Mine is a *great* bargain, I got at $8.

Dear Papa was well when I heard from him. I saw Capt. Twiggs[8] this morning, who married Lucy Wilkins. He is on his way home; he has had erysipelas. He telegraphed to her that he was coming. Capt. Twiggs saw Papa the other day; he was quite well. I saw Col. Barrow this morning, and he promised to call and see you and Mother and tell Mother that he had seen me. I've been to the Telegraph office here to see if I could get any news further from the fight of the 3rd Geo. I hope, however, by this time dear Mother's anxiety is relieved. For myself, I am very anxious, but *hope everything*. Cousin Will reasoned me into that.

I sent a note to Blandy thro' the P. office today. She won't get it before tomorrow, so I may not see her until the day after. I will keep my letter open, as I shall see her soon, and besides you'll hear from me thro' Mrs. Barrow. I am so sorry I did not get your dress before the trunk left. I would have put it in the trunk and Grandma would have had it made for you. Richmond is no place for people but millionaires. I never heard such exorbitant prices in my life. It is perfectly awful. I bought the muslins here. There are some beautiful goods here, of the kind so fashionable in Richmond, silk and linen—a kind of poplin. I would certainly buy one but for the cost, and money is so very scarce now.

I have concluded, daughter, that I will finish this letter and let you know how to address my letters—*not* to Charlotte, as I hear that is not Cousin Baxter's P. office, but to "Mrs. W. E. Bird, c/o A. B. Springs Esq., Fort Mills, S.C." . . .

Be a good little girl; perhaps I may soon be home, perhaps not, I cannot tell. You know I'll have to come home for summer clothes before long. In Richmond merinos were pleasant. Here, thin dresses are beginning to be worn. I must close now, as I am going out to try to get Bud a jacket of some kind. Kiss Mother for me. I sent a message to John by a lady, a real lady who lives in Goldsboro. She promised to hunt him up and deliver the message. Dear Richard is, I hope, well. Write me the news from the Texas boys.

Goodbye, darling. God bless you. Bud sends love and kisses to you and Grandma.

Your devoted Mother

I had a long talk with Mr. Flinn[9] yesterday. He saw Papa the day before. He went back to Yorktown today. I sent a long message to Papa by Mr. Flinn.

1. Willie Seymour was a resident of Athens who took part in a meeting there following Lincoln's election to discuss what needed to be done. Stegeman, *These Men She Gave*, 143.

2. Cousin Jule Curry was related to Jabez L. M. Curry, who was in Richmond. He married (in 1847) Ann Alexander Bowie, daughter of Alexander Bowie and Susan Barnett (Jack) Bowie. See Owen, *History of Alabama and Dictionary of Alabama*, 3:444–45.

3. Not identified. Thomas J. Semmes of Louisiana was in Richmond in the Confederate Senate, but Sallie Bird probably would not have misspelled the name of this family friend.

4. Anne O'Neal married Robert P. Trippe in 1842. He was a member of the Confederate House of Representatives. A first honor graduate of the University of Georgia in 1839, Trippe served on the Georgia Supreme Court and in the U.S. Congress. *Biographical Dictionary of the Confederacy*, 416.

5. Margaret Nisbet was the daughter of John Nisbet and Harriet Cooper of Athens. Hull, *Annals of Athens*, 470.

6. Cousin Will was William Springs of Charlotte, N.C., brother of Baxter Springs, the husband of Blandie Baxter.

7. Lieutenant Colonel James Barrow of Athens, a staff adjutant of Howell Cobb's Sixteenth Georgia Regiment, was wounded in the fighting along the Warwick River on the Virginia Peninsula and was

returning home to recuperate. Two years later, still only twenty-two, he was shot through the heart while commanding the Sixty-fourth Georgia Regiment in an engagement near Jacksonville, Fla. Stegeman, *These Men She Gave*, 44, 68, 103–5.

8. The only Captain Twiggs in the Georgia Roster is H. D. D. Twiggs, Company G, First Regiment. *Georgia Roster*, 1:325.

9. William Flinn (sometimes Flynn), chaplain of the Sixteenth Regiment, Georgia Infantry. *Georgia Roster*, 2:480.

Edgeworth Bird to Sallie (Saida) Bird

In the trenches near Yorktown, 28 April 1862

My dear daughter,

I know you've looked anxiously for a letter from Papa, for I well remember how earnestly you expressed a desire to have letters from me. And you must have desired it the more of late, since dear Mama has been separated from me, and you are not able to gain such frequent intelligence of me. Yes, Mama has been advised by friends to leave Richmond and is now in Charlotte at your Cousin Blandy Spring's. It is a great trial for us not to be able to see each other now and then, as we so earnestly hoped and believed when she came on. I know it is a greater trial to her than to me who have so much excitement around me. We can only resume an old plan of frequent interchange of letters.

Meanwhile, by her waiting a while in Charlotte, some event may transpire whose light may dispel the thick clouds which gather around Richmond now, and she may be able to return near me. Indeed, it is already the news today in camp that Jackson has whipped Banks near Orange, which may prove a check to one of the columns which are advancing on Richmond. Down here on the Peninsula, I know not what we may be able to do. We are not clearly advised of the intentions of the enemy. Many think we will have no fight here. I think they intend to take Yorktown, if possible, and they can do so if they undertake it by slow approaches and the assistance they can bring to bear from the heavy batteries on their ships. They may possibly be able to shell them out of their works there.

Toombs Brigade are several miles to the right of Yorktown. We have a line of trenches and batteries entirely across the Peninsula. Our Regt. takes its turn in them every other 24 hours and have been doing so for ten days past. When we go in, we lie in them for a day and night, rain, hail or shine, and it has mostly been our luck to be in them in the mud and rain. There is our Battery at Dam No. 1 where it is very dangerous. The Enemy's Battery is just opposite, in plain view, about 600 yards off, and is constantly filled with sharpshooters, who pick a fellow off if he shows so much as his head. We have been there twice and each time had the misfortune to have one of our Company wounded badly. First, Corporal Cone,[1] who was shot through the left lung from imprudently exposing himself, and I fear will hardly survive it; and the next time Wingfield Butts[2] had a piece of shell driven through his thigh. It passed between the bone and large artery. The wound is very dangerous, but it is not believed mortal. The shell exploded about three feet above the heads of nearly a dozen of our Company, and also wounding Doc Pierce,[3] Pete Harris,[4] and John Stafford[5] very slightly in the face.

We don't go there any more, having had our turn. We are in the trenches last night and today, and before dinner had a slight brush with the yankee's across the swamp, exchanging shots with them for half an hour. I think [we] must have killed several; the balls whistled over our heads but that was all the damage they could do us. They had finally to leave. Now all is quiet and I concluded to write you, as you so richly deserve a letter from the nice ones you've sent me, tho' it has been a long time since I heard from home. My dear daughter, you must write often to me. Always direct your letter to 15th Regt Geo Vols, Toombs Brigade, and at present send them to Yorktown. It seems at present very uncertain about their reaching me, but that must not discourage you. I hope your dear Grandma will write sometimes, too. I love her very much and think of you all continually.

There is hardly an hour of the day but some of you are in my thoughts—and you my dear child have a place in my heart. It was a source of inexpressible comfort to me to have Mama and Bud near me and see them now and then; and as for Mama, I never saw her happier and brighter. It is a bitter trial to her to have to leave and go from me, so she earnestly writes me. I know she has written you and Grandma all about the kind, very kind friends we had near Orange C.H., Mr. James Newman and family. We can never forget them. I have not had an opportunity of writing to them, but she has done so. Tell Grandma it is nearly time she had run down to Granite Farm for a short time. I hope she may find it convenient to do so, if Mama does not go home shortly. She can put things to rights there in a very few days, and the negroes, I know, would be overjoyed to see her. I expect they long for a sight of some of the white family.

I wrote Grandpa a long letter the other day and I hope it will go safely to him. I am very sorry and distressed about his lonely situation and I know he suffers a good deal about me. Oh! The horrors of this war are endless. We heard New Orleans was taken, but now it is contradicted, and we learn that our own iron clad boats sunk two Yankee steamers that succeeded in passing Fort Jackson.[6] I hope it is so, and that the Crescent City is safe from their polluting hand. Mama found many pleasant acquaintances in Richmond. Cousin Will Yancey[7] and wife was there, and Mary Harrell, his daughter, and others of whom she has no doubt written you. She was down at the wharf when our Brigade steamed off down the James River, and I did not then think our separation would be so long.

I've seen several Athens friends. Dr. Bob Smith[8] was in our camp yesterday, and before that I saw Bob Thomas,[9] Willy Lumpkin,[10] and Miller Lumpkin,[11] also General Howell Cobb.[12] I haven't yet seen Col. Cobb,[13] but he and all the others are well. They are camped quite near me. I've seen Mr. Flynn several times. My daughter, you must be a good girl, study hard, obey your Grandma, and never forget to say your prayers night and morning, and always think of me in them. Kiss Grandma for me. Howdy to Violet and Can and Peggy and all the rest. I think of them all. Remember me with love to Mr. and Mrs. Hull and Mrs. Hayes and family and all friends. Love me always as I do you, my dear daughter. Your affectionate father, Wm. E. Bird

1. Jonathan B. Cone, private, Company E, Fifteenth Regiment, 15 July 1861, was wounded at Rapidan Station, Va. (*Georgia Roster* says 1 May 1862, but

this date must be incorrect). He died of wounds in a Richmond hospital 10 May 1862. *Georgia Roster,* 2:444. Judge Frank L. Little of Sparta, in his unpublished memoirs (1911), said the men had been careless about sharpshooters because of an early morning fog and that Cone "unguardedly arose and stretched himself fully." He immediately fell, "pierced in the breast by a sharpshooter's bullet." Little and his brother Wilbur, George White, and Pete Harris "carried him to the camp whence he was sent to Richmond to Hospital and died, the eighth day after being wounded. He was the first man killed in our companies from Sparta or Hancock County in Virginia."

2. Wingfield S. Butts, second corporal, was wounded at Rapidan Station, Va., and died of wounds in a Richmond hospital in May 1862. *Georgia Roster,* 2:442. Frank Little reported that Winfield Scott Butts was wounded the day after Cone's shooting. A fragment of an artillery shell, bouncing off an oak tree, passed through his thigh near the femoral artery.

3. Doc Pierce was Lovick Pierce, son of Methodist Bishop George F. Pierce.

4. Pete Harris was Samuel P. Harris, then a corporal in Company E, later second sergeant, and finally assistant quartermaster, Fifteenth Regiment, Benning's Brigade. *Georgia Roster,* 2:409, 445.

5. John Stafford, private, Company E. *Georgia Roster,* 2:447.

6. New Orleans was occupied by Union forces the day after Edgeworth Bird wrote this letter. Union gunboats succeeded in passing the forts below New Orleans the night of April 23–24.

7. William Lowndes Yancey (1814–1863) was in Richmond in 1862 as a member of the Confederate Senate from Alabama. He earlier headed a Confederate mission to Europe to secure recognition of the new government; the mission failed. Yancey left Richmond in 1863 because of failing health and died at his home near Montgomery, Ala. He was the son of Edgeworth Bird's Aunt Caroline, whose first husband was Benjamin Cudworth Yancey. William Lowndes Yancey was born at his mother's home, the Aviary, and grew up in the household of his abolitionist stepfather, Nathan S. Beman.

8. Dr. R. M. Smith was one of seven physicians practicing in Athens during the Civil War, but his name does not appear in any lists of Athens military units. Coleman, *Confederate Athens,* 151.

9. Robert Thomas of Athens was brigade quartermaster of Cobb's Brigade at the time of this letter. *Georgia Roster,* 2:480; Stegeman, *These Men She Gave,* 62, 68.

10. William Wilberforce Lumpkin was the son of Joseph Henry Lumpkin (1799–1867), first chief justice of the Georgia Supreme Court, and the nephew of Georgia Governor Wilson Lumpkin (1783–1870). He was a member of the Mell Rifles, an Athens company that became part of Cobb's Legion. The entire company was surrounded and captured on Lee's final march two days before the surrender at Appomattox. Stegeman, *These Men She Gave,* 151.

11. Miller G. Lumpkin, a brother of William W. Lumpkin, was a member of Company C, Cobb's Legion, Georgia Cavalry. *Georgia Roster,* 1:537.

12. Howell Cobb of Athens was a brig-

adier general at the time of this letter. He commanded a brigade throughout the Peninsula campaign.

13. Thomas Reade Rootes Cobb (1823–1862) was the brother of Howell Cobb. A pro-Unionist until the election of Lincoln, he led the secession effort after that, raising a regiment called the Georgia Legion, composed of infantry, artillery, and cavalry companies. In the fall of 1862 he took command of the brigade formerly commanded by Howell Cobb and was promoted to brigadier general. He was killed near Fredericksburg 13 Dec. 1862. *Dictionary of Georgia Biography,* 1:203–5.

Edgeworth Bird to Sallie Bird

[Virginia] 29 May 1862

It is the eighth hour after breakfast of as beautiful day as ever greeted mortal eye. My precious darling old Birdie, no further orders have come to us. We are quietly on our camping ground still. No fierce battle rages, as the order to prepare provisions, and coming in after night, seemed to foreshadow. I add this half sheet to relieve your precious heart. I have several letters to write this morning. Bill Alfriend, the mulatto boy who was run away so long, came to camp this morning. He was sent to wait on Ben.[1] He brings news from Sparta. I learn from him, and also through letters to others, that Father has sold his house to Ed Soullard[2] for six thousand dollars. Bill says he will take everything down to our house, negroes and all. This secures to us good management of our affairs there, but I fear Father will regret his doing so. I am sorry he sold the house, but as it is done, will not be disturbed or disquiet him about it. If he lives with us, we will try to make him happy. I will write him soon, and as he is there, will suggest that he have that work done on the roof that we often talked of. Jack Mitchel[3] is doing nothing, Jim tells me.

Whilst that fight was going on day before yesterday, the yanks had two balloons up in plain view.[4] One of our batteries took a crack at one of them. Billy Green has joined our company—is now with us.[5] I am very glad to have him. I see our old friend Dr. Church[6] has gone, too, with Dr. Reese,[7] two of the most excellent of men. I hear very, very seldom from Athens. Jack Lane's[8] regiment is at Richmond, or nearby. Dearest, I will write often. Remain where you are for the present. Isn't old Stonewall[9] a grand Fellow? Goodbye, my own precious wife. God bless and keep you. Kiss Bud. Love to all, your own Edge

1. Benjamin A. Alfriend, who was in Edgeworth Bird's company.

2. Edward A. Soullard, Jr., Savannah businessman, grew up in Hancock County. The handsome home of Wilson Bird and its history is described by Mrs. Terrell Moore in "The Bird, Pierce, Moore House," Sparta *Ishmaelite*, 28 March 1963.

3. Jack Mitchel[l], Sparta workman, listed in the 1860 census.

4. Balloons were used for reconnaissance.

5. Dr. William Hudson Green transferred to Company E, Fifteenth Regiment, Georgia Infantry, 26 May 1862, from Company I, Forty-ninth Regiment. He returned to Hancock County in August after being discharged for physical reasons. At home he served as an assistant surgeon with Georgia state troops. *Georgia Roster*, 2:445. An interesting account of life on a Hancock County plantation during the war written by his wife, Rebecca Sasnett Green, appears in Smith's *History of Hancock County*, 1:60–65.

6. Dr. Alonzo Church died in Athens, Ga., 18 May 1862. A native of Vermont, he was among many Middlebury College graduates such as Nathan and Carlisle Beman who came South to teach. He became president of the University of Georgia in 1829 and held that post for thirty years. *Dictionary of Georgia Biography*, 1:189–90.

7. Dr. Charles M. Reese, a leading Athens citizen, helped to organize an academy, an agricultural society, and the Georgia Equitable Insurance Company. Ernest C. Hynds, *Antebellum Athens and Clarke County, Georgia* (Athens, Ga., 1974), 35, 62, 145.

8. Andrew Jackson Lane was elected colonel of Company I, Forty-ninth Regiment, 22 March 1862.

9. Confederate General Thomas Jonathan Jackson (1824–1863) won the nickname "Stonewall" when he rallied the troops at First Manassas, "standing like a wall." Edgeworth Bird's comments followed the campaigns in the Shenandoah Valley of Virginia in May 1862, when Jackson neutralized McClellan's 175,000 troops by his astute maneuvers.

Edgeworth Bird to Sallie (Saida) Bird

The Picket near Richmond, 21 June 1862

My dear Daughter,

It is long since I have written you, but equally long since I have heard from you. Why are you so silent? Do you determine to count letters with

Papa? . . . I am anxious all the time to hear of Grandma and you, and all the good friends in Athens. So, on receipt of this, send me a good, long, neat letter and tell me all that goes on.

Your Grandma will be glad to learn that I have seen Richard[1] at last. My company was on picket duty one day quite near the 3rd Geo. Regt. I managed to send him word, and he came over and stayed with me most of the day. His health is excellent; never been sick yet. George Hayes[2] was unable to come with him, but he was in first rate health. That has been two weeks ago, and I have not seen him since, as the next day our brigade was moved off to its present position. He is not more than two miles off and well. On Tuesday last the 3rd Geo. were engaged in a skirmish and drove back the enemy by a charge. I heard from Richard next day through Mr. Tom Murray[3]—he came through safe. I thought your Grandma might be uneasy, if she saw an account of the skirmish.

Yesterday, I was agreeably surprised by a letter from your Uncle John.[4] He is stationed at the 3rd Geo. Hospital in Richmond. Dr. Green of Macon[5] is surgeon in charge, and your Uncle John asst. surgeon. It is [a] good place for him. He will perfect himself greatly in his profession, and in the meantime is in comfortable quarters. He told me your Grandma and you had just returned from Macon, having been there to bring little Tracy to Athens. Kiss the dear little fellow for me, for his sweet mother's sake. Up to the reception of his [John's] letter, I thought he was surgeon of the Battallion to which he belonged. He promises to try and get to see Richard and me soon at our Rgts. I hear very often from Mama, but I have not had a letter in the last four days.

I learn through a letter from Mrs. Waddell to Major Waddell[6] of the 20th Geo. that she had gone to Columbia; I presume on a short visit to Mrs. Sallie Taylor[7] and maybe to see Aunt Lou.[8] She has been speaking of going to see both and then go home, but as she has stayed so long awaiting the result of the struggle before Richmond, I persuaded her to remain longer. I look for a letter today. The 15th is now out on picket at a very dangerous post, but we manage to keep friendly with the Yankees, exchanging papers with them. Their pickets are in sight, a short distance off. There is a mutual understanding there is to be no firing on either side. They can drive us in whenever they choose to make the attack, and our orders are to give way. We are only a post of observation, and not required to hold the position.

The weather is now beautiful and dry, and I can't imagine why the Yankee Genl halts so long in his "on to Richmond." Genl Johnston is nearly recovered from his wound and has been out on horseback within a few days.[9] Isn't it a blessing from God that he is spared to us? He is our greatest general and 'twould be a terrible blow to lose him. Whilst he was so ill, they had ropes stretched around the streets leading by the house in Richmond where he lay, to prevent all noise from passing. I think he can wake up McClellan when he assumes command, if the Yankee Genl delays so long. I suppose you read accounts of the great battle. We were not in it, but close enough to hear the most horrible din I ever listened to. We were ordered in on Sunday just as the battle stopped. I saw a great many of the wounded and dead, and it was sickening.

Dear daughter, you must be good, obedient to your Grandma, and never neglect to say your prayers. Pray that all of us may soon be re-united at our home at Granite Farm. Ain't you sorry Grandpa sold his house? I am, but it was best for him, and therefore I am contented. Kiss Grandma many times for me. I love her and want to see her very much. Remember me in love to Mrs. Hayes[10] and family. Tell *Teedee*[11] she might write to me if she would. Remember me to Mr. and Mrs. Hull, when you see them. Tell them I often think of them. Howdy to Violet and Can and Peggy and Dinah and Gus and all the servants. Goodbye, dear Daughter. Remember that I love you very much and am always your affectionate Father, Wm. E. Bird

* I've just got a letter from Mama. She is with Mrs. Sallie Taylor in Columbia to stay a short time, and then goes back to Mr. Springs. I have no ink out here but write on my knee with pencil, seated on the ground. I hope you and Grandma together may make it out. Sammie Wiley is well, and all my friends.

1. Richard Baxter, Sallie Bird's brother and Saida's uncle. He was wounded a few months later at Sharpsburg, Md. (Antietam, 17 Sept. 1862).

2. George E. Hayes, second lieutenant, Third Regiment, was the son of Sarah Ann Hayes, sister of Mary Wiley Baxter. He rose to the rank of major and was killed at Weldon Railroad, Va., 21 Aug. 1864. *Georgia Roster,* 1:532.

3. Thomas A. Murray began service as a private in Company A (Sydney Brown Infantry of Hancock County). He was a junior first lieutenant at the time of this letter, serving with Carlton's Battery, Troup Artillery. *Georgia Roster,* 1:757.

4. John Springs Baxter, Macon, Ga., physician. He had just been appointed assistant surgeon and was appointed chief surgeon of the Forty-sixth Georgia Infantry Regiment later that year. *Georgia Roster,* 6:784.

5. There were two Doctor Greens in Macon, both brothers of Dr. Fitzgerald Green of Milledgeville, longtime director of the state mental hospital. Edgeworth Bird is probably referring to Dr. James Mercer Green, who was appointed surgeon in the medical department in February 1862 and who was sent to Richmond later that year. Spencer B. King, *Sound of Drums* (Macon, Ga., 1984), 286–87, 371.

6. James D. Waddell, a major, began service with Company D, Twentieth Regiment. He later became a colonel. *Georgia Roster,* 2:790. He was the son of the Rev. Isaac Waddell and grandson of Dr. Moses Waddel, for many years president of the University of Georgia. Waddell Papers, Special Collections, Emory University.

7. Not identified.

8. Edgeworth Bird's Aunt Louisa Bird married Robert Cunningham of South Carolina.

9. General Joseph E. Johnston was badly wounded at the Battle of Seven Pines (May 31–June 1, 1862), where he attacked but missed the opportunity to destroy McClellan's army. Johnston's forces were driven back to the gates of Richmond. The severe losses (Confederate wounded and dead 5,700, Union 4,300) brought Robert E. Lee to command the Army of Northern Virginia. *Biographical Dictionary of the Confederacy,* 259–60; Randall and Donald, *The Civil War and Reconstruction,* 212–13.

10. Aunt Sarah Ann Hayes of Athens.

11. Teedee (Teadee) was probably Sarah, youngest daughter of Sarah Ann Hayes.

Sallie (Saida) Bird to Sallie Bird

Athens, Ga., 11 July 1862, Friday morning

My own precious Mama,

It is almost a week since I have written to you and fully a week since I have heard from you. I know you can't write as often as you used to, and that you [are] very busy, but still Grandma and I would feel better if we could hear from you at least once each week. I know your health is not good and you can't stand much exertion, and I know also, that is I am afraid, you will task yourself too heavily. If you can only sleep good at night, it will not hurt you, but I know how hard it is for you to do that at home where all is quiet, and I know it must be harder in the midst of so much noise. I am perfectly well now, though I suffered very much with headache and backache. You may laugh, Mama, but it is the truth. I am well now and intend to remain so.

Last Sunday was commencement Sunday. Dr. Lipscomb[1] preached the sermon. They did not have any senior class and consequently no commencement, only the sermon. I did not go, although the Dr. said I was well enough, but Grandma thought it would not be prudent and might make me sick again. I send you a sample of the dress Auntie gave me, and a piece of Tracy's hair. Grandma got Mrs. Clark[2] to make it, and it fits me like "a bug's shirt," as dear Papa says. Oh, Mama, I wish you could see Tracy.[3] He is so sweet, and I think very much like Aunt Carrie. His eyes are the image of her's and so is his mouth. The rest of his face is not so much like her. Mama, he is *so* smart. He has been calling Jeff [the dog] Jeff Davis all morning. I don't know where he got the idea, for no one told him. I expect he heard someone speaking of Davis, and he remembers everything you tell him. Sometimes he is *very* pretty. I wish Uncle John could see him when he is in one of his *sweet humors*. I know he would love him harder than ever.

It was just one year ago yesterday since dear, sweet Aunt Carrie died. I expect you remember, dear Mama. I am so sorry for poor Uncle John, for I know it was a sad day for him. Did you notice, Mama, it was just one month after our baby left us? June 10–July 10.[4] Grandma received a short letter from Uncle John day before yesterday. He said Papa had gone back to camp. I hope he did not go until he was perfectly well, for if he did, it may make him sick again. How does Uncle Richard get along? Uncle John said in his letter that he was sick, and expected into the city that evening. I hope he will not be sick much. If he is there, give my love to him, and tell him I want him to write to me, if he can get time and is well enough. Grandma says she feels very unhappy about him.

I saw Mr. and Mrs. Hull not long ago, and they both told me to give a great deal of love to you when I write. Seabrook[5] has gone back to Mr. Johnston's to school. I must say goodbye now, dear Mama. Give a great deal of love to Uncle John and to Bud. Why don't he write to us? I think he might, for he has time. Tell him that I keep writing to him just as I used to, but I never hear from him in return. If he won't, I will stop. Good bye, my precious Mama. Write to us whenever you have time, yr affectionate child,

Sallie E. Bird

1. Dr. Andrew A. Lipscomb (1816–1890), chancellor of the University of Georgia during the Civil War and Reconstruction. Only a handful of students remained at the school by the time of this letter; in the fall of 1863 it shut down for the remainder of the war.

2. Martha L. Clark, forty-five, was listed as a dressmaker in the 1860 census.

3. Tracy Baxter, the infant son of Dr. John Baxter.

4. Saida's sister, Mary Pamela Bird, died 10 June 1857 at age 3 years, 9 months, 13 days.

5. Seabrook Hull, son of Henry Hull and Anna Thomas, went to Rockby, the school conducted by Richard Malcolm Johnston on his plantation.

Edgeworth Bird to Sallie (Saida) Bird

Richmond, 29 July 1862

My dear daughter,

Dr. Carlton[1] has just called to say he leaves for Athens in the morning. I avail myself of his kindness to send you a "wee" note, and enclose a memento of the battle fields around Richmond. It was the only thing I've met up with that seemed suitable to a little girl like yourself. George White[2] picked it up in the Yankee camp as we passed through in pursuit. What use the aforesaid Yankees could have for it in camp, my mind don't conceive, unless it be a relic of some loved one at home, a tender reminder of sweet pledges given by some straight nosed Yankee damsel. At all events, I begged it from George and send it to you. Mama also puts in some Yankee envelopes. I contracted a severe cold sometime back and haven't been entirely well since. I have been in camp for a while, but having constant headache, I am here in town again with Mama, having a resting spell. In a day or so, I'll be back to the Regt.

We are now in Longstreet's Division, and yesterday it was moved some 15 miles down from Richmond—and we are entrenching ourselves pretty close to McClellan. He seems to be sending heavy reinforcements to Pope[3] up about Fredericksburg, and our generals are strengthening Jackson, and it is to be presumed the next fight will come off up there. By God's blessing, we'll beat them again. One or two more signal victories will so disgust the North with abolition rule, that a peace party, and one willing to grant our demands, may spring up there and this cruel war have an end. Richard and Sam Wiley are here. Your Mother has written what nice people we are with.[4] Sam's erisypelas foot gets along slowly, otherwise he is quite well. Dick is about all right again. He begs me to thank his mother for the shirts and drawers by young Wilkins.[5] He got them today. He's got all of his old merriment about him. John's hospital is close by, and of late he comes up and sleeps in the boys room. So, we have quite a family meeting every night.

Mr. Gresham,[6] too, was added to the gathering, until a day or so back when he left for home. We were all truly glad to meet the squire. He was with us a good deal. But in a day or so we will all be scattered to our hard soldier life. We are all heartily tired of this hateful war, but must fight it out nonetheless. Give ocean's of love to Grandma and say I love her all the more for the kind solicitude she expresses for me in her letters. I, too, pray daily that we all may be spared to meet again in peace and happiness. Kiss dear little Tracy. Kind regards to all our friends, the Hulls, Wares, etc. Bud and Mama send many kisses and all join in love.

Your affectionate Papa,
Wm. E. Bird

1. Dr. Joseph B. Carlton went to Virginia in July 1862 to nurse wounded soldiers. Accompanying him from Athens were William King, the Rev. Joseph S. Key, and Young L. G. Harris. Coleman, *Confederate Athens*, 62.

2. George White was a private in Company E, Fifteenth Regiment. He fought to the surrender at Appomattox. *Georgia Roster*, 2:448.

3. Shortly before this letter, Union Major General John Pope (1822–1892) was given command of all Union forces in the East except those under McClellan on

the Peninsula. After his disastrous defeat at Second Manassas (Aug. 29–30), he resigned the command. Ezra J. Warner, *Generals in Blue* (Baton Rouge, La., 1964), 376–77.

4. They were staying with Mr. and Mrs. Henry James.

5. Grant Wilkins, from Athens, was a member of the Troup Artillery, which was a part of Cobb's Legion at the time of this letter. Stegeman, *These Men She Gave*, 148.

6. John J. Gresham of Macon, husband of Mary Baxter.

Sallie Bird to Sallie (Saida) Bird

Richmond, 7 August 1862

My precious child,

Altho' I've written to dear Grandma, yet I must write you a letter all for yourself also, that I may cheer and comfort you as much as possible. I grieve deeply that you should have suffered so much pain when I am away, but I feel assured that you are well cared for. Nothing would keep me away from you, or from your dear Grandma, now that her heart aches so heavily about dear Link,[1] but your Father's immediate danger. In all human probability he will be in a desperate fight tomorrow, perhaps tonight. May our gracious God spare his dear life.

Oh, my little daughter, as you suffer pain in your face, think of the horrible torture of our poor soldiers. Perhaps before this letter reaches you the fight will be over, and your own beloved Father among the slain! But I pray with all my heart and soul unto Him who is mighty to save and . . . shield our darling one from danger and death. I will send a dispatch to you if there is a battle, so as to relieve yours and dear Mother's anxiety. A gentleman just from the Brigade has come in and says they are drawn up in line of battle and expecting a fight every hour. Now that they are again in immediate danger, I dare not leave, for if Edge were wounded and I far away, he might die before I could see him.

The worst is over with you, I trust, my darling. Your Uncle John understands it all perfectly and says it is the natural result of scarlet fever, and tho' causing you great pain, yet is a safety valve for the disease. I pray it may be so. Mrs. James,[2] who knows all about scarlet fever, says she has had three of her children to be so afflicted, and that after the swelling is lanced, nothing is required but to wash it clean and let it run. As you regain strength, it will cease to run of itself. She says one of her children had a tumor on the gland that ran two months, and the best physicians in the city said it was the best thing for the child. It prevents deafness, or sore eyes, or any disease of the throat.

God grant, my dear child, that you may have no more pain. Just as soon as this danger is over, I will come home. I should have come before, but for circumstances explained in my letter to Mother. I rejoice to hear you are so patient and good about bearing the pain. That is my own dear, brave little darling! You deserve all praise, your Father says. I regret deeply that your Grandma should have been distressed about you, in addition to her sorrow about your dear Uncle Link. I have been so distressed at this sad news, I pray that John's and Richard's feelings about it may be correct. They do not believe it, for they had heard the rumor before. And as we have not received the letter from Teadee to which Mother refers, we have no particulars and only the allusion to the fact, as given in Mother's letter rcd today to John. Still my tears have fallen long and bitterly, for the thought of one of my dear brothers dying away from home and among strangers makes my heart ache heavily.

God comfort and sustain dear Mother in this, her first bitter trial of the war. Ah, how glad I am now that I have been able to minister to the comfort of so many dying soldiers. Perhaps some kind lady will be near our dear ones when they need attention. I've seen so many heart-rending scenes here, such awful agony, that I think it would kill me if my dear Edge were to suffer unaided and away from my tender love. If he *is* wounded you shall be telegraphed and you shall come to see him, if you can get an escort. Be assured of that, darling. But I pray he may be spared again to bless our hearts and home, and if he is safe I shall come immediately to you. I hope, as far as you can, my daughter, you will cheer your dear Grandmother. She has an aching heart, but she will, I trust, remember all God's mercy to her in sparing this long so many of her children.

Your dear Father has been on sick leave for two weeks, and tho' he and Major Waddel leave in an hour or two for the Regt., neither of them are fit for service. Yet they will go, because the fight is coming on and in a few hours they may be exposed again to the murderous fire of the wicked foe. As we have not received Tea Dee's letter, we of course don't know how Mother got the news of our dear Link, nor whether he was wounded or ill. I sent a dispatch to her this morning. Hope she'll get it tomorrow—to let her know why I can't come. I think we've lost several letters from you and her. I did not know anything about your face hurting so much until I got Dr. Long's[3] telegram yesterday and your Grandma's letter today. I knew you had the rising, but I did not dream it lasted so long, for in the last letter from Mother she said you were better.

I had a visit from Mr. Orme[4] of Milledgeville yesterday. His son was wounded in one of the last fights, shot thro' the lungs and tho' the wound is healing, yet his lungs are diseased by it, and Mr. Orme fears the worst. And so ends this terrible war for him. The dear friends who were so kind to me at Orange, Mr. and Mrs. Newman, had three sons in the fight, two of whom were wounded, and one carried from the field with sunstroke. One died three days after they got home. The other, tho' wounded in four places, is recovering, but the one who had sunstroke is ruined as regards health, and has had a discharge. All these came in the same battle (the one in which Col. McIntosh was shot[5]), and just see what affliction to one family, in one day's fight.

Your Uncle John does not think I ought to leave, just on the eve of battle, and says you will suffer yet more pain; after the rising was lanced, he said, you would be easy. My darling little daughter, your dear Father and I love you, talk of you, and pray for you. Be good and obedient to dear Grandma and comfort her all you can. God bless and restore you. Write to me as soon and as often as you can. Your dear Father will get the letters. Richard and Sammy send love to you and Mother, as does Bud. We are all eager for news and want to hear more about our dear Link. My dear, dear Link, poor fellow. Your own devoted Mother, S.C.B.

1. Eli Leroy (Link) Baxter, Sallie Bird's brother, was killed in the war in Texas.

2. Mrs. Henry James of Grace Street, Richmond.

3. Dr. Crawford W. Long (1815–1878), the pioneer of ether anesthesia in surgical cases, moved to Athens in 1850 and practiced there until his death. *Dictionary of Georgia Biography*, 2:630–31.

4. Richard M. Orme, editor of the *Recorder* in Milledgeville, then capital of Georgia. His son, Dr. Henry S. Orme,

was wounded. James C. Bonner, *Milledgeville: Georgia's Antebellum Capital* (Athens, Ga., 1978), 168.

5. Colonel William M. McIntosh of the Fifteenth Georgia Infantry Regiment was killed at Garnett's Farm, Va., 27 June 1862.

Wilson (Bud) Bird to Sallie (Saida) Bird

Richmond, 10 August 1862

My dearest Sister,

Mamma is now writing to Aunt Eliza Wiley, and as she is going to write to you this morning, I thought that I would write a little note to put in it, in reply to the one I received from you yesterday, enclosed in Cousin Teedee's to Mamma giving us the particulars of Dear Uncle Link's death. We were so glad to hear that he had a kind friend to nurse him during his illness. . . .

Well, Sister, I must tell you about our trip to Drury's Bluff[1] yesterday morning at ten o'clock. Uncle Richard, Mamma, Mrs. Waddell, Mrs. James, Miss Grant,[2] and myself got aboard of the gunboat Beaufort[3] and steamed down the river for Drury's Bluff, and, as you know, it was my first trip on board a steamboat. I, of course, enjoyed it very much.

We passed on down the James and, on the way, we saw Powhatan (where Pocahontas saved Smith's life) and other beautiful residences. In the course of half an hour, we arrived at Drury's Bluff and there we landed and had to climb (I reckon) the highest hill I ever saw, and steeper and longer than the one from the house to the spring [at Granite Farm]. After we got there, a gentleman went around with us and showed us all the works. He said that he was the chief gunner on the *Virginia*.[4] I have not room to say any more about it, but Mamma will, as she is writing you now. Give my love to Grandmother, Tracy, Cousin Teedee, and all the servants.

Your devoted brother,
W. D. Bird

1. Drewry's Bluff, a key point on the James River below Richmond.

2. Not identified.

3. The Gunboat *Beaufort*, a steamer armed with one gun, guarded the coastal waters of North Carolina until the naval

defeat off Roanoke Island, when it escaped to Virginia waters. Scharf, *History of the Confederate States Navy,* 157, 162, 164, 369, 392, 708.

4. The *Virginia* was the Confederacy's famous ironclad vessel. It was created from the steam frigate *Merrimac.*

Sallie Bird to Sallie (Saida) Bird

Richmond, 10 August 1862

My darling,

I sent you a long letter, and one to your Grandma the other day, and a long letter to her the day before. This is my fourth letter in four days. I pray you all may get them all. I have been very unhappy about you, my dear child. Your Uncle John and others assure me positively that there is no danger, and Mother wrote me that Dr. Long said so, and yet, but for your dear Papa's critical and *exposed* condition, I would have gone to you before this. But he has been within 200 yards of the Yankees at Malvern Hill, and a fight expected every hour. But day before yesterday, just as our men marched forward to drive them back, they found that the Yankees had retreated in the night.[1] Our forces fell back again a mile to [illegible].

A great battle is coming off without doubt in two quarters; one is with Pope near Gordonsville where our glorious Stonewall is in command, and again with McClellan down here. Our Brigade is now in Longstreet's Division, so you can see where Longstreet is engaged and know whether your father has been in a fight. Your dear Papa has not been well, but he is a great deal better. He will, I hope, be able to keep up. His strength has been severely taxed by the heavy work of the last two months. Oh, darling, if you could see the frightful, horrible wounds I've seen here, you would not wonder that I feel reluctant to leave our precious one here exposed to all these perils, when, if wounded, he might die for lack of food and ice. But if you need me, or dear Mother [does], I will come anyway, unless Edge was wounded or ill.

And so, I've wanted to go to you so much, and if things settle down here quietly, I'll come away home to see you. My sympathy with dear

Mother in the loss of our dear Link prompts me to go home, too. I long to comfort and cheer her and will when I can. I hope my frequent letters will do her some good. I grieve bitterly for my dear brother and pray our Father in heaven to grant that there be no more links broken in our family chain. How sad is the fate of the soldier who died far away from home and kindred. Alas, I've seen so many die here. I've tried to *devote* many a dying man[2] and hope that the labors I've had here in nursing the wounded and sick may be bestowed by some kind lady on my dear, dear brother, if any other should be ill. I know, almost, that Richard's life was saved by the good care of him.

Yesterday, [Mrs.] Waddell, [Miss] Grant and I all went down on the boat with Richard to Drury's Bluff and spent the day there with him. He was only a mile from us there. I should have been so very glad to have seen George and Liney Hayes,[3] but it was so very warm, and the boat left at 3 o'clock to return to the city, so I could not walk over. Richard met with [illegible] and some men from the 3d. He walked over to camp. Mrs. James made some delicious ices and gave him a splendid ham and a lot of nice biscuit. Now, isn't she one of the nicest women in the world? Yes, that she is. She charged him, if he got sick or wounded, to come straight to her house. Now, that is a comfort to Mother to know that he has a dear female friend here who will care for him always.

Richard says he loves her next to his mother and sisters and his sweetheart, of course. All are gone now but Cousin Sam, and he says he feels as if he ought to go, but his foot is not well yet. Mrs. James says he shan't go until he is well. She tried to keep Richard a week longer, but he said he felt he ought to go, and then John gave him a recommendation requesting them not to put him on heavy duty for a fortnight. We parted with him at the boat. He had a shady walk through the woods to his regiment.

I am very sorry, my dear daughter, that you had to suffer pain, and as I said in other letters, glad to hear you are good and patient. I'm so sorry my dear Mother has been anxious about you. I know she is easily alarmed about you, but I do think your presence would be great company and comfort for her. When you get well, Darling, I pray God you already have, you must do all you can to cheer her up. I did not receive Tea Dee's letter til last night. I can't imagine where it has been. I am grieved, indeed, to hear confirmation of the sad news about Link. John and Richard did not believe it at first. I wrote at length about this in my last. Dear Link! I had not seen him in 5 years. I pray for his dear young wife. What a terrible loss for her. Tell T I'll try to write. I hope to get a dispatch about you today.

Howdy to all the servants. Tell Can[4] to take good care of you. I am so anxious for letters now. . . . God bless you and dear Mother and restore your health.

Your devoted mother,
SBB

1. The Federals suddenly disappeared from Malvern Hill 7 Aug. 1862 just as a fight was about to develop between Lee's forces and McClellan's. They went back to Harrison's Landing on the James River, which Federal gunboats could protect. See Douglas Southall Freeman, *Lee* (New York, 1961), 227.

2. The writer omitted some words. She was devoting her time to comfort the dying in Richmond's military hospitals.

3. George E. Hayes and Samuel L. Hayes were members of Company K, Third Regiment. Both were sons of Sallie Bird's Aunt Sarah Ann Hayes. *Georgia Roster,* 1:532, 536.

4. Can [sometimes Candice, Candus] was a servant often mentioned at Granite Farm. She seems to have been in Mrs. Mary Baxter's Athens home at this time.

Sallie Bird to Sallie (Saida) Bird

Richmond, 20 August 1862

My dear, dear child,

I am up today for the first time from quite a sharp attack of the flu, which prostrated me for ten days in bed. I am quite well now, but very languid, and I am not sure I shall be able to finish this letter to you, but "c'est egal." It will be finished, I hope, some day. I recuperate so rapidly, generally, that a couple of days will set me all right again, so you are not to be anxious and I hope you have not allowed dear Grandma to feel so. I got John to write to her, then Bud, and I wrote a poor letter myself in the bed.

John has, as you know, accepted the appointment of Chief Surgeon of the 46th Geo Regt, Col. Colquitt commanding, and to the Major (Speer) of which, he is warmly attached.[1] I regret it sincerely on some accounts. His presence here was a great comfort to me, when I thought of your dear Father and Uncle Richard. Then, too, his position was pleasanter and very healthy, being in Church Hill,[2] which is a high and delightfully airy bluff. On the other hand, he is promoted by this change, ranks as Major, with a Major's pay—and then he is very anxious to be in the field, he says. He talked it over with me today. He makes his application for transfer to the Surgeon General tomorrow, but knows not how long a time it may take to pass it through.

Therefore, after you receive this letter, address my letters to the care of "Hunt and James,"[3] Richmond, Va. But unless a battle occurs at Orange C.H., where your Father is, I shall leave for Athens, myself, about the 26th or 27th of this month. I trust it will be so that John can go with us (as he has to go), as far as Charlotte. There I shall have to stop a day to get my things and see the friends who were so kind to me. Wright's Brigade[4] has gone through and passed on up to Gordonsville, too. We did not see Richard, but it was accounted for by a letter rcd by John today. In that, he said he was going to stay behind with the sick, so as to get a ride. This was very wise and John and I were glad of it.

Aug. 21st—I laid aside my pen and have not felt like writing since. I am up and dressed today, and feel a great deal better, tho' I'm sorry to see I've lost all my full plump cheeks and am very thin. Cousin Sam says I don't look as thin, yet, as I did before I left home. Mr. Lewis[5] has called and sat some time with us. He says all his children, from Merriwether down, have had scarlet fever. It has been very prevalent in Hancock. He lost two negroes with it—his children have all recovered. I suppose it was about the time Dilsy died with it. I am so thankful we were not at home. You might have had it much worse, and Bud, too. Col. Lane leaves today with his wife, Drafton Haynes, and Evans,[6] the horse and sugar man.

Mr. Sexton,[7] the member of Congress from Texas, is coming up to see me. He wrote me a note thro' the office inquiring where I was. I sent him word to call after yesterday, as I was too unwell to see visitors up to that time. He says he may bring me some Texas news, at any rate can tell me much about affairs in Texas. John makes his application to the Surgeon General for transfer to-day, I think. I don't know how long it will be before it passes through the Department, but perhaps it will be so that we can all start off together. If he goes a day or two later than we have arranged to start, I'll wait for him, to have his escort part of the way. Everyone here believes another great series of battles inevitable, within a week or two.

I do not know how I shall be able to leave just then, but my call home is urgent, even if I come back in the course of a month, or later. But if the fight begins, I shall not go until I am assured of the safety of Richard and Edge. Richard's Brigade, as I said, has passed thro' the city, but it is not supposed to be far from here, and it may not be sent on. All say that they never saw troops pass thro' as rapidly since the war began. 20,000 passed through in one day. I wish, my daughter, you could see them—some brigades of Mississippians filled up by conscripts, where the Regts were reduced by battle and disease, made a splendid appearance. It is raining now, and I am very glad, for the dust has been oppressive to our men on the march.

Richard wrote John that he was fast getting back both flesh and strength and was *perfectly well*. Dear fellow, I wish Mother could see him. John, too, looks unusually well, and is so. It will not be long before we meet, I think, my child. Unless a battle occurs to keep me, I shall leave as I said for Athens, stopping only a day or two on the way.

Sammy Wiley had a letter from Sallie by Mr. Lewis. She says Pete Carnes and Berrien Eve[8] have joined the church. Cousin Philo and Eva[9] went up to attend the meeting. . . .

I am going out to drive with Mr. Lewis tomorrow to see if Mr. Hutchison's[10] grave is distinctly marked at Oakwood, and to get some things left by one of our poor men at Chimborazo, a Mr. Hammock[11] who died last week. Also to see all the Yankee trophies collected at the Capitol. Mrs. Waddel and Bud go with us. I will try to have my picture taken for you, darling, if I feel well enough, and it can be done here. Cousin Sam is cutting you a pretty ring from ivy root which came from Orange C.H. Poor Cousin Sammy! He feels so awfully about our all going off, and wants a furlough very much, but the chances are very slim indeed for him.

Give my dearest love to your dear Grandma and Tracy. Howdy to the servants, always including Laura.[12] Tell Mother I have only tasted two peaches this year and want some terribly. John and I sit and talk about Aunt Peggy's[13] vegetable soup often, and the broiled steak and good coffee. Goodbye for this time, darling. If you write again, direct to the care of Hunt and James, Richmond. You had better write, because if a battle comes off, it will detain me for a while. God bless you, my dear darling, your Mother

1. Peyton H. Colquitt had been elected colonel of the Forty-sixth Regiment in March. He died of wounds received at the Battle of Chickamauga in September 1863. Alexander M. Speer was appointed major of the regiment in March. *Georgia Roster,* 4:924.

2. On Church Hill, a high spot in Richmond, stands the church where Patrick Henry made his famous "Give Me Liberty or Give Me Death" speech.

3. Hunt and James, commission and forwarding merchants, Richmond. James C. Hunt and Henry James were partners.

4. Ambrose Ransom Wright, an Augusta, Ga., attorney and pro-Union man, became a secessionist, like many Southern moderates, after the election of Lincoln. He was promoted to brigadier general in June 1862, following his services at the Battle of Seven Pines, and was badly wounded at Sharpsburg (Antietam) in September. Wright was elected president of the Georgia Senate in the fall of 1863, but never took his seat. Promoted to major general, he saved Augusta from a sacking in late 1864. He practiced law in Augusta after the war and edited the Augusta *Chronicle and Sentinel.* See *Biographical Dictionary of the Confederacy,* 447–48.

5. David William Lewis, Hancock County planter, lawyer, and educator, was in Richmond to represent Georgia's Fifth District in the Confederate Congress. *Dictionary of Georgia Biography,* 2:618–19.

6. Draughton Stith Haynes attended Carlisle Beman's school at Mt. Zion, Ga., and Georgetown College (class of 1862). He taught briefly at Rockby for Richard Malcolm Johnston, subsequently enlisting in the Pierce Guards at Sparta, 4 March 1862. Haynes, *The Field Diary of a Confederate Soldier* (Darien, Ga., 1963). Evans is not identified.

7. Franklin B. Sexton of Texas served in the first and second Confederate Congresses in Richmond.

8. McPherson Berrien Eve was the youngest son of William Joseph Eve and Philoclea Edgeworth Casey of Augusta. He enlisted in the Confederate army at fifteen when war broke out. Myers, *Children of Pride,* 1516. Peter Carnes does not appear in the 1860 Georgia census. The Carnes and Wiley families were linked by several marriages.

9. Philoclea Edgeworth Eve and Eva Berrien Eve, mother and sister of Berrien Eve. *Children of Pride,* 1516–17.

10. Mr. Hutchison's grave in Oakwood Cemetery not identified.

11. J. R. Hammock, private in Company E, was discharged from a Richmond hospital for disability in August 1862. His death is not indicated. *Georgia Roster,* 2:445. Chimborazo was a military hospital.

12. Laura, a servant in the home of Mrs. Mary Baxter.

13. Aunt Peggy, a servant in the home of Mrs. Mary Baxter.

Sallie Bird to Elizabeth Harris

Granite Farm, 29 December 1862, Sunday afternoon

I received your kind note by Ted, and as he has just notified me that he will leave this P.M., I seat myself to send you a hasty reply. We have had a very pleasant Christmas, the chief blessedness of it being (to me) my dear Edge's presence.[1] If our country could only be blessed with peace, and our dear ones be given to their homes once more, how glorious would the New Year seem! For myself, I seek no boon of Heaven greater than my husband, children, and friends spared to me. For worldly goods, wealth, I care not.

The same good Lord who has preserved my darling's life mid the dangers of war will, I trust, protect him again; and tho' whenever I think of the parting before me, a sinking-shivering dread comes over me, and my heart aches; yet I try to be perfectly resigned and to wear as brave and cheerful a face as possible. For the trial is so hard to my dear Edge and to all soldiers who have happy homes, that I think we ought not to add one pang to what they must suffer. For to them are the hardships, the privations, the cruel bodily sufferings.

Yes, dear Cousin Lizzie, none know what I feel, for my husband is not only cheerful and good, but oh! so tender, so careful of me! So watchful for my health! And now says that if I say so, he will take me with him again. He will not say it himself, because he fears the cold would be too much for me. My plans are indefinite, but come down, you and Cousin Jimmy, by all means, to see Edge before he goes, and I can tell you all about our vague hopes and plans for the future. Nothing but the feeling that Edge is going to the post of duty would serve me to bear up.

We had a good many xmas invitations. So had the children. We anticipated having company, too, but had these invitations and did not have any at home. A good many say they are coming down this week. You will be welcome and acceptable at any time. Edge will not leave before the 15th, I imagine. I have never asked, nor do I want to know the day. The time slips by—ah! so rapidly. Richard will go on with him, and he has some few recruits, I believe. Mother is better, having been able to attend General Cobb's[2] funeral, her first going to church in 8 weeks. She is still far from well. Sister's little Leroy[3] is not so well, either, and she is very anxious. Sallie had a very gay week at Mrs. Soullard's.[4] Wilson was invited to several places, too. I must close now as Ted is waiting. Kiss Moses[5] for us all. Edge sends love to you (Never call him Mr. Bird, Cousin Lizzie, I was glad to see your correction), and to Cousin Jimmy. We are both sorry he should have encountered poison oak. It must be very disagreeable. We have not killed a hog yet. I expect you are nearly through. Wishing you a happy New Year, and hoping soon to see you, I remain your affectionate—Sallie[6]

1. Edgeworth Bird was seriously wounded in the Battle of Second Manassas, 30 Aug. 1862, and was home at Granite Farm on sick leave for several months.

2. Thomas R. R. Cobb died 13 Dec. 1862 while leading his men at the Battle of Fredericksburg. Little girls brought flowers along the train route from Virginia to Georgia, and in Augusta's city hall he lay in state. Back home in Athens the town turned out, young and old, black and white, to accompany the remains to Oconee Hill Cemetery. Stegeman, *These Men She Gave,* 73–78.

3. Leroy Gresham.

4. Mrs. Edward A. Soullard, Jr., of Savannah and Sparta. Her husband had earlier bought the Wilson Bird home in Sparta as a place of refuge for his family.

5. Moses Wiley Harris, one of the numerous children of Samuel Harris Wiley, was adopted by James Harris and his wife Elizabeth, who was the child's aunt. He became a Sparta banker.

6. This letter from Sallie Bird to her cousin Elizabeth Harris is from the collection of Mrs. Ann Harris Marbury of Sparta, Ga.

THREE

The Road Past Gettysburg

"Ah, my darling,
these are sad, sad times. I sicken
and weary of them . . ."

EDGEWORTH BIRD

Early in 1863, after a stay at home recovering from war wounds, Edgeworth Bird returned to Richmond, where he was appointed brigade quartermaster. In July he was present at a major turning point in the war, Gettysburg, where many of his friends died. He had held a friend who died in agony while his legs were amputated. The optimism he always showed in his letters home began to fade. He urged Sallie to pay off their debts in Confederate currency. One dollar in gold was now worth five in paper. July was a fateful month. Vicksburg fell and with the surrender of Port Hudson the South lost control of the Mississippi. In that sad and heated month Edgeworth Bird lost a powerful friend in the death of his cousin William Lowndes Yancey.

The tensions in Georgia increased. Robert Toombs spoke in Sparta, attacking measures taken by the Davis government such as the conscription act and the Confederate tax in kind. The news was dispiriting. Bird was astonished at reports of men back from furlough that "Georgia was almost whipped." He wrote his wife that the state "has hardly ever had an armed heel on her soil." He reminded Sallie that some of their circle had never taken up arms in their cause. Nonetheless, he wrote, "They can never subdue us and our people are staunch." As for the army in Virginia, "It thinks it can whip its weight in wild cats."

Edgeworth Bird to Sallie Bird

Richmond, 27 February 1863

Dearest Darling,

I believe it is harder to write from the city than the camp, for I did not write you again yesterday, as I had thought to do. One meets so many friends and acquaintances, and there are so many long tramps to take, but only one day's interval between letters is not so bad, is it? Sam came in from camp day before yesterday and brought me two letters from you; sweet, dear letters to me, darlie; long ones, too, and for them I am so grateful.

You may dismiss all uneasiness in regard to my obtaining the position of Brigade Q.M. It is only a slow process, as all matters are that go through the high government mills. My nomination has been sent in to the Senate by the President for confirmation, as is usual, but such matters go along slowly.[1] Day before yesterday, Genl Toombs told me to go up and see Mr. Yancey or Semmes and let them have my name and Capt. Troup's,[2] as his Hdqt. Genl, passed through as soon as possible. I accordingly did so. Tom Semmes[3] says I have disgraced myself and renounced glory by becoming a Quarter Master and he expects Senator Foote soon to be after me for embezzlement of the public funds.[4]

I am still in town, having a pleasant easy time. I write this morning from Mr. Greanor's,[5] where I am most of the time, with Mr. Lane. These kind people insisted so pleasantly that I should be with Jack[6] at their house while he remained, that I have done so, with the exception of one night spent with the James's.[7] I consider Mr. J's my home and made Sam take my clothes there, for when he brought me a change. I can't say how long we are to be here. I shall stay part of the time with them, as Jack heads for home tomorrow. Shall send this letter by him. If we are here long, I'll have to go elsewhere, if they won't take board from me.

I call up every day to see Genl T[8] and learn our movements and prospects. It is still quite possible we may go to Savannah. But let none of our good friends set their hearts on it. Toombs will take us there if in his power, but those sort of matters work slowly and are very uncertain. If he were sent to Savannah, he would be the ranking officer, and I expect there is one of the difficulties. It would remove others from command and cause heart burning. There is still hope, however, but the friends at home are not to be sanguine.

Darling, you must pay attention to little Fanny Greanor.[9] Send for her to come over and stay, now and then, with Sallie. These good folks are very kind to me, and I know of no other way you can show your appreciation of it. I never saw nicer living. Mrs. G is the finest of old ladies. Mr G is very wealthy, retired from business and a fine, jolly old gentleman. They all seem very much attached to Mr. Lane, and it is in his account they are attentive to me. If Mrs G goes to Georgia, you must let her feel your kindness. There are two or three married daughters living close by, very nice ladies. They spoke of having seen you two or three times on the street, and knew you by sight, and expressed a desire to make your acquaintance should you come on again. As for Bud, they all seemed to know him and pronounced him a nice little fellow. Mrs. Greanor says he promised to call and take a bundle to Fanny. I'm sorry he forgot it. I told her your illness must have made him forget it. I think I have seen but few as nice old ladies as she is.

I am sorry my matters are not arranged. Jack would go on my bond with Waddell[10]—would remain a day or so, if we could only know what day it could be done. Well, the only consolation is the delay keeps me off duty and gives me an easy time. I have not written to Henry C, but told Pete Harris to explain everything. He could do it better than I could write. I still think there is great doubt; he might be elected by a bare majority with good management, but I would not have the place in such a case. I doubt that Henry will ever be fit for field duty. Hearnsberger[11] has been elected Lieut. Col. to my great regret, beating Capt. John

Culver. Hearnsberger is clever enough, but John is about the best officer we have.

I am glad you always tell me of the plantation work. See Mr. Rhodes[12] often and keep yourself posted, and me. My regards to him. I hope everything will go smoothe and fair. Is the guano at home? Don't put any more acres in cotton than your hands allow. John[13] can show Mr. Rhodes the least productive part of the field—and you have some watermelons and a roasting ear patch.

Did I tell you I lost all the money I had as I went up from Richmond? Some 30 or 35 dollars. Was on the cars without a cent—bad fix, borrowed. Prepare me some white shirts, nice ones, and a handkerchief or so. Did you know you only put up 3 pr socks? Want three more pair.

Precious, give my love to Mrs. Dawson and her mother.[14] Kind remembrance to Miss Trezvant.[15] The scarf and head gear those dear friends gave me saved me from being converted into a pillar of ice. Couldn't have travelled without them.

Tell Mrs. Camel[16] I smoke to her frequently. Kiss and dearest love to Sallie and Bud. Howdye to all the negroes. Tell Mr. Edwards he'd better have Comet killed for his skin. He's ruined on the shoulder. Then you can get Mrs. J cards. I had a long talk with her yesterday morning. Mrs. G[17] says nothing about "Manassas." She's finer than any. My own precious darling, goodbye. I hope to hear from you today. Love to John D. and Mr. Edwards and all friends. Be good and prayerful and true and loving ever to one who prays God's choicest blessings on you always. Your Edge

1. Edgeworth Bird was appointed brigade quartermaster 30 March 1863. *Georgia Roster,* 2:442.

2. J. Robert Troup, captain and aide-de-camp, June 1862. Jones, *Georgia in the War,* 96.

3. Thomas J. Semmes was in the Confederate Senate from Louisiana.

4. Henry S. Foote served in the Confederate House of Representatives until expelled 27 Feb. 1865. He was a member of the committee supervising the quartermaster and commissary department. See Bell Irvin Wiley, *Embattled Confederates* (New York, 1964), 263.

5. Draughton Haynes in his diary wrote of Mr. and Mrs. William Greaner of 20th and Broad, Richmond, saying they

nursed his uncle, Colonel Andrew Jackson Lane of Hancock County. Haynes himself was carried to the Greener home after being wounded at the Battle of Fredericksburg. *Field Diary of a Confederate Soldier,* 13, 26.

6. Colonel Andrew Jackson Lane.

7. Henry James of Richmond. He was a partner in Hunt and James.

8. General Robert Toombs.

9. Fanny Greaner of Richmond was visiting the Lanes in Georgia.

10. Major James D. Waddell.

11. Stephen Z. Hearnsberger began service as a first lieutenant with the Lamar Confederates of Lincoln County, Ga. He was officially made lieutenant colonel 4 March 1863 and was captured at Gettysburg in July 1863. *Georgia Roster,* 2:454.

12. The 1860 census lists George F. Rhodes, thirty-six, as an overseer.

13. John, a slave at Granite Farm.

14. Lucy Terrell Dawson and her mother, Eliza Rhodes Terrell.

15. Miss Trezvant. The Trezvants from Memphis, Tenn., were refugees in Athens at the time. Hull, *Annals of Athens,* 260.

16. Possibly Mrs. Ned Campbell.

17. Mrs. Greaner.

Sallie (Saida) Bird to Edgeworth Bird

Granite Farm, 21 June 1863, Sunday morning

My dearest Papa,

. . . Oh, I wish you were at home while Cousin Eva and Cousin Sallie[1] are here. We all (Cousins Eva and Sallie included) wish a dozen times a day for you. They both say they will come up to see you, if Cousin Eva has not gone up to "that" house on the corner of Drayton and Liberty Streets in Savannah.[2]

Cousin Sallie is too pretty and, oh, you just ought to see her dance the "Highland Fling," "Fisher's Hornpipe," "La Chuca La Coska," and some others that I do not remember the name of. She danced all the other dances, it seems to me, that were ever invented. She has taught me the polka, schottisch, mazurka, and is going to teach me to waltz. Cousin Eva, too, is just as sweet as she can be and pretty.

You know, Cousin Sallie Casey says she is nearly frantic to see you; says she had hoped you would come home while she was here. I will take my last music lesson next Friday. I am very sorry . . . he (Mr. G) gives six weeks vacation. Since I commenced with him, I have taken a piece from the opera of Martha, one from "La Prophete," one from "Lucretia Borgia," and am now taking the "Carnival of Venice" and one of Goss's Transcriptions. He is giving me the last two with "La Reve" to practice during vacation.

Mama had a long sweet letter from Uncle Richard yesterday evening. He seemed so glad at the idea of getting with you. Cousin Eva says I must tell you that she and Cousin Sallie Casey went around to cabins to pay visits to all the negroes. They went to Aunt Sally's house and made her kiss her hand to them. Went to Betsey's house, complimented her on her child, and finally went to Lou's house. Tried to make her name her baby Cupid; explained who Cupid was. Rather Cousin Eva wanted to name it Cupid, and Cousin Sallie wanted it named David Jackson after a gentleman friend of hers, she says. She says when she goes to her father's plantation she is going to name one Jackson, and then no one will know. They will think she named him after Jackson (Stonewall). Cousin Eva and I walk out to the rocks almost every evening. Sometimes Mama and Cousin Sallie go. Mama is reading *Vanity Fair* aloud to Cousin Sallie and Cousin Eva. She read a long time last night. Cindy made those little pallets on the floor for Cousin Eva and Cousin Sallie and myself, while Mama was on the iron couch and read aloud. Cousin Eva has read it before, but Cousin Sallie never has. Cousin Sallie is reading *Jane Eyre* and Mama and Cousin Eva *Lucile,*[3] when they do not feel like reading aloud.

There was quite a large party given to Cousin Sallie in town last Friday night. She, Wilson, and myself went and had a nice time. The Saturday before we went to Mt. Zion to a dance at Cousin Jane Connell's.[4] We had a nice time there, too. Cousin Sallie met a school boy there that we, in fun, tease her about. He is the ugliest boy I ever saw in my life, but Cousin Sallie declares that she is very much smitten. Aunt Philo is talking a little about coming up next week. I hope she will, for I love her very much, and then Cousin Eva says she will have to go home, if she does not. Mama has written a note to Col. Jones[5] inviting him to come up and make a visit while Cousin Eva is here. Cousin Sallie, myself, and Wilson signed the note. I hope he will come.

Dear Papa, I must close. Give my love to Uncle Richard, if he is with you and Cousin Sam. Tell him I saw Birdie[6] at church last Sunday and she is as pretty and bright as ever. Goodbye, dearest Papa. Your devoted daughter, Saida

1. Eva Berrien Eve and her cousin Sarah Berrien Casey. Eva was the daughter of Philoclea Edgeworth Casey and her husband William Joseph Eve. Sarah Berrien Casey's father was Dr. Henry Rozier Casey, Philoclea's brother.

2. Eva Eve married Charles Colcock Jones, Jr., in October 1863, a few months after this letter. His home was at the corner of Drayton and Liberty streets in Savannah. See Myers, *Children of Pride*, 1486, 1516.

3. Sir Robert Lytton (1831–1891), English diplomat and poet, wrote *Lucille* (1860) under the name Owen Meredith.

4. Jane Baxter Connel(l), daughter of Eli H. Baxter and wife of Dr. Alva Connel(l).

5. Charles Colcock Jones, Jr., lawyer, historian, and archaeologist, was first married to Ruth Berrien Whitehead, a cousin of Eva Berrien Eve, his second wife. He was mayor of Savannah (1860–61) and served as chief of artillery for the military district of Georgia with headquarters in Savannah during the Civil War. *Children of Pride*, 1568.

6. Samuel H. Wiley's daughter, Sarah Bird.

Edgeworth Bird to Sallie Bird

Williamsport, Maryland, 7 July 1863

It is towards sunset, and I've a moment ago learned that possibly I may get a letter off in the morning to my own precious darling. I've so longed to send you a line, so longed to receive some of the many letters that I know are on the way to me, and yet have been entirely debarred from all communication south.

Since we crossed the Potomac, and indeed days before, there has been no opportunity to send a line. Indeed, I wrote you after the receipt of your last two, dated the 12th and 14th June. Since then not a word, and you can half imagine, my own loved wife, the burning desire I have for a *pile* of your dear assurances of love.

Since you heard from me, our army has seen pretty rough times, long and heavy marches to the Potomac. The whole army and transportation has crossed over at Williamsport, a small town on the Md. side. We passed across the western and narrow portion of the state 7 July 1863 into Pennsylvania. Moved along by easy marches in Greencastle and thence to Chambersburg, a mile beyond which place we remained in a camp a day or so. From there I wrote you, tho' mountains twould go through. I told you of how beautiful and highly cultivated the country was, the splendid grass, clover and wheat fields; of how methodically we tramped them down along the turnpikes and grazed cattle and horses on them. From thence we passed on, changing our course towards Gettysburg. There we found the enemy posted in a terribly secure position. Now, I know, we should not have attacked him there on high hills and mountains, but we did so.

I sat on my horse and looked on from the distance. Certainly there has been no fiercer conflict during this, or any war. The Yankees were impregnably posted and on their own soil they fought undoubtedly well. They had rock walls built on the mountain side and tops. Our men were rushed at their positions, performed heroic deeds, and died heroic deaths. We could not carry the points. After several days hard fighting, the transportation was ordered back. Arriving here, we found the river so swollen we could not cross. The Yankee cavalry attacked our trains, destroyed a few waggons a short distance in front of us. Yesterday evening they attacked our camp, a large body of cavalry with artillery. It was successfully defended, tho' at one time it looked bad. The drivers turned out and helped the troops.

For several days we've been separated from the Army. I learn they are near us now, and I hear that we whipped them bad the day we left. Our loss of noble men is terrible. . . . In our own Brigade Col. Jones[1] of 20th Ga., Lt. Col. Wm. Harris,[2] of 2nd Ga. were killed. I helped bury Col. Harris, a half brother to Ben Harris. Ev Culver,[3] Joe Dickson,[4] John Laughlin,[5] Munt Harrison,[6] of Co. K were killed. Lyons[7] of Co. E the only one killed. Lt. Hardwick[8] of Co. K mortally wounded. Tom Culver[9] and Doc Pierce[10] shot through the calf of the leg, doing well and now with us in a spring waggon. Jimmy Reynolds[11] lost his left arm. Jimmy Medlock[12] wounded in the side by a shell. Jimmy Middlebrooks,[13] Jasper Boyer,[14] Doc McCook,[15] and several others of our Hancock boys missing. . . .

Dud and Ben Alfriend are here in camp with us. Dud is worn down and had to come back with us. . . . Major Ballard,[16] commissary of our Brigade and myself spent the night of the first fight at Hood's Division Hospital. His brother Capt. Ballard,[17] 8th Geo. was killed. He was in great distress. I assisted as best I could. Held legs while they were taken off.

At daylight we went to the picket lines and brought off the Captain's body. Oscar Dawson[18] is shot through the leg—flesh wound. Genl Hood[19] is wounded in the arm. I hear today Genl Benning[20] is also. . . . Every brigadier in Hood's command is wounded except one, Genl Robertson.[21] I hear he is now in command. I will try and enclose a list of casualties so you will understand exactly our losses. God bless you . . . my own loved darling, your own Edge

1. Colonel John A. Jones, who enlisted in May 1861 with the Muscogee County, Ga., "Southern Guards." He had just been elected colonel a few weeks before his death at Gettysburg on 2 July 1863. *Georgia Roster,* 2:824.

2. Lieutenant Colonel William Terrell Harris joined the Meriwether County "Jackson Blues" in July 1861. He died at Gettysburg 2 July 1863. *Georgia Roster,* 1:382.

3. Everard Culver, a private with Company K (Hancock County), died 3 July 1863. Ivy Duggan wrote that Culver was quite young when he enlisted in 1861 and was "noble, gallant, and good; and we all loved him." *Georgia Roster,* 2:475; Duggan Papers, Emory University.

4. Joseph C. Dickson, private with Company K, killed 3 July 1863. *Georgia Roster,* 2:475.

5. John Laughlin, private with Company K, killed 3 July 1863. *Georgia Roster,* 2:477.

6. Montgomery Harrison, private, Company K, killed 2 July 1863. *Georgia Roster,* 2:476. Duggan described him as "quiet, unassuming." Duggan Papers.

7. B. F. Lyons, private, Company E, killed 2 July 1863. *Georgia Roster,* 2:446.

8. William H. Hardwick, junior second lieutenant, Company K (Hancock Confederate Guards), wounded 2 July, died of wounds 25 July 1863. *Georgia Roster,* 2:476.

9. Thomas H. Culver, second lieutenant, Company K, wounded at Gettysburg, was killed in the Battle of the Wilderness 6 May 1864. *Georgia Roster,* 2:473.

10. Lovick Pierce, Jr., son of Methodist Bishop George F. Pierce. The bishop went by train to Richmond and removed his son and Henry H. Culver from the hospital. Lovick Pierce recovered at home from severe wounds and gangrene, fighting on to Appomattox. Smith, *The Life and Times of George F. Pierce,* 481–82.

11. James R. Reynolds, private, Com-

pany K, wounded and captured at Gettysburg 4 July 1863. Reynolds's left arm was amputated. He was paroled and exchanged in August. Duggan called him an excellent soldier. *Georgia Roster,* 2:478; Duggan Papers.

12. James E. Medlock, private, Company K, was slightly wounded by grapeshot, according to Duggan. He fought on until Appomattox, married a Virginia woman, and returned to Hancock County to farm. *Georgia Roster,* 2:477; Duggan Papers.

13. James T. Middlebrooks, private, Company K, was captured 3 July 1863 and paroled at Point Lookout, Md., 18 Feb. 1865. *Georgia Roster,* 2:477.

14. Jasper J. Boyer was severely wounded in the head 2 July and captured 3 July 1863. Exchanged 20 March 1864, he ended the war in a Macon, Ga., hospital. *Georgia Roster,* 2:443.

15. Dawson McCook's record does not show him missing at Gettysburg. He was captured near Knoxville, Tenn., 3 Dec. 1863 and released at Rock Island, Ill., 19 June 1865. *Georgia Roster,* 2:477.

16. Walter S. Ballard, commissary sergeant with the rank of major, Benning's Brigade, fought on to Appomattox.

17. C. M. Ballard, captain, Company C, Eighth Regiment, killed 2 July 1863. *Georgia Roster,* 6:934.

18. George Oscar Dawson entered the war as a captain with the Greene County "Stephens Light Guards." He was wounded at Second Manassas in 1862, promoted to major, and wounded again at Gettysburg 3 July 1863. *Georgia Roster,* 1:913, 1:980.

19. John Bell Hood won a promotion to major general following the loss of an arm at Gettysburg. Two months later he lost a leg at Chickamauga. Despite his physical impairments, he led the Atlanta campaign and fought to the end of the war. *Biographical Dictionary of the Confederacy,* 238.

20. Brigadier General Henry Lewis Benning was not seriously wounded. He took part in campaigns at Chickamauga in September. Severely wounded in the arm in the Wilderness campaign 6 May 1864, he was incapacitated until the final days at Appomattox when he surrendered with Lee. Fort Benning at Columbus, Ga., is named for him. *Biographical Dictionary of the Confederacy,* 98.

21. Jerome Bonaparte Robertson had earlier been wounded at Second Manassas. He led Hood's Brigade in July 1863, despite being wounded again at Gettysburg. He later clashed with General James Longstreet, under whom he served at Chickamauga, and was sent to the Trans-Mississippi Department in command of the Reserve Corps. *Biographical Dictionary of the Confederacy,* 370.

Edgeworth Bird to Sallie Bird

Williamsport, Maryland, 9 July 1863

Yesterday morning I sent on the way a letter. I don't know that it got off, but I hope so. This evening I begin another draft, My Own Precious, and hope to be able to send it off. The postman tried to get over the river today, but the rains of the day and night had caused it to rise, and he is still here. It is probable he may get over in the morning. We are still in camp here with the immense army trains. The Army has moved down near us in the vicinity of Hagerstown, and the large trains are now safe.

I wrote you of the attack made on us the day after we got here. The teamsters turned out with all the guns that could be scraped up and assisted the troops, and the Yankees were driven off. The Army had not then come up. Now they are within five miles, and their positions cover us. I rode up to the Brigade today for a few hours. Genl Benning won laurels for himself in the Gettysburg fight. His men, I hear, are delighted with him, and the men of the other Brigades in the Division cheered him as he passed along since. They say Hood's Division attacked a terrible position. Hood, himself, thought it should not have been done. Our troops did all men could do, but could not carry the mountain. Finally, another order was sent to charge it again, and Genl Benning refused to have his troops butchered and sent word back that he wouldn't obey the order. This caused a closer reconnaisance, and the order was countermanded. All applaud his firmness and judgement.

Genl Hood was wounded in the arm. I hear the Yankee's acknowledge to a loss of thirty thousand. Ours could not have been half of that, tho' the number of officers killed or stricken down was very heavy. Today the Brigade reports only 836 effective enlistments for duty. The troops are all in fine spirits. They inflicted a much heavier loss on the enemy than they received, notwithstanding their terrible disadvantage. The Yankees army retreated at the same time our fellows fell back and did not attempt to follow up, tho' we left such of our wounded as could not bear to be moved. You will have learned before this reaches you that Tom Camack[1] was killed. I could but sorrow for his poor wife. I fear this will cut the frail tenure she seemed to have on the thread of life. But, darling, you will learn more from the papers than I can tell you, and earlier. Capt. Harris will be cheered to know his brother was buried in a coffin, and the burial service read over him by a minister.

Oh, my darling, these are sad, sad times. I sicken and weary of them, and my heart turns to you and longs so earnestly for your presence. But still, I would not have you out here, did your health even permit it. I would prefer your remaining at home. The war seems to change nearly all, and times are rougher. I'll have you at home, dearest darling, to care for our children and keep our house in order, and if it please God to let me return to you again, we'll stay by each other the balance of time allowed us here. Kiss again and again our children. When Sam is entirely well, send him on, but it better be when there is a good chance; some one to come here. I hardly know how he could get here from Richmond. A great many negroes have gone to the Yankees. Antony, Waddell's boy, has. And, darling, you must send me some money. I do not really need it now, but I do not wish to be restricted. Send me by first safe opportunity five hundred dollars. If I do not require it, I can send it or take it back some day.

Everything is very high. I need another horse, but darling, my own loved old Birdie, my heart needs you more than aught else on earth. I despise my business here, but why should I trouble you? Doc Pierce and Tom Culver are in camp in a spring waggon, and well cared for by Henry Culver. I tell them in jest, they'll get well so fast before they reach Richmond, they'll miss a furlough. A great deal of love to the girls, if they still be with you, as I trust they are. God bless you darling, and our children. Always *ever* remember my heart's most cherished wishes about you and them. Goodbye, your own longing, loving Edge.

1. Thomas U. Camak, member of a leading Athens family, had commanded the Mell Rifles since the company was mustered into service in 1861. Part of Wofford's Brigade at Gettysburg, they drove the enemy back nearly two miles, but at great cost. A shell almost carried Camak's leg away. Doctors could not control the pain; the officer suffered in agony several hours before death came. Stegeman, *These Men She Gave*, 92, 151.

Edgeworth Bird to Sallie Bird

Williamsport, Maryland, 12 July 1863

Dear Sallie,

I am seated in front of a fly tent this midday, Dearest Darling, to write and thank you for the dear treat that has been afforded me this morning.

"Old Mac" returned this day from Winchester [several words illegible]. I opened the headquarters package and found you, dear precious old fellow, six letters for me. One from the children and balance from you.

You cannot suppose that my pleasure was diminished by getting them in bulk. True, I had been deprived for many days of agreeable pleasure, but had you seen me pick a seat to myself and, with mounting satisfaction, arrange in order my mail package, you would have realized the proper feast I proposed to make, and it was a regular journal of home matters to me. Every word was pure enjoyment, and I perused slowly to drag out and prolong the feast.

Tom[1] got one letter, but in the regimental mail there was another of July 2 from Mary Gilbert.[2] Dearest, before this reaches you, you will have learned that it was a memorable day and a sad, sad one, too, to many a hearthstone in the south. Three major generals wounded—Hood, Heth, and Pender,[3] and some eight or ten brigadiers. Then the loss of officers and privates was very severe. I have sent you a detailed account of the loss in Hancock companies. . . .

I don't know whether Jimmy Reynolds was brought off or not. He lost his left arm. Joe Dickson, son of Tom Dickson, I put down as killed but his leg was taken off, and he died afterwards. I saw him in the hospital the night of the fight, before and after his leg was taken off, and sustained him. He asked me to speak to Dr. Haynes[4] to attend to him. I did so and [several words illegible]. Hardwick is a first cousin of Faring Johnston.[5] Doc Pierce and Tom Culver have started for Staunton, or some point on the railroad. Henry Culver has them in charge. They travel in a little one-horse waggon and are cheerful and lively. Henry has got himself sent back to hospital and will make another effort to resign. I think they certainly did him injustice. Mr. Hardy Culver's boys were very distressed that poor Ev's body[6] could not be recovered from the hands of the enemy for burial.

I can't understand, at last, whether you heard Toombs' speech. How does it seem to go down with our people? Would be a shame to have such a man beaten.[7] [Several sentences are illegible at this point.]

Yes, do keep that pretty Sallie[8] with you, if she can be contented with your quiet life. Will it not improve our own rustic Sallie or Saida, as you seem to like, to have the association of such nice young women? I suppose I am to be scolded for that phrase. I return as many kisses as Sally C. will accept, and a great deal of love, and hope, one day, we may know each other well. I barely remember her as a little wee fellow, when Ponce and I went down to Appling years ago. Sallie tells me her music lessons are over for the present. I am sorry for this discontinuance, but she will not lose much if she continues to practice faithfully. [Several lines are illegible.]

I should very much like to have been at home when Rozier[9] was there. I am glad he met with so much attention. Tell him I say, if he'd send that sweet, graceful daughter of his, when he proposed to be in a place, and follow on a week or so behind, he'd always find himself feasted and made much of. I suppose Rozier found nobody but Bud to play billiards with. You should have seen him play. I'm told he plays an elegant game.

If you have started Sam[10] along with a box, he may reach me, but the box never will. Remember how many miles we are from a railroad. I hope he'll think to take out the shirts and pants. It is possible he may have great difficulty in getting along a box. Indeed, I don't know how he can do it, though Sam is very managing. I wish he could have come under tow of some one. I've certainly missed him a great deal.

I'm so glad, Darling, you have plenty of wheat, and indeed of everything, around you. It's a great comfort to me [illegible] know you manage everything superbly. You did just what I wished and directed about Flawral[11] and Dennis. It would not be right to put them under Mr. Rhodes[12] in utter defiance of him. I hope you may make a superb crop of corn and everything. Before all things, take care of and push your hogs, and kill as large an amount of pork as possible. You can eat some of the male lambs, Dearest. I only care to turn out, or retain in the flock, two rams. Have a strong plow force, by all means. You have plenty of horses or mules—it will not hurt your horses. But never use them, except when you don't wish to drive yourself. Most assuredly your presence at home is a blessing there, and being as you can improve and make it agreeable to yourself, hope you will not be absent any long time.

I wish so earnestly your mother could come to you. Certainly you should be together. I'm very sorry she is not well. I'm greatly obliged to Dawson[13] for the cigars and hope they'll reach me, and that he may soon regain his shattered health. Give for me a great many regards to Mrs. D. and Mrs. Terrell.

Hurling our army against the heights and mountains at Gettysburg was certainly very unfortunate. I think Genl Lee proposes to cross to the Virginia side. The river is too high for fording, and they are constructing pontoon bridges. Our army is drawn up in an arc of a circle around Williamsport. It is now 5 p.m., and whilst I write, the cannon are pealing around on the left, some distance off. The Yankee's are longing to make a general pitch in, no doubt, but fear to do so.

We cannot subsist long here. Our space is so contracted to forage our horses in. We feed together on wheat, and clover, and timothy hay. At present there seems plenty of that. From the attack this evening, the Yankee's plan a grand demonstration tomorrow. I think they will be badly whipped. Our losses have been very heavy since we came over the Potomac, but Lee's genius may yet turn the tables on them. He had met with no defeat, but certainly failed in his plans at Gettysburg, and at a great loss. We hear nothing from Vicksburg.[14] We have seen no paper later than the 2nd of July. First, we have a rumor that Johnston has driven Grant off. Then, that the place has fallen, but I place no confidence in either and suppose, when this grand blow comes this way, we'll hear soon enough, and that it will be completed with a great blast. Meanwhile, my own dearest, we lead this unpleasant life here.

Certainly Edgar Dawson is right. Quartermastering is a calling that don't suit me, but there is no help for it now. As soon as I can, I certainly intend to get out of it, but there is little use in talking about it. It has rained and leaked through the fly until writing paper is soiled, but my darling won't mind that. I send a longer letter than of late. I'm half ashamed of the pencil scrawls I so often get off, but I can't do well or better. I had proposed to write to Father, also, this evening, but persons coming in, and the heavy rain, broke me up. I haven't written him in a long time, and he never writes to me, but once, I believe, since I left. This is a hard world, Precious, at all times, and particularly so now. Grab is the game, from nations to individuals, and you know I'm not good at that, but, so we love truly and fondly, we'll bear the balance and trust to God.

I hardly think it best to leave those funds in Athens. I think you had better pay the money owing your Mother. *Now* is your time to pay *all* debts. I owe the Wynn estate some money. I think we had better pay all indebtedness. Confederate money is at a great discount below gold, but in paying one's debts, it's as good as gold. One dollar of gold is worth five of our money—to pay off. Let's be clear. Talk to John[15] about it. I think he is the best counselor you can find.

The money in Athens will clear our stocks, together with the bonds. After that, you and the children shall have everything you need or desire. It is necessary I should have plenty of money. Send me by first chance five hundred dollars. I have that amount due me here, but, nevertheless, send it by first chance. Sell nothing of the present crop at present except to oblige an intimate friend. We will need a great deal of wheat to sow. You may probably have applications for corn, etc., in advance. Last year I sold most all at 1.00. Others waited and doubled, but I don't care for that. Only exercise ordinary prudence. [The close is missing.]

1. Thomas A. Murray, junior first lieutenant.

2. Mrs. William H. Gilbert, the former Mary Wiley.

3. John Bell Hood lost an arm. Henry Heth was severely wounded, but fought on until Appomattox. William Dorsey Pender, severely wounded in the leg, died 18 July 1863, following amputation. Ezra J. Warner, *Generals in Gray* (Baton Rouge, La., 1959), 133–34, 233–34.

4. It is not clear which Dr. Haynes is referred to.

5. Faring Johnston not found in the *Georgia Roster.*

6. Everard Culver was eventually buried back home in the Culverton, Ga., cemetery. Smith, *History of Hancock County,* 1:x.

7. Robert Toombs made a speech at Sparta 17 June 1863 in which he said all Southerners had the same objective in view, differing only on means. He pronounced the conscription act unconstitutional and condemned the Confederate tax in kind. Phillips, *The Life of Robert Toombs*, 248.

8. Sarah Berrien Casey.

9. Dr. Henry Rozier Casey, father of Sarah Berrien Casey.

10. Sam, Edgeworth Bird's body servant.

11. Flawral and Dennis, slaves at Granite Farm.

12. George F. Rhodes, overseer.
13. Edgar Dawson.
14. Vicksburg had already surrendered on 4 July 1863.
15. John DeWitt.

Edgeworth Bird to Sallie Bird

Camp near Bunker Hill, Va., 19 July 1863

My own dear precious darling,

Day before yesterday I sent you a letter. I am trying to get off a hurried one this morning. This I shall direct to Athens as, doubtless, you have gone up by now. Yesterday's mail brought me no letters, but I shall look for two by the next. My own precious, you've spoiled me. . . . I don't think Sammie and his wife deal fair by each other. They don't write often enough, tho' it is not my business. And I am so sorry for Cousin Sallie.[1] She has such a trouble to bear with.

It is certainly a comfort to have John DeWitt there. If he don't attempt to manage the farm atall, his advice is always sound and good. Whenever Sallie comes down to see you, try and have John come also. You can then consult him if you have any matter on hand, but I forget you are in Athens. Dearest, if you find yourself improving and strong enough, you must not remain away from home very long at the time. Get the children to school, and you and your mother—or it may be Mrs. Hunter[2] would take pleasure in running down with you. Go for a week, taking only a small valise. If you stay off very long, there's liable to spring up some stew among the negroes and overseer, or some new complication. Besides, you'll find it a pleasant change.

I haven't the same implicit faith in your improvement in Athens as at home, at a time when rest is absolutely essential to you. Your friends will have you go about too much. You rarely find them with consideration enough to consider one's health—and, indeed, they are not posted as to your real situation. But let me impress it on you, dearest, to lay aside pleasuring, and tea drinking, and such as interferes with your perfect quiet until you are restored. Now, you know in your heart of hearts, that I am not giving an idle warning, but that always you have been on the pad in Athens, and that it requires a great deal of moral courage to withstand the solicitations of your Athens friends. But this time you can plead the state of your health, and the condition of your country, for verily misfortune and evil times have come upon us suddenly.

A few short weeks ago we were confident and jubilant, but Vicksburg, Port Hudson,[3] and the *unfortunate victory at Gettysburg* have changed greatly the fall of our fortunes. Charleston, too, is in a terrible straight. I fear it will go—the proud old city—I hope its people may prefer to lay it in ruins. Lee's army is now the great hope of the South. There is a terrible band of veterans here yet. There is a very current rumour here among the troops that we are to go back and try our fortunes north of the Potomac once again. I don't know . . . ; it seems a desperate yet probably a prudent move.

We can whip Meade's army if they don't have all the position, and badly, too. We did whip them at Gettysburg, but at awful loss, and the heavy ordnance was all exhausted. Nothing you've ever heard or read of can give you an idea of the terrific fire Lee opened on their heights. Not less than 300 cannon belching forth at once. It had to be discontinued from exhaustion of ammunition. Captured officers say they would have had to abandon all their positions, if it had kept on thirty minutes longer. They finally had to retreat, but Lee had to do so at the same time.

July 19th—Dearest, I write you to pay off *all* our indebtedness. I think it is best, decidedly best. The Dickson[4] land is not to be bought, but even then they would prefer notes to money. Pay the Wynn estate,[5] your Mother, and anybody that has a claim. Let us not owe a dollar. Give Mr. DeWitt authority to pay the Wynn money. You can pay your Mother. Richard[6] was to see me yesterday. He is camped 2 1/2 miles off, is quite well. All . . . [except] his wounded hand, which he says still unfits him for service in the ranks. He is to come again. He had a letter from you or Sallie. I am going to try and find where his application has lodged. It went approved from Genl Wright's office. Must be either at A. P. Hill's or Genl Lee's. I shall send this telegram to Athens, believing it will find you there. Do Precious, don't think hard of me for writing so hurriedly. Kiss our dear children. Tell them not to grow into forgetfulness of Papa. They see very little of him as they verge with maturity. Dearest love to your Mother. Dick says George Hayes was quite well. Love to his Kate.[7] I wish she could see him as I did. God bless and guard you in these times of peril, my own and all our loved ones. Your own Edge.

P.S. Frank Burnet[8] not in Richmond. If Sam could get under care of some one it would be best, but I suppose he has started. He'll find his way. Goodbye, Precious.

1. Sallie Carnes Wiley, wife of Samuel H. Wiley.

2. Perhaps the wife of Professor B. T. Hunter, who taught in Athens. Hull, *Annals of Athens*, 380. Or Mrs. Hunter could be the wife of John Hunter, who served with the Troup Artillery. Stegeman, *These Men She Gave*, 147.

3. With the fall of Vicksburg, Miss., 4 July 1863 and the surrender of the Confederates under siege at Port Hudson, La., five days later, the South lost control of the Mississippi.

4. David Dickson and his brother Thomas were major landowners in that part of the county.

5. The male Wynn heirs died young of tuberculosis. The 1856 Hancock County tax digest listed 4,600 acres and 136 slaves in the estate, all valued at $125,000 for tax purposes.

6. Richard Baxter, Sallie Bird's youngest brother.

7. Kate Rucker of Athens, who later married Richard Baxter.

8. Frank Burnet, private, Company J, Forty-ninth Regiment (Pierce Guards). Smith, *History of Hancock County*, 1:139. Burnet was a brother of Julia Burnet Whitehead, a friend of Sallie and Edgeworth Bird. Reduced to poverty after the war, he obtained a job as conductor on the Georgia Railroad, but gave it up rather than wear the blue uniform imposed by the company. Sparta *Times and Planter*, 9 and 15 May 1879.

Edgeworth Bird to Sallie Bird

Culpeper, Va., 29 July 1863

My own Precious old Fellow,

I am dressed and sitting by my trunk before breakfast. A glance at the portfolio reminds me that I might begin a letter to you, so I begin the good work, and I recall what a grunty, complaining letter went off before, telling of divers ailments and evils that were assailing this poor body of mine—and mentally resolved there should be less of that style. I am not yet in a robust state, and have continued under the weather longer than I expected. After gradually getting better in every other way, a kind of neuralgic pain continues in my forehead. I haven't been clear of it in ten days. It is constantly annoying, but, of course, it must soon pass.[1]

Dearest, I did not get far with this before breakfast was announced and I wrote no more that day. In the evening came your letter of the 19th and 20th. A long sweet letter written after your confinement to bed for fourteen days. This is the 30th I now write. What could have frightened you so badly? You tell of the fact, without giving the cause. I expect it was that Scamp Peter's deviltry. In any case I agree cheerfully to what you wish about that fellow. Sell him by all means, and as far off as possible. One should not have such a negro on their place in such times as these. I am half sorry Dennis is there, for he is not much more to be trusted.[2] Those fourteen days were long, weary one's, darling, I know. Your friends were all gone and your children alone were left to solace you. I hope they exerted themselves to wait on and amuse you.

Dr. Alfriend[3] tells me Bud is growing finely now. I hope so. It is time he was looking up. Tell him to remember what his Uncle Eli says, and drink plenty of buttermilk. Mr. Latimer[4] is also here. In the long letter by Dr. A you speak of, you wish to send Sallie to Mrs. Ford. I have already written you to do as you thought best. I hope it may prove a good school and doubt it not from the description given you. Anything to remove you from the toil and burden you've borne so long and faithfully. I am a swift witness for you, my own, that you've never wavered in your duty to your children. I am not so certain you did a wise thing in allowing Wilson to have his pony in Athens. He should be put immediately to school and kept at it. And then, a spirited young man in Athens, scampering and racing with a half dozen other youngsters, is different from the gentler associations of the plantation. So warn him to be careful and never to run a race.

What has become of the Toombs mare? Has she been sent for? I can't gather whether your carriage has arrived. Sometimes your proceedings are obscure. Was it to be sent to Athens or to Sparta? Dr. Alfriend, who is a very scattering fellow, says, as he came on, there was a carriage on the platform and some of them there at the depot said it was to be sent back. And he understood it to be yours, and that you didn't like it, but in your letter of the 20th, written many days after, there is no mention made of it. So, I suppose there is nothing of it.

Yes, I suppose I had better write Mr. Rhodes and tell him what I want done on the place. I do wish that piece of branch land cut down below your garden. It adds no beauty and will make a nice piece of meadow ground. It is to extend back to where the road crosses the branch at the mulberry gate. Then the pine thickets are to be cut down in the spring—March 1st. I wish to open that like the other fields. After that, the whole plantation must be put in thorough repair as to fencing. Dr. Ed Alfriend sent me a long letter by his brother. He speaks cheerfully of your improved condition. I imagine your last attack was a set back, and you are to be very careful not to have another. No more fainting spells. Lead a quiet life and try to have no cares or crosses.

July 30th—This letter drags its slow length along. As I wrote so far yesterday, Richard came up. Pete[5] had gone into the country for a load of hay, Sammy to the creek to wash, so I stopped to talk to Dick who staid all day, not riding off until nearly sundown. And then, Precious, that incessant pain in my head annoys me so much, it's a trial to write. Richard is in fine health and spirits. Yesterday George Hays,[6] who is acting Adjt Genl for the Brigade, loaned him his horse to come over. You know he has been ordered back to his company. I would not mention it before, but he told me he wrote his Brother. His Brigade was in a terrible little row on Manassas gap the day it relieved Benning's. They were attacked by overwhelming numbers and driven out, losing heavily. Richard says, at one time, the colonels of his regiment and those of the enemy were not 25 yards apart, but he came through safely, without a scratch, as did George Hayes. I think it was the 23rd.

Richard says Genl Wright[7] (who, by the by, was not in the fight being under arrest, something about a spring waggon) called him up yesterday and enquired what had become of his paper. After [Richard's] telling him he had never heard from it, Wright concluded it must be lost and told him to go and have another drawn up and started, then get a pass and come over here and let me have it signed up. This was all done. He took it back with him, and it goes out today. The other went off at an unfavourable time, just as the move towards Pennsylvania was initiated, and was lost in the confusion incident thereto. Wright looked at Richard's hand and told him it unfitted him for active field service. He, moreover, offered him the place of Brigade Clerk. I think he was quite kind.

In the evening, Darling, I got your letter of 24th from Athens. Gave parts of it to Richard. I see the carriage has arrived. Tell me candidly if you are pleased with it, or are somewhat disappointed. Has it been used enough to take away the good looks? I wish to know if you are pleased. In that case, I shall be. You didn't tell me enough of Jimmy Harris,[8] of his condition; if he is in better spirits and more reconciled to his unfortunate accident.

I think I will write Mr. Rhodes and tell him some things I wish done, but I've been away from home so long and have become such a stranger to the business, I am hardly fit to instruct in the details.

Drafton Haynes came by this morning—is in good health and spirits and thinks the war is to soon end, but . . . on what basis he predicates his opinions one can't imagine. Dr. William Alfriend is to remain here a couple of weeks or more, I believe. He slept with me last night. Mr. Latimer and he were, of course, delighted to find their boys safe and [to] be with them for a while. Is not B. Yancey now living in Athens? If so, you will see him and Cousin Sarah and Caro.[9] Give them my love. Ah, old fellow, you've seen the sad news of the death of William Yancey.[10] He died at his residence near Montgomery. I saw it announced under the telegraphic head in yesterday's paper. It sorely troubled me. We need our strong men now. William looked terribly broken in the Senate last winter.

I wrote Father the other day; I told him, as he had gotten back to his old comfortable room again, I thought he had better occupy it permanently, and that it was my sincere advice that he should buy it back again, and I do really think so.[11] What better investment could he make of our so greatly depreciated Confederate money? I hope you will not defer very long paying up whatever be my indebtedness to the Wynn estate. You must remember that under many more reverses there are people who will not wish to receive it at par in discharge of debts. It is not well to speak of this, but wisdom will always look ahead. Pay all our debts, then we can go to investing.

I hope your Mother is well again. I know you've both improved since you were together. Dick and I discussed you all up there. Bud and Sallie must go at their books with a will. I never wished Sallie at the Institute,[12] but for the present it may be best. I would make the other arrangement as soon as I could. Many howdy's to the black people, Aunt Peggy, Vilet, Candus, etc. Remember me to all of them. Tell Henry to see to it to stay on the lot and keep out of trouble. Athens is a great place for Darkey's to get into trouble. How is Teedee? I had like to have forgotten the little lady. Send stamps each time. We cannot get them.

Clarence Simmons[13] is detailed to go home . . . to get clothing appropriated for destitute soldiers by the State. He will take a small package for you and deliver it to John DeWitt. He can send it up by express, if you want it. I expect he will send me five hundred dollars. You seem not to have received any of my letters about it, tho' I suppose they may have reached you by this. I wish that amount by first chance, and Clarence will be the best. A great deal of love to your Mother and our dear little folks. Kind regards to all friends. Sam and Pete are well. Goodbye, my own darling. God bless you always. Edge

1. Edgeworth Bird was severely wounded the year before at Second Manassas. It is not clear whether these complaints were related.

2. As master of Granite Farm, Edgeworth Bird usually spoke kindly of the slaves there. This reference to Peter and Dennis is the first critical one.

3. Dr. William Alfriend.

4. John Latimer, the father of Captain Mark Latimer. A few months after this letter, Captain Latimer was badly wounded at the Battle of Chickamauga, but he survived the war.

5. Samuel P. Harris.

6. First Lieutenant George E. Hayes, Third Georgia Regiment.

7. Ambrose Ransom Wright, a brigadier general at the time. With the strong support of Jefferson Davis, Wright was later promoted to major general.

8. Probably James M. Harris, husband of "Cousin Lizzie."

9. Benjamin C. Yancey, son of Edge-

worth Bird's aunt Caroline Bird. He first married Laura Hines and had a daughter, Caro, by that marriage. After the death of his first wife he married Sarah P. Hamilton and had a son, Hamilton, and a daughter, Mary Louisa (Mary Lou).

10. William Lowndes Yancey, brother of Benjamin C., died at his home near Montgomery, Ala., 27 July 1863. He left his Senate seat in Richmond early that year because of failing health. His sons Ben and Dalton refused to live in the U.S. after the war. They went to Brazil with several thousand other Southerners. Ben spent the rest of his life in Brazil as a planter and real estate investor. Dalton eventually returned to Alabama. Eugene C. Harter, *The Lost Colony of the Confederacy* (Jackson, Miss., 1985), 87–90.

11. Edgeworth Bird's father had sold his Sparta home to Edward Soullard, Jr., of Savannah.

12. Lucy Cobb Institute, an Athens school for girls.

13. J. Clarence Simmons, quartermaster sergeant, Company E, Fifteenth Regiment, fought until Appomattox. *Georgia Roster,* 2:447.

Edgeworth Bird to Sallie Bird

Camp near United States Ford, Va., 8 August 1863

My Dearest Darling,

I am going to send you only a half sheet today, but it shall go full and be a good, long letter, too. We've been on the move a great deal of late, and I've had no opportunity of writing until today. We are in the midst of a warm, oppressive spell of August weather; have been making marches under . . . as hot a sun as I've ever felt. I've had to quit my horse and take to the waggon for fear of sunstroke, for one day I thought I felt premonitory symptoms. It is a wonder to me how the men stand it. A great many do not, but fall out and follow on at leisure, coming into camp probably next day.

We went down to Fredericksburg, passing through the edge of town and camping a few miles off. As you go out of town, the road runs along the rock wall behind which Tom Cobb's Brigade fought and dealt such terrible destruction to the enemy. I saw the very tree under which he fell,[1] and my sad thoughts flew to his stricken wife and family. Oh! How we miss such men as he, as our country's troubles become deeper involved in gloom. Yes, I had received the sad news of the death of Mr. Yancey and written you about it. Another strong, manly intellect gone, another broken column that supported the great arch of liberty we are trying to build. I was very, very much grieved to hear of his death.

From near Fredericksburg, we were moved up to this point, on a sort of picket duty, I judge. None of the army are down this way, except our division, and we are at least ten miles from any portion of it. We are a few miles from U.S. Ford and have pickets there, tho' I believe, at present, there are no Yankee's showing themselves on the Stafford Side. It is too hot to fight, such weather as this, and there *seems* no prospect at present for a battle. I wrote you that Richard had sent me up another application by advice of Genl Wright, and that he had also offered him the place of Brigade Clerk, so you see he is likely to have a good place, even tho' his application for transfer should fail. I very much wish he was with me, for I am much attached to him, as it seems I am obliged to stay where I am, but I do not like the place.

Dearest Old Fellow, evening before last I received two sweet letters from you, 29th and 30th July, one enclosing Miss Janey Dickson's[2] note, and one from Miss Sallie Newman.[3] They are very kind friends, the Newmans, to send such petition and urgent invitation, and I hope it may some day be in our power to show our appreciation. But you are right not to think of coming on. First, the state of your health utterly forbids it, and then, the state of the country is such that a Lady had better be at home, unless she has sick or wounded friends, or relatives. If we were stationed in winter quarters, and you, in good health, could come to such a place as Mr. Newman's, that would be grand, and it may be, darling, that you'll get well and strong, and we be quartered near them. Then you *can* come. But you must write Miss Sally your grateful thanks. If we get near them, I'll certainly go and see them.

I hope Mr. Stanley Newman[4] came up, and you had it in your power to show him some attention. You did perfectly right to pay the $500. We are obliged to have a manager and could not replace Mr. Rhodes. I have full confidence in him, and he has learned my way of doing business. I should have said to consent to pay, if necessary, but we are short of money now. I have written for $500, and you need some. We mustn't try to grow rich too fast. Some of those bonds must be turned into Confederate notes, if necessary. Darling, when the factory makes another dividend, and the plantation begins to yield a return in money, I wish several thousand dollars kept on hand. If we are lucky enough to have more, we will invest.

I've written you, and now repeat, sell Peter. In Richmond he would bring $2,500 or more. I do not wish you annoyed, and I am very certain there should be no such negro on a place *in such times*. I am gratified and very thankful that the balance of our people behave so well. And so our little man is established at school at last, a new episode in his young life. Tell him he is to study hard and try to excell, be always truthful, never tell an untruth. He must write me and tell me how he gets on. It will not be much of a trial for Sallie to begin school in Athens. I hope to hear fine reports from both. You must return with interest the kind messages sent me. A great deal of love to your Mother. What do we not owe her for her many kindnesses? Love and kisses to our dear children, and to Teedee. Be careful of yourself, my own loved treasure. God bless you and care for you and let us soon meet in peace. (Send me postage stamps.) Your loving Edge

I have no means to get stamps. Make up a rule to put one or two ten cent stamps in each letter. Howdy to Henry.[5] Tell him to mind what I say. If he ain't careful, he'll get in trouble. Howdy to all the servants.

1. Thomas R. R. Cobb of Athens died at Fredericksburg 13 Dec. 1862. He led his infantrymen to the base of Marye's Heights to a sunken road bordered by a rock wall. His troops helped rout General Burnside's men, but Cobb died that day when a shell fragment struck him. Stegeman, *These Men She Gave*, 73–75.

2. Not identified.

3. Sallie Newman, member of the family of James Stanley Newman of Orange Court House, Va.

4. James Stanley Newman of Orange Court House.

5. Henry was brought up from Granite Farm to be Sallie Bird's driver in Athens.

Edgeworth Bird to Sallie Bird

Camp near United States Ford, Va., 15 August 1863

My own Darling,

Richard wrote you yesterday, which deferred my writing until today. Before this reaches you, you will have learned that he has succeeded in getting his transfer and is now regularly installed as Q.M. Sergeant of the Brigade. The duties are all new and unfamiliar at present. But we are, for the time, quiet in camp, and he can have an opportunity of becoming gradually familiar with them. The man Whitney[1] I have with me is a first rate business man and understands this all well. He is not an enlisted man, so his name must go on the rolls, and he is not paid by the government. I pay him out of my own private funds, and it is no small tax. But, still, he is so useful I shall retain him as long as I can.

Dearest, I have been very uneasy for fear of losing Sammy.[2] There came an order, a few days back, requiring all clerks who could not produce a certificate . . . of disability for field service to be returned to their companies, and their places be filled by wounded or disabled men—a very unjust order, for it takes a long time for men to become familiar with the duties of clerk in the Q.M. Department. They are intricate and troublesome; there are so many forms.

In this Brigade the order only bore upon Major Ballard[3] and myself. Our clerks are invaluable to us. We each addressed a communication to Genl Lee asking . . . that they be allowed to continue. . . . I appended to mine a pretty strong certificate of surgeon showing Sammy's unfitness for field service. . . .

I had a letter from John DeWitt a day or so since. He tells me Burwell Taylor[4] has been up and paid the debt of his father to the Wynn Estate. You know they owe us some two thousand dollars personally. He promises to pay that shortly. I reckon John will have to draw that $500 to be sent on by Clarence[5] from Turner. If you need money, borrow it till the factory makes a dividend, and then be sure to invest no more till we have a surplus of several thousand on hand. In these times, it is necessary to keep that much on hand. We never know what will turn up. I wish I had about fifty thousand in one of those iron establishments. They pay so well, and then perhaps I might get out of the confounded quartermastering. . . .

There seems to be a lull in the storm of war. The great depression our people laboured under, after the fall of Vicksburg and Port Hudson, was uncalled for. The Battle of Gettysburg so disabled Meade, that he is unable to resume the offensive. Charleston seems able to defend herself. Johnston[6] says Mobile is the most defensible point on the coast. He has a growing army and is our ablest gen'l. Bragg has a fine army and position. We have fifty thousand troops west of the Mississippi. Lee will be able to take care of any force the Yankee's can bring against him or Richmond. The draft seems to progress slowly. The Yankees will realize money, but very few men by the operation. $300 lets a man out. There are many exemptions.

They *can never* conquer us, but still our late losses and failures may protract the war for years, unless a kind Providence provides something in our favour at present veiled from human ken. Ah! Old fellow, I'm very weary of it all. I long for home and you, but when heavy misfortunes come upon us, I feel that I should stay. But there are so many within our circle who have never raised a finger in defense of home and family, who have never borne for an hour or a second the heat and burden of the day. Richard does need a horse. The government is so hard run for horses to keep up transportation and particularly the artillery, that it is hard to obtain a public animal. I advise him to buy one for himself. It will always bring the same money or more. He can well afford to pay that much for his change of position. Besides, it is customary. Nearly all the sergeants own their horses. I believe he has written for money. Send it to him, by all means.

I received Sallie's letter and am much obliged to the young damsel, particularly if she'd write oftener and not always be in a hurry to go out visiting toward the close. Bud must send me his experiences as a school boy. I am glad your carriage pleases you. From your description, I doubt not you have a most excellent one. It's carrying six is a decided advantage to a family which may increase !!! some fine day. Tell me how Henry deports himself. Make him stay on the lot, and don't let him learn to roam the town; he'll be sure to get into trouble. You know he is famous for getting into small scrapes, and large one's too.

I wrote so far soon after breakfast, and now resume quite late in the evening. I thought I would be sure and get a letter this evening, and there might be something I wished to reply to. Alas, none has come and I am about to begin to get in a stew. . . . I wrote Mr. Rhodes one or two days ago, giving him directions concerning the work to be done, now that the crop is laid by. I told him to walk into that piece of woods in front of the house, clearing it all as far as the road that leads from Mulberry gate, past Ted and John's[7] potatoe patch towards the rocks. We'll get a very nice piece of land, mostly meadow, and I think the opening will add much to the appearance of the place. The small batch of woods immediately at, and partly at the side, must detract from the appearance. It will also assist to deliver your flower garden from the depredations of the rabbits.

Dr. William Alfriend has gone home. He remained in camp with us for a week or two. Mr. Latimer is still here. He seems very much devoted to his son. Stays with him in camp and takes camp fare. Dear, dear Darling, you are the only person in the world who would risk for me the dangers . . . of this life. . . . Even we have a chasm between us that seems to widen,[8] but why need I refer to it. My children have been baptized by a Presbyterian, are educated at schools and Sunday Schools of the same kind. Between our hearts, darling, there is a *bond* nothing can ever disunite, for God and a pure love have cemented them. Meantime, I am here in this life. Should I be taken off, it would make no difference. Were I deprived of you, I would indeed be isolated, and alone. These are my reflections a thousand times over, as I look into the future. Please excuse me for expressing them. They will haunt me, as I lie on the grass and watch the stars, as I do almost nightly.

Col. Waddell[9] went off in an ambulance a day or two ago, some affection of his throat. I did not know he was sick 'till he was gone; there have been a death or two from diphtheria around here. His was not that; some trouble about his tonsils. I am entirely out of postage stamps, and begging, except what I let others have. All go to you; send one or two in every letter. Oh! My precious, beloved Sallie, you know not how earnestly I pray for one thing, and while I have life I'll never despair, night and morning it goes up from an eager, hopeful heart. Goodbye, Dearest, God bless you and direct you as you should go. Love to your Mother, and kisses to the children. Ever and always, your Edge

1. Whitney is not in the military roster. He seems to have been a clerk hired independently by Edgeworth Bird.

2. Samuel H. Wiley.

3. Walter S. Ballard, commissary sergeant with the rank of major.

4. Burrel [possibly misspelled by the census taker] Taylor of Thomas County is the only Georgian by that name in the 1860 census.

5. J. Clarence Simmons, quartermaster sergeant. Turner was probably Thomas Mickleberry Turner, Sparta planter and businessman.

6. General Joseph E. Johnston.

7. Ted and John, servants at Granite Farm.

8. Edgeworth Bird's Catholicism often clashed with his wife's Presbyterianism.

9. Colonel James D. Waddell.

Edgeworth Bird to Sallie (Saida) Bird

Camp near U.S. Ford, Va., 21 August 1863

My dear Daughter,

The different letters you have written me are very deserving of an answer long since, and it has ever been in my mind to send you a "wee" letter. But then you know, Daughter, Mama must be served first, and she keeps me very busy answering her letters, and I reply to every letter that she sends me, at that. Your last was received last night and was very nicely written for the first two pages, then you had to dress to go visiting. You must be a great visitor. Nearly all your letters begin well and neatly, but your industry and perseverance give out before you have finished. Now, daughter, I have referred to this several times and don't do it in a spirit of fault finding, but for your improvement.

Laying aside that motive, it would make very little difference to me that one part of a letter should be written less neatly than another. To write a letter is not so easy a matter to you as to your Mother, but still it is a slight job, and you should show more perseverance. If you are going visiting today, don't write; tomorrow write, and don't go visiting. Try and acquire the habit in your youth of resolutely carrying out what you undertake. There's a lecture for you, young Damsel. I'm quite a lecturer nowadays. In my last to Mama, I believe I lectured you and her and Bud and the teachers. It may be that my lectures may gain me the sobriquet of "Grumbler." But young people must have someone to point out their faults.

I can't say I am delighted that you are going to school. I fear for you that you are about to pass from the sure, loving guidance of your Mother and mingle with those who care so much less for you. You will have many temptations to do wrong, many trials to your good temper, and small troubles innumerable. But if you will govern yourself by a few simple rules, you will come through unscathed. Always be truthful, also always act the lady, and preserve your own self-respect. Never hurt another's feelings, and if you do so inadvertently, never be ashamed to apologize openly. Try and be first, always, but don't let ambition be your first motive, but a solid improvement of your mind. Be kind and approachable to all and try to gain the good will even of the humblest. Love your neighbour as yourself. Try to act up to that great precept of our Redeemer.

If Latin is taught you, I wish you to study it by all means, and, daughter, do so willingly, and cheerfully. Your argument against doing so is easily met. Your Cousin Lucie and Sallie Casey are undoubtedly very sweet, but would they have been less so had they studied Latin? Mama is sweeter than any of them and she *did* study Latin. It is not difficult to attain, and you can never have a correct knowledge of your own language until you have acquired a good knowledge of Latin. I wish you to go at it with an intention to master it, and so with French, which is the universal language. Indeed both, one or other, will take you over Europe.

There is nothing of interest happening now. We are lying quietly in camp. I believe the Q. M. Department is the only one kept very busy. We have to send long distances for supplies and forage. From what Mama says, I expect your prospect of going to Mrs. Ford's is broken up. I'm sorry for it, from the account given of the school, I would prefer much that you be there. Tell Bud to slave ahead and study hard. Always go to school prepared to recite a good lesson. You will have to lay aside your evening dresses and promenades to accomplish that. You have but few years in which to store your mind with book knowledge, and you'll have to be diligent.

Pray write me as often as you can. T'will improve you, for as I prove such a critic, you'll take pains. Richard said his Mother must send his books, clothing, etc., by Sam Hayes. I ask for messages to his mother but his modesty keeps him silent. Give my love to any of your young friends whom you think will value it, among others to Miss Kate Rucker, and oceans of love to Mama. I've just written her. Love to Grandma and the Hayes cousins.

Your Uncle John, I presume, will have left before this reaches you. Kiss Bud, and Mama, and Grandma for me. Love to our Yancey kinfolk. All your friends here are generally well. The health of the troops is unusually good. Goodbye, Daughter, God bless you and guide you, your affectionate Father,

Wm. E. Bird

Edgeworth Bird to Sallie Bird

Camp near U.S. Ford, Va., 23 August 1863

My dearest Darling,

I wrote our Sallie yesterday, and a day or so before a long letter to you, but I feel like chatting a little with you today. I rather hope to hear from you this evening, but the clerks in the Richmond P.O. have been on a strike, and we had no mail yesterday. If that matter is not arranged, we shall not hear today. . . . I generally carry each letter a day or two in my pocket and reread it several times. So, you are to understand that you are not wasting your sweetness on the desert air, when that poor thumb is being exercised.

I am looking for Sam today. I think that he and Forbes's boy will come up with Mr. Pierpont Jordan,[1] now sutler to the 15th. He is brother to our Mr. Jordan. We are just about through with a hubbub of work. Have just issued to Regts several hundred pair each of jackets, pants, drawers, shirts, socks, shoes, and sundry other things. You see all these things are issued to me, and invoiced and charged to me. So I have them all to account for. Today, I believe it all right. So it is with money. I receipt for all that is required by the Brigade, and have to account for all to the Government, and then every small article such as curry combs, spiders, have to be accounted for. Indeed, everything you receive. When I turn them over to Regimental Q.M.'s, I take their receipt, and that is my voucher.

Just here I stopped for dinner, and since then have been handed your letter of the 17th. I am quite exercised on the subject of your horses. The government is very hard run for artillery horses, and such as yours are just what they need. Still, I hope you will not be disturbed. T'would be sad indeed, were you to be deprived of what is so necessary to your comfort. In Petersburg they just bought everything, splendid pairs of Northern horses, bought before the war and belonging to private families, were taken, and I afterwards saw magnificent animals hitched to the heavy artillery wagons, in a few months to be completely ruined. They are a reckless set, and the hardest horse masters in the world. I heard of a splendid buggy mare for which $1500 had been refused—that was taken. As for Bud's mare, she is too small, for either draft work, or for cavalry, and I think would be passed by. Still, it is wise to take precautions. There is nothing at the plantation that they might make useful, except Lizzie. Mr. Rhodes should be written to state that she is a brood mare and plow animal.

I would like to accommodate this little Confederacy as far as may be, am giving it myself, but $2500 wouldn't buy Lizzie, if she only proved a good breed mare. Bye the bye, there shouldn't be less than that asked for Peter.[2] Mares are bringing much higher prices than horses. People begin to learn their value. I wish I had one or two fine ones in addition. I don't see how you could send the filly to John.[3] There is no transportation by railroad. . . .

They are piling the agony on Bud, but he must work bravely. In the assistance that is rendered him, he must be sure and understand everything, or it will simply be plastering him over, and when left to himself, he'll be afoot. In studying Latin, let him [illegible] by his dictionary, look out every word, again and again and again, as he forgets it, noticing the declension and the gender. It will soon be indelibly impressed on his memory.

Sallie pleads not to study Latin, if it is taught there. I desire her to do so, by all means. But, let me make this suggestion about that young lady. Always dress her neatly, but once a day is sufficient. Lay aside her evening dresses; don't run home from school to change dresses for a tramp on the streets. Goodbye then to books. She can walk in her neat school dress when she chooses to, but for heaven's sake, let her be a stranger, rather than otherwise, on the streets. In the observance of this, there is a multitudinous multiplicity of *good.*

Don't pout, dear Darlie, at my presuming to advise. I'm sorry she is to stop her music, but you know what is best. About a piano, my precious, you are right. No one could deserve a fine one more than you, but Darlie, it might not do to go into such a luxury now. We know not what emergencies may come upon us, and soon, perhaps. We have no surety of preserving our lives, and property necessary to life for a twelve month, and I should not feel it was right, with our means, to buy a fine piano, and I would have no other sort. I know you agree with me, dearest Darlie, don't you? Hire at any cost first.

I can judge you do not fancy the teacher now in Athens. If it's the little man I think of, he won't be big enough to hold a sufficient quantity of music to distribute to others. But I can't see when she'll have the benefit of Mrs. Lowery[4] again. I'm puzzled about her schooling. I'm not pleased with the present status of things. I would like to have her very thoroughly educated, but the times seem to conspire against it. Darling, we could afford to pay any price in money, and more in love, if Miss Janey Dickson would come and live a year or so with us. . . . Bud can get along after he gets underway. A boy can go through life with ordinary help, but for a woman to do her part well, she must have early training and advantages.

Well, we must rock along for the present. I understand Old Sumpter[5] is knocked into a cocked hat. The villainous scoundrels, but they are no nearer taking Charleston than if the pile of bricks still stood. Col. Waddell has returned and brings the news. I haven't seen him yet. Forbes[6] wants four or five bushels of barley. Write Mr. Rhodes to let him have it, if he has it to spare. He should sow a lot for me about first of September. Another about 1st October. John has left you before now. I know how grieved you all are. The four stamps are received, and thank you. Do keep me supplied. It is very inconvenient for me to get them. Put them in dry.

Bud is right to look askance at $500 for his mare, if she was bona fide sold, but his Uncle John was very kind. Dearest, give a great deal of love to your Mother. Stay in that bed and keep quiet generally. Love and kisses to the children, love to the Hayes cousins, howdy to all the servants, and a Pacific ocean of love to yourself. Your Edge

Richard, Sammy, Pete, all well. Tell Henry[7] he'd better take that bushel's worth—his horses, rather than let them take them away from him. Note what I said about peach or apple brandy in a former letter. Can't Dr. Linton[8] put you in a way to get it? God bless you and care for you, Dearest,

Ever your own Edge

1. Pierpont Jordan, sutler to the Fifteenth Regiment, not further identified.

2. Peter was a slave, not a horse.

3. John Baxter, Sallie Bird's brother, the Macon, Ga., physician.

4. Mrs. Lowery, Athens music teacher, is not in the 1860 census.

5. Fort Sumter received its first bombardment from Union land and naval batteries 17 Aug. 1863. Thousands of shells fell on the fort in Charleston harbor, but caused relatively few casualties. After Swamp Angel, the pride of the Union battery, blew up 22 Aug., the Federals stopped the shelling, leaving a mass of rubble still in Confederate hands.

6. H. W. Forbes of Hancock County, captain and assistant quartermaster.

7. Sallie Bird's driver.

8. Dr. John S. Linton, Athens physician and businessman.

Edgeworth Bird to Sallie Bird

Camp near U.S. Ford, Va., 28 August 1863

I have been sending you letters quite often of late. . . . The receiving, opening, and reading of your letters is the greatest pleasure I have left me. . . . I think I have rather come out in the epistolary line, having written Mr. Rhodes twice, John Dewitt once, and Sallie once. . . . Sallie will find my letter rather admonitory, and I share with you a great anxiety on her entering the outer court of the temple of love.

There are a thousand perils for the young and inexperienced of which they dream not, and it would indeed be culpable of a parent not to give such teaching as they may. I would, of all things . . . have Sallie's friend receive a strong desire for self improvement and a consequent love for study, the only means of acquiring a high cultivation.

"Knowledge is power" in this life and is, besides, a greater source of enjoyment than all other sources afford, unless we except the natural and domestic affections. As the beauties the diamond shows are only made apparent by an exceeding high polish, so the mind can only be made capable of following the loftier . . . emotions by rubbing off the coarser and lower aspirations. . . .

Sallie has only a few years before her in which to lay the foundations of a finished cultivation. Let her set herself sternly and earnestly to the task. Teach her this, that her first object now be to study and learn, and prepare herself with a capability for future enjoyment and usefulness. And so with Bud. So far, he is a pretty good boy. Knows how to groom colts and may one day be a pretty good horse jockey. This is all very well, a very excellent addition to a gentleman's education, but t'would indeed be sad were this all. No, let other aspirations now seize his mind. Study steadfastly and determinedly to acquire all the knowledge that this opportunity may allow him. . . . The times seem averse to our giving the children the best advantages. So far you have acted the part of a noble and loving mother, and they have not been neglected. In the future, they shall have every advantage the state of the times will allow, if I be spared.

I wrote Mr. Rhodes about the new carriage house and crib, but only gave definite instructions to move the crib and where to put it on the lower side of the steer pen, so there would be nice shelter under the shed on one side for the oxen, and suitable troughs for feeding them along the major shed on the lower side. . . . I fear the sawed logs have not length enough to make your carriage house large enough. There should be room to hold two carriages, and several buggies. Cutting so large a door as would be necessary would weaken the carriage house. I told him to measure the logs and write me about it. A neat frame house, large and ample, would be so much better.

Jack Mitchell, Wes, and Arthur[1] could hew out one, that is the framework. Pine poles for sheds, rafters, shingles, weatherboarding, and nails would have to be bought. They would have to hew four sills, four corner posts, and four plates, and then the sleepers for laying the floor on. Mr. Lane[2] has a large, roomy one. It is as well to put up neatly and conveniently what must stand so long. Were you to defer building it till you go down, you could have Jack Mitchell there and have it done neatly and well. Your carriage would be safe for the short time it would take to build it, and t'would not be a trouble to you. Write me your thoughts and wishes about it, darling. I directed that all nails be carefully saved in taking down old cribs.

I have been wonderfully mistaken about Sam.[3] You know, I wrote you he had arrived in Richmond, and I looked for him daily. He is still at home with rheumatism. I'm sadly perplexed what to do. I know no other negro to bring here and don't know how long he is to be laid up. I am now hiring. It is hard luck. Bill Sasnett[4] has just come and says Alfriend told him Sam was not yet fit to stand this life. I think I'll write Alfriend. Well, my precious Darlie, I'll just halt here until evening. I may have a letter, and there may be something to reply to. Always give my love to the Yancey's and the friends who feel an interest in me.

August 29th—There came two letters for me, Precious old fellow, but I did not resume until this morning, dates of 19th and 21st. It is refreshing to hear you speak so cheerfully of yourself. The decrease in the length of your attacks is most encouraging. Assuredly, if you will persevere, you will entirely recover. Success must not make you negligent. You should remain the seventh day in bed and never resume an upright position until everything is in a perfect state of rest. Don't let us have half a cure. Darlie, do you hear quite often from Gresham's folks? You have not mentioned them lately. I like to hear from them all along and how poor Leroy[5] gets on with his sufferings. Do you not expect them this summer atall? You've made no reference to them as coming to Athens.

About the nice gold ring I . . . got Frank to have made for you in Richmond, I'm so glad you like it. Ain't I a good old fellow? Bless your dear heart, if I'd a just thought about it, I'd have sent you forty bushels of gold rings. Frank Burnet is at home for 60 days. His direction is simply to Richmond, care of Box 61.

Your conclusions about slavery are not a sure thing. I think it entirely dependent on the results of the rebellion. If we come out with flying colours, it is established for centuries. I am astonished at the state of public feeling in Georgia as represented by the returned furloughed men. They say Georgia is now almost whipped, and she has hardly ever had an armed heel on her soil. The army here thinks it can whip its weight in wild cats and has no mistrusts or apprehension. I hope there is no truth in these reports.

All of us are well. Sammie gets, now and then, the best letters from his mother.[6] I tell you, she is a "Cracker" to write. The simplicity of style is quite charming. Dr. William Hoyt[7] is a very nice gentleman. We had a long chat last evening about our friends and Athens people. He is quite well. I only lately learned he married Florence Stephens. Richard has been quite in the dumps, but a whole bundle of letters that had gone to Second Georgia came yesterday, and he has laid aside several desperate acts he contemplated.

Any man who advocates reconstruction should be hung to the nearest tree. Disband our armies, and mind never dreamed of such a scene as the South would soon represent: murder, rapine, conflagration. But Poh! They can never subdue us, and our people are staunch. Goodbye, Precious Darling. God bless and care for you and direct you to truth. I love you *best on earth* and my heart yearns to rest on yours. Love and kisses to our darling children and your Mother—Goodbye,

Your own Edge

1. Jack Mitchel(l), Sparta workman listed in the 1860 census. Wes and Arthur were servants at Granite Farm.

2. Colonel Andrew Jackson Lane.

3. Sam was Edgeworth Bird's body servant who went home because of illness.

4. William Pembroke Sasnett, a fourth sergeant with the Hancock Volunteers (Company E, Fifteenth Regiment). He died on 30 Dec. 1864. *Georgia Roster,* 2: 442.

5. Leroy Gresham, son of John J.

Gresham and Mary Baxter Gresham of Macon, Ga.

6. Eliza DeWitt, the Connecticut-born wife of Edwin Wiley and the mother of Samuel Harris Wiley.

7. William D. Hoyt, son of Nathan Hoyt, pastor of the Presbyterian church in Athens. He married Florence Stevens. Hull, *Annals of Athens*, 457. He was surgeon of the Seventeenth Georgia Regiment at the time of this letter. Later, while in charge of a military hospital in Richmond, he was captured, 3 April 1865. *Georgia Roster*, 2:559.

FOUR

Chickamauga, Home, The Wilderness

"How I long for peace and home. But, dearest darlie, there are fearful battles yet to be fought."

EDGEWORTH BIRD

EDGEWORTH BIRD was among the 11,000 men rushed from Virginia to aid General Braxton Bragg in Tennessee. Bragg's forces won the bloody battle at Chickamauga in September 1863, but the opportunities presented by the Confederate victory were lost. During October trouble broke out among the blacks in Hancock County and some of the Bird slaves ran away from home. Eighteen slaves were jailed for attempting to incite an insurrection. Edgeworth Bird spent the winter in rugged and often hostile country in mountainous East Tennessee where Richard Baxter, Sallie Bird's brother, was captured by Union troops.

By February 1864 Edgeworth had found his way back to Granite Farm. Sallie Bird wrote their daughter, then in school in Athens, "Oh, daughter, how happy I am to be in your precious Father's arms once more." That happy time lasted only a few weeks. In May Edgeworth Bird was again sending home a list of friends who had been wounded or killed, this time at the devastating Battle of the Wilderness. In early summer General Jubal Early gave Confederates a brief heart-stopping lift when he crossed the Potomac at Harpers Ferry and was within range of Washington, but the thrust could not be maintained. Far to the South, Georgia was beginning to feel Sherman's strong hand as the hot months rolled on.

Edgeworth Bird to Sallie Bird

Camp near Chickamauga Station, [Ga.][1] [30] September 1863

This morning, before I got out of the blankets, yours of the 27th was handed me by the postman. . . . There is sad news conveyed in it for which I was totally unprepared. I read your first allusions in utter amazement, but as I got further I comprehended that poor Eddie had lost his life,[2] but am now utterly ignorant of the circumstances. You write evidently on the supposition that I had received previous letters detailing these. You can imagine how my surprise augmented, until the cruel truth burst upon me that the poor, dear fellow was no more.

My Darling, my heart warmly sympathizes with your poor, dear Mother and yourself, under this sad stroke. I gather he was shot in a private difficulty and by one who took advantage of him. May God comfort you both and poor bereaved widow Jule.[3] . . . My whole soul melts in pity for her. . . . Her child is now her comfort and Ellen, I know, will be her sister. Andrew,[4] too, will do all that a brother can do for her. . . .

Richard does not know it yet. He has gone to Chickamauga Station to draw corn, and tho' I had read your letter before he went, I would not speak of it to him 'till he had finished his business—time enough for the sad news when his business is over. Dear Darling, just here I have been several times interrupted. Among others, John Berrien Whitehead[5] came in, inquiring the way to some friend. He has been by Sparta; saw Mrs. Julia Whitehead. I am now at liberty to continue. Meantime, your half sheet of the 25th was handed to me by a courier of General Benning who came to me with orders. It had found its way to General Roberson's[6] headquarters (Texas Brigade) and was sent over to Benning's. . . .

It took us three days after the evening we left Mr. Whitehead's to reach our post. . . . No, Sammie did not go by home. The railroad man in Augusta told them the train could not get off until evening and afterwards started it much earlier, and he and several others, being uptown, were left and had to come up on another train about night. In this way he failed to get word from me and came on. I was so sorry. He has learned the state of affairs at home now and has been in great distress about it. . . .

Richard has just come in and is feeding his horse and whistling merry tunes. You know, I wrote you he had bought a very beautiful horse on our route up for $800. Poor fellow, I'll let him get through all before I give him your letter to read. I hate to do so. If I had my way, he never should have the pain it will cost him to know he has lost a loved brother, if such things were only possible. There is a letter for him lying by me from Kate also.

I rode up to the Brigade yesterday, or rather the day before. Staid all night and returned last night. I slept and ate with Waddell. They have no tents up there, but are in the woods a little way from the breastworks and ready to fall into them at a moment's notice. We have a strong set of breastworks along our whole line. This extends from the foot of Lookout Mountain, entirely around Chattanooga, to the river above. I see Rosecrans[7] says he'll be able to resume the offensive shortly. If he comes to our lines, not many will go back; our men are well protected. Meantime, I presume General Bragg is arranging to injure him all he can by cutting his wagon trains and supplies, etc. We might take Chattanooga and drive him out, but their guns on the other side of the river command the place, and we could not hold it. Besides, it is of no value to us. It rained all night and has continued to do so all day today—from unsupportable dust we are to have mud and mire.

October 2nd—We have a beautiful bright morning today, dearest darling, after raining one day and two nights. I didn't finish last evening, it was so dark and gloomy. John[8] is camped a few miles off. He has been to see us several times. He came early this morning, bringing the copy Sallie made from Andrew's letter, so I have the particular's of poor Eddie's death and I am shocked to think how little cause those miserable men had. No cause, for not even an enmity is referred to, tho' there must have been a grudge in their hearts, the brutal murderers. Oh! How I sorrow for you all, my darling. You can look above alone for comfort.

My Precious, Col. Waddell says you treated him royally at Union Point, that he was hungry and you fed him bountifully. He thirsted and you gave him drink. Says he was fifteen hours with Medora. He went through the battle untouched, and is now in fine spirits. My darling, as soon as you feel like going down home, send for Sam and see how he is. It may be he is unable to fill Henry's place and drive you. He ought not to stay at Mrs. Brookings,[9] but at our place. Food is too high. If he is unable to come or fill Henry's place with you, who had better come? It would seem Robert would [be the] only choice. I cannot get along without a boy.

I have two horses now. Have purchased a mare from Houston, not handsome to the eyes but five years old, sound in every respect and the finest walker I ever backed. Gave eight hundred dollars, or rather my note. She lopes very finely also. I hate to reduce our force, but hope it will only be temporary. Send several hams, more catsup, pepper sauce, or something on that order. Fill in with onions. We are on very short rations now. All of us keep in good health. Pete is at present at the Brigade, attending to forage matters up there. Richard is visiting this morning. John did not stay long and has returned. Mr. Latimer gave the bundle for me to Forbes at Augusta. He forgot it and left it at the Southern States Hotel. I wrote to Capt. Thomas who keeps it to give to someone. I forget whom. I expect it will come up all right after a while.

My own loved darling, may God bless and comfort you and your dear Mother. Pray for me always, and may He direct you. Kiss our dear little folks. Love to Teedee and howdy to the servants. God care for my own love is ever the prayer of your own Edge.

1. Edgeworth Bird wrote from Chickamauga following the bloody battle near there 19 and 20 September. Confederate General Braxton Bragg routed Union troops under W. S. Rosecrans. Each army lost nearly a third of its men, making real the Cherokee meaning of the word Chickamauga, "river of death." Bird and his fellow Georgians were among the 11,000 men under James Longstreet that Lee had rushed from Virginia by rail to bolster Bragg.

2. Edwin G. Baxter, the next-to-the-youngest of Sallie Bird's brothers, was killed in an altercation in Texas.

3. Edwin married Julia Hardwick. Their children were Edwin and Leila. Hull, *Annals of Athens*, 443.

4. Andrew Baxter was Sallie Bird's oldest brother. He married Martha Williams. Their children were Thomas W., Alice, and Narcissa. *Annals of Athens*, 443.

5. John B. Whitehead is listed in the 1860 Georgia census, living in Jefferson County.

6. Jerome Bonaparte Robertson clashed with General James Longstreet later and was court-martialed. He spent the rest of the war in Texas and Arkansas. *Biographical Dictionary of the Confederacy*, 370.

7. Union General William Starke Rosecrans suffered a rout at Chickamauga which cost him 35,000 casualties and effectively ended his military career. He was replaced by Grant.

8. John Baxter, Sallie Bird's brother.

9. Robert N. Brooking married Martha Clayborn in 1820. Smith, *History of Hancock County*, 1:172.

Edgeworth Bird to Sallie Bird

Near Chickamauga Station, 21 October 1863

My own Precious Darling,

Yesterday morning I rode off early to the Brigade and returned late at night. The box of good things reached me an hour or so afterwards, but [I] only had an opportunity of opening it this morning. Dr. Tom Raines[1] was here at the time and assisted me in opening one of the bottles. He is here making an effort to be reinstated in his old position. You can imagine better than I can depict what a reception the box met with. Many thanks to Teedee for the snug manner in which she managed to store away so many nice things, and a thousand to you, dearest, for your kind forethought in providing all. We are grateful here for good things to eat and drink, and I only regret there were not a half-dozen times as many bottles. Jugs, two gallon jugs, are the only things to send soldiers drinkables in.

I learn John Boyer[2] has peach brandy to sell at twenty to twenty-five dollars per gallon. Had you not better provide some? In a few months it will be much higher. Richard was delighted with the wine. He has gone to the depot for corn, and I'm not sure he was not a little boosy. I gave one of the bottles to Whitney,[3] with Richard's consent. He's never touched anything else but wine. They both say they never drank better. There was only one bottle of catsup, and that marked to Sammie from his mother. He brought several with him in his own box and gave that to me. Do make up *gallons* of it, and pickles. Give ten or twenty dollars per gallon for vinegar, if [it] can't be had cheaper. Such things are actually necessaries. I'm very desirous to have a box come on now and then. It is next to impossible to convey an idea of how acceptable such arrivals are.

I shall let Whitney go home in a few days on a short visit. He will go up to Lexington depot and thence to Elbert. If possible to collect them, I'll send some bottles back by him. I shall direct him on his return to go by Athens for the purpose of bringing anything you may wish to send up, my clothing, etc. Be sure and send a box of good things. If necessary let him remain over a day. You can get a good bridle in Athens, if not in Sparta. Set him to work. There's no end to his ingenuity and industry. He'll knock up a box and hunt up a suitable bridle and fix up everything. I want you to notice him and give me your woman's instinct and intuition. I trust him fully, often with very large sums of money.

It is best for him to remain over a day. . . . Send me two or three towels. I need them very much; so does Richard. I have three shirts, but they are threadbare and full of large rents. They talk about taking up a subscription for me. Whitney can bring the overcoat. I will instruct him to go straight to Mrs. Baxter's and be there while he is in Athens. I know she'll receive him cordially.

Sam had better remain at home until he is fully able to "substitute" Robert. He must stay at the farm and do what he is able, when able work out with the others. Our force is small enough already. He'll never get well lying about [at] Mrs. Brookings.

Dear old Darlie, I have very little hope that your horse will escape the impressing officer. I think they are very highhanded in their measures, but bear it cheerfully, if it is done you. You *shall* have others. I will see John and get him to write your Mother, directing her to keep Bud's mare until further orders. About the wheat crop, I think this is the best. Sow all the best parts of the Red field in wheat as far as it will go. The red land is best for grain; and then sow balance in oats, not to be cut but be ready for the hogs as soon as the wheat is taken off. Sow the Road field in oats. I propose putting the entire 10 acre lot in ground peas and the seven acre lot in potatoes. If Uncle Fed[4] will take good care of his hogs and have a hundred to kill next winter, they will turn out something handsome. The loss of the two plough hands was severe upon us. The grass must have been terrible to have cut off the crop so much. We ought to have had two thousand bushels to sell. But we'll make no complaints. It has been my lot to see hundreds of places without a negro or horse left to work them, or rail to fence them. Are we not blest? Should we not be thankful?

I do not wish Dennis to return to my place again. Tell Father so. Read him this. I expect he'd better sell him, but I expect it will be required to have him sent off. Flawral is not a bad boy, and I can easily understand he had been misled. I am astonished at Isaac. I thought it was enough to be Sam and Allen's brother and Bill and Cornelia's child to keep him out, and then he had so much sense. I acknowledge my judgement completely at fault. Let matters take their course about March[5] and don't be troubled one second.

Certainly Father's eyes should be opened about woodland now. It will not do to leave negroes alone at night, and in all rainy weather and time of sickness, when he is compelled to be absent a week or two at a time. But do not you say a word to him about it. He will pursue his own course. Bless you, dear old precious heart. You were sadly mistreated about the syrup without so much as "by your leave, Madam," but doubtless Father proposes to purchase it, but if he don't, we'll not be troubled about a few gallons of "long sweetening." We'll plant enough to make twice as much. Take your Mother up as much as she needs, ration out the balance to the negroes as they need it. It ain't good nohow, certainly not worth troubling our dear old hearts about.

Darling, here I stopped for dinner, and while eating your dear, sweet letter by Tom Culver was handed me. Thank you for that and the delightful volume by Ben Alfriend. Old Fellow, you never waste your sweetness on me. Never fail to send me such when an opportunity offers. I've just sent General Benning some by a safe hand. I'll try and save one of the 3 bottles of real drinkables for Dubose and Waddell[6] to

Thomas Baxter, brother of Sallie Bird, was named for their father. Like Sallie herself and many other Southerners, he sought refuge from Reconstruction in Baltimore following the Civil War.

The University of Georgia (then Franklin College) had attracted many of the state's leading families to Athens by the 1840s, the era of this drawing. Sallie Baxter grew up there, living near the campus where her brothers and later her son attended college. Sallie wrote of Athens, "No place is more dear to me."

Sallie and Edgeworth Bird made a "wedding journey" after their marriage in 1848 in Athens, Georgia. Among other places they went to Baltimore, where this photograph was taken. They had important kin in the North, including Sallie's uncle, Leroy Wiley, then one of New York City's wealthiest men.

Sallie Bird sits at the right front of this family gathering at Cape May, New Jersey, in the 1870s. Also seated in front is her son Wilson Edgeworth. In the center is her sister, Mary Gresham; on each side, Sallie's daughter Saida and Saida's husband, Victor Smith; at the rear, Mary Gresham's son and daughter, Minnie and Tom.

Granite Farm, Hancock County, Georgia, from the front carriageway in 1887. The house had extensive wings and a widow's walk from which the family could survey the plantation. Sallie Bird's brother, Richard Baxter, lived there following the death of Edgeworth Bird.

Lucy Cobb Institute, founded in Athens before the Civil War, taught the classics and social graces to Georgia's most privileged young women, including Edgeworth and Sallie Bird's daughter, Saida.

After the war Saida Bird (left) and her cousin Minnie Gresham, financed by their uncle Leroy Wiley, went north to school.

Major W. Edgeworth Bird was described by a fellow Georgian as "a perfect gentleman by instinct, by education, and by habit." He was severely wounded at the battle of Second Manassas.

Sallie Bird moved her husband and her infant daughter from the Sparta, Georgia, cemetery to Oconee Hill Cemetery, Athens, to lie beside her parents, Thomas and Mary Baxter. The larger monument is to the Baxters.

take a hand to. I sat down to a superior dinner today, a fine goose killed several days ago, nice gravy, Irish potatoes, fresh nice Granite Farm butter, sweet potatoes, and pepper sauce.[7] That'll do a soldier very well.

Tom Culver brought a letter also to Sammie. Today is Wednesday. Cousin Sallie mentions you were expected at her house last night on your way to Athens, tonight at Jimmy Harris's. So I shall write this to Athens, tho' I rather inferred you might stay longer at home. . . . Dearest love to your Mother and to Teedee and friends. Get my overcoat, pants, etc., ready when Whitney comes by—and a box of goodies. Remember, direct to "Army of Tennessee." That is the best direction. Goodbye, Darling. God bless you and guide you. Your own loving,

Edge

1. T. A. Raines had resigned as surgeon in March. He later became chief surgeon of the First Division, Georgia Militia. *Georgia Roster,* 2:559.

2. John Boyer is listed as a planter, age fifty-seven, in the 1860 Hancock County census. He had a wife and thirteen children, of whom the oldest was a son, an overseer, age eighteen.

3. Whitney seems to have been an employed clerk rather than a soldier.

4. Uncle Fed was one of the slaves at Granite Farm.

5. Several months later (17 January 1864) Edgeworth Bird wrote his wife to sell March "if he is caught." The troubles with the Bird slaves occurred at the time eighteen Hancock County blacks were jailed for attempting to incite an insurrection. Milledgeville *Southern Recorder,* 6 Oct. 1863. Judge Thomas W. Thomas of Elberton was asked by Judge James Thomas of Sparta to preside at the trial the first Monday in November. The Elberton judge wrote: "I think it is fortunate for the country that if we were to have an attempted Negro insurrection it should first develop in Hancock County where it would be met and managed by a sensible, firm, and discreet people. I tremble for what the consequences might have been had it developed in some other parts. A fatal notion seems to prevail in some parts of the country that our safety and refuge in an emergency consists in breaking doors and trampling under foot our own laws and hanging, burning and torturing, without delay and without discrimination. All honor then I say to your people and county and it is my earnest wish that that lofty spirit and wise prudence and forbearance that have marked her people in a peculiar manner at least since my acquaintance with them 26 years ago shall continue to mark and characterize her generations forever and ever." James Thomas Papers, Emory University. The Milledgeville *Southern Recorder* of 15 Dec. 1863 reported that four of the eighteen jailed slaves were convicted. One of the four was recommended for commutation of his sentence by the governor.

6. Colonel Dudley M. Dubose and Colonel James D. Waddell.

7. Edgeworth Bird and his Georgia companions were enjoying being near their home state's rich agricultural supplies, untouched by war. When they retreated to Virginia from Gettysburg in July, the soldiers were almost barefooted, rations were "menacingly" short, railroads could scarcely haul what food and forage was found, and the horses received so little grain that they recovered slowly. Freeman, *Lee*, 348.

Edgeworth Bird to Sallie Bird

Winter Quarters, Morristown, Tennessee, 17 January 1864[1]

My own Darling,

At last, after a dark night of time, a tiresome, cheerless blank of sixty-four days, I am brightened and revived by the arrival of a package of letters from you. "Old Mac" returned from Bristol yesterday morning, bringing a large mail. There were nine letters for my share, one from Bud, two from Sallie, and six from you, one from Father enclosed and one from Mr. Rhodes. . . .

Ah, dearest, you don't know the half of what a long weary waiting I've had of it. Hope deferred makes the heart sick. For a while I stood it bravely, continued to send you letters till we left Knoxville. Then got off a pencilled note or so, as sudden chance presented. When we got up toward Kingsport, I had opportunities of sending a letter or so to Bristol, and indeed have continued to do so ever since, whenever there was an opportunity. Tho' you have had, I know, long intervals, I trust some of my letters have reached you along, sufficient to keep down a full grown anxiety. For a while we were so entirely cut off from communication with the South, that I well know all of your friends were solicitous for our safety, and your dear heart surely troubled about me.

I was very sorry for you, Precious, and half forgot my own loneliness in the absence of your letters, in solicitude about the anxiety you were undergoing, but could lend no strong hand. . . . It takes at least ten days for a letter to go through. It is strange. I've received none of your present letters, the latest is Dec. 9th, written more than five weeks ago, in fact last year. You should direct to Bristol with the Brigade, Division, and Corps.

It is a relief that I knew nothing of Sallie's sickness and only hear of it to know she is well, tho' you are always right to write promptly of such matters. I am thankful her attack was no more serious. Kiss this young dame for me and tell her to try to avoid such pranks. . . . Thank her and Bud for their letters. I hope that Bud begins to find that letter writing is not as Herculean a labor, but he must continue to practice. . . .

Your purchase of the hides was very judicious. Now Mr. Rhodes should fix up a vat and let Wesley tan them. If sent to a tan yard, you only get the half, or pay an exorbitant price. I should think he could get bark where they cleaned in front of the house. We will also be able to kill two or three beeves. It isn't worthwhile to try to get too large a stock of cattle. The government agent will be along to take them, if he has not already visited you. We had better use what we need. He will only leave you the milch cows and work oxen. At least that is obliged to come after a while.

When they come, you must have Mr. Edwards[2] to assist you. We've all got to contribute to feed and pay these soldiers here. So kill any we can spare that are not too young. They'll make beef another year, maybe. Let us try and make everything we need that we can. I would not care to sell the blooded cattle. Let the young bulls be altered, and when large enough, we'll kill them for their hide's sake. I would only part with a fine calf to oblige a friend. I would rather have a well grown Durham calf of one year old than two hundred dollars of Confederate money. In another year he'll be a splendid beef with a magnificent hide.

Dearest, I hear Forbes is at Carter's Station. He sent me word he had a box for me that would weigh 700 pounds and whenever it was moved it would cry Goody! Goody! Goody! I'm so thankful. We are living on a slim diet. Our only vegetable is lye hominy, and I'm sick unto surfeit with beef so lean that it does not cast a shadow. We get, now and then, a side of meat in the country. That's my diet now, a streak of lean and a streak of fat. We had a beauty yesterday, and last night some poor devil of a famished soldier came in and stole it and left us without a drop of grease to make up bread with. So you can judge how acceptable your contribution will be.

It is my custom to have a feast about eleven every night. I toast two or three biscuit before the fire and a flitch or so of bacon on the end of a stick and then have a very royal snack. When your box comes, Dearest, I'm to do better. I know of a dozen mouths now that are distilling humid drops at the expectancy of a few drinks in that box. The wagon leaves today that will probably bring it, but it is sixty-eight miles distant. I hope the overcoat and some clothing [are there] and the fine bridle that I thank you so much for, tho' I shan't care if it is kept at home for a while. I have a fair one and I learn there is an order that will reduce us all to one horse, forage is so scarce. I think it a very necessary and most judicious move. Then I know there is some good eating and drinking, dear old fellow, when it comes. I'll write you all about it, and how we enjoyed it here.

But when am I coming home? Dearest, most precious darling, I am utterly unable to say. I have not applied, because I am convinced they would refuse me. One quartermaster applied, and Longstreet endorsed upon it, "If ever there was a time when quartermasters were needed, it is now," and so refused it. I wait till the times look more propitious. Darling, I'm so longing, longing to see you and home. My thought is intent on getting there, and when I do, I'll have my stay out, if they break me for it. The application to go to Georgia has been refused, and the disappointment was dreadful to us all, tho' we were not sanguine. We are sorely tried to procure forage for man and beast. Richard and Peter are out now. They have to be careful to avoid the Yankee cavalry. They annoy us all the time and, now and then, capture some majors. But Longstreet is after them now. . . .

Yesterday there was heavy cannonading and heavy skirmishing in plain hearing. Our brigade was not engaged. They are driving the enemy before them and [have] not yet got up a heavy battle. The day is half passed, and I hear no sound of anything yet. I saw an ambulance driver just now, who brought some wounded. He says there was heavy skirmishing until dusk yesterday, and our troops are moving in pursuit this morning. . . .

Richard sends love. He got a bundle of letters from Kate. Sammie and all of us are distressed at Mrs. Beman's death and mourn with Mr. Beman.[3] He is indeed the gnarled oak stripped of its branches and hastening to decay. Bob was in high glee over his letter from Nancy.[4] Tell her to send him more. Kindest remembrance to Mr. Edwards. Tell him I fear I am to chase no more foxes with him this winter. It'll be too late before I get home. Love to Father. Tell him for me that I do not wish Dennis to stay at my place, or be sent there to work. I fear it will make him angry, but I know no other course.

I don't expect any of us will have much left when this war ends. Meanwhile, I wish no such annoyances about me as that chap. Sell March or get someone to do it when he is caught. Let us cheerfully abide by the decision of the committee, if they request him to be sent off, tho' I don't think it right to put bad characters on other communities.

Tell Mr. Rhodes[5] to plant the next year's crop thus: the fork field, and low grounds, and spring branch field in corn—that will be 130 acres. Make up what more he can tend in corn from the fresh lands in the lower field. Put the sorghum cane there also. Put the sixteen acre lot in ground peas; the seven acre lot in potatoes. The red field is in wheat. The meadow field must lie out. The sheep can winnow that. Let him save all the manure he can to put on the corn. We'll plant no cotton atall.

Our boys are all well. Give a great deal of love to your dear, good Mother. She and you must manage to have a fine, cozy time. . . . Bob sends love to Nancy and all the rest. Tell John we are in a new year and he must brace himself to make a good crop. Always give howdys to Arthur. Tell him I don't forget him. Tell Uncle Fed he must send me word what his hogs averaged and with so much small grain and peas and ground peas next year he must try and put [several lines illegible].

Your own Edge

1. Edgeworth Bird was with Longstreet, who had attacked Burnside's forces at Knoxville but was repulsed. Longstreet had only 15,000 men opposing a larger force in mountainous country. Meanwhile, Braxton Bragg lost the battle of

Lookout Mountain–Missionary Ridge 23–25 Nov. 1863. The opportunities presented by the Confederate victory at Chickamauga had been lost. Bird wintered in rough and often unfriendly country in Tennessee.

2. James B. Edwards.

3. Avis DeWitt of Connecticut married Carlisle P. Beman 30 Jan. 1823; he became a notable educator. The Bemans lost two children shortly after closing their Villa school in 1857: Dr. Edward Beman, graduate of Philadelphia Medical College, and a daughter, Katherine DeWitt Beman. Another son, Thomas S. Beman, fell at Second Manassas, leaving a widow and three children. Three months later his widow died. With the added death of his own wife, Carlisle Beman was indeed "a gnarled oak stripped of its branches." Smith, *History of Hancock County,* 2:71.

4. Bob, a slave at Granite Farm, replaced the long ailing Sam as Edgeworth Bird's body servant. His wife Nancy, despite Georgia's law against teaching slaves to read and write, was able to write to him. Methodist Bishop George F. Pierce kept slaves at his Hancock County plantation. Nonetheless, in urging repeal of the law he told the General Assembly of Georgia in 1863, "Our Heavenly Father certainly never intended any human mind to be kept in darkness and ignorance." Smith, *The Life and Times of George F. Pierce*, 474–75.

5. George F. Rhodes, overseer.

Sallie Bird to Sallie (Saida) Bird in Athens

Granite Farm, 16 February 1864

My dear Child,

. . . Oh, daughter, how happy I am to be in your precious Father's arms once more. . . . He is so good, so sweet, so beloved, and making me so *full* of *repose!* Oh, how I have sighed for *that!* My darling precious Edge! He is *so* happy himself. Tell dear Mother I *am* her happy child now. I thought of dear Richard[1] instantly and constantly since, but Edge speaks so hopefully, cheerfully of him, I am more than ever cheered.

This letter is to say that if your Grandma can't come with you, I will send Bud and a servant up for you. Edge says he longs to see his dear, good Mother, but if she cannot come, you must, of course. . . . Oh, daughter, it is so inexpressibly sweet to see his dear face again, to hear his footstep on the floor, to hear his voice, to *smell* his cigar or meerschaum even!

He and German Culver[2] came all the way from East Tennessee on horseback. That is the way the letter came from Washington, Wilkes County. He got here about four o'clock Saturday P.M. Bob is well and lively. Edge brought three fine mares with him. He sold Richard's horse for $1,000 and has his saddle here. . . . He will hold the money for Richard or pay it over to Mother. He'll want it to get another horse. Your Grandma ought to hear Papa give the experience of some of our returned prisoners. They went to New York, spent a month, and were as happy as you please. Had plenty of money, then came thro' home. They escaped.

Edge says as soon as he knows where Dick is he'll write to his old friend, Ned Donnelly, by flag of truce. I have no time for more. Let me hear from you all. I will send Wilson and a servant up as soon as I hear from you. In the meanwhile, *study* hard; you'll have less to make up. Bring the jeans for Papa's coat. Mother knows about it. Also the scraps, if they are there, of the two pair of pants . . . I made him. He has spread so that his pants are too small, and I've got to gore them.

Two of the mares that your Father brought were his Army horses. The other is one he purchased on the road, remarkably fine, which he christened with peach brandy "Sallie Baxter," for me. He had so announced it. The other two are to name. I must close hurriedly. Love to Thomas.[3] Can't he come down? Your Father would be so glad to see him. All of us would. I've just written to Sister. I hope dear Grandma will come with you, if she is able to travel again so soon. I don't want her to fatigue herself, but it would cheer her to see Edge. Edge says, "Dick is as true as steel and no finer boy treads the soil." Tell Kate what Papa says, also that he declares he'll be back all right before long. God grant it. Bring all my letters from Edge and the one from Ellen. Write soon what Mother says.

Your devoted Mother, S.C.B.

Lucie and Edgar[4] drove down in an hour after they heard Edge had come, just to express their joy and sympathy. The next day Lucie sent me this sweet note, so purely sweet, so incomparably sweet, that I must send it to you that you may enjoy it. . . . My lettuce looks finely. Tell Mother to hunt up something for the fine vinegar I made for her and send it when you come. I know she'll be pleased with our good luck when she gets her vinegar. A great many gentlemen have been here to see Papa.

1. Richard Baxter, Sallie Bird's brother, was captured by Union troops while on a foraging expedition near Knoxville, Tenn., in January 1864. He was not released from prison at Rock Island, Ill., until 21 June 1865, more than two months after Lee's surrender at Appomattox. Smith, *History of Hancock County,* 2:70.

2. German Pierce Culver, one of six sons of Hardy Culver fighting on the Confederate side, was detailed to the quartermaster department at the time of this letter. *Georgia Roster,* 2:474.

3. Sallie Bird's second brother was named Thomas W. Baxter after his father. The first son of Andrew Baxter, her oldest brother, also bore the name. In later years Richard Baxter named his youngest son Thomas also. Hull, *Annals of Athens,* 443.

4. Lucy Terrell Dawson and her husband, Edgar Dawson.

Edgeworth Bird to Sallie (Saida) Bird in Athens

Granite Farm, 19 April 1864

My dear Daughter,

. . . Are not you and Grandma both surprised to find me not yet gone? Circumstances have so transpired that I still breathe the flower scented air of Granite Farm, to the great joy of Mama and no small gratification to myself. Recent movement's of Longstreet's Corps[1] have quite changed our plans. Only the night before I was to set out to join the party at Washington, Col. DuBose's boy reached here, telling me of the late army news and the change in programme. Robert left early Monday morning with him. He is to take my horse on with Col. D's horses under charge of one of the 15th.

Our party now all go on by the cars. I leave for Mayfield[2] tomorrow, and Mama was so elated at my staying two days longer that she promised to behave beautifully tomorrow. It is her greatest trial to be left alone. It is scarcely less a burden to me, but we all have our duties and must perform them faithfully.

You, too, must bear this in mind and try to do well in every obligation of life. Be truthful under all circumstances, and to be this means to be true and good in a thousand ways. Study, study, study; an enlightened, well polished mind, well regulated and stored with useful knowledge, is the greatest blessing you could prepare for yourself, after a true piety. Unite the two and you have the Philosopher's Stone. I must slip in a little lecture. Can't you persuade that kind Miss Lipscomb[3] to get underway a Latin class? I do so much desire you to understand Latin thoroughly and consider it indispensable to a polite education.

Give oceans of love to dear Grandma and make her understand how much I regret not seeing her. I have a bright hope it will not be long before Dick is back to rejoice her heart and dear Miss Kate's.[4] Give her, too, my kindest love. Mama is now packing my trunk and stowing away a small box of good things, a pleasing but sad task to her. The last day at home will always be gloomy in spite of one's resolves.

Bud has been making prodigious efforts to capture a wild turkey, but his early risings and patient sittings have hitherto been in vain. Mrs. Wiley[5] is decidedly better, and there are hopes of her recovery. Give love for me to all our family kindred. Kind regards to Dr. Linton. Kiss Grandma and Cousin Caro for me. Write me quite often and take pains to compose well. Be kind and loving to Mama and *cheerfully* obedient and you will always have the warmest love of your affectionate Father.

William E. Bird

1. Edgeworth Bird had been on lengthy home leave. Longstreet on 7 April 1864 was ordered to move from Bristol, Va.-Tenn., to Charlottesville, Va.

2. Mayfield was in 1864 the western end of the rail line planned from Augusta to Macon, which was finally completed in 1867. Only a few miles from Granite Farm, Mayfield provided rail transportation east to Augusta. The line had been under discussion for many years. One proposed route would have cut off a corner of Hardy Culver's house. "Don't vary it an inch," the public-spirited Hancock citizen said. "I can move my house if necessary." Milledgeville *Southern Recorder,* 25 Oct. 1853.

3. Sarah A. Lipscomb taught at the Lucy Cobb Institute at the time. Coleman, *Confederate Athens,* 128.

4. Kate Rucker of Athens, who married Richard Baxter shortly after his release from the Union prison at Rock Island, Ill., in 1865.

5. Mrs. Edwin Wiley (Eliza DeWitt) died the next year.

Edgeworth Bird to Sallie Bird

Battlefield [The Wilderness, Va.], 6 May 1864

My own Darling,

I've barely time to send you a hasty line telling of the day's battle and some casualties. There was some fighting yesterday. At daylight this morning the fight opened in earnest. The enemy were driving one of our divisions back, just as Longstreet went and moved them back. Since then, we have been successful all along the line, as far as I can learn. It has not been decisive today, and the heavier battle is looked for tomorrow. God be with us, and I believe he is. We have done well tho' we are greatly outnumbered.[1]

Hoke's[2] Division is looked for tonight. McLaws[3] Division has hardly been in yet. Our loss in high officers is pretty heavy. Benning's Brigade suffered a good deal. General Benning[4] himself is quite severely, tho' not very dangerously, wounded. He asked me to get his exact case from the doctor and telegraph his wife. I sent this by their direction, "Severely but not dangerously wounded. He is shot through the left shoulder, bones of course fractured. He is sent to Orange Court House."

Col. Hodges,[5] 17th Regiment, severely wounded. In the 15th Tom Culver[6] is killed. In Company E, Joe Wright[7] hurt badly in arm. Dud Alfriend,[8] contusion on hip. Joe Hines[9] killed. Bill Seals[10] wounded in hand. George Waller[11] [wounded] in [one] hand and slightly in other hand. Matt Parker,[12] leg amputated below knee; and some few slightly wounded.

In 2nd Georgia, Lt. Fogle[13] killed. In 20th Lt. Bostic[14] and Richards[15] killed. Lt. Cleghorn,[16] leg amputated and wounded in arm. Henry Middlebrooks,[17] painful bruise on foot. General Longstreet[18] is severely wounded. General Jenkins[19] killed. General Lee was among the thick flying balls on the front lines, waving his hat and encouraging the men. Tody Alfriend[20] is all right and, the boys say, acted gallantly. All others safe. German, Sam, and myself found poor Tom Culver's body. Brought it out on a mule, dug the grave and buried it.

Your friends are all well. Dearest darling, I've had an anxious day. God bless our friends and watch over them tomorrow and give us a great and crowning victory. Grant is commander against us. Losses in Benning's Brigade—208 wounded, 10 killed. Col. DuBose[21] is in command. General Field[22] was very slightly wounded; is in command of the corps.

Dearest, be brave hearted and hopeful. Tell Mrs. Newman we camped one day only four miles of her father. I was so busy I couldn't get off to see them. Our camp was in 200 yards of the Miss Cowherds, two old maiden ladies related to his mother.[23] Sent messages by them and talked of home. I sent German to telegraph Mrs. Benning. Will write tomorrow if I can. Merely a line if I can send it off.

My heart overflows with love for you. May our Father in Heaven watch over you and make you strongheartedand well. Dud's hurt is only a bad bruise. He wishes himself home.

I wrote Father two days ago. The Yankee loss must be tremendous. Our boys gave them "hankins" today. Dear, dearest Darling, goodbye. Love to Father and all friends.

Your own Edge

1. The Battle of the Wilderness began when the Army of the Potomac moved across the Rapidan on 4 May 1864. In two days of fighting in the thick woods near Fredericksburg, Grant lost 18,000 men, of whom 2,000 were killed. The Confederates lost more than 10,000. Nonetheless, Grant continued south for a month's bitter fighting.

2. Confederate Major General Robert Frederick Hoke.

3. Confederate Major General LaFayette McLaws, who ran afoul of General Longstreet in the Knoxville campaign. In 1863 his family had refugeed to Sparta, where they boarded at the Edwards House. Letter of Richard Malcolm Johnston to Judge James Thomas, 18 May 1863, Thomas Papers, Emory University.

4. Confederate Brigadier General Henry Lewis Benning.

5. Colonel Wesley C. Hodges was wounded 6 May and was on wounded furlough at the end of the war. *Georgia Roster,* 1:411.

6. Thomas H. Culver, lieutenant in Company K, son of Hardy Culver. A monument was erected to him in the Culverton cemetery. Smith, *History of Hancock County,* 1:x and 2:20.

7. Private Joseph Wright died of his wounds 9 May. *Georgia Roster,* 2:448.

8. Dudley Alfriend survived to surrender at Appomattox. *Georgia Roster,* 2:443.

9. Joseph S. Hines, private in Company K, had been previously wounded at Second Manassas. He died 6 May 1864. *Georgia Roster,* 2:445.

10. William D. Seals survived. *Georgia Roster,* 2:479; Ivy Duggan Papers, Emory University.

11. George L. Waller, third sergeant, died of wounds at a Richmond hospital 30 Sept. 1864. *Georgia Roster,* 2:474.

12. Private M. E. Parker, Company K, died 26 May. *Georgia Roster,* 2:478.

13. T. T. Fogle died 6 May 1864. *Georgia Roster,* 1:414.

14. Lieutenant Patrick N. Bostick died 6 May. *Georgia Roster,* 2:784.

15. Lieutenant John B. Richards was not killed. Captured at Fort Harrison, Va., 29 Sept. 1864, he was released 17 June 1865. *Georgia Roster,* 2:804.

16. Lieutenant Samuel B. Cleghorn, Jr., was in a Columbus, Ga., hospital many months later. *Georgia Roster,* 2:810.

17. Sergeant Henry L. Middlebrooks fought on to surrender at Appomattox. He farmed near Culverton, Ga., after the war. *Georgia Roster,* 2:446; Duggan Papers, Emory University.

18. General James Longstreet saw no more action for several months, following his wounds at the Wilderness. He fought again in the fall and surrendered with Lee at Appomattox.

19. Brigadier General Micah Jenkins had been severely wounded at Second Manassas, but recovered to fight in all the major battles from Gettysburg to Chickamauga. On the second day of the Battle of the Wilderness he was mortally wounded by one of his own men in an accident similar to the one that killed Stonewall Jackson a year earlier at almost the same spot. He was not yet thirty. *Biographical Dictionary of the Confederacy,* 253–54.

20. It is not clear which of the Alfriends from Hancock County the nickname Tody applies to.

21. Colonel Dudley M. DuBose of Washington, Ga.

22. Charles William Field led Hood's Texas Division and saved Lee's right wing at the Wilderness. He fought on until Appomattox. *Biographical Dictionary of the Confederacy,* 185–86.

23. The 1850 census listed Mary and Tabitha Cowherd in Orange County, Va.

Sallie Bird to Sallie (Saida) Bird

Granite Farm, 8 May 1864

My dear Sallie,

I sent a short line to your Grandma a day or two since asking her to let Gus go to the factory and get any tallow from Mr. Bloomfield,[1] as it is too late to have it sent down before I go up to Athens. I mean, it is too late to mould this spring. I want Mother to take care of it for me, at the present. We are all jogging along as usual, only Master Florral cut up his usual trick day before yesterday, and left for [as] a slight threat. Wilson was present and saw and heard all. I am only too glad and humbly trust I am not to be annoyed with any of them any more. Peter (Archie's son) did the same some weeks ago, only he ran away from John, who gave him a trouncing.

Sallie Wiley and her family staid a week with us; left Friday evening. I am going to Cousin Lizzie Harris this week to stay several days. Shall go probably on Wednesday. Mrs. Beman invited me to dine there on Tuesday to meet a friend of hers. Lucy urges me to go, but I feel very little like it. Lucy thinks the change will do me good. But I do not rally from the sad parting with your dear Father. My heart feels sore and aching. Then, I have been particularly troubled about dear Tom and Richard. Oh, that Richard was free once more! I will write him again soon. The truce boat with Yankee prisoners was turned back the other day, so I suppose there'll be no exchanges for a few weeks.

Thank God for our victories out West and one in N.C.—in Va.—in Fla.—everywhere so far—and may the God of Battles be our aid in the great contests about to come on. I feel, indeed, that all of us ought to be on our knees. The very warm weather for two days past makes me think of getting to Athens where all my clothes are, for summer wear, and I do long to be with dear Mother. I will try to get all things arranged, so that we can get off before very long, but I have much to do. Things are getting pretty straight in the building line. The logs for the hen house are hauled up. I shall make Frank get up the pieces for the shed to the kitchen and I do that first, I think. Negro clothes are to be cut out, and many things done, but the necessity of cool clothes for myself becomes urgent. All the little laurels Mother planted are growing beautifully.

The air is full of the fragrance of flowers. The basket of white pinks is superb, and the roses are getting to be grand. The pit plants look well. My vegetable garden is in beautiful order, but late. The apple trees have a good deal of fruit on them. I want to know exactly when your vacation comes on. Then I want all of us, dear Mother, you, and Wilson, to come down here and enjoy melons, and we can dry apples, etc., etc. When your vacation is over, we'll all go up again. Mother can go to Macon easily from here. I'll send Wilson with her, and they can easily go in a day—by going either to Milledgeville or Sandersville—that is, provided she does not go after I come up to Athens.

Give my love to all Cousin Ben's family and thanks and love to Caro for her kindness to you. Give my love to Emma Huger, Walton and Lucia Johnston.[2] Mark J spent the day here Thursday—and oceans of love to you. Who do you think spent the day here yesterday? Old Mr. Rogers![3] He is a good old man. Dr. Connell[4] has been worse again. There is not a particle of news stirring that I can hear.

Our boiler came from Atlanta yesterday, 75 gallons. I've only one more load of tithe tax to send off.[5] Sent two loads yesterday. Tell Caro I wish she could see my flowers now. Mrs. Terrell has been quite sick and is still unwell, so my darling Lucy couldn't come down, but she writes to me nearly every day. Goodbye, daughter. *Study hard.* I implore you, improve your time and don't lag behind your classes in *anything*. Never be content with mediocrity. . . . Love to all my friends. You know how many I love in dear Athens. Don't neglect your Bible, or prayers. *Never* forget God. Love and kisses to darling Mother. Your devoted Mother, S.C.B.

1. R. L. Bloomfield, Athens businessman, operated the Athens Manufacturing Company in which Mrs. Mary Baxter was a stockholder. In 1867 Bloomfield bought the old Confederate armory in Athens, converting it into a weaving mill. In the paternalistic style of the time, he built cottages for the employees. He also built St. Mary's Church, honoring Mrs. Baxter, who had recently died. Hull, *Annals of Athens*, 332.

2. The daughters of Richard Malcolm Johnston, who were in school in Athens.

3. Henry Rogers, sixty, is listed as a planter in the 1860 Hancock County census.

4. Dr. Alva Connel(l), husband of Jane Baxter.

5. After reserving certain amounts of food for his own use, each farmer was required to pay the Confederate government one-tenth of his wheat, corn, oats, rye, buckwheat, or rice, sweet and Irish potatoes, cured hay and fodder, sugar, molasses, cotton, wool, tobacco, beans, peas, and bacon. Randall and Donald, *The Civil War and Reconstruction*, 257–58.

Edgeworth Bird to Sallie Bird

Near Richmond, 1 June 1864

My own loved Darling,

I didn't write yesterday . . . . because of a short move, but this evening I prepare a half sheet for you. Nothing of great interest has transpired. Ewell's Corps had some work yesterday on the right, driving the Yankees to their breastworks for the purpose of ascertaining their position. Today there has been heavy cannonading and musketry, but I haven't been able to ascertain the exact whereabouts, tho' I've been on the stir a good deal . . . I am able to say none of our Hancock people are hurt.

Doc Pierce[1] left me a few minutes since and reports all in good condition. He had come back to our camps for man and horse grub. . . . Your long, sweet letter came by Warren Clarke[2] and was deliciously delightful. . . . We had been anticipating a heavy battle today, but it didn't come off. Butler[3] has absconded from Bermuda Hundreds and, it is presumed, has joined Grant. Beauregard's[4] forces have joined Lee. The 6th Georgia passed by our camps. Mac Arnold[5] and Gene Burnet stopped a short time. I missed seeing them, but some later saw Toby Stewart[6] and Billy Martin,[7] also Capt. John Grey,[8] the A. Qr.M. of the Regiment, all of them in good health.

Lee's army is now greatly strengthened, and it is probable he will resume the offensive. He must be nearly equal to the enemy in point of numbers, and Grant has before him an impossible task. He cannot take Richmond, and I hope and believe is destined to a more hopeless defeat than fell to the lot of McClelland.[9] We all here imbibe the confidence of the Georgians and believe everything there safe in Joe Johnston's hands. I look upon Sherman[10] as gone up. He is too far from home and runs counter to sixty-five thousand muskets (Waddell told me General Bragg[11] said that was Johnston's force) and a hundred percentum more of brains than he can bring to bear. Waddell came out an hour or so one evening. I've sent in a horse for him this evening and look for him to stay all night. His voice is still very weak. He tells me the Yankees got some of his negroes that were hired out. Mrs. W is in Athens. You'll see her there. Tell Bud I've come into possession of the little red fox spoken of before. He is a wonderfully smart, sharp little fellow and very amusing.

Dear old beautiful, blessed darling, I haven't had a cent of money since I came to camp. In a day or so I had loaned out all and the Govt has not turned over a cent of public money since. There is more than six months due the troops now; there are four months due me. Everybody is out. If you had the surplus you had some time ago, I'd say send me some by first chance, but I know your purse is empty. Be sure to send me stamps frequently. . . .

What say you to my proposition to call Lizzie's colt "Wilderness?" Oh! How I long for peace and home. But, dearest darlie, there are fearful battles yet to be fought. Tomorrow, or any day, I look for it. Severe skirmishing goes on every day. Sammie, Pete, Forbes, and Clarence and German Culver—all our Sparta people—are well. Many kisses to Bud. Love to Father, to Mr. Edwards, and the Dawsons. God forever bless you, my own, for you are the light of my life. Be, oh so careful of yourself. Howdye to all the servants. Bob is very well and very faithful. He looks finely.

While I am near Richmond, I'll write very often but necessarily shorter. Dearest love to Daughter and to Grandma. Ever and always, your own

Edge

1. Lovick Pierce, son of Bishop Pierce.

2. Sergeant W. H. Clark of Company E. *Georgia Roster,* 2:444.

3. Benjamin F. Butler, hated in the South because of his conduct in occupied New Orleans, was pushed back to Bermuda Hundred Neck 16 May by Beauregard.

4. P. G. T. Beauregard had defeated Butler at Petersburg in April.

5. William McIntosh Arnold of Hancock County's Sydney Brown Infantry was killed two months later at Petersburg. He had earlier suffered wounds at Malvern Hill, Sharpsburg, and Chancellorsville. *Georgia Roster,* 6:751.

6. There were three Stewarts from Hancock County in Company A, Sixth Georgia. It is not clear which one was called Toby. Benjamin Stewart enlisted in April 1861, was captured in December 1864, and took the oath of allegiance to the U.S. government. *Georgia Roster,* 1:759.

7. William A. Martin had been captured and exchanged two years earlier. He was paroled at Augusta, Ga., in May 1865. *Georgia Roster,* 1:756.

8. John H. Gray, captain and assistant quartermaster. *Georgia Roster,* 1:754.

9. General George B. McClellan was removed from command of the Army of the Potomac 5 Nov. 1862 when he allowed Lee to retreat in safety across the Potomac after the Battle of Sharpsburg (Antietam). Never again offered a command, he ran unsuccessfully for president on the Democratic ticket in 1864.

10. William Tecumseh Sherman (1820–1891) became commander of the military division of the Mississippi in March 1864 when Grant became general-in-chief. Sherman began his invasion of Georgia before Edgeworth Bird wrote this letter. By September he had taken Atlanta from the Confederates, and three months later gave Savannah to Lincoln as a Christmas present. Jefferson Davis replaced Johnston with Hood in the Atlanta campaign, a very controversial decision.

11. Braxton Bragg was assigned to duty in Richmond in February 1864, following his failure to follow up his victory at Chickamauga. A friend of Jefferson Davis, he accompanied Davis on his flight south into Georgia.

Sallie Bird to Elizabeth Harris

Athens, 16 July 1864[1]

Dear Cousin Lizzie,

I reached my dear old home after a safe and comfortable day's ride one week ago. The deluge of rain that fell before I left made me apprehensive of the creeks, so I made a boy go with us on horseback to try them before we drove in. They were very high, but not swimming, tho' Stewart, the stage driver, said they were swimming that day, about two hours before we crossed. I found Cousin Ben Yancey's comfortable carriage awaiting me at the depot and Caro in it. Mother and Sallie were both well and rejoiced to see me, but severely regretted Aunt Eliza's disappointment. Mother hopes yet to have a visit from her this summer, and I do hope she will be able to get here.

Mother sends you and Mary[2] a thousand thanks for the nice butter, no present could be more acceptable. She sent Mrs. Richardson[3] more than half of yours. As Mary and I together only made about half as much as yours, I would not let Mother send it all. Mrs. R. was very grateful and says you are too kind. She sends a world of love to you and to every member of your family. Mother says Cousin Jimmy must not pay her in money the balance due. She is only thankful to have such a glorious farmer to fall back on to ward off starvation from her household. Give our love to him.

I've received three dear, long letters from my precious Edge, since I came up. He writes in the finest spirits about our cause in Virginia and has unbounded faith in our success. He feels the same confidence in General Johnston, in whose brains he has immense faith. General J has 65,000 muskets, so General Bragg told Colonel Waddell who told Edge. That, in addition to cavalry and artillery, makes his force a great one.

My friends, the Hugers, refugees from New Orleans, had a sad affliction yesterday. One month ago, Lt. Willie Huger,[4] a gallant fellow who lost his leg at Murfreesboro, married a daughter of General Polk[5] to whom he had long been engaged. Yesterday, news came of her noble father's death! Poor young bride! What a sad end to her honeymoon! God pity her! I believe I can feel for the sorrows of others. All the Hugers were here yesterday to see me and were so bright and happy.

The crowds of charming refugees who fill the college buildings are all to be turned out, and the buildings to be used as hospitals. It is right, but I am very sorry for these nice people, who had just managed to make themselves comfortable. They were like the dove that Noah sent forth.

Wilson has been dreadfully afflicted with large boils soon since we came up, day before yesterday. The doctor lanced a very bad one, and today he seems much better. I had a dear, precious letter from my darling captive boy, Richard, a day or two since. He had, at last, received a letter from me and he says that the first tears he had shed, in a long while, fell from his eyes as he perused it. He said it made him happier than he had been since his capture and that he could almost whistle in good earnest. He sends his love to Sammie and Pete.

Dear Miss Lizzie continues her kindness. God forever bless her. She wrote to Dr. Dickson of Philadelphia, and he copied the sentence in his last letter by Flag of Truce to his daughter in Carolina. "Sallie Bird's youngest brother, Richard, is a prisoner at Rock Island, Illinois. He is well and cheerful, and I will supply all his wants." Oh, Cousin Lizzie, you can scarcely imagine our deep, deep gratitude. Edge said he had received my letters written from Long Cottage [Elizabeth Harris's home] and felt so glad to hear directly from you and Cousin Jimmy. He says he "knows Jimmy is going to beat the world at a crop this year." I gave him glowing accounts of my pleasant visit to your dear home.

Have you heard of the red fox that ran up to a man in the 15th during the fierce battle of the Wilderness? He [the fox] was in the front lines during the subsequent battery and escaped unhurt. He is quite a hero and a great pet among the men. Edge has succeeded in getting him and intends him for Wilson. They have called him "Gavroche" for a famous little fellow in Victor Hugo's novels. Edge says he is very smart and is a great pet with all the Brigade. Tell Sallie I sent Sammy's knife down to her by Henry; directed him to give it to Mr. Edwards for her.

The Richardsons are all well and send more affectionate messages to all your families than I have space to write. I've written four long letters today and, as I am going out to dine, I must now wind up and lie down awhile. I am getting along finely in regard to health. I'm always better when with my dear, sweet Mother. Do give my love and kisses to Aunt Eliza—to Mary and Sallie. My regards to Mr. DeWitt and kisses to all the bairns. I've seen nearly all my friends here and received my usual cordial welcome. I hope you will all keep well and that when we come down for the summer vacation, you'll all come to see us. All send love to you. Goodbye for the present. Tell Cousin Jimmy to save a piece of his heart from the claims of his dearest friend for Edge and me!

And with cordial affection for you both, I am your own true

Sallie

I sent you and Mary packets to the post office before I left.

1. Sallie Bird's letter to Mrs. James Harris at Long Cottage, Hancock County, is from the collection of Mrs. Ann Harris Marbury of Sparta, Ga.

2. Mary Carnes Wiley, wife of William Wiley.

3. The 1860 census lists Mrs. Elizabeth B. Richardson, forty-five, in Athens with her daughters Cornelia, fourteen, and Ann, ten.

4. Mary Ann Cobb wrote her husband Howell Cobb 14 Oct. 1863 that Mrs. Huger, "who has a husband and five sons in our army," was living in New College

with a family of daughters. Mrs. Cobb said, "Two of the sons have one leg each left." Coleman, *Athens, 1861–1865*, 70.

5. Leonidas Polk, the famous fighting bishop, was killed near Atlanta 14 June 1864. A West Point graduate, he was Episcopal bishop of Louisiana and resigned to lead Confederate troops.

Edgeworth Bird to Sallie Bird

Petersburg, Va. 17 July 1864

My own loved Darling,

At last a letter from you of July 10th, the day after you reached home. . . . I know your mood the instant I open your letters. You learn many things that you suffer to annoy you on your return home. Such always happens, more or less, during the absence of owners. I have no idea, of course, what troubles you, but I recognize it in your handwriting and style. My Darling, don't let it be so.

Never mind, if the yield of wheat is small. It can't be helped. If the hogs will die, we've used every precaution, and it is Providential. Precious, don't mind it atall. There is scarcely any misfortune we may not look for in these wretched times. Those are so very, very far removed from being the greatest that we must only thank God we are removed from heavier ones. Were I only at home, I know we'd have a greater abundance on the plantation, for it has always been a very peculiar business and one that I love and, of course, I could conduct it more successfully. But it would seem that cannot be, tho' so many others enjoy that privilege—and then we really do very well.

I think the copperas and sulpher, ashes and salt, and corn soaked in tar water will stop the disease among your hogs. Let those that die be buried *deep, deep,* so they cannot be scratched up. See that the sheep have a good chance and are in fine condition to enter on the winter. For the rest, my darling wife, trust all to God. I don't believe He intends we should be too wise in our providing. We have plenty to encourage us. Make all the syrup you can, and let us keep an abundance on hand to feed the negroes. Continue to plant such vegetables, after rain, as do well later in the season. Save all the peas you possibly can, and if we have rain, we'll do very well.

Have the colts well cared for and Brown Bess worked enough to ascertain she'll work kindly in the carriage. You know your horses may be taken at any time. That investment in mares was a very good one, the best we now have. Horses here are very high, and they must continue to go up. If the enemy keep off us, we will not have to purchase and shall be able to replace many of our deficiencies by them. You see how rapidly they grow up. I wrote you "Newcome" was stolen and recovered again. He and Perry's mare were gone two days. Some stray borrowed them for that length of time. They were not injured. Wilderness will bring a round sum one day. Let him be well cared for and reared for purpose of sale.

Darling, look on the bright side and don't allow yourself to be ruffled by any annoyance from home affairs. I am very glad you like Dr. England's[1] works and sorrow, from the depths of my heart, that the truths he annunciates do not meet your approving judgement. Isolation is to be my lot, I sadly fear, through life. T'is hard, but others have borne it. My own dearest, my darling, I try to live rightly and each day I pray that you may have God's kindliest blessings.

My great anxiety about your health is greatly relieved by what Dr. Alfriend told me, and with returning health and strength, you will bear up under trials well enough, I know. Why didn't your Mother come down with you? And Mrs. Waddell? You say nothing about them. I was sure both were with you, and have written Colonel W he had better direct his letters to Sparta. I hope you will induce her to make our house her home. I say so, darling, because I think it would be agreeable to you. I am sure that Col. W is greatly pleased at "Medora's" having what he considers so pleasant a refuge in her exile.

It is very desirable for me to have two horses, but of course I must consult my finances. For a month, I've been riding one of Ballard's[2] horses, and you know how disagreeable it is to me to borrow. A lameness or a sore back may, at any time, put one afoot with one horse. "Newcome" is now about right again. It is desirable that we sow a large wheat crop this fall, and we must take more pains. The land must all be well broken up first. I wish to put the Fork field in wheat, but it will take at least seventy bushels; that will cost pretty heavy. What does Dr. Green[3] propose to charge? I hardly know what to say. Let us talk it over in our letters, but don't let it trouble you.

I've sent you some doleful letters of late, but I can't help it. Sometimes dyspepsia makes me low down and sometimes half takes away my voice—and I am so utterly worn out with this life here. Oh! you don't half know how I long for your love and caresses. For news about our affairs here, the papers are teeming with it. Early[4] is careening around Washington and Baltimore and frightening the eternal Yankee nation into fits, but I fear will not be able to capture the former. Grant has thus been forced to send off many of his forces. We are looking for a move of some sort. I don't know what is on hand, but we rather believe we will force Grant to go and defend his own territory. This is Sunday, no papers. Tomorrow we look for important news.

We lose a few men in the trenches every day. The sharp shooting on both sides is murderously active and accurate. Yesterday, a Capt. Jones,[5] 17th Georgia, and a private of 2nd Georgia were passing each other in the narrow covered way of the main trenches. Each raised his head a little too high, and a ball passed through the brain of each. The Yankee sharp shooters kill the town milch cows that are grazing as far as 700 yards in rear of our trenches—1100 yards from them. And then they have killed our boys who venture back to them to cut off the beef. It would almost seem a minnie ball never loses its force.

I have confidence that Joe Johnston will yet demolish Sherman. God grant it. Darling, give our children a thousand loves and kisses. Daughter's letter hasn't come to hand. Bud's of June 25th and one of the same date from Father reached me yesterday. Yours was postmarked 12th July and reached me today, the 17th—quick time. Love to Father. I wrote him yesterday. Love to all our dear friends. Your letter enclosing Mrs. Dawson's letter has not reached me yet. I know I shall enjoy it. Give them both my kind love. I am glad Alfriend has returned for her sake. Bob received a letter from Nancy yesterday. Sent her a letter and money by Alfriend. Remember me kindly to John, Lewis, Uncle Ted and Aunt

Sallie, Eliza, Wes, etc.; to all our people. I hope to be with them one day. Don't forget Rachel, Judy, and Dinah.

Kindest regards always to John and Mr. Edwards. Have the latter with you all the time. He's a glorious old friend, ain't he, Darling? I hope Mrs. Waddell and Grandma are to join you soon. Love to Mrs. Whitehead. I saw Gene[6] two days ago looking well. I wrote you of his good luck. Goodbye, my own heart's love. God care for you and our dear children. And write me soon.

Your own Edge

1. John England (1786–1842) was the first Roman Catholic bishop of Charleston, S.C. The isolation Edgeworth Bird speaks of is his Catholicism; his wife raised their children as Presbyterians.

2. Major Walter S. Ballard, commissary sergeant of the brigade.

3. Dr. William Hudson Green had extensive farms in Hancock County. He had come home from the army in 1862 after being discharged for physical reasons.

4. Jubal Early distinguished himself at Gettysburg and protected Lee's flank at the Wilderness. Douglas Southall Freeman wrote that "Early's name was on every tongue late in June, and his prospects were discussed in every council and at every bivouac. He would be in position to threaten Washington. For a time he made a continent hold its breath." *Lee,* 429.

5. Captain A. M. Jones was killed 16 July 1864. *Georgia Roster,* 2:610.

6. Eugene P. Burnet, brother of Julia Burnet Whitehead, had just been appointed captain and inspector general of Colquitt's Brigade.

Edgeworth Bird to Sallie Bird

Near Petersburgh [Va.], 18 July 1864

My blessed Darling,

As I sat under the bush arbour, before my tent, smoking after supper, a stranger came up and announced himself as Mr. Sneed,[1] clerk of "the board" of which Waddell is a member in Richmond—and the bearer of a letter which I was to open in Ballard's absence. It was a call for money that Ballard owed him, as he was just on the point of leaving for

Georgia. It seems that the three officers who compose the Board have a leave of absence for 30 days. Lucky dog, isn't he? I sent him a note, telling him I think he'll find Mrs. W in Athens with trunk packed and ready to accompany Mrs. Baxter to Granite Farm.

I'm so sorry you made no mention of her plans in your letter, but I urged him to take her and go straight to our home to spend his short vacation. It is quite likely he'll have some business to look after, but he can be there a portion of the time. My conclusion was that you had gone ahead, with the children, to put matters in trim, and she and your Mother would follow. It was quite late when his clerk arrived and now, as I begin this *billet doux* to you, it is after midnight. . . .

I was greatly pleased to hear of Dear Sallie's improvement and good standing. Am very anxious to get the copy of her composition. Urge her for me to give all her thought to the adornment of her mind; a highly cultivated, virtuous mind only knows true pleasure. Tell the big boy that also, bless his dear heart. What you tell me of him, too, is unutterable pleasure. No one can know anything of the guile of this world without having been in the army three years in a Revolution. God grant that present depravity may not survive the army and the Revolution, but I doubt not there is much purity and truth, also.

There is rumour tonight that Johnston has been superceded in command by Hood. If Johnston[2] is removed, I despair, but I don't credit a word of it. Early is said to be south of the Potomac with a large booty.[3] I hope that is not to be the end of the raid, tho' I didn't believe he could take Washington, which is said to be the best fortified city in the world. We've had unusual quiet today and tonight. Only the incessant sharp shooting greets my ear as I write. . . .

Don't let smutty wheat or choleratic swine disturb the serenity of your soul, but just bear the ills of life as they come, feeling assured that the good Lord will not put more upon us than we can bear. . . . I hear there is a great deal of injured wheat from the wet weather, and you must be careful what you buy for seed and then have a perfect understanding about the price. We cannot buy wheat and pay in money. It is worth thirty dollars per bushel here, schedule prices. If you can pay in cloth at old prices, or some such way, it will take seventy bushels to sow down Fork Field, but write me what the prospect is. Let us have plenty of seed oats. We have to sing small on wheat and go it on oats and plant what is allowed of cotton to raise a revenue. But we won't trouble ourselves about that yet awhile. Consult with John about anything you wish to do with bonds. . . .

Go and see Father often—never mind, go. He's a very lonely old man. 'Tis your duty, darling, and a reward is always sure for doing one's duty. Love to those to whom you know my heart goes out. Always kind love to Mr. Edwards. Kisses to our darlings. Howdey to all the servants. Bob is well. I pray God's cherishing love for you ever, Edge

Tell Nancy her talk about the butter in Bob's letter makes my mouth trickle water. Tell Uncle Fed to stand by his hogs till Rabun brings the cows home, which you know is quite late.

1. A clerk with the Board of Slave Claims.

2. Joseph E. Johnston was replaced by John B. Hood in July 1864. Johnston ended the war in North Carolina, where he surrendered to Sherman at Greensboro 26 April 1865.

3. Early withdrew to Virginia 14 July at White's Ford.

Edgeworth Bird to Sallie Bird

Near Richmond, Va., 4 August 1864

Yesterday's mail brought me Sallie's letter and your "leaves from the blank book" written whilst you all were in such excitement and dread of a raiding visit from our hated foes. My own best loved darling, whilst I read, I was fully aware that you had escaped the danger, that their route was not immediately in our neighborhood, and that elsewhere they had been routed and dispersed. But yet my innermost heart was moved, and my very soul troubled to learn of the deep anxiety and distress you had been subjected to. I sorrow for all of our people, darling, that such times have come upon us. . . .

Revolution in all its horrors is indeed upon us, and there is but one trust . . . that can save us. . . . Your brave hopefulness and self reliance fill me with pleasure, and are a double assurance of your improving health. God grant that all our ladies may be alike, calm and resolute. A firm front always goes far to intimidate a cowardly foe, but dearest darling, if possible I never wish you to be in their power. At this distance I cannot advise what course of action would be wisest. . . . Under sudden emergencies, the advice of friends is best. Should they come on our little town suddenly, be with some tried friends. I do not think they would harm a few resolute ladies who stood by each other.

Should they overrun our immediate country, I don't know where you'd go, unless to your cousin, Mrs. Springs.[1] Augusta will be a prominent point of interest to them. So much for the gloomy side. But, precious darling, I don't believe they will reach Hancock. They have already made their outer circle. Hood's army is strengthening every week. Our people are arming and organizing. The defense of Macon has taught them these itinerant horse thieves can be checked and beaten, and Iverson has shown how they may be torn to pieces.[2] Lieut. General S. D. Lee[3] now commands our cavalry, and he has acquired a habit of victory. So cheer, dearest, all will yet go well. Hood is an able man, and his industry and perseverance are endless. Tho' much inferior to Johnston, I have great faith in him, and he is so ably supported. . . .

S. D. Lee brought reinforcements to Hood. Others must be coming. The fable that Forrest[4] is to be turned loose on Sherman's rear must one day become a fact. And, darling, there seems a general, accepted idea that the rout of that army would ensure peace. The North seems almost ripe for it, it's a growing sentiment there. We are nowhere unsuccessful except in Georgia. Here [in Virginia] Grant is at a deadlock. His last well planned and desperate move of blowing up a way into Petersburg[5] is a total and, to him, disastrous failure. . . . His gunboats and position on the river is all that have saved him so far. Early's main force has not crossed the Potomac yet, but his cavalry has taken a little turn. Pennsylvania has burning homesteads and desolate wives. The beautiful town of Chambersburg[6] is a black, charred mass. There is retribution at last. We all recall the defiant and scornful faces of its ladies as we marched through a year ago. I then and still respect them for their spirit, but their scorn has been turned into wailing.

Each month's continuance of this war will witness an increased ferocity, but the very violence of the contest will sooner bring peace. Precious old fellow, how troubled you must have been, you and your daughter, alone. And all those terrible summons coming in on you thick and fast. You do right to supply any demand that may be made upon you under such circumstances and do so promptly and cheerfully. . . . It strengthens me away off here to read your letters. May you never be subjected to such another trial, tho' our loved state is welcome to the last horse we have . . .

What do our black people think of the hubbub and near approach of the Yankees? When they come, if ever, such as wish to go with them are welcome; those of the men who do not should take to the woods, for they will seize every one of them and enroll them in their army to meet such fates as the poor creatures at Fort Pillow[7] and the other day at Petersburg. They force every negro man they get hold of into their army. The negro women I do not think they'll interfere with.

It is not worthwhile for your Mother to persist in staying in Athens in case of a raid there. She could do no good, and [it] seems to me you should all be together to mutually sustain each other. I wish Mrs. Waddell would come to you. I feel quite sure the Colonel will bring her down before he returns. He'll be dogmean not to do so, that he may tell me how you are. I readily understand how anxious you were about your dear Mother when you thought they were coming towards Athens.[8] I feel with you through it all, my Darling, fully and truly. Would to God I could take the burden from you and that I could be there to assist in defending our own homes. Bud would be a comfort to you now, but I suppose it best for him to be with his Grandma. Alone as she is, she surely needs him, but I wish both were with you.

I know now that the enemy did not go to Athens and that all there is safe, including that very necessary factory. It would indeed be a blow to us to lose that. But 'twould take a pretty strong raiding party to take Athens if they are fortifying it. Sallie expresses undying confidence in

Cook's battalion,[9] and there is considerable local force. Ah, dearest, could we only be near each other in such times, but it has not been given us.

Dr. Jervey Robinson[10] paid me a visit, a day or so since. He is on duty with 1st S. Carolina, McGowan's Brigade. Has been a prisoner since we saw him. He desired particular remembrances to you. He is not very far off, and I promised to ride by and see him. Said he wrote you as soon as he heard I was wounded. Did you get the letter? I couldn't remember to have heard you speak of it. He sought out my company to learn the extent of the wound. Very kind, wasn't it? Doc Pierce has a letter from home telling of the excitement there.[11] He is quite well, as is also Sammie, Pete and Dud Alfriend. Ben Alfriend has been quite sick with dyspepsia; is now about well. Everything here [is] quiet just now. Field's division[12] and several other brigades are on [the] northside of [the] James. Our troops here are having a comparative time of rest, after their several hardships in Tennessee and around Petersburg.

Dearest, I'm afraid you've lost ground this time. Do make it up by extra care. Tell me how your contrabands all behaved. Neither you or Sallie speak of having had a rain yet. I am so profoundly thankful the hateful Yankees have not fed upon our cribs or polluted our grounds with their presence. Darling, present my congratulations to Mrs. Lucy upon her contribution of strength to the Confederacy.[13] I am very glad for her and I hope Mrs. Terrell is in health again.[14]

Thank dear Sallie for her letter, only I don't look for half sheets from a young and healthy damsel. Will her school be interrupted? Love to Father. How does he bear our adversity? Bob is well and sends love to all our people. Says he wishes he was at home at these times of trouble there. Remembrances to all our Negroes.

My own darling, may God bless and care for you in these days of trial. Look to him for strength and guidance. Let me hear often. A thousand loves and kisses to dear daughter, Bud, yourself, from your own loving Edge

1. Blandina Baxter Springs lived at Fort Mill, S.C.

2. Confederate Brigadier General Alfred Iverson, Jr., defeated Union Major

General George Stoneman near Macon 31 July 1864. Stoneman, the highest ranking officer captured by Confederates during the war, had been sent by Sherman to destroy the Macon and Western Railroad. He had twice the men Iverson commanded. *Dictionary of Georgia Biography,* 1:510–11.

3. Stephen Dill Lee, recently appointed lieutenant general, had assumed command of Hood's old corps of the Army of Tennessee. He led them until Joseph E. Johnston's surrender in North Carolina in April. Warner, *Generals in Gray,* 183–84.

4. Nathan Bedford Forrest is considered by some to be the greatest cavalry officer produced by the U.S. In April 1864 he captured Fort Pillow. In June he routed a superior force at Brice's crossroads, and a month before Edgeworth Bird's letter he stood off General A. J. Smith at Tupelo. He commanded all of Hood's cavalry in the Tennessee campaign that followed in November and December. Warner, *Generals in Gray,* 92–93.

5. In the siege of Petersburg, Grant's forces cut a huge mine underground behind the Confederate lines and loaded it with explosives. It was set off 30 July 1864, killing many Confederate soldiers and creating the famous Crater, 30 feet deep and 170 feet long. Lee's men rallied and finally won in desperate hand-to-hand fighting with nearly four thousand Union men lost. Grant called it a stupendous failure. Randall and Donald, *The Civil War and Reconstruction,* 423–24.

6. On the same day Union forces set off the explosion at the Crater, Confederate forces burned Chambersburg, Pa., to avenge Union General Philip Sheridan's destructive raids on the Shenandoah Valley.

7. General Forrest reportedly killed several hundred black Union soldiers at Fort Pillow, Tenn., 12 April 1864.

8. The previous month men from Stoneman's brigade came near Athens and were captured by cavalrymen commanded by Colonel W. P. C. Breckinridge of Kentucky, who brought the prisoners to the University of Georgia campus before sending them on to Andersonville. Athens gave the Kentuckians a banquet. Hull, *Annals of Athens,* 263–64.

9. Major F. W. C. Cook of the Cook and Brother Armory commanded the local Athens defense unit. Coleman, *Athens, 1861–65,* 88.

10. Probably Dr. P. Gervais Robinson of Charleston, S.C.

11. Edgeworth Bird refers to an earlier letter, but on 5 Aug. 1864 Bishop George F. Pierce wrote his son: "Since Sunday last we have had great excitement in old Hancock about the Yankee raiders. Such commotion, running, hiding, you never saw. The raiders never came nearer than the river. They visited Henry Fraley's plantation, took all his mules, drank his brandy, ate his preserves, and left going toward Greensboro. They have done great damage to the railroads—the Central Georgia, and Macon and Western. Our cavalry are after them." Smith, *The Life and Times of George F. Pierce,* 485.

12. Major General Charles William Field retook the Bermuda Hundred line and fought in August 1864 from Chapin's Bluff to New Market Heights.

13. Lucy Terrell Dawson gave birth to Joseph Hill Dawson 22 July 1864 in Sparta.

14. Eliza Rhodes Terrell, Lucy Dawson's mother, died the next year.

Edgeworth Bird to Sallie (Saida) Bird

Near Richmond, 10 August 1864

Dear Daughter,

Your letter and Bud's under the same envelope reached me quite recently. I am always pleased to get your letter and the young man's, the more so as they, in one sense, resemble angel's visits, being "few and far between." . . .

I should be very sorry to know that you had lost the benefit of Miss Lipscomb's[1] instruction, for tho' I do not know her personally, Mama's high opinion of her and your affection convince me of her great worth. . . . I am too far off to have a finger in the pie of your education . . . but there's one ingredient I shall insist be under the pastry (where the real good things are), that is a thorough knowledge of Latin. . . .

In French you are doing well, I presume. Try to be perfect in it. I would have you neglect nothing, my child, that will contribute to giving you a vigorous and cultivated mind. . . . Your opportunities are none of the best, owing to the stormy times we live in, and any great progress must be owing to *your own industry and perseverance*.

I hear frequently from Mama, as she writes nearly every day—her letters are an inexpressible comfort and pleasure, by far the greatest I experience in this miserable war life. She has many trials and burdens at home; the care of a plantation is a new onus and not properly belonging to her department, but under necessity she assumes it bravely, and right ably and skillfully does she direct. Little one, you may well be proud of your Mother. Imitate her energy and faithful performance of all duties. You can never be *half so beautiful*, so I won't try to create an emulation on that point.

Have you written Colonel Waddell?[2] He urges you to do so; will reply and send his photograph as promised. You will be amply repaid if you can coax him out of spare time for occasional correspondence. He is peculiarly happy in letter writing. . . . Your Cousin Sammie Wiley is sitting nearby at the desk. . . . His health was never better. He hasn't been at home since little Lizzie was a wee baby of a few days. . . . Mr. Pete Harris is absent most of the time . . . to procure forage for the Brigade. Benning's [Brigade] and the Texas Brigade of Field's Division are on the north side of the James, and for some weeks have been having quite a period of rest. Balance of Division are at Petersburg.

Our men hold the trenches all the while and keep an active watch for any demonstration against Richmond from this side. . . . Our army in North Georgia seems unfortunate. Reverse after reverse falls to its share. It is composed of splendid material and was effective in the hands of a master mind like Johnston. Hood is a nice fellow, but isn't owner of sufficient mental calibre for the crisis. . . . General Lee[3] spent nearly a whole day in consultation with the President, t'is said, so tell your Grandma to feel easy. It is all arranged to gobble up Sherman. If the old "Butcher" [Grant] wasn't so pertinacious along the Weldon Road, we'd send our Lee down to solace the Georgians for a week or so, but Johnston would do equally if our pigheaded President would replace him [Hood]. . . .

You seem greatly attached to Miss Emma Huger.[4] In view of your mutual friendship I claim that you present her my respectful compliments and desire to meet and know well my daughter's friend. How does Bud come on with his studies? You are the senior, Miss Sallie . . . remember you are to look after and advise him and generally play the role of "Big Sis." . . . I was very much distressed to hear of the death of poor George Hays[5] and most fully sympathize with his mother. . . . Ah! the hearts that are bleeding today from this cruel strife. . . . Tell Bud "Gavroche" has gone home carried by Bill Alfriend, but he is not to think of him till his study time has passed. God bless you, dearest daughter, and care for you in all things.

Your affectionate Father, William E. Bird

1. Sarah A. Lipscomb taught at Lucy Cobb Institute in Athens.

2. Colonel James D. Waddell, grandson of Dr. Moses Waddel. (Earlier generations

spelled the name with one *l.*) Colonel Waddell and his wife, Medora Sparks, had no children; he took a fatherly interest in the Bird family. Waddell quit active combat in 1864 because of physical disabilities and was assigned to the presidency of the Court of Slave Claims. His wife wrote him from Woodville, Ga., 27 Aug. 1864, that she was going to Granite Farm to visit within the next week or so, if Sallie Bird was not going to Athens. After the war he practiced law, edited the Atlanta *Times* briefly, and wrote the biography of his friend Linton Stephens. Waddell Papers, Special Collections, Emory University.

3. Lee was reportedly not pleased with Davis's decision to replace Johnston with Hood.

4. Emma Huger was a member of a New Orleans family living as refugees on the University of Georgia campus.

5. Major George E. Hayes, the son of Sallie Bird's Aunt Sarah Ann Hayes, was killed at Weldon Railroad, Va. *Georgia Roster* 1:532 gives the date as 21 Aug. 1864, which must be incorrect if Edgeworth Bird's letter is dated correctly.

Sallie Bird to Sallie (Saida) Bird

Granite Farm, 22 August 1864

It is Monday morning, my dear Sallie, and I imagine you and Bud off to school. I wrote to Mother the day after you left. I hope this P.M. to get a letter from some of you. Looked in vain on Saturday. I've been in bed Saturday and Sunday and write from there today. No news from Walton[1] of the beads, so I've just written a note to her for them, and Sam will go by with it this P.M. She could not have received your note, or she would certainly have sent the beads. I am not so well as usual, but keep [to] my bed and hope to improve. Miss Caroline[2] is kind and no trouble. You should see your room now that she stays in it; not a pin is out of order, and it is so clean, and sweet, and cool that it does one good to look in there. Oh, if you could only keep it so! I had the front room wash stand put in there, which was the only difference made, and it is just as nice a little bed room as any one could desire.

I hope you received the letter enclosed from Minnie.[3] Write to her soon. The correspondence will keep your hearts warm towards each other, and always take pains with your letters to her. Mrs. Dawson started down to see me yesterday. Met our servants going up to church and heard I was sick and turned back. I am excused from sending a negro to Hood's army for the present, but may have to do so ten days from now. I wrote sister a long letter yesterday from my bed and sent by Frank Burnet, who leaves today. I wrote Edge a long letter, also. I sent Frank B. two pounds of butter yesterday for his own eating. He was greatly obliged; wrote me a very pretty note. . . . Now I'll save for Mother, to go by Frank. Frank is doing as well as possible.

Henry is "laid by" with his cut foot, Isaac with general debility. Ed had some sore throat and fever, which I cured in one night by turpentine inside and outside. The rest are well. Before I got sick, I made pretty sleeves to my pretty white lawn, and Judy is going to wash it today. Do, Sallie, take care of your clothes. I have no idea they can be renewed. The supply that I started the war with is greatly reduced. I send a full white waist of my finest homespun to be made for you. Let it be made by the little striped white. I don't think you'll need it immediately. It must have strong pieces put under the arms. . . . I'll cut the pieces—bands on the shoulder, length of the inserting in your striped waist. For a variety, wear linen collar and cuffs with it. It will look so nicely over your new calico when made.

Don't forget to get me a box of wafers from White's.[4] Make an engagement with Dr. Lowrance[5] to have your teeth examined, and Bud also. Take care of your teeth, also. *Both of you.* You'll bitterly regret neglecting them. Tell my dear boy I'll write him next. I'll send his Father's letter by Frank. Be good children. I charge you both to *obey strictly* your Grandma who has your interest *always* at heart. No tramps down town in the sun, no washing, no liberties which you know I'd disapprove. How does your hat look? I imagine it very pretty. I think the shape extremely pretty and stylish. Miss Caroline sends love to you all. We drove to town Friday evening. Met Mrs. Whitehead and Annie Burnet[6] coming out, and I was obliged to go on to see about the impressing of negroes.

Goodbye, dear daughter. Neglect me if you neglect anyone, but never your dear, dear Father. Kiss my dear Mother for me. Ever your devoted Mother,

S.C.B.

1. Walton Johnston, daughter of Richard Malcolm Johnston.

2. It is not clear which Caroline this is. Mrs. Caroline Bird Yancey Beman died at the home of her son William Lowndes Yancey in 1859. Caroline, the daughter of Benjamin C. Yancey, was called Caro; Sallie Bird would not have referred to her as "Miss Caroline."

3. Minnie Gresham, Sallie Bird's niece who lived in Macon, Ga.

4. William N. White's bookstore in Athens stocked books, writing paper, sheet music, musical instruments, valentines, greeting cards, and garden seed. Coleman, *Confederate Athens*, 2.

5. H. A. Lowrance advertised as a surgeon dentist and had offices over the jewelry store of Talmadge and Winn on College Avenue in Athens. In 1861 he charged a dollar for extracting teeth, one dollar and a half for cleaning teeth, and from four and a half to five and a half dollars for gold plugs. *Confederate Athens*, 152.

6. Anna Burnet, daughter of William H. Burnet and niece of Julia Burnet Whitehead.

FIVE

Sherman Marches Through Georgia

"Our house will soon be in Yankee hands and at Yankee mercy, so cheerfully as I can, I submit to the necessity. Tho' I know they will sweep me clean, t'is only what a hundred thousand others have suffered."

EDGEWORTH BIRD

ATLANTA was evacuated by Hood and taken by Sherman in September 1864. By late November Sherman's men moved into Milledgeville, then the capital of Georgia, only a few miles from Hancock County. Kilpatrick's raiders burned the mills at the Shoals of the Ogeechee which Colonel William Bird, Revolutionary War veteran and Edgeworth Bird's grandfather, had built. They spared the Aviary, the original home of the Birds. Raiders destroyed much property on plantations near Granite Farm. They took livestock, burned mills and barns, demolished wagons and farm implements, wantonly spoiled or stole food supplies, leaving a trail of hunger and desolation.

Edgeworth Bird was named to the Slave Claims Board in Richmond and in November Sallie went there to join him. Mary Baxter, Sallie Bird's mother, left her Athens home for Granite Farm, where she managed to hide the cattle and hogs from Yankee raiders. Saida fled from her refuge in Savannah at the home of her cousin Eva Berrien Jones. She and Eva Jones sought safety with relatives in Augusta, leaving the splendid Jones library to the mercy of the invaders who took Savannah in time to make a Christmas present of it to President Lincoln.

Edgeworth Bird to Sallie Bird

Four Mile Church near Richmond, 28 August 1864

As lovely a Sabbath day beams upon us this morning, my darling, as is ever the good fortune of mortals to witness. It is bright, cool, and bracing. Of late, we've had fine rains, there is no dust and the fields are putting on a fresh suit of velvet green. . . . The surroundings are in perfect antithesis; the strong passions of men sweep like a desolating sirocco over all this summery beauty, and there is no pleasure, no peace. I wrote you day before yesterday. Since then there is no change, except that negro troops hold the picket line in front of us.

General Lee has taken some of the Yankee works near Ream's Station and holds an advantageous position for finally driving them from Weldon Road. He captured, at the same time, two thousand prisoners and nine pieces of artillery. Grant's losses in prisoners, killed and wounded, have been very heavy within a few weeks. At this rate, he must soon be shorn of his strength. Have you noticed the large number of Northern papers that call for peace, as shown by extracts from them? Surely the public mind there has perpetrated a complete somerset.

Bah! the paper maker forgot to mark this sheet. Don't our little Confederacy put up an abominable article of paper? . . . The steel pen I write with would be magnificent on good paper.

My Precious, I had yesterday a letter from Sallie and Bud, a half sheet from each. Bud has dived into his books again, but seems to doubt his ability to keep up in Virgil without Mama to assist him. I rather feared it, because they've hurried him forward too rapidly, but if he'll persevere, scuffling by himself will help him. Two weeks longer vacation will help her . . . give her ample time to do all the frolicking, and then she must bend all her energies to hard study. Darling, you don't know how much solicitude I have about that child. Young girls are so simple and heedless. I want her to completely realize that the next three years of her life comprise the most essential time of her improvement. . . . Sallie has a fine, capable mind, and I wish it thoroughly developed and cultivated. . . .

Waddell has just come out to spend the day and night with us, and DuBose and Doc Pierce are here to dine with us—and John Waddell.[1] So you see we've quite a dining. I've just slipped away from them; they are talking in the next tent. I wish to have this finished for Waddell to take back and mail. A few days ago I mailed you a letter in which was enclosed my photograph. I had six struck off. It is not good—a defect about the eyes, too strong a glare. . . .

Tell Bud and Sallie I gave their letters to the Colonel to read. Let Doc's people know he is quite well, and also Henry Middlebrooks and Dud. Ben Alfriend is in Richmond and still quite unwell. I understand he has written for Dr. Ed or Bill. Sammie, Peter are both in good health. The latter has just returned from a ten days forage trip. The wagons had to go a hundred miles to load with oats and clover hay. Meantime, we buy fields of green corn and feed away. The soldiers *will* take the roasting ears, and then we buy for the animals the green stalks and fodder.

Perry[2] went on the lines yesterday and exchanged a Richmond paper for a New York Herald of the 24th. I'll send it to you. One of the men went out afterwards and waved his paper, the usual signal for an exchange, and out walked a nigger soldier with a paper. The Confed "cussed him out" and retired in disgust. Perry has executed for Bud a free likeness of "Gavroche." I enclose it, but I think I'd let it remain until he comes home. He's too easily distracted from his books now. Col W says if Sallie will write him, he'll reply and send her his photograph as promised. He tells me a sad piece of news. He has heard that George Hayes[3] was very severely wounded at Petersburg, and the person who told him feared he was killed, but remember, this is not certain. I am very much grieved about it.

Monday 29th—I am up before breakfast to finish this. Waddell goes in after breakfast and will mail it. I kept it open that I might have a chance to speak to him about that affair of mine. He says he has set it agoing, and it progresses most favourably. Hasn't the least doubt of its perfect success. In ten days I shall most probably be relieved from field service in this department—and, darling, I do assure [you] I feel under extremely great obligations to my friend J.W.[4] for arranging the matter for me. He and I shall probably keep house, after a fashion. Of course, then I shall want all the supplies that can be furnished by home, butter, lard, meat (after next killing), flour, pickles, catsup, etc. Sam can make trips and bring on supplies. Please have an eye to this from now on.

We'll have a room apiece for you and Mrs. W, and you can spend a month or so with us when you feel like it. My own precious, are you not glad? I am so, only I am very much troubled about these boys. But I shall do my best to retain all that I can. If Houston succeeds me, there'll be no trouble about most of them. I've talked to Sammie about it. Do keep it all to yourself. Waddell says I can get a 30 days furlough now. Would you like to see me? I need clothing and my trunk fixed up. Shirts are about out; only one pair of pants. I shall try to get government cloth enough for a suit. Waddell has a pair of boots made at the Athens factory for 75 dollars, very good ones, only made for stockholders. Please write to Bloomfield and order me a pair at once. Let them be made on the same last he made Waddell's on. They fit me exactly. I wonder you'd never found that out before.

My darling, dearest, dearest of old fellows, goodbye. God bless you always. I write you often and will continue. Love to all friends. Howdy to the servants. Love to Father, kisses to our dear little folks and your Mother. Your own Edge

1. John Waddell, brother of Colonel James D. Waddell, was a member of the Troup Artillery of Clarke County, Ga. Stegeman, *These Men She Gave,* 148. DuBose was Colonel Dudley M. DuBose.

2. Heman H. Perry was a captain in Benning's Brigade.

3. Edgeworth Bird mentioned the death of George Hayes in a letter to his daughter 10 Aug. 1864. The *Georgia Roster* lists the death date as 21 Aug. Hayes may have been critically wounded at the time of the earlier letter and may have died later, or one of the two letters may be incorrectly dated.

4. Colonel James D. Waddell.

Edgeworth Bird to Sallie Bird

Four Mile Church, Richmond, 3 September 1864

Your long, sweet letter of Aug. 28th has just been read, My Own Precious Darling; you see it reached me in quick time. . . . I thought I'd draw you out on the subject of my change of position. I knew you must have been thinking about it and could not be entirely passive about what concerned deep ponderment for me, and my interpretation of it was not far wrong. You were somewhat at fault, as I was myself, and hardly knew how to cast your judgement. In a letter written one or two days ago, I gave you at length the reasons which influenced me.

You argue the pro's and cons very lucidly. So far as the permanency of the Board goes, here stands the case. Three millions of dollars have been appropriated for payment of these negro claims against the Government, and they have not yet paid out fifty thousand. So it may exist a long time before the present sum is rid of—and as long as the war lasts new claims of similar nature must continue to arise,[1] and I suppose further sums be appropriated. I do not think the city life will suit, and there is one of the drawbacks, one great reason why I hesitated so much; and for the rest, my darling, three years of absence from you has proven to your old fellow that he can be thoroughly trusted in cities or elsewhere.

The matter of expense is a serious consideration, and one that every one addresses himself to who lives in Richmond, but we must try to weather that. My pay will be about $400 a month during September and from October about $500 a month. You perceive my regular pay is the same, $162 per month. The increase is the summer allowance as commutation for quarters, etc. It is much increased in winter. I was in town yesterday to draw money and clothing for the Brigade. Went in very early, having been notified by Major DeShields,[2] division quartermaster, to meet him there by 9 a.m. After attending to those matters, I went up to the office of the Board and saw Waddell. I declare, he's a sharp fellow and manages matters to a nicety.

He introduced me to Major Brockenbrough,[3] the member of the Board I hadn't yet met. He seems to have enlisted him warmly in the matter. He seems a very nice, gentlemanly fellow, and one of the F.F.V.

[First Families of Virginia] and W says has influence at court. He was very kind and declared the matter must be pressed through at once. W then would carry me up to the War Office . . . where he introduced me to Major Briely,[4] one of the officials of eminence up there, as W would express it. Major Briely remembered to have met me at Centreville in Jasper Whiting's[5] office and mentioned his telling him I was a college mate and warm friend of his brother Henry Whiting.[6] Was extremely cordial and agreed with Waddell to take a strong pull to put the matter through at once.

We then returned to the office, and while there a note came from General Somebody, chief of Engineering Bureau, saying the application for another member to the Board was granted, and requested them to nominate some one to fill the place. As soon as W read the note, he dashed his cap on the floor and brought a very unboardly whoop and immediately wrote in reply, sending in my name. . . .

One reason I am anxious to leave here is the heavy money responsibility attached to the situation. At Waddell's suggestion, I obtained from Dr. Gregory,[7] Brigade Surgeon, a certificate showing my condition from hemorrhoids and how they frequently disabled me from field service. It is now quite dark. I resume tomorrow.

Sept. 4. . . . I heard more from the transfer last night. Morton[8] came from town quite late and sent down a note, after I'd gone to bed, to tell me that he had heard at the War Office I was assigned to duty on that Board. So Dearest, I presume you may look on the matter as finished. . . . Altho' I've gone and done it, I can't help feeling badly and rather depressed. I've been associated here a long time, and there are many here to whom I am really attached. . . . Yes, my own, you shall come to see me. Major Brockenbrough and Waddell are for renting a house,[9] but of all plans you shall hear at length when I have been able to "view the landscape o'er." My darling, Waddell deserves our lasting love for the friendship he has shown me. . . .

About money matters, we must try to help our income from the plantation. We must plant the quantity of cotton allowed. A few bales bring a large sum of money, and the tending of it will not interfere with corn, cane, etc. I think there are seven bales in the gin house. The sale of these will bring a good sum. Raiders might come along and burn them. Then there are other bonds, 8 per cent. It is doubtful if we will be benefitted by keeping them. The cotton and 8 per cents will carry us on a year or two. Then surplus meat will bring a good deal. We'll kill as much as last year. Must slip in a beef now and then. Give out syrup and not meat, except a piece to boil a pot. So don't be downhearted, darling. You *shall* buy yourself and Sallie what calicoes you wish.

Why, darling, if you and our children are to be straightened, I'll take to going in my shirt tail (excuse the phrase). Why, my blessing, that style is not to be. I'll arrange it so we'll have money from our place. I've already written about sending Peter or March. Peter is the one, if his finger is well enough. It don't matter if they do keep him. Let us take it as it comes. I do not wish to be exempted from sending a driver. Darling, it is after dark. Perry, Ballard and I have just returned from dining with Col. Dubose. He gave us an elegant dinner, and we had a good time. Doc Pierce, of course, was there and well. I'm so glad you've heard again from dear Richard.

My darling, we are in the midst of very unpleasant rumours about Atlanta.[10] Tis said it has fallen and Hood is thirty miles toward Macon; that at one time his army was cut in two, tho' now united. I won't believe it till I hear the official news of it, but I can't help being depressed. . . .

Tell John I look to him to be true and faithful. Ten or fifteen of the negro soldiers in our front have come in the past few days. Two came over this morning. A negro who knows what is for his good will never let the Yanks get him. Oh, my darling, how I wish I was with you this moment. I'll hope and trust in our good God. My faith never waivers that all will be right. . . . Give dear Grandma and our dear darlings oceans of love for me. Love always to Father. Don't let the Yanks get our cotton. Save one bag. Had not the rest be turned to money? Always give my love to Alfriend. Tode can bring the money.

Tell Mr. Edwards I have received his letter and thank him. Love to Lucy Dawson and Edgar and Mrs Terrell and Whitehead. You must all stand by each other. Howdye to all the servants. I hope they'll be true and faithful. For yourself, my own love, do be quiet and careful. I am sorely distressed at your backset. It made my heart ache. . . . God bless and care for you. He can and will strengthen you to bear all that he sends upon you. Ask him. Love and trust always your own Edge

1. Edgeworth Bird was about to be appointed to the Board of Slave Claims in Richmond. On 23 Sept. 1864 official orders were issued by John W. Riely, assistant adjutant general. Major A. H. Davenport replaced Bird as quartermaster, Benning's Brigade.

2. Major H. C. DeShields, quartermaster on the staff of Major General Charles William Field. Confederate Military Records (microfilm), Georgia State Archives.

3. The Slaves Claim Board was created by a special order 1 April 1864, followed by the appointment of Colonel James D. Waddell, Major J. B. Brockenbrough, and W. A. Spence, surgeon. The board was to examine claims for slaves who escaped to the enemy or died from injuries or disease contracted while in Confederate service. Henry Putney Beers, *Guide to the Archives of the Government of the Confederate States of America,* 155.

4. John W. Riely, assistant adjutant general.

5. Jasper Whiting of Centreville, Va.

6. Henry Whiting, Edgeworth Bird's classmate at Georgetown, brother of Jasper Whiting.

7. Dr. W. B. Gregory, Second Georgia Infantry. Confederate Military Records (microfilm), Georgia State Archives.

8. Not identified.

9. Colonel Waddell wrote his wife Medora 19 Sept. 1864 that they had gotten a house on 5th Street between Clay and Leigh, "comfortable and pretty well furnished, not elegantly, but neatly enough." There was a parlor, a bedroom, and a dining room on the first floor and three comfortable bedrooms on the second floor. "Good grates [fireplaces], carpets, bureaus, wardrobes. No towels." Waddell Papers, Special Collections, Emory University.

10. Atlanta was evacuated by Hood 1 Sept. 1864 and occupied by Sherman the following day.

Sallie Bird to Sallie (Saida) Bird

Washington, Ga., 7 September 1864

My dearest Sallie,

I had expected in this [time] to have received a letter from one of you directed to this place, but have been disappointed. I still hope I shall before I leave. Are you all so dumbstricken by the fall of Atlanta that you cannot speak? For ourselves, I am glad we were here when it occurred, for were we at home, we should have given way to deep depression. As for depression here, it is impossible to give way to it. We are surrounded by such cheerful circumstances, and everyone is so kind to us. Mrs. Toombs is as sweet as she can be and just as good, and Mrs. DuBose[1] is bright and sparkling, and one of the most entertaining persons I ever saw. She makes us scream with laughter in spite of ourselves.

And we have just spent a day and two evenings with our dear Barnett cousins.[2] Oh, Sallie, they *are* lovely, and I long to have you know them. I never visited a more charming household, every member of the family, and I want you to know them. I have promised that you shall, some day, if nothing happens. Anne is lovely, girlish, fresh, quite pretty, and so *very* pleasant. She talks remarkably well, and is altogether, your Cousin Lucy and I think, one of the prettiest . . . girls we ever met. She is very anxious to know you—says you are one of the people she most desires to know. Sam has given a brilliant account of you. . . . Cousin Lizzie is lovely, too, and *everything* is pleasant here. Emma and Mary are just as good . . . as can be. Mary is *lovely* in the highest sense of the word. She is an invalid and a great sufferer. . . .

Wednesday night—I could not finish this morning, so I close hurriedly tonight. I received yours and Bud's letters this P.M. Glad to get them. Cousin Sam says tell Mother his earnest thoughtful advice, which is to stay at home, and for you children to remain also. But whatever Mother does will be right to me. Can she get Dorsey[3] to see about the piano? I wish she could. I'll pay his expenses. I sent to Tennille again the day before I left—not there. Janey Reese[4] wrote to Mrs. Lamar Cobb[5] about it yesterday. We took tea at Judge Reese's this P.M. Have just returned. Saw Sam Harris[6] there from Athens. Says his mother and sisters will remain in Athens. Says he heard Mother was going to leave. I am of the opinion that we had all better remain at home. That is the universal opinion, and I agree with it.

For myself, I've no place to go if they destroy my home, for Mother's is equally exposed. I hate for Bud to leave school. I should prefer his remaining if Mother and you leave, and staying at Dr. Linton's, if they'll take him. He and Hal can hide where they would be safe. His education, if possible, must be pushed on. As for your school, I expect that must be left to Mother's judgement. Of course, I prefer you to be at school, but if Miss Lipscomb is not there, I fear the school will be very inferior.

I am truly sorry my dear Mother is again harassed. Bless her heart, it is too much. Well, if she leaves, I hope she'll stay with me. Most people think they'll hardly reach Hancock again. The fall of Atlanta is a great disaster, but not irretrievable. I trust every energy will be put forth. Some of the scenes Mr. Stephens foretold are upon us. I am not depressed yet. We leave tomorrow, a day earlier than expected. I never had a sweeter visit. Dear Mrs. Toombs is so good and sweet, and Mrs. DuBose is fascinating indeed, so sparkling, that is the word to apply to her.

Mrs. DuBose goes with us to Barnett tomorrow. So does Jane Reese. Anderson[7] is here too. . . . Good night. I am tired. A world of love to Mother and my darling boy. God bless and protect you all. I think Edge will be crazy [with worry] about me. Your devoted Mother, S.C.B.

1. Sallie DuBose, daughter of Senator Robert Toombs of Washington, Ga. Her husband, Dudley M. DuBose, a colonel with the Georgia regiment in which Edgeworth Bird served, later became a brigadier general.

2. Samuel Barnett and his wife Elizabeth Stone. Barnett was the first railroad commissioner for the state of Georgia and at one time edited the Augusta *Chronicle*. His son Samuel was a noted mathematician and attorney. The Barnett home is now the Washington-Wilkes Historical Museum. See Barnett Papers, Special Collections, Emory University. The Barnetts and the Wileys were related through the Jack family. Eliza A. Bowen, *The Story of Wilkes County, Georgia* (Marietta, Ga., 1950), 56.

3. Captain William H. Dorsey of Athens, the town auctioneer, a man of many services. The Athens *Banner* said, "Everybody calls on the Captain to sell property, buy property, collect debts, catch thieves, recover stolen property, and do a great many other things too tedious to mention." Coleman, *Confederate Athens*, 112.

4. Jane Reese, the daughter of Charles M. Reese and his second wife, a Mrs. Meriwether. Hull, *Annals of Athens*, 471.

5. Mrs. Lamar Cobb was Olivia Newton, who married the son of Howell Cobb and Mary Ann Lamar. *Annals of Athens*, 448.

6. Sampson W. Harris, son of Sampson W. Harris and Paulina Thomas. *Annals of Athens*, 453.

7. Anderson Reese, son of Charles M. Reese and brother of Jane Reese.

Edgeworth Bird to Sallie Bird

near Richmond, Va., 9 September 1864

My own Darling,

You have not had your dues in several days. . . . Yesterday I went up to town and proposed to write in Waddell's office, but was prevented. One is so taken up during a single day in Richmond, that he can do little else than walk around and submit himself to others. Yesterday, Ballard and I were in together. Got off quite late and 'twas nearly 1 o'clock before we arrived there; then, of course, the matter of my transfer has to be canvassed. Like all military arrangements, it draws its slow length along. It seems it had to pass through different channels from what was anticipated. It has passed clearly and prosperously through all the Richmond departments, thanks to our friend Waddell. When it reached the Qr. Master Genl's office, Gen'l Lawton[1] referred it to Col. Corley, chief QM of A.N.V., for remarks, and there it has gone at present.[2]

Today I sent Whitney over to Major DeShields, our Division Q.M., asking him to see Corley and try to secure his approval. Sent him a letter explaining all. Major Scott of Hill's Corps had also promised Waddell to do the same. It has passed Mr. Siddon, Genls Cooper,[3] Gilmer,[4] Lawton all right, and I imagine Col. Corley would not strike it a blow after that. But Corley has the reputation of being a straight-laced West Pointer and rather gruff—and I can't help feeling a little uneasy, but still hope all will go right.

If the matter succeeds, Waddell and I propose to rent a small house with four or five rooms and arrange to keep house. During the winter months my pay there would be about six hundred dollars per month—Waddell's a little more. By getting our boxes from home with lard, butter, meat, and redeploying our own servants, we'll probably do. Then Richmond is the safest place now and will be a refuge for you. A portion of the time you can be with me and, such time as we wish, at home. You know, dearest, you'll be needed there some times to keep matters agoing.

If we succeed with the transfer, Waddell wants me to get fifteen or twenty days furlough and go on home to bring you ladies on. What say you to that, ma cherie? Would that comport with your idea's of nowadays? Darling, I want you to think over and consider well about the matter of keeping house. Note that *we* are going to keep house and invite you ladies to see us. It is the cheapest way to live. It will be nothing more than a mess. The house isn't even obtained yet, but the lard and butter are. Don't sell any more lard. I'm half fearful you've already been depleted.

There is a Major Briely in the War Office who has been very warm and cordial in his assistance. In a note to me, Waddell says, "So and so went straight through thanks to Briely (God bless him!)." I sent for that thousand dollars because I found myself six hundred and thirty-six dollars short in balancing my books—this includes the whole eighteen months I have been in the department. At first one blundered, and there are so many ways to get behind. I'm thankful to have got off so well. A portion of this was captured on Richard, who had it to purchase forage, and in getting rid of so many hundred thousand dollars reg.[ularly], one does very well to be so near even. Then I owed Pete Harris for the boots and I have paid him. So there was only a hundred and sixty odd left of the thousand. I had to advance the money captured on Dick. He was not here to certify to the exact amount. I hope you may be able to send on the money soon to refund to Mr. Johnston who is very kind.

If I go to Richmond, Maj. Briely will take my horse and keep him, as he is entitled to one. That will enable me to have time to make a good sale of him. I think he will bring $4,000. That will keep a fellow living for some time, may be till the war ends. Houston and Forbes are recommended to remain with the Brigade, and they needn't leave unless they prefer and can get situations in Geo. I went to the Qr Master Genl and explained how these recommendations had been made without consulting Brigade QM's. This caused a change in the whole division. The matter was referred back and Brigade QM.'s made their own nominations. Houston will be transferred to Georgia. If I leave then, Forbes will be in charge of the Brigade. I don't know whether there is a chance for him to get an increased rank. I had a chance offered in conversation and I talked mighty pretty for him to Maj Lester,[5] one of the assistants to the QM Genl, but I believe Forbes had rather go to Geo., too, if he could get a place where he could be at home now and then. I think they are all right in that.

Darling, Atlanta has fallen. What a triumph for Johnston at the expense of our cause. Hood was outgeneraled. He is not able to cope with Sherman. But don't be downhearted. All will yet be well. Every advance is peril to Sherman; our head men will yet devise a plan to crush him. God will yet bless our cause. Lincoln has postponed his draft—he's afraid to try it. Everywhere we do well except in Georgia—and we'll succeed there, too. I have got me a pair of govt. pants. Very good blue ones. I need shirts. One of the calico's has "gone up," so I have but two and they are slazy. Is that hat to reach you soon? Ain't I a troublesome fellow? Bless your dear, loving heart, I know you don't think so. Have Bloomfield to make that pr. boots for me like Waddell's, on same last. Cost $75. Darling, have on hand all the money you can. 8 percents are quoted in Richmond at a hundred and twenty five. Your cotton is worth a small pile.

Love to Father and all the family. Tell Father I am still alive and would be glad to hear from him. I've written him twice since he wrote me. Keep my three pups for me. It is a cross I've been intent on making, so indulge me, darling. Sammie is very ill. Pete is gone most of the time on forage trips. Sends love to you and Mrs. Whitehead. Send up kisses and love to your Mother and the dear children. You are, as ever, my all. Do, do take care of yourself. Remember your promise to keep in bed *all* the while you are sick. I trust you in this, as in all things, and love you best on earth.

Your Own Edge

Howdy to the servants. Bob got a long letter from Nancy. He's been a little sick and I think it cured him immediately. Yes, send Peter on that trip. He can be best spared. He ought to be well clothed when he starts. The [illegible] won't lose any of his colts with distemper. Tell him I am counting heavy on him in these times, indeed on all of them. Who knows but I may turn up home some fine day. There's no other prospect than such as I've mentioned. Love to Mr. Edwards, to John, the Dawsons, Wileys, etc.

Hope you had a pleasant time with Mrs. Toombs. Kiss dear Eva with my warm love. Wish I could share her visit.

1. Alexander Robert Lawton (1818–1896) was appointed quartermaster general of the Confederacy in February 1864 by Jefferson Davis and filled that position until the end of the war. An alumnus of West Point and Harvard, he married Sarah Hillhouse Alexander of Washington, Ga., and practiced law in Savannah. He served in the campaigns in Virginia and was severely wounded at Sharpsburg. *Biographical Dictionary of the Confederacy*, 278.

2. Lieutenant Colonel James L. Corley, chief quartermaster of the Army of Northern Virginia. John M. Carroll, *List of Staff Officers of the Confederate States Army* (Mattituck, N.Y., 1983), 36.

3. General Samuel Cooper (1798–1876), adjutant and inspector general of the Confederate army. An organizational genius, he was a close friend of Jefferson Davis. *Biographical Dictionary of the Confederacy*, 150.

4. Major General Jeremy Francis Gilmer, onetime chief of the Engineering Bureau of the Confederate War Department. A West Point graduate and outstanding military engineer, he helped fortify Atlanta. *Biographical Dictionary of the Confederacy*, 202–3.

5. W. W. Lester was assistant quartermaster general.

Edgeworth Bird to Sallie Bird

Four Mile Church near Richmond, 22 September 1864

. . . So positive do you seem in your belief that we are soon to have the Yankees around our home, that I look the more anxiously each day for letters from you that I may know the exact state of your own feelings.

My darling, I feel so very, very anxious about you and our dear children. I have some fears, also, you are having an attack of sickness. Bud must have written for you. My Precious, don't be sick in these times. I would have you strong and braced up. Then, I know you'll be equal to emergencies and meet every new trial with a brave, hopeful heart. I am so very glad your Mother is now with you. I feel deeply for her that she considers it necessary to give up her home. Bud tells me many, many people are preparing to leave Athens, and that a party of the enemy may be looked for any time there.

Bless her dear soul, while one stone stands upon another at our home, it is her home, but she knows that very well, and she may well feel "at home" there, for we are indebted to her for many of the comforts we have. I wish I were there to welcome her with my warmest love as a permanent inmate. But I do not feel we'll be interrupted much this winter by the vandals, tho' I fear Hood is not equal to the great emergency. Oh! for Johnston. It is believed here that Sherman is sending large bodies of troops to reinforce the armies that encompass devoted Richmond.

Sheridan, in the Valley, has been largely strengthened from some source, and we are all pained this morning by a reverse to Early; and worst of all, the statement is, he was surprised. Our affairs do wear rather a gloomy look just now, but, by God's blessing, I hope better times are ahead. If Sherman sends much of his strength here, Georgia will be, in a measure, relieved from present pressure. Our Lee is equal to any crisis, if he can be strengthened. The trick of getting up the decisive fight of the campaign, with two of his corps against six of the enemy, cannot be played on Lee, as seems clearly was the case with Hood. I believe it is generally agreed he was maneuvered out of Atlanta, and it is further thought the three of ten days had been employed by the enemy in sending forces to Virginia.

However, it is useless that we should discuss these points now. What are all our people determining to do? Do many propose to leave their homes, or is the intention general to remain and face the worst, hoping to save something from the storm, if it blows over us? I haven't been to Richmond in several days and know of no further progress in my matter. I am needed here for many things, and Major Briely told me 'twas in a secure way and best let it arrange itself. I am trying to bring all my matters to a close. I am more than ever solicitous for a winding up of the affair, as I hope to get a short run home. If so, we can all advise together.

I still have but few days at home and am anxious for you to return with me. I am obliged to stand this separation when an impossibility for us to be together exists, but when all such obstructions are removed, I must have you with me. Six hundred dollars a month will go a long way towards defraying expenses, and we must try to raise what else is needed. I shall surely stand aghast if you demur to coming with me. Indeed, I can't imagine you'd prefer being anywhere else than with me. . . .

Darling, I hope every day to see my shirts arrive. I have but two, and they are all in holes. High as they are, I'll have to purchase some if they don't arrive in a few days. Mine are barely fit to wear. I've sent my hat to Richmond to be done up, and will have it in a day or so, so I can wait about that. I've seen no chance yet to get any government cloth, but hope I may be able to do so. Boxes for soldiers of the Brigade arrive every day by the arrangement with the express and Relief Association. The Culver boys have received two within a week or so. They send them clothing and fill up with as nice ginger and tea cakes as I ever eat. Pickles, etc. in that many boxes can continually come to me. They seem to be sent to the Georgia Relief in Augusta, as there is printed on them Georgia Relief Association, care of E. Saulsberry, 111 Main Street, Richmond; so I presume they are sent to that office in Augusta and freight paid there—money sent in same way. When one gets the hang of it, there is no difficulty.

Waddell sends me word the house I spoke of is taken, and we are to be in possession 1st October. So that die is cast. My own best beloved, how are you this day? I am fearing you are sick. More and more my heart centres on you, as troubles thicken around us. Of all desires on earth, my greatest is to have you near me; with me, dear Sallie, and Bud, and your Mother. You are all together at home this morning and happy. Would I could be with you, and no secret mistrust that the dear union of hearts would again be broken. And there are other absent dear ones we'd quickly add, a world of love and kisses to them all.

Howdye to all the servants. Tell them I continually think of them and wish, for their sakes as well as ours, the enemy may never come near us. Have our hogs in the field as soon as possible, then on ground peas. We want them in the shambles as soon as possible. Love to Father, always.

Sallie, his condition is very lonely. Go and see him often, won't you dearest? Tell Bud to be careful of Gavroche when he is eating (He has no gratitude) and never to be cross with him. He does not readily forget. . . .

It is nearly dark, and I'm a little unwell today. Sammie and Pete are quite well. We have some few chills among us. Kiss our darlings again and again for Papa. Your own Edge

Bob is well and sends love to Nancy and all

Edgeworth Bird to Sallie Bird

Richmond, 18 October 1864

My own Precious Darling, I sent you a short note telling that I had turned over property to Forbes and was no longer on duty with the Brigade. I write today from Richmond. Came in last evening, but shall possibly go out again this evening, as I have many things, of course, to look after in winding up my affairs, but consider myself as belonging here now. The orders about returning detailed men to their companies are very stringent. All have to go who have not a certificate from a Medical Board of Army Surgeons. The intention is to supply their places with disabled or infirm men.

I do not think it will work well altogether. Teamsters should be able-bodied to attend well to the teams and do the heavy, rough work generally before them, but of course it is best to try it. In the present stress of the country, all these men are required, at least that is the verdict of those in command. As I before mentioned, I think the Certificate of Medical Board of Army Surgeons Sam W.[1] now has will be sufficient to retain him in his place. Most sincerely do I hope so, as I do not believe he can long stand the exposure of the trenches and the marches.

My coming away cannot affect his staying or going. It all turns on whether the certificate is still good. I think it is, and then there is no infirm man in the Brigade who can fill his place, because it takes one some time to learn to keep Quartermaster accounts and make out the returns. Pete is already with his company. The others will soon have to go. It is quite a breaking up of old associations and messes that have existed since the war began. At least there are many such.

I have a letter from you since the last pencil note I wrote. In this you speak quite confidently of Mrs. DuBose coming on and messing with you. Dearest, you don't exactly know about the accommodations. There are but three rooms of comfortable size. The only room not occupied is a very small affair and no fireplace, but Miss Yerby[2] told Col. W that she thought a room could be obtained next door, which is almost like the same house. He will see something about it this evening, but I will put in a slip of paper after I hear more about it. You know it would not do to take any step which would affect the rooms of those now in the mess.

There is also a Dr. Hines,[3] medical purveyor to A.N.V., who will be with us and occupy a small near room. He was with the mess before I came in and is a very nice gentleman. You see, it would affect him to take another lady and she have a small room with no fireplace, so without discussing any of these points, which be sure not to do, we probably had best not take another lady, but I am in hopes a room can be had next door, which is the same as being in the house. Will add a slip. You ladies travel faster in your arrangements than men. I don't feel very well or bright today. Do all you think best in the way of preparation.

Love unbounded and kisses to our dear children. Sallie's letter was very nice, she must write quite often, and always when she feels like it and has time. Col. W talks of sending his little brother, about Bud's age,[4] to stay with and go to school with him. That would be more company for your Mother. How would it suit? I am looking to hear from you since I suggested the bringing on Nancy.[5] My direction now is simply, Box 1455, Richmond, Va. All letters that come to me will be kept and sent on to me from my old quarters. [Letter ends here. Page missing.]

1. Samuel H. Wiley.

2. Miss Yerby in Richmond unidentified.

3. Dr. James W. Hines, medical purveyor to the Army of Northern Virginia.

4. Colonel James D. Waddell had a younger brother named Isaac. Hull, *Annals of Athens*, 476.

5. Nancy was the wife of Bob, Edgeworth Bird's body servant.

Sallie Bird to Sallie (Saida) Bird

Richmond, 21 November 1864

My dear, dear Child,

How often, how tenderly, how yearningly my heart has gone back toward you since that morning in the early dim light I kissed and bade you goodbye! And more frequently, if possible, since I reached Richmond and heard the news that our beloved Georgia was likely to be overrun. I feel that you are as safe as you can be anywhere, and that Col. Jones,[1] will call for you, as he does for Eva, in case of immediate danger. Your dear Grandmother is my special anxiety. So hard is it, that in the evening of her noble, well-spent life, she should be harassed by our insulting, brutal enemies.

She and Mrs. Terrell will join forces, and Bud will be her grand guard, grand consoler, precious little friend to both! Our dear little man! Don't *we* love him, daughter? And don't we pray heaven to guard his dear life? For next to Papa, he is our main stay. And that brings me to Papa, our quiet, grave, tender, true Papa! Ah, Sallie, *love him ever.* He is so true, so good, so entirely trusty. And we are to comfort and caress him always.

Our trip on was without serious accident and but slight delay, tho' in all my numerous journeys, I have never travelled in such crowds. From Augusta on, the trains were crowded to overflowing, jammed. We met no acquaintances, but our own party was quite large enough. The *big* trouble of the trip was that *both* Mrs. Waddell's trunks were left in Augusta. By a miserable mistake of the baggage man, the trunks checked through from the Georgia road to the S.C. depot failed to appear, and we did not know it until the last moment.

Then it was too late, or we should have gotten off (horrid word, don't use it) and staid ourselves. But it was too late to get our baggage off and we had to come on. For two hours Mrs. Waddell was in a terrible fix; after that she bore it beautifully. But your Father was greatly troubled. He telegraphed back to Cousin Yancey to ask Capt. Williams[2] to bring them on next day, and I do hope he will appear with them today. Mrs. DuBose wrote back to Mrs. Barrett to get her son Hall to see to it, also.[3]

In Charlotte, I found our friend Mr. Brown[4] of whom you have heard me speak. He promised to do all in his power. I feel very anxious and unhappy about it. I share Mrs. Waddell's, or rather she shares the contents of my trunk.

I have a very pleasant room, a sweet comfortable chair, and with my own nice bedding I do finely. Mrs. Fry is very pleasant. Dr. Fry is extremely so. He is a brother of the General Fry you saw at your Aunt Philo's in Augusta that night.[5] Mrs. Waddell and the Colonel, Dr. and Mrs. Fry, and Dr. Hines, Medical Purveyor of the Army of Northern Virginia, your Father and myself, are the household. It is quiet and agreeable, and I like it as well as I could any home, away from my own. I mean any *army* home.

Edge goes to the office at 10 o'clock and remains until 3, after which time he is free and belongs to *me,* and much do I love and pet him, I assure you. His spirits are still sad. He is always quiet, speaks little, but those dear eyes look love unutterable at me, twenty times a day, slyly or not, as the chance allows. My dear Sallie, you see how I dwell upon papa. Dear, darling papa. You are old enough to appreciate him, and my child, listen and obey. Love your Father supremely. Love him next to your God. He is far worthier than I am.

Just here I had a visit from dear Dr. Moore.[6] He is his own dear self, so warm, so cordial, so very glad to see me. Offers to do anything in his power for me and is as lovable as ever. Asks kindly after you and sends his love to you and Bud. Your Father and I pictured Eva and yourself at her home in Savannah, getting things put away and set up for the winter. We both feel very secure and very thankful that you are with our precious, our well beloved Eva. Kiss the lips I love so well and ask her to cheer me with one of her . . . letters. Bless her heart! I do so fondly love her.

Mrs. DuBose could not get in the same house with us, to our infinite regret, but is boarding quite near us at a Col. Elliott's.[7] Dr. Moore says I'm within a stone's throw of his house. I must go to him often. Says Mrs. Moore will be around as soon as it stops raining. It has rained steadily ever since we came, so of course I have not been out of the house. Col. Waddell praises your letters so warmly that it did me good, and Dr. Fry, who is one of the nicest men I ever met, says that it was the best letter from a girl of your age he ever read, so easy, so well dictated. I tell you this, darling, not to flatter, but to encourage you to persevere. You can make a grand letter writer, I think, if you will practice it. But to do that, you must *read, read, read,* closely, indefatigably. I sense the guidance of my precious Eva and her cultivated, excellent husband. *Study, study,* oh my little one, study. An uncultivated woman is so unlovely.

Never mind your looks, if you are only intellectual, refined and high-bred. Those who love you best always tell you this. Write regularly once a week to Mother, once a week (or oftener) to me, and practice your music faithfully. Papa sends his sweet daughter a kiss and a prayer for her happiness and usefulness. Col. and Mrs. Waddell send you their love and Nancy sends her *best* love, she says. Bob desires to be remembered, too. All are well but Papa. He is not well. I bore the trip wonderfully, tho' it was very fatiguing. My cordial remembrance to Col. Jones. God bless you, dear Daughter, and make you *all* our hearts desire, Your devoted Mother,

S. C. Bird

Mr. Gresham was here for two days. Left with Thomas[8] for Macon and succeeded in getting him transferred to the Engineer Corps in Georgia. Write to Minnie—a nice letter. Papa will write you soon. He says you must write weekly, always.

1. Charles C. Jones, Jr., lawyer and historian, was mayor of Savannah (1860–61) and chief of artillery for the military district of Georgia during the war. After the death of his first wife he married Edgeworth Bird's cousin, Eva Berrien Eve, 29 October 1863. Following the fall of Atlanta in September 1864, young Sallie Bird went to the Jones home in Savannah. Mrs. Mary Baxter, her grandmother, left her Athens home for Granite Farm. When Savannah was evacuated in December, Sallie Bird and Eva Jones fled to Augusta. Myers, *Children of Pride,* 1568.

2. Possibly Thomas C. Williams of Company C, Delony's Troopers, Athens. Stegeman, *These Men She Gave,* 151.

3. Mrs. Barrett and her son were possibly members of the family of Thomas Barrett, listed in the 1860 census as president of the State Bank in Augusta.

4. Not identified.

5. Dr. and Mrs. T. B. I. Fry of Richmond. Dr. Fry was the brother of General Birkett Davenport Fry.

6. Dr. Richard Moore was a prominent Athens physician. Stegeman, *These Men She Gave,* 80, 81, 108, 109.

7. There are several Colonel Elliotts in the list of field officers.

8. Thomas B. Gresham, a private in Company B, Second Battalion, Macon Volunteers, transferred to the Engineer Corps in 1864. *Georgia Roster,* 6:787.

Edgeworth Bird to Wilson Bird

Richmond, Va., 26 November 1864

My dear Father,

I have hesitated about writing you for several days, scarcely knowing if a letter would reach you, fearing that the hated Yankees had already passed our county and held the country between us. But I got a dispatch this morning from Augusta and gather hope that they have not yet reached you. I reached Richmond safely with Sallie, Mrs. Waddell, and Mrs. DuBose in reasonable time, after leaving home without accident on the route, for which we should be thankful, for they are of very frequent occurrence nowadays. In coming out, there was a man killed in a few feet of me. I was first apprised of the advance of Sherman[1] whilst travelling on the road. When I left, there seemed to be no apprehension of such a move.

I think there has been a great mismanagement about our Georgia affairs, and, when Johnston's great intellect was taken from us, their solution became much more difficult. Our subsequent misfortunes have all proven his long sighted sagacity. But it is needless to complain. Our homes will soon be in Yankee hands and at Yankee mercy, so cheerfully as I can, I submit to the necessity. Tho' I know they will sweep me clean, t'is only what a hundred thousand others have suffered. I am very sorry, dear father, you have to undergo the great annoyance of being amongst them.

I hope you will leave until the storm blows over, as you can render no service. You might go over to Aunt Lou's. As for me, I believe I have arrived at that point where I have a heart for every fate. Little Sallie is in Savannah and in safe care, but I have some uneasiness about Bud, who with his Grandma is at my place.[2] Their being there is my greatest assurance that my affairs go on, but on this advance of the enemy, I hope they, too, have left.

I have already told my negro men, that in such case, those of them who wish to go to the Yankees could do so; those who did not must take to the roads and keep out of the way. I shall take much pleasure in hearing from you. Give me an account of all transpiring events. We have no stirring news in the city. Address me as below. God bless you, dear Father, and keep you in health. Sallie joins me in love to you.

Your affectionate son,
Wm. E. Bird
P.O. Box 1455, Richmond

1. Advance columns of Sherman's Twentieth Corps entered Milledgeville, the state capital, Tuesday, 22 Nov., after a cold rain that left icicles hanging from roofs. Sparta was little more than twenty miles away. A few miles farther east Judson Kilpatrick's cavalrymen raided the Shoals on the Ogeechee, burning the mills that Wilson Bird's father had begun there. Bonner, *Milledgeville*, 182–83.

2. Edgeworth and Sallie Bird's daughter Sallie was in Savannah at the home of her Cousin Eva, Mrs. Charles C. Jones, Jr. In December, as Savannah fell to Sherman, they fled to Augusta. Bud, the Birds' son, had gone with his grandmother Mary Baxter from Athens to Granite Farm. Athens was felt to be less secure. Mary Ann Cobb wrote Howell Cobb from Athens earlier (3 Aug.) that Mrs. Baxter had left Athens to visit her sick daughter, Mary Gresham, in Macon. Hearing that there was a raiding party at Sparta and that the road to Macon was cut, she had stopped at a safe place in Columbia County. Coleman, *Athens, 1861–1865*, 98.

Samuel Wiley to Eliza DeWitt Wiley at Mt. Zion

Near Richmond, Va., 26 November 1864[1]

Dear, dear Mother,

I propose to close the week by writing to you. It is Saturday night after supper, and I am sitting at my desk and have a candle. So I thought, as I may be employed tomorrow, I will at least begin a letter to you tonight.

Since I last wrote home, which was to Sallie last Sunday, we have changed our camp. We moved last Wednesday to this camp, where I suppose we will stay for the winter. We consider that we have gone into winter quarters. We are, I suppose, about the same distance from Richmond as our last camp, about 5 miles, and on the Darby-town road—about three quarters of a mile in rear of the line of works occupied by our Brigade. It is a low, flat, and wet spot in winter, but the best to be found, and, by the way, we can make it a passable camp. Water is scarce, though it will soon be abundant.

Wood is the principal object, and with economy from the start, there will be enough to keep us comfortable. Every tent, bunk, and hut will soon have a chimney, which will economise the consumption of wood, and you have no idea how comfortable it is to sit by a fireplace. There are several already in pleasant operation. I would have been sitting by my own fireplace, too, by this time, but I am all alone now. German is out with the wagons all the time, and Whitney went up the country last Tuesday. So I cannot do it by myself—tho' I could have done much towards it, but there are only 3 or 4 axes in our camp, and they have been in constant use.

Ben Culver has been sleeping with me for some time. To-night I went to the hay-stack and brought in a turn to put our blankets on, so I think I will rest better tonight. Last Tuesday night it cleared off and turned very cold and has continued so ever since, though it is moderating now and, I think, will rain tomorrow, as it is now cloudy all over.

To-night the negro teamsters, so long talked of, were sent in to Maj. Davenport[2] to fill the places of the able bodied white drivers. German left this morning with ten wagons to procure forage, so Major D will employ these substitutes in building such houses as are needful, and in cleaning up the woods, etc. He says he will have a chimney to my tent tomorrow. I suppose he will assign some of them to me, and I will superintend my chimney. I would rather let the negroes rest tomorrow, but I suppose I must yield to his plans.

I think, about the time we get fixed, we will have to fall back, for if an assault should be made on our front, the shells would just about reach this point. Every time I have written, lately, I have said "all is quiet." So I have to report now. The long expected fight still hangs fire. It was expected last Thursday morning that it would begin, as our men had orders to be prepared, but it did not. It is rumored again this evening that "Field's Div. is going to Georgia"—an idle rumor tho'—

My dear Mother, I received your kind letter which you intended to send by our good friend Edge, day before yesterday. I have not seen him yet, though he sent Sallie's and Sister's letters out soon after he came, and yesterday I received one from him. They have sent several messages and invitations to me to come in town. . . . I think I will go in next week. They sent out my coat by Capt. Perry who was kind enough to bring it, and I am delighted with it. It is just the very thing. It fits just right and is so nicely lined. But I am afraid Sallie deprived herself for the lining. I also find a nice elegant pair of suspenders in the pocket. I want nothing now. I drew a good pair of shoes the other day—have a good pair of pants—a sound jacket, two pair of socks, etc. I took a good wash and put on clean clothes to-day. (It is beginning to rain now, and as my old tent is leaky, I must put up for tonight and arrange my furniture and move my bedding into the middle of the tent, so as to keep dry tonight. So goodnight, my dear Mother and Pa.)

Sunday morning. My dear Pa and Ma, how I wish I could step in to your room this morning, if you yet have a room—if you yet have a home. It did not rain much last night and is quite pleasant this morning, tho' it is cloudy. I have just finished my breakfast and will resume this before I am put to work. Slept unusually well and am in good health. I am restrained from enjoying my good condition and the comforts I have from constant reflection that you may be stripped of everything—negroes stolen away—stocks and provisions all taken—all your clothing destroyed—your house burned, and you all perhaps turned out without anything and even without a place to put your heads!

All these reflections are caused by the knowledge that Sherman's army is abroad in Middle Georgia, and I am obliged to conclude from his having been near Macon, next near Augusta, that his route must have been through Sparta.[3] There is scarce room or reason to hope that you all have escaped. It is most tantalizing, distressing, saddening. The last we have heard from Sparta was the 16th. Captain Forbes received a letter from his wife. Nothing said about the approach of an invading army. No more allusion to it than yours contained. Every one here is painfully anxious to hear.

We conclude that our homes and property are scathed and plundered and we all imagine the worst. When I think of what may possibly be the situation of my dear, aged and infirm parents, and my dear wife and little innocent children, and other near and dear relatives and friends I chide myself for being a drone; for not doing something active, actual and practical. Here I am in a safe place, behind an army of invincible soldiers, a great part of my time with nothing to do, comfortably clad and enough to eat and a tent to sleep in; what the government does not furnish me is contributed from your strained resources. Every day with you all brings its cares, disquietudes and anxieties. There is no want of industry on your part, and with rigid economy and restricted indulgence in all things for years back, to my knowledge we have only about managed to keep together.

We have not grown rich before the war began and are rapidly going down hill now. What is the cause? I will tell you what I think. It is the presence and expense of an idle, lazy, sickly, deceitful, discontented family of negroes. I believe they have been a sponge to soak up all the substance and increase and profits of a few who have always rendered reluctant, compulsory service. With you, especially, there is always some sick, and all these things go together. The prospect of Billy's[4] going away soon, his work so far behind, so many sick, the demand of the Government for a tenth of what is produced when the negroes do not produce enough to support themselves, and when every article of necessity which is not produced at home commands such a fabulous price; how can I drive the thoughts away and find any comfort in the future?

In the midst of all this state of things, comes the probability of the crowning disaster, viz: Sherman's raiders among you in your house, stealing, plundering, and destroying everything; then burning your house, dear old "Rocky Hill," and my own home, and you all perhaps despoiled of everything, turned out to seek the charity of a district equally impoverished. My only hope is that Sherman's peculiar situation obliged him to be very hurried, and therefore we are not clean stript of everything. I say I often chide myself for occupying such a place of comparative ease and freedom from danger, and I feel impelled to rush to the front, regardless of my "surgeon's certificate" and—well, if I should everything is quiet there and what could I do to avenge your private wrongs and insults?

Oh, that I could resolve myself into a host and throwing myself among them utterly destroy them from the face of the earth. Indeed, I would disregard my privilege of remaining in the rear, rouse and shake off my frailty, and assume the strength and will of a defender of our dear and sacred rights, but for the remonstration of S. and you all. I am not well pleased, anyhow, as I once was. Pat is gone. Edge is gone; the Culvers are always away. Capt. Perry, whom I liked very much, is transferred. Capt. Forbes is trying to get an assignment somewhere. Quartermasters and their attaches are subjects of universal criticism and disrepute. Selfishness, blasphemy, obscene conversations, gluttonous and beastly indulgence in disreputable and sinful practices which I witness, make me shudder, and long and pray for restoration to the pure precincts of our own humble and dear circle.

As in the day preceding the flood, God saw that the wickedness of men was great in the earth; so it seems to me it is now. O, how long must it continue! To-day, dear Parents, I suppose is the day that Mr. Pitzer[5] would have preached in Mt. Zion. But he has told you goodbye, and then you may not be in a condition to assemble, even to worship! I am so anxious to hear the fate of you all, and our neighborhood particulars. Your allusion to the last communion surely touched me! The coincidence made it the more solemn to you. I thank God I have not yet lost my interest for the welfare of our church in dear old Mt. Zion and I am thankful that I, an unworthy member and officer, was remembered on that day. Give my love to Uncle Beman. Does he come over to see you sometimes? You ask me how I like the new major. I have not had much to do with him yet. He is a very stirring man, a great blower, mighty fussy; is about to assume charge of things now. Is busy today directing these negroes in building some stables. I am troubled about Billy. Where has he decided to go? I suppose you have seen Pete,[6] and he will soon have to return.

Well, I reckon I have about written enough. I will say here that I discover that my shirts are getting ragged. Those colored osnaburg two shirts—have worn them a long time. The wristbands and collars only are wearing out. I wish I had two more just like these—thick and strong and smooth flat felled seams. I need no socks. Drawers getting thin, tho' I believe they will hang together this winter. The under clothes issued to the troops are very badly made and of sleazy, thin homespun. I would rather S would make them at her leisure—in 2 or 3 months from this will do. I doubt whether this letter will go directly to you. Communication, I reckon, is interrupted.

I wrote to Cousin George[7] about in time to miss a safe transit. Give my love to Sister Mary when you write. Give my love to Uncle John,[8] too—to sisters and brothers and to all the children. Also to Hal and Cousin Bell.[9] My kindest regards to your good neighbors and friends in Mt. Zion and Sparta. My grateful remembrance to Mrs. Terrell and to Col. Johnston for their kindnesses. Howdy to the causes of all our woes. You will let Sallie see this, my dear Parents, as I will not write her today. I must now say goodbye. May our God preserve and bless you and yet bring you to joy.

Most affectionately your son,
Samuel H. Wiley

1. This letter is in the Samuel H. Wiley Papers, Southern Historical Collection, Library of the University of North Carolina at Chapel Hill.

2. Major A. H. Davenport, quartermaster, Benning's Brigade.

3. Some of Sherman's men swept within a few miles of Sparta to the west; Kilpatrick's raiders hit the Ogeechee River to the east, but none reached Sparta. Samuel Wiley's fears about his parents' home were unfounded as troops did not raid the Mt. Zion area.

4. Billy was Samuel Wiley's oldest son.

5. Alex Pitzer, Presbyterian minister, preached at Mt. Zion and Sparta.

6. Samuel P. Harris.

7. Cousin George is unidentified.

8. John DeWitt.

9. Hal and Bell Beman were Henry D. Beman, son of Carlisle P. Beman of Mt. Zion, and Henry's wife Isabella.

Edgeworth Bird to Sallie (Saida) Bird in Savannah

Richmond, Va., 30 November 1864

Mama has written you, dearest daughter, more than once, and I have written Grandma and Bud. Did so immediately on arriving here, to try and give some directions in regard to our little worldly plunder. Several days after leaving home, I noticed for the first time Sherman's advance, which, you remember, was totally unlooked for when we left. Mr. Rhodes and Bud are our only representatives to arrange for hiding away in any manner what little of valuables we have that are moveable—and Grandma, whose wisdom and ingenuity are by no means to be underrated. I have no doubt the hated swarm of Yankees have passed over us, and our loved home has been partly stripped and desolated.

We have news of fighting on Buffalo Creek[1] and at Sandersville, and one speculation was that the separate columns would unite at Sparta. It is certain that they moved from Milledgeville, and seemed to be aiming at some points between Augusta and Savannah. All of these assumed facts assure me that our immediate section lay in their route, and we can scarcely hope that Granite Farm has escaped, tho' snugly hid away from the highways. Mama is very much depressed, but bears it more bravely than you would imagine. I cannot but congratulate myself on having her with me and removed from the scenes of excitement that are transpiring at home. She can hold up under a great deal here, but would scarcely be able to witness the destruction of the place on which she has so liberally lavished both care and affection.

I am very much disturbed about Grandma, and Bud, and Father on account of the terrible anxieties to which they have been subjected, tho' I have no uneasiness whatever on account of their personal safety. I am quite sure the two former did not remain at the farm. Presume they united forces with Mrs. Terrell and tried to sustain each other. Doesn't it seem almost impossible for you to realize that a Yankee army has passed our quiet county! And how do I feel about you, young Missy? Quite comfortable and no disquiet whatever. I have an assurance that you are in the best of hands, that dear Cousin Eva will share with you the kind care she will be sure to receive. You are a lucky lassie to be under such loving, kindly shelter in such boisterous weather. Remember that. So try to occupy a modest corner and deserve the love of these dear, kind friends.

Your letter to Mama came day before yesterday. . . . I think you are right about Miss Jenny Bryan.[2] She is so cordial in manner, and intelligent. You musn't have Cousin Eva's sayso alone about Col. Jones's good opinion of you. Your own assurance of deserving it will be your better test. I will give you a wee suggestion that will help you gain the goodwill of others. Keep out of rocking chairs, then you won't loll ungracefully, or acquire lazy attitudes, and in forgetfulness you won't sway yourself to and fro' till all around are nervous. And when you haven't a rocker and are obliged to sit still, the inability to be in perpetual motion won't make you stiff and ill at ease. I don't say you have this habit, but young people often have, and you may avoid it.

I am very willing, my daughter, for Cousin Eva to make you a good Catholic. I feel my loneliness in that regard, tho' I have the most perfect assurance that my faith is right. I don't think Mama would weep bitter tears over such honest convictions on your part. She is as sweet as she can be in all ways. I have this item in my creed, that God will arrange us all for our good, if we act our parts according to our most sincere convictions of right. Under some circumstances, we are dismayed at the full Glare of truth, and the bravest heart quails with indecision. I think the path to safety and happiness lies in a diligent search after Truth, and the honest acting our convictions.

Does Bud write to you? I hope you will keep up a regular correspondence, the Yankees permitting. I feared at one time they were making for Savannah. Now the impression here is they will pass direct across to Beaufort, S.C.[3] I think the management of affairs in Georgia has been wretched. Since the removal of Johnston, the preponderance of brains has been terribly against us. If our people could have arranged to hang a mammoth bell around Sherman's neck, they might have divined his movements.

It is to be hoped Hood is having a good time in Tennessee. Sherman surely is in Georgia. The former fairly proposed the exchange, and the latter chose—when he got ready. The only unfair thing about it was that he should have kept our head men in such blessed, benighted ignorance. But what avails it to clamor! At last we must accept the situation. Mama is quite well and joining Papa in boundless oceans of love to our darling child. Out of this great abundance, please dip enough for a great shower bath. Place Cousin Eva underneath and pull the string.

My kindest regards to Col. Jones and ask him please to keep you out of rocking chairs. Remember me to Miss Jennie Bryan. Nancy and Bob are well. All quiet here, but a movement on Grant's part looked for quite soon. Col. Waddell sends love and says he will write you this week. Mama will tell you about our mess arrangements. Write me often, my dear child. Try and be all Papa wishes you to be and be very, very obedient and affectionate to those dear friends. Your own Papa,

Wm. Edge Bird

1. Eliza Frances Andrews of Washington, Ga., crossed Hancock County in mid-December trying to reach her relatives in southwest Georgia. The rail ended at Mayfield and she went by "four-mule" wagon from Sparta to Gordon at a cost of $75. "About three miles from Sparta," she wrote, "we struck the 'burnt country' as it is well named by the natives and then I could better understand the wrath and desperation of these poor people. I almost felt as if I should like to hang a yankee myself. There was hardly a fence left standing all the way from Sparta to Gordon. The fields were trampled down and the road was lined with the carcasses of horses, hogs and cattle that the invaders, unable either to consume or to carry away with them, had wantonly shot down to starve out the people and prevent them from making their crops. The stench in some places was unbearable. . . . The dwellings that were standing all showed signs of pillage and on every plantation we saw the charred remains of the gin-house and the packing-screw, while here and there, lone chimney stacks, 'Sherman's Sentinels,' told of homes laid in ashes. . . . Hay ricks and fodder stands were demolished, corn cribs were empty, and every bale of cotton that could be found was burnt by the savages. . . . I saw no grain of any sort and there was not even a chicken left in the country to eat . . . crowds of soldiers were tramping over the road in both directions." Eliza Frances Andrews, *The War-Time Journal of a Georgia Girl* (Macon, Ga., 1960), 32–33.

2. Unidentified.

3. Most Georgians thought Sherman was headed for Augusta. By the time Edgeworth Bird wrote this letter, Savannah was a more obvious target.

Mary Baxter to Sallie Bird

Granite Farm [undated, possibly December 1864]

My dear Sarah,

Yesterday my eyes and heart were gladdened by the return of my dear child. When he came, I was at the flower garden; he ran out to me, and for the first time since the harassments of this raid commenced, I broke down. I hugged him, kissed him, and sobbed over him till I expect he thought I was crazy.[1] He is well and says he had a fine time. He wrote you on the bank of the Savannah River, he said. I hope you got it and my two long letters, one eight pages, the other four, giving you some account of things that have taken place in this county and other counties. They got Dr. Green's mules[2] and cut up carriages in many places. They got [illegible], and one of the men asked Beck for some water. She handed it to him and said, "My Bible tells me if our enemy thirst, give him drink."[3] They said, "We are not your enemy." She pointed to the destruction and they said, "to put down rebellion."

Mrs. Whitehead came to see me yesterday morning, but promised her mother to go back. Her mother said she would be uneasy about her. She has promised to come and spend the day and night with me. She says Mr. Bird and Soullard[4] has had a dispute about fattening the hogs he got from Mr. B. Mrs. Soullard told her of it, but they have patched it up. Mr. B has not sent the mule home yet, no work going on. People are afraid to put their horses and mules [out]. Laws on the other side of old Mr. Bonds place had his mules ploughing in wheat and they took them from the plough. A negro came to Sparta to tell it, and some men went out to see about it.

These are our own men stealing horses. Here, they don't seek out them for government purposes, but they are afoot and want horses to keep out of the way of Yankees. I heard Henry[5] say he saw 13 in Sparta wanting horses, but no one troubled themselves to mount them, for they did not believe they wished to go into service. I feel now I have a friend, since my dear Wilson has got home. I live in a state of alarm all the time. The negroes came in and told me they [Yankees] were in Athens, and so this morning Arthur said a negro man told him they were in Athens on the way to Mayfield. But Mrs. Whitehead told me yesterday there were none nearer than Louisville, at last account. We can't get reliable news. They caught those at Tom Turner's[6] and sent them off, chained, in the hack to Mayfield, thence to Augusta.

The terrible freeze we had, Mrs. Whitehead thinks, has killed many rose bushes. Some of your euonymus is as brown as fodder. The freeze only lasted three days. Now I am writing by an open window, no fire in the house. Vilet cooks. Sam is in camp. Arthur has made the cart wheel, every spoke in it new. It broke down. . . . I am so glad to have my dear boy back with me. He was at no expence, except to get a tin cup, while he was gone. I will leave it for him to tell of his travels. While they were in Columbia County, Col. Fulton[7] came to their camp and brought them sugar and coffee. I don't know what else. Mr. Yancey[8] sent Wilson word to come to him. Sam[9] says, if Mas Edge will trust him with the keys, he will take better care of his interests, better than Rhodes. He asks me to write this.

Rhodes asked me, a day or two since, if I thought it was worthwhile to try to make a crop. I told him I would work till the Yankees destroyed everything. I believe he is afraid of them. I told him I thought much could be accomplished by uniform treatment, and constantly being with the negroes, and planning well. I told him I was not much acquainted with plantation life, farming not at all, [but] that I knew negroes ought to have their overseer with them all the time. He always says, *just so, Mrs. Baxter.* Sam says I must tell you he has had his mares and colts out now 11 days, that they are all in fine condition. Up to this day, Rhodes has not been to the lower field that I know of. The cavalry [illegible] men rode through there. Isaac left the fence down. He and John just [line illegible]. I sent March, Peter, and Isaac there and told them not to quit till they got every place secure for our hogs. They have just come in and report no hogs in the field and they put up every place that looked weak.

I fear finances will be very high in this county. I have received 63 dollars for 14 pounds of butter the two weeks you have been gone. Tomorrow is my day to send it to Mrs. Sledge.[10] I send seven pounds a week at $4.50 per pound. I will do the best I can for your interest. Mrs. Whitehead brought her basket yesterday and wanted butter. I told her I had none to spare. Mrs. Sledge will take all I can send her all the winter. Mrs. Whitehead wants to engage hams and lard from you. I think I will tell her she can have the pork and cure it herself, but that is as you say. I have had no application for pork, but no one appears to think of getting anything now. . . .

The negroes send howdy. They are all well. Wesley cut his leg. I have been dosing that. It was inflamed and swollen; it is better today. I think he has made all the shoes except Aunt Sally's and Dinah's. He is working on them today. He has not made Vilet's or Candace's yet. . . . Mr. Bird has just sent the mule home. I think I will send you a piece from my paper. Tis a mistake about the mills not being burned. There are many of them. Latimer's[11] is safe, as I wrote you in a former letter. The enemy in Milledgeville committed outrages on ladies, tho' I only know of Mrs. James Nickels,[12] poor thing. She is again out to the asylum. Mrs. Whitehead did not recollect the names of others. How the Yankees missed this place I cannot tell, as they were so numerous 8 miles each side of this. [Remainder of letter is missing.]

1. Mrs. Baxter's "dear child" was her grandson, Wilson (Bud) Bird, then fourteen.

2. Dr. William H. Green. Discharged from the fighting in Virginia because of disability, he had gone to serve with state troops near Atlanta at Lovejoy when Sherman's men raided his Hancock County plantation.

3. "Beck," as Mrs. Baxter called her, was Dr. Green's wife, Rebecca Sasnett Green. Mrs. Green wrote an interesting account of the raid at her place where troops burned her ginhouse, the whole crop of cotton, the seed of the prior crop, the carriage house, wagon shelters, and every carriage, buggy, and wagon. "Men and horses seemed to rise out of the ground," she wrote. "Not a panel of the yard fence was left intact. In their search for gold and silver and other valuables they did not leave an article of furniture untouched. Bedding was stripped off and thrown on the floor; every lock on doors, closets or wardrobes was broken and the doors smashed with the butts of guns; every bureau drawer was thrown on the floor, contents strewn in every direction." An officer from Kentucky rescued the trunks of her children's clothes being thrown about the place. He told her he would never have joined the Union army if he had "thought to see women and children treated as he had seen them." Smith, *History of Hancock County*, 1:61–62.

4. Wilson Bird, Edgeworth Bird's fa-

ther, and Edward Soullard, Jr., Savannah businessman and native of Hancock County, who had bought Wilson Bird's Sparta house as a place of refuge.

5. Henry, servant at Granite Farm and Sallie Bird's carriage driver.

6. Thomas Mickleberry Turner, Hancock planter, had 872 acres and 35 slaves according to the 1856 Hancock County tax digest. His town house in Sparta was opposite that of Wilson Bird.

7. Not identified.

8. Benjamin Yancey of Athens.

9. Sam was Edgeworth Bird's first body servant who came home from the fighting in Virginia because of ill health.

10. Possibly the wife of James A. Sledge, editor of the Athens *Banner.* Sledge was an unusual Georgia editor, defending Jefferson Davis against Governor Joseph E. Brown. Coleman, *Confederate Athens*, 145–46.

11. A grist mill named Latimer's was in the district near Granite Farm.

12. Mrs. Nichols, the wife of Captain James H. Nichols, was raped by two Union soldiers at her home near Milledgeville; she eventually died in a mental institution. Captain of an elite group, the Governor's Horse Guards, Nichols served in Virginia where General "Jeb" Stuart said he was too gallant in the line to be appointed to staff duty. Bonner, *Milledgeville*, 172, 190.

Sallie (Saida) Bird to Sallie Bird

[Augusta, December 1864]

. . . in a buggy for wagons to carry the rest of the party over that night.[1] Well, Mrs. Kirkland, her three children, her two cousins, Willie and Pearson Hardee (Mrs. K was Miss Hardee, niece of the general[2]) and Cousin Eva and I all crowded into a wagon and rode over to Col. [illegible]'s camp. There I met Alva Connell[3] quite unexpectedly. [A largely illegible sentence tells about going in an ambulance to Pocataligo,[4] getting there at three in the morning.]

I cannot tell you the horrors and discomforts of that ride. Suffice it to say, we were [illegible] in the roughest old ambulance imaginable, within a heap with a little of our large quantity of baggage. I, with Mrs. Kirkland's two oldest children, one five and the other four, both very fat and [illegible], asleep upon me. That was the only part of the journey I really minded, but I tell you it wore me out. When the ride was over we went in the cars at P[ocataligo] and slept until daylight, all very much fatigued, consequently entirely unmindful of the unpleasant stiff seats we used for benches.

I woke up very much refreshed the next morning, tho' Cousin E and Mrs. K did not. At nine, the rest of the party came up and we started for Charleston. Got there at five in the morning (Tuesday). Spent Tuesday night in the ticket office at the Augusta depot and came on here Wednesday. I never expected to take such a trip and I hope never to take such another and tho' I had a very funny time—enjoyed the adventures. I was positively sorry we came on so soon from the Coosawhatchie,[5] tho' Cousin Eva and Mrs. K seemed quite glad they got away in time.

The poor women and children who stood waiting the arrival of General Beauregard's[6] waggons had a gay time. They say about eleven o'clock the enemy (whose batteries were planted only five hundred yards on one side from the track, while our fortifications were not quite so far on the other) turned to find that a train was standing a little distance down the road, for they changed the direction of their guns, and the shells fell thick and fast all around. The train ran back to Hardeeville,[7] and the passengers, who were expecting the wagons every minute, got down in the ditches for protection, while the rain fell heavily. They did not connect up with them until nine that night. From this, you will see the Georgians are beginning to feel, in no slight degree, the sufferings of the Virginians and others.

However, we are safer now in Augusta, so I can enjoy laughing it all over with Cousin Eva and Sallie, but I can tell you it wasn't so pleasant at the time. And now, what am I to do? Cousin Eva tells me to ask you this question. Cousin C's glorious library is gone, and we have no books.[8] Cousin Eva says I must stay here and study, as well as I can. She can't devote near so much of her time to me. She is busy all the while, and besides, no one thinks we will be here very long without yankees. Many are going to Athens for safety. Aunt Philo[9] is very sweet and kind and seems to take my staying here as a matter of course. Nothing has been said on the subject except Cousin Eva's remark that I must do as well as I could, for all her books were gone. Still, I do not like to take up my abode here without some arrangement [several illegible words]. Of course I shall be perfectly satisfied with whatever you decide on, but you know poor Aunt Philo, I imagine, is very much put upon in this way. Her house is always so full.

Don't think for a minute she thinks anything of the kind, for that would be a great mistake. She is as kind and affectionate to me as she could possibly be, and I love her dearly. I sent you a telegram yesterday stating my arrival in Augusta, etc. Please write me your plans. Cousin Eva thinks if I am here for any time I had better have French and music teachers. I am agreeable to anything. I wonder if Grandma will go back to Athens and if the Institute will be opened. Aunt Philo says the Lucy Cobb[10] is immensely puffed up now.

I wish the yankees were in the Hellespont, I was going to say, but that is not far enough away. (Our precious Cousin Eva and I have been reading of Leander.) I was having such a happy, happy time in Savannah and was getting devoted to the place. I had begun to know so many nice people and had so many delightful books. Cousin Eva was such a darling, and Cousin Charlie so nice, though such a tease. Everything was so pleasantly arranged, and now everything is broken up. Cousin Eva says she consoles herself with the thought that they can't do her much more harm. [Conclusion of letter is missing.]

1. The first part of this letter is missing. The letter was written at the end of 1864 from Augusta, Ga., where Saida Bird and her cousin Eva Jones took refuge after Savannah fell. Saida and her cousin fled into South Carolina and eventually to Augusta.

2. Lieutenant General William Joseph Hardee (1815–1873), a native of Savannah, served with distinction in the Mexican War and was commandant at West Point when he resigned to join the Confederacy. He became commander of the Department of South Carolina, Georgia and Florida in October 1864 and escaped from Savannah with his troops prior to Sherman's taking it. Jones, *Georgia in the War*, 83.

3. Alva Connel(l) served in Company B, Terrell Light Artillery, which was organized by Dr. William Terrell's son-in-law Edgar Dawson. Connel married Jane Baxter of Cornucopia plantation, Hancock County. Smith, *History of Hancock County*, 1:137, 175.

4. Pocataligo, a town between Hardeeville and Charleston on the Charleston–Savannah road.

5. Coosawhatchie, river and town between Hardeeville and Pocataligo.

6. General P. G. T. Beauregard was assigned to the Carolinas the last months of the war.

7. Hardeeville, a town near Savannah on the South Carolina side of the Savannah River.

8. "Eva and her cousin, Miss Bird, left Savannah the Sabbath before the evacuation upon a few hours' notice, taking only their trunks with them and all the servants. Library and everything else was left behind, and Eva has heard that the house is occupied by Yankee officers." Mary S. Mallard to Susan M. Cumming, 10 Feb. 1865. Myers, *Children of Pride*, 1249.

9. Aunt Philo was Philoclea Edgeworth Eve, the daughter of Dr. John Aloysius Casey.

10. Lucy Cobb Institute, a school for girls.

SIX

The War Ends

"There is wonderful power and recuperative energy in the South yet, if only wise counsels prevail."

EDGEWORTH BIRD

The war was rapidly coming to an end. Wilmington, North Carolina, the last Confederate port, fell in January 1865. When Confederate Vice-President Alexander H. Stephens led a peace commission through the lines in late January, the soldiers on both sides applauded, but the peace effort was abortive. By early April Richmond was evacuated, followed quickly by Lee's surrender, Lincoln's assassination, and Joe Johnston's capitulation in North Carolina.

Sallie and Edgeworth Bird were back home at Granite Farm as the Georgia spring unfolded. The house was full of guests; Nancy was cooking "delightfully," and Saida was with her grandmother in Athens, attending Lucy Cobb Institute. The family's energies were concentrated on clothing Saida fashionably for the May dance. Union troops finally appeared in peaceful Athens 4 May. Edgeworth traveled to Augusta 20 May to surrender and be paroled. For the Birds of Granite Farm, the war was over. Unlike many of their fellow Southerners, the fortunate Birds were neither hungry nor homeless.

Edgeworth Bird to Sallie (Saida) Bird

Richmond, 7 January 1865

I am at a loss how to direct you, my precious child, but shall send it to Athens, care of B. C. Yancey. Your Mother and I have concluded it was best for you to get to your books as soon as might be, and thinking Cousin Sarah and Caro would take you in charge for a while, she has already written for you to go up there and begin your studies with Miss Lipscomb,[1] who we think is in charge of the Institute. Your Grandma will probably be in Athens before very long, and you can enter on the pleasant life with her.

We are both greatly disappointed that the pleasant and very improving management with Cousin Eva has been broken up, but first and foremost is the great sorrow we feel for Col. Jones and Eva on account of their great losses and the breaking up of their home. Already are we deeply indebted to them for their care of you, and if possible the measure would have been greatly increased. Mama and I both received great pleasure from your letters in which improvement was clearly perceptible. I love you, if possible, more than ever, dear Sallie, that you show so much desire to cultivate the talents God has given you and to fit yourself to fill well any station in life. Go determinedly to work in Athens and apply yourself to make hay while the sun shines, for we know not when the next interruption may come.

If means are left me, you shall have every advantage. Our affairs look rather gloomy, but I hope yet for a favourable turn in our fortunes. There is wonderful power and recuperative energy in the South yet, if only wise counsels prevail. I do not think our resources have been used to the best advantage, but it is useless to discuss the past, except to draw from it wisdom for the future. I much fear the good people of Savannah are yet to have a hard time, tho' for a selfish purpose our enemies now encourage and make fair weather for them. I am sorry Miss Jennie Bryan had to remain in their clutches and I presume Mrs. Law[2] remained also and, as her means are rather limited, she may have to undergo privation.

I see by the papers, Judge Wayne[3] of the supreme bench of the United States, a native and resident of Savannah, applied for leave to visit his home as soon as the city fell and was refused. The papers and people here are quite indignant at the resolutions passed by a meeting of some of the citizens of Savannah in which they propose to let bygones be bygones and bury the past.[4] Of course this is unconditional submission and reconstruction. I don't think the people of any state in the Confederacy have shown themselves equal to the Virginians. Their spirit is still unbroken, and their patriotism, under the greatest trials, beyond praise.

You heard of our losses. They amounted to quite a large sum, but your Grandma did admirably and showed a wonderful fortitude. There are few such women, and I shall always love her very, very dearly. If she takes up housekeeping in the spring in Athens, she must supply herself with meat and lard from our smokehouse. She saved it in the panic and had it killed and cured in the smoke house, and she is entitled to all she needs of it. . . . If this finds you in Athens with Cousin Sarah, give her and Caro my warm love. . . . Tell Cousin Ben I won't trouble him with you very long, and you are going to be such a good girl, you won't be much in the way.

Your letter by Mrs. Cone[5] only reached us yesterday. I am glad you liked the sisters at the convent and like "Papa's religion." I trust you may learn to like it still better; nothing gives me greater pleasure than to hear you express yourself as you do. Mama and myself are both well and long to clasp you and dear Bud to our hearts. My daughter, we live in evil times. Cultivate truth and purity of character. Keep away from the idle gaieties of the day. You are too young to mingle in them and should improve all you can. No late news from Uncle Richard. Love to Miss

Kate and all friends. Write me very often. I love to get your letters. Ever your loving Father, William E. Bird

1. Sarah A. Lipscomb, who was associated with the Lucy Cobb Institute.

2. Possibly Alethea Jones Stark, third wife of Judge William Law. Sherman wrote his wife from Savannah on Christmas day 1864, "There are many fine families in this city, but when I ask for old and familiar names, it marks the sad havoc of war—the Goodwins, Teffts, Cuylers, Habershams, Laws, etc., etc., all gone or in poverty, and yet the girls remain, bright and haughty and proud as ever." Mills Lane, ed., *Marching Through Georgia: William T. Sherman's Personal Narrative of His March Through Georgia* (New York, 1978), 186.

3. Judge James Moore Wayne, a native of Savannah, was associate justice of the U.S. Supreme Court (1835–67). He had earlier been a congressman, a judge, and mayor of Savannah. Despite his ties to Georgia, he remained loyal to the Union and served on the bench in Washington until his death. His son, Henry Constantine Wayne, was a Confederate officer. Jones, *Children of Pride*, 1718.

4. Savannah citizens, at a meeting called by Mayor R. D. Arnold, passed a resolution praising Sherman for placing General John W. Geary as "military commander of this post." They spoke of Geary's "urbanity as a gentleman and his uniform kindness to our citizens" and urged that he be kept in his post there. The resolution appeared in the Savannah *Republican* less than a week after the city was occupied. It was reprinted in the New York *Times*, 5 Jan. 1865. Randall and Donald, *The Civil War and Reconstruction*, 432.

5. Not identified.

Sallie Bird to Sarah Hamilton Yancey in Athens

Richmond, Va., 8 Jan. 1865

Dear Cousin Sarah,[1]

An officer who leaves for Georgia tomorrow offers to mail letters for me in that state, and as the mail is so very slow and so very uncertain, I avail myself of his kindness. I write to beg a favor of you. Edge and I both hope that you will receive and take care of Sallie until Mother returns to Athens, which will be in a few weeks. I am certainly anxious for her to be at school as steadily as possible, and as she is broken up in Savannah, I prefer placing her with Miss Lipscomb, in whom I have all confidence, provided you will receive her on any terms until Mother comes.

She can attend school with Mamie Lou, and you and dear Caro will look after her health, physical and mental, for a little while. Won't you, dear Cousin? I feel encouraged to ask this of you, because you so kindly offered to take Sallie for a few days once before. This is for a longer time, but I think (and most people say) Sallie is a good child and will not be much trouble. Tell Caro she will, I know, relieve you of the care a great deal, not only for her Cousin Edge's sake and mine, but to assist in making Sallie as good as Caro herself. I don't think Sallie will be troublesome, and yet I realize fully that it is an additional care for you; and therefore, my dear Cousin, shall most gratefully appreciate it. I wrote to Sallie and to Eva Jones of our wishes, and requested Sallie to write you immediately on the subject. . . . I suppose the Lucy Cobb will open soon, if it has not already done so.

Richmond is full of people, and suffering, and crime. One can hear anything here. I steadily decline all invitations into the *beau monde,* not caring to get into the vortex of fashionable society. I am here to see my dear husband. He does not go out at all save to his office, and I have him from 4 P.M. until 9 next morning. He is not very well, but is, I think, better than when I came on. Our mess consists of Mrs. DuBose, Mrs. Waddell, and myself, and our lords, with Dr. Fry (brother to General Fry of Augusta) and Dr. Hines, Medical Purveyor of the Army of Northern Virginia. Mrs. DuBose is just now on a visit to her husband at the front. General DuBose, General Longstreet, and General Kershaw[2] have their wives there now.

We live as economically as our appetites will allow, and yet expenses are frightful. Yet Confederate money has this virtue. It enables us to be near our husbands for a while. I spent one evening with Mrs. Stanard and breakfasted with her one morning, and one would not suspect scarcity from her superbly spread "dejeuner." I have accepted no other invitations, save to one old friend's. In fact, I didn't bring my best clothes, so I have a good excuse.

Tell Caro an extremely fashionable trimming for skirts of dresses is a tiny box plaited frill about one inch wide, sewed at the bottom of the skirt, either of the same or some contrasting color. Plain waists are trimmed. (The latest tip—Mrs. Davis[3] gave Mrs. Stanard the pattern from a Paris dress with velvet laid on in curious blocks. A peculiarity being that there is a block on the back just below the collar. It is very striking and pretty.) Prices are anything the fancy suggests, from $800 for an ordinary doll baby to $1,800 for a cloth coat!

Blessed are they who want nothing! There has been and is still considerable depresssion here, and yet people have dances and weddings, and bands serenade (delightfully, too), and ladies dress and walk the streets as if there was no war. Only the soldiers, the full hospitals, and the wails of the bereaved tell us constantly of this dreadful war.

Mr. Stephens[4] comes to see us frequently and promises to tell me when I must go. If the road at Branchville is cut, I may have trouble in getting home. Tell Caro we all blessed our knight, Capt. W, for the arrival of the trunks. Mrs. DuBose and I felt sure that the telegram to her was the plan, for we thought Capt. W would do anything to oblige her. Mrs. Waddell was very grateful. So were Edge and I. They, the trunks, reached here about ten days after we did.

Edge joins me in sincere love to Cousin Ben and yourself and Caro, also Ham and Mamie Lou.

Kiss Mamie Lou for me.

Hoping to hear from you soon that you will receive, for a while, my poor little girl, who is so eager to be at school. I am most sincerely yours,

Sallie C. Bird
Box 1455, Richmond

1. Sarah Hamilton Yancey, wife of Benjamin C. Yancey. Letter in the Benjamin C. Yancey Papers, Southern Historical Collection, Library of the University of North Carolina at Chapel Hill.

2. Major General Joseph Brevard Kershaw soon opened the attack at Cedar Creek during the final phase of the siege of Richmond. He was captured at Saylor's Creek, 6 April 1865, a few days before Lee's surrender at Appomattox. *Biographical Dictionary of the Confederacy,* 272–73.

3. Varina Howell, wife of Confederate President Jefferson Davis.

4. Alexander H. Stephens, vice-president of the Confederacy.

Edgeworth Bird to Wilson Bird

Richmond, Va., 17 January 1865

My dear Father, Some days ago I received a dispatch from Augusta, from Sallie, stating that you were ill and desired to see me. It did not convey to me the idea that you were dangerously ill, but still caused me the greatest anxiety, and I dispatched immediately to Cousin Philo for particulars, but the telegraph wires were down, and no communication existing between this place and Augusta. The avenue of travel was also broken up by the washing away of several bridges, and I cannot learn if yet open.

Yesterday, Mrs. Baxter's[1] letter came, written the day before the message was sent to Augusta, and from it I gathered fresh courage about you, as Alfriend did not consider you in any danger, and the severe cold from which you were suffering would have to develop worse symptoms before you would be in danger. As I wrote you in a former letter, the fine habits of life you've always led have so much contributed to preserve your constitution, that I had no fears about you from an ordinary attack, and I trust this letter will find you quite restored.

I am rejoiced, dear Father, that you have again taken up your residence with us, and I pray you may be long spared to enjoy the quiet of life in your old age. I've never felt satisfied that you should live elsewhere than with me, since you parted with your own home. Now you must make yourself comfortable and feel as if at your own home. I know you've received every attention that could be rendered under the circumstances, from Mrs. Baxter, who has proved herself one of the noblest and kindest of friends to me and mine. I can never sufficiently love and thank her. Bud, too, is one of the best and most attentive of nurses for one of his years, and his heart is full of affection and love. So I feel you've been as kindly cared for as could well be, unless Sallie and myself were at home.

The affairs of our country are in rather a gloomy condition and there is a general tone of depression. The country seems to have lost confidence in the ability of the chief magistrate, and all sorts of opinions are afloat as to what is best to be done. I think Mr. Stephens has indicated a wiser policy during the whole war than anyone else, and had his course been followed our situation would now be different, but they have always been rejected and are still.

He is here now, and I shall be sorry to hear that he has left. I think there are quite a number of congressmen who take counsel with him. The fall of Fort Fisher has just been announced, and the port of Wilmington is closed against us.[2] An immense quantity of food and clothing for the Army came through that port. Well, it is not worth one's while to bemoan past misfortunes, but hope for the future. I can't now see the way and the manner, but I trust a change for the better will soon come. Anything is better for us than to submit to Yankee rule. That people are determined upon our ruin and will carry it out if in their power.

From all I learn, Rhodes[3] has acted badly. He had no right to complain at my not wishing to keep him, for the understanding has ever been that either of us could withdraw at any time. It was not for my interest to keep him on and pay the wages he received. Under present circumstances and the uncertainty of the times, I could not calculate to make even a support on the plantation, but if I agreed to do so, would have to support and feed him and his family anyhow.

Please give my best love to Mrs. Baxter and to my darling boy. Dearest love and kisses to Sallie, if she is at home. Howdy to all the negroes. As soon as you are able, write me. If I knew you were dangerously ill, I would make every effort to reach you, if allowed to do so. Earnestly trusting you have recovered from your illness, Sallie heartily joins me in warmest love. Ever your affectionate son, William E. Bird.

1. Mary Baxter, Sallie Bird's mother.

2. A large Federal fleet began bombarding Fort Fisher on 13 Jan. 1865. Two days later the Union flag flew over the fort and Wilmington, the last port of the Confederacy, was closed.

3. George F. Rhodes, the overseer.

Sallie Bird to Sallie (Saida) Bird

Richmond, 20 January 1865

My precious Child,

After your various and even alarming adventures, I am indeed rejoiced to believe that you are once more quietly at school in dear Athens, the beloved home of my early life. I feel such confidence in Miss Lipscomb that I rejoice to have you under her care and entreat that you'll not lose a moment of time, knowing how precious every hour now is. Let pleasure be a secondary thing and knowledge your first aim. Dear, darling Eva! I feel so grateful to her and to Cousin Philo for their unvarying kindness to you, and now your dear Cousin Sarah, and Caro, and all are, I know, as sweet as possible to you.

Indeed, with all the trials this war brings, we have much to be grateful for, and chief among our blessings I rank friends. It is a very great pleasure to your Father and me to feel that you are never cast among strangers, but always among loving and kind relatives. Thank Mamie Lou and Caro for their kind letter to you. It did us good, and we are glad you enclosed it. Do assure them of my earnest, grateful appreciation of their readiness to receive you. Tell Cousin Sarah that I sincerely value her kindness and I am sure Caro will keep a watchful eye upon you and Mamie Lou.

I send this letter by Sam Wiley, who I am most happy to say, has a furlough at last. It is true it is short, but it is better than none, especially when we remember that his mother is in so low a state.[1] I pray she may recover, for when she passes away there will be few left like her. If you've been home, you've heard all the home news. I was very glad to hear your Grandpa expressed such a desire to see you. Poor old man! He finds, at last, that there are none so true and faithful to him as his *good* child's family. Yes, indeed your precious Father has been a model son. I, who know him best, say so unhesitatingly. He is a *good* son, and isn't he a precious Father, my daughter? Who could more tenderly love and desire all purity and excellence for a child than he does? Love him as much as you can—that can *never* be too much.

And how much are you going to love me? I can never be satisfied with any but an eager, heartfelt love—such as I know my children do give me. And, ah, what does *not* a child owe a mother? I hope Miss Lipscomb will bring you on rapidly, but always remember, darling, that more depends on the pupil than the teacher. Do your part faithfully and well. I think Cousin Philo's suggestion about your trunk going to Athens was very wise. You'd not stay long at home, because your school would open soon; I presume on the 15th of this month. Write me all the news of the town that you think would interest me—and that is all—for I do dearly love Athens.

How are our dear friends, the Ruckers?[2] And why didn't Kate answer my letter? And did they ever get the two muslins I asked them to buy for me? And how is dear Ann Hull?[3] I've thought of her very often and hoped she was more cheerful. Do give her my love and tell her Mrs. Felix Alexander[4] is very kind to me, and I think her very sweet and lovable. I go to see her oftener than anyone in Richmond. Mrs. DuBose is down at the front with the General. She spent the day with us yesterday; was as bright as ever. I am so sorry when she leaves.

Mrs. Dorsey,[5] poor child, has lost much of her life and vivacity. She is still very sweet, and I love her. She is in one of the Departments; is absent from 9 till 3 every day. The four years of her married life have been the four years of war and are fraught with events. She is only about 22 now, the age when she might *think* of marriage. She had a fearful illness, typhoid fever, which kept her prostrate for three months, and from which she has never entirely rallied. But her voice is still very sweet and her singing is a treat.

She is going to tea at Senator Semmes's to meet Capt. Raphael Semmes of the *Alabama* tonight.[6] She declares she has "nothing to wear," which is nearer the truth than in Flora McFlimsey's case,[7] for these Marylanders are more and more cut off from home and from their friends, and hence she felt obliged to accept a place in one of the Departments. She is anxious to see her little darling once more, as she calls Wilson.

Every one here who knew my boy in 1862 wants to see him here again. Everybody loved him, and indeed he deserved it. The little man has his hands full as overseer, waiting on Grandpa, and being Mother's chief comforter. We feel deeply grateful to my dear Mother for remaining with Bud, after his Grandpa was taken ill. It seemed hard for him to bear all the cares alone. The future is dark, dark, yet I do not despair. I will stay here a while longer; shall certainly try to come home before Sherman cuts the road at Branchville, which, of course, he means to do. But will remain with your Father as long as I can, as both of us are miserable at the very thought of separation so soon again.

But I shall go home in the spring, at all events, perhaps sooner. You must, none of you, be uneasy about me. I am in good hands. If cut off from you, will manage somehow to get thro'. Give my love to our friends the Hugers, always. Go to see Mrs. Hunter[8] if she sees company and give mine and your Father's love to her. Our love to all Cousin Ben's family. I hope you'll preserve your good character and prove a pleasure, rather than a trouble, to our friends. Goodbye, darling. A thousand prayers and good wishes follow you from your Mother's heart. Your own devoted Mother S.C.B.

1. Mrs. Edwin Wiley (Eliza DeWitt) died in 1865 and was buried in the churchyard at Mt. Zion Presbyterian Church, Hancock County.

2. The Ruckers of Athens were descendants of Joseph Rucker (1788–1864), who was a highly successful banker and planter and the founder of the village of Ruckersville in Elbert County. His granddaughter Kate married Sallie Bird's brother Richard Baxter at the end of the war. *Dictionary of Georgia Biography,* 2:856–57.

3. Ann Hull, the former Ann Thomas, wife of Henry Hull, Jr. See Hull, *Annals of Athens*, 482.

4. Mrs. Felix Alexander was Lucy Grattan, daughter of Peachy Grattan of Richmond, Va., before her marriage to William Felix Alexander of Washington, Ga. Alexander was the brother of Brigadier General Edward Porter Alexander of the Confederate army. William Felix Alexander's first wife was Lou Toombs, daughter of Robert Toombs. Marion Alexander Boggs, ed., *The Alexander Letters, 1787–1900* (Athens, Ga., 1980), 3, 184, 261, 383.

5. There were two officers named Dorsey from Maryland in the Confederate army: Ed R. Dorsey, major and lieutenant colonel, First Maryland Infantry, and Gustavus W. Dorsey, lieutenant colonel, First Maryland Cavalry. *List of Field Officers*, 38.

6. Thomas J. Semmes represented Louisiana in the Confederate Senate. Raphael Semmes, a native of Maryland, resigned from the U.S. Navy when the war broke out. He became a rear admiral in the Confederate navy following his daring attacks on U.S. ships as captain of the

Sumter and later the *Alabama*. Toward the end of the war he was assigned to the Confederate fleet in the James River.

7. Not identified.

8. Mrs. Hunter in Athens was possibly Mrs. J. H. Hunter, whose husband attended the first Athens meeting about secession in December 1860. John Hunter was in the Troup Artillery. Stegeman, *These Men She Gave*, 144, 147.

Edgeworth Bird to Sallie (Saida) Bird

Richmond, Va., 30 January 1865

My letters seem fated not to reach you, dearest daughter, so I open one Mama has just sent down and add a half sheet, hoping for better luck in company with hers. I wrote you a long letter to Savannah and again to Athens in advance of your going. It seems you've received neither. I think I also wrote to Augusta. Well, quite a topsy-turvy has occurred in your status for the winter, since we last saw each other. I very much regret the pleasant and instructive Savannah arrangement has been disturbed. Your improvement was already apparent in the short time that passed, and you probably [would] have made such lifelong friends of those dear relatives, however I trust this is already so.

There was another acquaintance you were making, I would like for you to have cultivated, [that] of those good convent ladies. You would have had an opportunity to look at Papa's side of religious matters. But still, at last, we are all favoured that you are again so well situated. Make the best of your opportunities and try to win the love of your good kinfolk. I know Caro will love you and train you up in the way you should walk, as did your Cousin Eva. Tell Cousin Sarah, I say please to have you under her entire control, and to advise and direct you in all these things, as she does Mamie Lou. It will not do for a wayward missie like yourself to be left at full liberty.

From what Mama says, I have great confidence in the mental training you'll receive under Miss Lipscomb. We hear often from Bud and Grandma. They are faithful correspondents. I am sorry you did not go by to see your Grandpa when he was so sick. You owe him love and duty as your Papa's Father and must not fail to render him a full share. Write a nice long letter now and then to him; tell him of your studies, general surroundings, etc. Do this, my precious child, without fail, because Papa wishes it, than whom no one loves you better. He is near towards eighty years of age, almost alone in life, and needs the love and sympathy of his children. It is our sacred duty to render it.

Mama tells you most of the news here. The greatest excitement exists on account of the going to Washington of Mr. Stephens, Senator Hunter and Judge Campbell as quasi peace commissioners.[1] They go in consequence of something that has passed between Mr. Davis and Mr. Blair,[2] but are not yet regularly authorized. I hardly know whether or not to hope for much good to come out of their going. General Lee is to be made Secretary of War.[3] These changes and the peace talk have produced a better feeling here, and there is less depression than a few weeks since.

Give a great deal of love to Caro, and Cousin Sarah, and Ben, if he be at home, and to Mamie Lou and Ham. Some two weeks since, Col. Waddell had a letter from Richard. He was quite well. His letter was dated Dec. 3rd 1864. Had Miss Kate heard of it? Or perhaps she's had something later. Give her my kindest love. Col. Waddell says you must write him again; that probably his letter may reach you after a while. I have several to come to you. Correspond regularly with Bud. I long to see you, my darling child, and love you with my whole heart. Write me often. Lay frolicking aside for the present and study hard. Nancy and Bob are well. Nancy shows the greatest interest whenever a letter comes from you. Ever yours, lovingly,

Wm. E. Bird, Box 1455

1. Vice-President Alexander H. Stephens, Judge J. A. Campbell, and Senator R. M. T. Hunter went to the Federal lines Jan. 29 and on to Hampton Roads. Their unofficial meeting with President Lincoln ended in disappointment.

2. Francis Preston Blair, politician and journalist, was a native of Virginia and former editor of the Washington *Globe*. He had supported John C. Frémont and then Lincoln. After Lincoln's reelection, Blair persuaded him that Blair's friendship with Confederate leaders might help bring peace. He went to Richmond with Lin-

coln's blessing and conferred with Jefferson Davis, setting up the futile Hampton Roads Conference.

3. Lee was appointed general-in-chief 6 Feb. 1865.

Sallie Bird to Sallie (Saida) Bird

Richmond, 5 February 1865

My dear Daughter,

Mr. Oscar Scott of Mt. Zion has just called to say that he will leave in a few hours for Georgia and kindly offers to take letters for us. I've written a long letter to Bud and now begin one to you. I must write very hurriedly, for I am expecting him to call every moment. I've received only one letter from you since you reached Athens. You must find time to write me at least every fifth or sixth day. You gave no details whatsoever in that letter. I wished to know under whose care you went to Athens, etc. I am sure your Aunt Philo and Cousin Eva would see to your escort being proper.

Lt. Lofton,[1] a very nice fellow, returned from Georgia yesterday. He told Mr. John Waddel,[2] who returned also, that you were under his care from Thompson [Thomson] to Lexington. How was that? I hope you are studying faithfully and eagerly. I have every confidence in Miss Lipscomb and a great deal in your own desire to learn. Let me be convinced that your mind is bent upon the acquisition of knowledge. I wrote you several days ago a long letter and hope you received it. I wrote also by Mr. Waddel when he went South, and several other letters by private chance. Your Father has also sent you several letters. Some days since, your Father received a long, sweet yet sad letter from Eva. I grieve to hear that the terrors of the times are telling upon her, and that her health is failing. She writes that she is wasting to a shadow.

Ah, poor child, the loss of her lovely library alone is irreplaceable and Col. Jones's losses otherwise were heavy. When I see and hear the misery occasioned all over the land, my heart shudders and bleeds. What next? Heaven knows. Messers Stephens, Hunter and Campbell returned to the city with nothing done. Lincoln and Seward, it is said, met them at Fortress Monroe, and they decided at once that nothing could be agreed upon. So there remains only the alternatives, war to the bitter end or subjection. Of course, our people are equally resolved not to submit, and so this cruel, this interminable, this ferocious war goes on. More hearts are to wail, more blood [is to] be shed, and the end is beyond the reach of mortal ken. Everyone sees the fact and braces himself for the danger.

I wrote you to go to see Mrs. Henry Hull and always give her my love. I also told you to go to see Ann Linton,[3] if you had a chance. I don't care for you to walk out there, unless you had a good opportunity with married or steady people. Tell dear Caro I hope she'll keep a friendly eye upon you. I feel so grateful that I cannot express myself, for all the goodness shewn you. You must shew yourself equally so. Write your Cousin Eva every now and then. Write lovingly and affectionately and always assure her of your gratitude. Eva wrote Edge that you promised to write her, but she had not heard then. Her letter was dated 19th of January, and you left on the 11th. Don't fail to shew yourself grateful to these precious friends. . . .

God bless you, dear daughter. I am now compelled to close my letter, for Mr. Scott has called. . . . Take care of your clothes. Remember that injunction, old but important. Don't fail to read your Bible regularly, my child. I should feel very miserably if I did not believe you always attend to your prayers and your Bible. Write to your brother sometimes and love him tenderly. You can never love him too well. He is your own, only brother, and a darling. I want you to be faithfully devoted to each other always, and when I am gone, I want you to cling to each other closer than life . . . and be sure to be devoted to Mother, my good blessed Mother. Write her often, be affectionate and kind. Our best love to dear Cousin Sarah, Caro, and all the family. Be good and thoughtful for them. Shew yourself appreciative of their kindness. . . . Your ever devoted Mother, S.C.B.

1. James H. Lofton of Elbert County was at one time a lieutenant in Company C, Fifteenth Regiment, but he resigned early. *Georgia Roster,* 2:427.

2. John O. Waddell, brother of Colonel James D. Waddell.

3. The wife of Dr. John S. Linton.

Sallie Bird to Sallie (Saida) Bird

Granite Farm, 22 April 1865[1]

My dear Daughter,

I have your May party dress and other things ready to send you, but in the present state of excitement about the Yankees, I am advised not to send it by express. If your Father cannot go up and see you, I'll send them by Bud, as it will not do to risk them, save by special hand. I send you a beautiful pair of slippers for that occasion, but Sallie, I insist upon it, they are to be worn only on that occasion or a similar one, never to be walked in or danced in. You can get no more such. Lucy Alexander[2] has made some lovely little rosettes for them which you must tack on securely. She has also made you some pretty bows for your neck and one for the waist. The bow is to be worn a little to one side, not in front of the waist.

Engage Mrs. Clark[3] to make your May party waist and sleeves; the skirt is made. The narrow edging is for the neck. The broader piece, as I wrote in my other letter, is for the bottoms of the sleeves to be made frilled into a band, low neck and short sleeves. Your muslin dress, I have concluded to cut and baste myself. You can get Mrs. Clark to finish it for you, fitting it nicely. Tell her to make the calico high neck and long sleeved, in some pretty style. I enclose you a copy of the verses Mrs. DuBose[4] has kindly written for your address. She says she will not be hurt if you reject them, as they were written in a few minutes, when she was very unwell and in great trouble, fearing the approach of the Yankees and dreading Charlie's having to go into service.

But yesterday Mrs. Johnston spent the day here. Mrs. Whitehead and Soullard[5] called. Lula Lawton was here and our own circle, Major and Mrs. Alexander, Mr. and Mrs. Shepherd,[6] and all. I read it aloud and it was pronounced beautiful. Mr. Johnston[7] begged off. Said he was utterly unable. Mrs. DuBose also declined writing for the queen. Said she thought her address should be in prose and begged me to do it. I feel quite unequal to the task, so I have just sent a note to Mrs. D. urging her to write either prose or poetry for Mamie Lou. If she does it, I'll include a copy in a day or two. I have the most exquisite copy of your address, copied by Mrs. Shepherd. Mr. Johnston said I must tell you he wrote it. It is really a chef d'oeuvre.

I wish I could see your party. You must write me the fullest particulars. Mrs. Clark can make your waist and finish your dress off in part of a day. I know I could, and she is as smart in that line as I am. Thank your dear good Coz Sarah for her kindness to you. I love her dearly for it; so do we all. Kiss her for me, and darling Mamie Lou, also. Tell her I know she'll make a sweet queen. Love to dear Caro, if she is at home; also love to Delia.[8] All send love to Cousin Ben. My dear daughter, we all long to see you. Be good and dutiful. Be amiable and kind to all. I am glad you love Mamie Lou so dearly. I know she is worthy.

Walton and Lucy[9] came over and staid a day and night with Lula Lawton. They all slept in your room, the boys on the dining room floor, the Shepherds in the billiard room, the Alexanders in the front room. Last night I had a soldier additionally. Nancy is cooking delightfully. Lula has gone back to the Soullards. She enjoyed her visit very much and said she would like so much to come back. I'll send for her again some time. Walton says she received your letter and longs to see you and hear you talk. Take pains with all your letters. . . .

Your devoted Mother, S.C.B.

We were told the Yankees were at Jack Smith's[10] last night, so our stock is all hid out. The Armistice is filling all hearts now. I am thankful for a cessation of hostilities, even for a while. I hope things can be honorably settled.

1. Richmond was evacuated 2 April 1865. The Birds returned to Granite Farm before that time.

2. Lucy Alexander was Sallie Bird's friend from Richmond, Lucy Grattan, who married Major William Felix Alexander of Washington, Ga.

3. Mrs. Martha L. Clark, Athens dressmaker, listed in the 1860 census.

4. Catherine Ann (Kate) Richards DuBose was the wife of Charles W. DuBose, Sparta attorney. A prolific writer, she was published in national magazines. Her brothers, Thomas Addison Richards and William Carey Richards, achieved national distinction as artists and authors. They collaborated in producing Georgia's most elaborate antebellum magazine, *Orion,* and a handsome volume entitled *Georgia Illustrated* (1842), engravings of Georgia scenes done by Thomas Addison Richards. *Dictionary of Georgia Biography,*

2:838–40. The DuBose home in Sparta still stood in excellent condition in 1988, a favorite subject for books on Georgia architecture. See Linley, *Architecture of Middle Georgia*, 95–96.

5. Mrs. Richard Malcolm Johnston, Mrs. Charles Whitehead (Julia Burnet), Mrs. Edward Soullard, Jr. (Cornelia Ann Smith).

6. Lula Lawton (b. 9 June 1849) was the daughter of Sarah Gilbert Alexander and General Alexander Robert Lawton of Savannah, who was quartermaster general of the Confederacy and later United States minister to Austria (1887–89). *The Alexander Letters*, 377. Others mentioned were Major William Felix Alexander and his wife Lucy; Mr. and Mrs. Shepherd were possibly Mr. and Mrs. William S. Shepherd of Columbus.

7. Richard Malcolm Johnston, the author and educator.

8. Delia Jordan, who later married Eugene Burnet.

9. Walton and Lucy, daughters of Richard Malcolm Johnston.

10. Captain Theophilus Jackson Smith of Glen Mary plantation.

Edgeworth Bird to Sallie (Saida) Bird in Athens

Granite Farm, 26 April 1865

My darling Child,

Bud goes to you tomorrow to take your dresses and other "fixins," and tho' I've been lying on the couch all day and suffering a good deal, I try to send a word of assurance and warmest love. I am very anxious to hold you to my heart once more, but I am entirely unable to leave home at this time; had proposed to run up and see you for a few days, but you must accept Bud as my substitute and send me, through him, love and kisses.

Mean time, make good use of your time. Don't let fun and jollity interfere with your books. Give a great deal of love to all our cousins and assure them of our loving gratitude for their kind care of you.

Your Grandma will soon be in A[thens], I think. At present I think she [illegible] enacts the prisoner programme. I hope the dear old lady will be paroled soon. What a mine of startling events has been sprung upon us in the last fortnight.[1] The impression seems to be gaining ground that the war is over. A short time will develop all. Kiss Caro for me. I had so many pieces of baggage to look after at Camack [Camak] the day we met, I had only time to see her for a moment.

Goodby, precious daughter, Kiss the "Queen"[2] for me.

Your own loving Father,
William E. Bird

1. Lee surrendered at Appomattox 9 April 1865. Lincoln was assassinated 14 April. Joseph E. Johnston surrendered to Sherman in North Carolina 26 April. Within a week Athens had its first invasion. Mrs. P. H. Mell, then a student at Lucy Cobb Institute, wrote: "The Federal troops came to Athens Thursday, 4 May 1865. They came without a note of warning. We were at school; Miss Lipscomb was called hurriedly from the room about ten o'clock. Of course we suspected something wrong, and rushed to the windows, although this was forbidden, and to our utter horror saw the street in front of the Lucy Cobb Institute full of bluecoats. I will never forget my terror. Miss Lipscomb came in very quietly and with no emotion (but with a very pale face) she dismissed the school. She arranged us in bands for our mutual protection and sent us home." Hull, *Annals of Athens*, 300–301.

2. Mamie Lou Yancey was to be queen at the Lucy Cobb Institute festival.

Sallie Bird to Sallie (Saida) Bird

Granite Farm, Sunday, 21 May 1865

My dear Sallie,

John[1] arrived safely day before yesterday, Friday, to dinner, and it gave us great pleasure to see him and hear directly from you. That very day your Father had gone to Augusta to get his parole, and we are expecting him home today.[2] Mother, most unfortunately, has been sick ever since the evening he arrived, with severely disordered bowels. She is in bed and no better today, but as soon as the medicine acts, I hope she will be well. It is nothing serious. John is, of course, a very great comfort. Mother sends best love to you and to all at Cousin Ben's, and her thanks to them for their kind care of her beloved boy.

Thank Caro for her sweet note. I sent the other to Julia Whitehead immediately. Poor Julia! Her spirits are entirely gone. She is totally inconsolable. Every one says I must do my best for her, as they think I have more influence than anyone else. She was here just one week ago, and I found it impossible to cheer her. The loss of our cause affects us all deeply, but she is sorrowing bitterly over the loss of property. Poor thing! She sees other refugees returning to their homes and she has no home to go to.

I am very sorry for her. She tells me the sunshine is hateful, the flowers are dark, the birds don't sing save to pain her—in fact that she cares for nothing, hopes for nothing more on earth, and feels an interest only in two or three friends. Let Caro read this and tell her to write often and cheerfully to her aunt Jule. I seriously think, as do all her friends, that she needs cheerful society and some change. I urge her warmly, and so does Edge, to come down and stay some with us, but she only sighs heavily and shakes her head and only comes to call. Is unwilling to create any of that old feeling. I am so very anxious about her. I fear her health will give way.

I was as much disappointed as you were at your not getting my letter by Mr. Jordan.[3] I wrote it late at night after hearing he was going out, and sent it up very early in the morning. But the train leaves Mayfield at 8 a.m., and that made him leave Sparta so much earlier that my letter was too late. I had it mailed, however, and sent it on to you and hoped you received it. I hope our mails will soon be regularly reestablished.

I am very sorry to hear that the Hugers[4] are going off. That is a great break in our pleasant refugee society. It will be hard to give up these warm friends. Upon consideration, you had better not shew this letter, but tell Caro to write often and cheerfully to Mrs. Whitehead. She is deeply depressed. Mother and John will be going up soon. I'll try and let you know what day they'll come, if the mails are passing. I wish dear Richard[5] would come, bless his heart.

Do give my warm love to all the Ruckers and other friends, and a double quantity to the dear Yanceys. I couldn't thank them sufficiently for their kindness to you. Allen[6] is making you a nice pair of calf skin boots. Major Alexander gives you the French calf skin for them. I fear your beautiful balmorals are lost. It is strange Mrs. DuBose[7] does not send me word, if they were. I am so thankful dear General Toombs[8] is safe, or I hope he is. Everybody sends love to you. I long to see you and shall watch eagerly for your coming. God bless you, daughter.

Your devoted Mother, S.C.B.

Mother says Caro gets sweeter. Is just one of the salt of the earth. Kiss Cousins Sarah, Caro and M. Lou for me.

1. John Baxter, Sallie's brother.

2. Edgeworth Bird surrendered and was paroled at Augusta, Ga., 20 May 1865.

3. Probably Sylvester Franklin Jordan, father of Delia and Gunby Jordan.

4. The Hugers of New Orleans had been refugees in Athens. Mrs. Meta Huger and her daughter Emma were among them.

5. Richard Baxter, a prisoner of war, was in the last squad to leave Rock Island, Ill., prison. He must have reached Athens soon afterward; he married Kate Rucker there 9 August 1865.

6. One of the former slaves at Granite Farm.

7. Sallie DuBose, daughter of Senator Robert Toombs of Washington, Ga. She married her cousin Dudley McIver DuBose of Memphis, who later practiced law in Augusta and during the war was colonel in the Georgia regiment in which Edgeworth Bird served. DuBose was made brigadier general in November 1864, was captured at Sayler's Creek, Va., 6 April 1865, and was not released until late that summer. He returned to Washington, Ga., to practice law; his wife died there 27 Oct. 1866.

8. Robert Toombs made his way from Washington, Ga., to Florida and on to Paris via Cuba. His escape route led through Hancock County, where Colonel Andrew Jackson Lane and Edgeworth Bird were among those who helped him. Toombs and his wife lived in Paris for some months. He returned home in 1867. Pleasant A. Stovall, *Robert Toombs* (New York, 1892), 298–99.

SEVEN

Saida's School Days

"Be frank and pleasant to all. This is due to all your school mates but your deep affections are your own to bestow—be very careful they are properly placed."

EDGEWORTH BIRD

Much to the delight of her father, Saida Bird was enrolled at the Academy of the Visitation in Georgetown in September 1866. Edgeworth Bird was reminded once again of his school days at Georgetown College and his friends and teachers there. Granite Farm no longer produced the generous sustenance it provided before the war. Most of the forty slaves had gone, some to Liberia. However, Sallie Bird's Uncle Leroy Wiley had saved some of his fortune from the shipwreck of the war and offered to pay his great-niece's expenses.

The one great tension in the loving lives of Sallie and Edgeworth Bird was religion. She was a devout Presbyterian, devoted to the "simple faith" of her fathers. Edgeworth Bird, baptized by Georgia's first Catholic bishop and reared in the faith by a Catholic mother, found the puritanism of the Protestants distressing and the doctrine thin. This tension surfaced again as Saida entered a Catholic school. Her mother warned her about being taken with the "bridal veils" of the nuns. Her father expressed his delight that she was in their care. Her absence from Granite Farm brought a flood of letters that told of life at home immediately after the war.

Sallie Bird to Sallie (Saida) Bird

Columbus, [Georgia] 5 February 1866

Your letter gave me heartfelt pleasure, my dear child, altho' it contained the news of Caroline's[1] departure. I am so comfortably situated and surrounded by such well trained servants that it seems hard to realize the discomforts of a menage so entirely upset and changed as ours. I'll realize it fully and plainly enough when I return to it. I try not to think of it while away. You must bear the burden of housekeeping bravely, daughter. Shrink from no duty and be cheerful about all. Take care of everything and be sure to remember the keys. As for your washing, perhaps you have secured Caroline's services weekly. If you have, tell your Father I would not employ any other servant regularly. Until he rallies a little more from the poverty into which the war left us, I think we had better do with those we have.

Captain Fontaine[2] came to see me last night with four young cousins, all nice girls: Callie Hargraves, Betty Shorter, Annie Meigs and Lou Stewart. Callie has a very pretty, sweet face, and Betty has a very bright face. They are all nice girls, and Annie and Emma love them very much. We have quantities of nice things to eat. Last night Hermie[3] had a waiter with pineapple cake and dried figs brought us. Tomorrow I expect to go to Lucy Alexander's if the weather will permit. It rains today a little and snows ever so little, so that I don't know whether I'll be able to go. But it is the first cold or disagreeable weather we've had. The days have all been bright and beautiful, until this. We have rode and walked and shopped, etc., every day.

I have not been to Lucy A's yet. We have had so much company and so many calls. Emma Seabrook[4] and I drove by there one day to see her, but she was out. We were all to have spent an evening there this week, but her baby was sick from vaccination, and Lucy has been sick almost ever since she came. She seems quite well yesterday and today, and I hope will not be sick again. It was the result of fatigue, I think. I sent your Father six pages of this paper the other day, besides a shorter letter on my arrival. This is my third letter from Columbus, which does pretty well, I think, as I've only been here one week tomorrow night. I hope you all have treated me as well. I was so glad to get your letter. I hope daily for more and trust I shall get one from my dearest darling today. Tell him, with a loving kiss, that I think of him constantly, of his pain in his side, and pray for his recovery.

Edgar Dawson suffered from asthma all night. He looks better than he did in the fall, but is still very delicate in appearance. Hermie and Emma seem to be the only robust ones of the family. Dear Hermie is so sweet, so kind, so brave, bless her heart. She will not let me speak of a day for going and vows I shall not go to Lucy A's tomorrow. I have not found your music yet. The assortment is very poor, but the man expects more soon. Tell Papa I am reading *Barren Honour* by the author of *Guy Livingstone*[5] and so far like it very much, but I have but very little time to read.

Lucy Alexander has two lovely presents for you: a sultana veil, one of those long, black, spotted ones, entirely woven here; and a blue velvet bandeau for your hair, lovely; and a steel pin. Isn't she good and thoughtful? She has a present for Bud, too. Tell him, with my loving kisses, that I've bought one box of glazed collars for him and shall get him some more. There are some imitations of Marseilles (Willie Hill[6] has some), which the ladies say are beautiful. I'll get some when I go to that store.

Congratulate me! I have a superb gold thimble ($12) marked "Bird." Oh, I am so glad about it. I got it out of the money Mother sent, so I consider it a present from her. I've got a very fine and beautiful hat for Edge, black, soft and fine. Can't get the sort of one I wanted for Bud. Terrell[7] has one, very pretty, but the number for Wilson is exhausted. I tried for a 6-7/8. Is that his number? I can find one in Macon, if I don't here. I am afraid I can't get a coat for my two males. The assortment here is selling at reduced prices, but is strictly winter. I wanted something lighter for spring. They are selling off to make way for their spring goods, but prices are awful, $60 to $65 for coat and pants, even now. I mean for a nice article. That was what I was in search of. I've had your breast pin mended and some other things for you.

Do sit down and write Lucy Alexander a nice letter, a real nice letter. I know you can compose it, if you'll only try to write it nicely. Hermie Hill says she is so sorry I did not bring you. So was Maggie Flewellyn.[8] Tell Papa Captain Bartow came and spoke to me in the street the other day. He and Albert Lamar,[9] (clerk of the House in Richmond).

With devoted love,

Your Mother S.C.B.

another kiss to Edge and Wilson and yourself from your entirely devoted S

1. Caroline, a servant at Granite Farm.

2. Captain Theophilus S. Fontaine served with Company G, Twentieth Regiment, from 15 July 1861 until he surrendered at Appomattox. *Georgia Roster,* 2:810. His brother Benjamin was a captain in the Third Georgia Cavalry. They were sons of John Fontaine, the first mayor of Columbus, Ga.

3. Hermie was Hermella Hill, wife of Joseph B. Hill of Columbus.

4. Emma Seabrook. Not listed in the 1860 census.

5. George Alfred Lawrence (1827–1876), English novelist, published the first novel *Guy Livingstone* anonymously. It was followed by others, including *Barren Honour.*

6. Willie Hill was William D. Hill, son of Joseph B. and Hermella Hill, according to the 1860 census.

7. William Terrell Dawson, son of Lucy Terrell and Edgar Dawson, was named for his grandfather, Dr. William Terrell of Sparta.

8. Margaret Crawford Flewellyn, daughter of Joel Crawford and niece of Mrs. William Terrell.

9. Albert Lamar was a resident of Columbus, Ga., at the time of the 1860 census.

Edgeworth Bird to Sallie Bird

Granite Farm, 8 February 1866

Today brought us quite a budget of news from you, my darling, a long letter for Sallie and one for myself, all safely delivered by Henry Cook.[1]

Bud took us quite by surprise as it was not mail day and none of us expecting, hence the greater enjoyment. . . . I am very glad you are having so good a time and hope to see you come back to me brightened and refreshed. Have a dim idea I am "powerful" good to spare you so long a time.

Candour, however, compels me to state that my visionary organ completed quite a dilation at the cool announcement that after the 20th you might turn an inquiring look in this direction. Well, we are rather dullish hereaways, but try to be goodnatured and unenvious. We wish you and Mrs. Lucy[2] a marvelously good time and shall only be too glad to get you back atall. Meantime, our hearts grow warmer towards the good friends who spread such good cheer to you. . . .

Your description of the good time is perfectly harassing. We hardly believe it over here, but lips moisten and palates drip at the possibility of its truth. Had just finished a dish of middling and turnip greens when Bud handed your letters. Had they come ten minutes sooner, said dish of turnips, etc., would have been consigned to the poultry yard. . . . But still we have some pleasant resources among ourselves. Minnie[3] and Sallie are bright and cheerful through the day, and at night we get up a gala time over Caesar's Commentary. Lou's[4] rolls won't rise, but then our spirits do, which does as well. Our nerves are not stirred by the startling crack of champagne corks, our digestion not pained by jelly cakes, lobsters *et id omne genus*.

Au contraire, the life-giving, jolly "goodie, goodie" of the yellow bourbon quickens the pulse and lightens the heart. The stomach soothing jowl and turnip give strength and vigour, whilst an easy conscience lulls to slumber, sound and sweet. So we are not so bad off, are we? . . . I am glad you met Shepherd and Fontaine.[5] There were no two nicer men in the Brigade. Please remember me to them. Tell Fontaine, when he comes to see his brother, to make my house his home. Please remember me to General Benning,[6] should you chance to meet him. I have a lasting admiration for very many of his qualities and very much regret he couldn't get his crust of bread at Milledgeville, but he was too honest and straightforward to ever learn the knack of the loaves and fishes.

We have no washerwoman yet. Tomorrow I put Mandy at it. She has washed some for Lizzie Harris. Arthur[7] tried all over town today. There is a young woman formerly belonging to Austin Berry, yclept Malvina, brought up at such things, who desires to come here. I am to see her. We are all well. It is very late. No further news from the white men. Lou sends Rabun in to say, tell Miss Sallie howdye. Rabun "jines his hand" in. Please say lots for me to Mrs. Hill, Lucy A and Mrs. Fluellen. Bring your Lucy back with you. Willie and Joe Hill and George Fontaine[8] quite well. I went over and took the rabbit hunt with them. No news. "All quiet on the Ogeechee." Ever affectionately,

Wm. E. B.

1. Henry Cook does not appear in the 1860 Hancock County census.

2. Lucy Terrell Dawson. The other Lucy mentioned in the letter is Lucy Alexander.

3. Minnie Gresham, Sallie Bird's niece from Macon.

4. Lou, servant at Granite Farm.

5. W. S. Shepherd and Theophilus S. Fontaine. Shepherd was a captain in Semmes Guards, Benning's Brigade, and later a lieutenant colonel in the Second Georgia Regiment.

6. General Henry Lewis Benning of Columbus, in whose brigade Edgeworth Bird served at times. Impoverished by war, he returned to Columbus and reopened his law practice.

7. Arthur, like Lou and Rabun, was a former slave at Granite Farm.

8. Willie and Joe Hill and George Fontaine were students at Rockby, Richard Malcolm Johnston's school for boys.

Edgeworth Bird to Sallie (Saida) Bird

Granite Farm, 2 September 1866

Dearest Daughter,

Just thirteen days have passed since you left us, and not yet have we become accustomed to the absences. Mama groans and sighs for your companionship so much that I'm quite jealous. . . . Verily you're a wee mite to cause so large a void in our little household. Mama does take it heavily and wearily and computes the days in a twelve-month. But, though you know she belongs to a heathen tribe and does not fully embrace the great extent of your good Fortune in being under the care of those dear, good ladies,[1] . . . her confidence is very great. I am more of a philosopher about the matter.

You know it would never do for the daughter of your intelligent Mother to remain always an ignorant little puss, and the good Uncle[2] was so princely in his kind offering t'would never have done to reject it. . . . You had to go somewhere, and since you are gone into such excellent hands and will be so tenderly cared for in sickness and health, in mental and moral training, why—well, to be candid, I'm obliged to say I'm glad you're gone. I am sure you will be delighted with the school and soon dearly love those kind ladies. . . .

So, why should I grieve! Should I not rejoice? I'm sure I do that you are gone to meet your opportunity . . . I am sure you will avail yourself of it. . . . We pursue the even tenor of our way. Bud daily to his school and his nap after supper. Mama sighs and weeps a little, does her usual share of laughing and talking, makes her "Grover and Baker"[3] rattle a good deal, consults "Downing"[4] with renewed pertinacity and, with busy thought, plans future improvement. Your Grandpa still enthusiastically devoted to papers and I, well, if Mama were here to prompt the sentence, she'd say I vented my spleen upon herself and Bud when not better employed.

George Holmes[5] has returned to Rockby. Mr. Lee[6] spent Saturday with us, and we had quite a chess tournament. I was over at Rockby a day or so back. Walton well and sweet. Yesterday I spent in town, first time in many months. Saw Mrs. Dawson. She was a good deal moved to meet me and, as usual, very sweet. Jenny and Frances Lane,[7] I hear, intend to go to the Lucy Cobb. I should be glad to hear Mrs. Soullard was so well pleased that Mamie[8] was with you. We owe them many thanks for their kindness. Write me all your impressions. Your Mother was so much gratified you were pleased on your first hasty visit. I hope and feel your good impression has strengthened.

Do remember me with much affection to Fathers McGuire and Curley.[9] Tell them, I hope they remember me with kindness enough to look after my little daughter, now and then. Present my respectful regards to Sister Bernard.[10] I know she'll be patient with you and love and cheer you on your way. Emma Huger writes of some friends of hers up there, Miss Murray and Miss Hamilton. Your Mother has sent her letters to you. All send a Niagara of love. Mama and Bud have gone to town to church. Goodbye, my precious child. I pray you may be happy and well. Write us very often. Did you have a good time in New York? Always give our love to your Uncle Leroy and write him often. Goodbye, darling, your loving Father, Wm. E. Bird

1. The nuns of the Convent of the Visitation in Georgetown, D.C. Edgeworth Bird had just succeeded in enrolling his daughter in their school near his beloved Georgetown College, which sat "gracefully overlooking the Potomac and the heights of Arlington." George Parsons Lathrop and Rose Hawthorne Lathrop, *A Story of Courage: Annals of the Georgetown Convent of the Visitation of the Blessed Virgin Mary* (Boston and New York, 1894), IV, 6, 7, 10.

2. Sallie Bird's great-uncle Leroy Wiley had retained enough wealth after the war to send her to the Academy of the Visitation.

3. A sewing machine. William O. Grover, a Boston tailor, patented his double chain-stitch action in February 1851.

4. Andrew Jackson Downing wrote *The Architecture of Country Houses*, published by Appleton in New York in 1850.

5. George Holmes at Rockby, Richard Malcolm Johnston's school for boys, the school that Wilson (Bud) Bird attended.

6. Willie Lee of the Rockby faculty, who later went to Mississippi. He gave his desk to Sallie Bird when leaving Georgia.

7. Jenny and Frances Lane, children of Colonel Andrew Jackson Lane of Hancock County.

8. Mamie Soullard, daughter of Edward Soullard, Jr., of Savannah.

9. Father James Curley, meek and shy and a bit shabby in dress, possessed one of the best mathematical minds of his generation. Joseph T. Durkin, *Georgetown University: The Middle Years* (Washington, D.C., 1963), 1. Professor of mathematics and astronomy at Georgetown, he founded the observatory there. Father Curley served the Convent of the Visitation as chaplain and "contributed his invaluable scientific knowledge to the Academy." Lathrop and Lathrop, *A Story of Courage*, 380. Bernard A. Maguire, one of the great rectors of Georgetown, began a second term as president in 1866, adopting official colors of blue and gray, suggesting reunion. *Georgetown University: The Middle Years*, 35.

10. Sister Bernard (M. Bernard Graham) was for many years directress of the academy. She was of a distinguished Virginia family related to George Mason and was born at Gunston Hall. In 1839 she entered the convent at age twenty-eight, leaving a life of ease. *A Story of Courage*, 334–36.

Sallie Bird to Sallie (Saida) Bird

Granite Farm, 2 September 1866

My precious child,

When I came from church today, I was so tired that I thought I could not write to you, but I have concluded, since resting, that I can send a short letter, altho' your Father wrote this morning. I hope you received my long letter and those of Emma and Minnie by your Cousin Howard.[1] Since then another letter has come from Emma, and one also from Lizzie Phinizy,[2] which letter, from being written in pencil, is scarcely worth sending. Yet she writes so affectionately, I've concluded to forward it, as it will cheer your heart to receive such assurances when so far from home.

Walton I saw yesterday at Mrs. Terrell's for an hour. She says she is coming over "ere" long to stay some with me. Amy plans eagerly for her coming and thinks it the event of her life. You can imagine how glad and happy I was to see your dear Father able to drive to town again. We spent the day yesterday with our dearly loved Lucy,[3] who was her own sweet self and who sends you always some loving message. She says she will be sure to send you Hill's[4] picture from Paris. Your precious letters, short and hurried but inexpressibly precious, have all come safely so far—those from Atlanta, Baltimore, and Washington. I almost cried today when Dud Alfriend got our mail for us, handed only one letter that was from Alfred[5] to Wilson.

I looked confidently for your Philadelphia letter but *n'importe* I'll get it Tuesday. I felt so thankful and so relieved that your first impression of Sister Bernard and the school was agreeable. I know you'll study, and I know, my darling, you are capable of high intellectual culture. Remember, my beloved child, in this first separation from all your own kindred, remember my words when we parted that sad, sad morning. Be my good, pure, truthful child. Never neglect your Bible or your prayers. Stick to your Mother's teachings. Ah, I must say follow the precept rather than her example. . . .

We had a charming little flying visit from Coz Sam Barnett. He talked most affectionately of you and begged me to tell you how dearly they all loved you. He said your letters to Sam and Annie were very sweet. Mr. Johnston sends dear love and says he will write you soon. Mrs. Clinch says Walton is really unhappy over your going. The Clinches and Fords[6] have been down. Were very pleasant.

Your dear Grandmother says she will write you as soon as she can get your address. Mamie Lou said the same. Alf Alfriend writes Wilson that Goodloe Yancey[7] is again expelled. Had a fight with a young Comer.[8] I'm very sorry. And F. Lucas[9] and Timmie Rucker had a fight, also, in which Timmie got very badly cut in the neck. The Campbells will probably occupy Lucy's house while she is abroad. I kissed Hill for you, and he talked very sweetly of Coz Saida.

I only meant to send a note, and here's a letter. You can't imagine how much I want to get particulars of you in New York and at Georgetown. I am wondering whether you got to Georgetown in time for Monday's opening. God bless you, my dear, dear child. My heart follows you hour by hour,

Your devoted Mother

Write me about all the listing to whom you may recite. Tell me if you are happy, and if they are kind. Avail yourself of every opportunity in French and music. Speak French wherever you can. We may go to Europe yet. Tell me all about Uncle Leroy. Ah, how I do hope we shall be able to come on next summer.

1. Howard Tinsley, a cousin, had served on the staff of the Fourth Regiment (Doles-Cook Brigade). He surrendered at Appomattox. *Georgia Roster*, 2:810.

2. Eliza, the daughter of Stewart and Marian Cole Phinizy.

3. Lucy Terrell Dawson.

4. Joseph Hill Dawson was born in Sparta 22 July 1864.

5. Alfred Alfriend, a student at the University of Georgia from Hancock County.

6. Mrs. Henry A. Clinch was Ella Ford, daughter of Dr. Lewis D. Ford, of Augusta. Dr. Ford originally owned the Clinch house in Sparta, and his family frequently visited there. A description of the home by Mrs. Terrell Moore was published in the Sparta *Ishmaelite* 30 Jan. 1964.

7. Goodloe Harper Yancey, son of William Lowndes Yancey, entered the University of Georgia 1 Jan. 1866 after fighting in the General Morgan Cavalry Brigade when he was only sixteen. He became a prominent citizen of Athens and

later of Atlanta, where he was secretary of the Prison Commission of Georgia.

8. George Legare Comer of Eufaula, Ala., entered the University of Georgia in February 1866.

9. Frederick B. Lucas of Athens was in the University of Georgia class of 1870.

Sallie Bird to Sallie (Saida) Bird

Granite Farm, 9 and 10 September 1866

My own sweet child,

Your dear letter to your Father from New York has just been received and read. I know you will not understand why I cried over it so much. But my love for you, always devoted and warm, is so tender now that we are so widely separated, that I can scarcely read a line from you, especially if you write as you have done so far, affectionately, without my tears rushing to my eyes. Don't feel for a moment, my darling child, that you have a single trial into which we *all* do not enter. . . .

My dear child, I know the trial of going among strangers and being separated from all those you know best. But my hope is that the sisters will be very kind to you, and that you may find lovable girls and make friends among them. And now that your letter expresses so plainly how much you feel in parting with Minnie and Mamie,[1] their going together and you to yourself, my heart overflows in love and pity for you. But you will soon be all right, precious. Don't despair and feel lonely. . . . You will make friends and be happy, and I cannot doubt the excellence of the school we have selected.

Col. Jones'[2] sweet little notes did me good. I am so glad you sent them, for their tenor assures me of the kind reception which he gave you. We are glad to think of you today as with our darling Eva. Tomorrow, we judge from your letter, you were to go to school. . . . I have been much better for a week past and will, I trust, continue to improve. Your Father, too, is rather better. Bud has been suffering considerably from a large rising on his neck, from swollen glands, I think. The pain has been great, yet he only missed Friday from school.

He was so much better Friday evening that we kept an appointment we had made and went to Rockby to stay a day and night. They kept us till this morning (Sunday), and we had an extremely pleasant visit. I told Walton what you said about tying her ribbon and tied them on for her yesterday. The Fords dined there and the day was quite pleasant, Dr. and Mrs. Ford, Miss Lily[3] and Mrs. Clinch. The colonel was sick and could not come. All asked lovingly after you, and this morning, when your letters came, Mrs. F and Walton gathered round to hear it read. I read most of it to them. Papa sits close by, leans over me and reads and listens together, stopping me occasionally with, "What is that? Read that again." Fanny and Walton send you warm love. So does Mr. J. He says he'll write soon to you. Walton says she is looking eagerly for your letter.

Jack Battle[4] left Saturday. He goes to the University of Virginia soon and wishes to be at home for a while. He is positively engaged to Miss Braddy. George Holmes is back and sends special regards to you. So do Malcolm[5] and Willie Lee. Willie Hill asks often of you and Howard Williams. Malcolm has been to Washington on a visit to Sam Wynn;[6] returned last night. Mr. Hollo[7] joined us one night and played his clarinet delightfully. Dear Lucy, she is sometimes quite bright, considering all things, and sometimes very sad, almost crushed by her sorrow.[8] Mrs. Burnet[9] has returned from Atlanta and I went to see her. She told me all about you, the day you came in Atlanta. Ah, I knew you were feeling the parting from all you loved best on earth. But you have seen such grand sights, such wondrous things, that I know you have been diverted and delighted.

I had a short letter from Uncle Leroy[10] after your arrival. He told me he thought I need not spend one unhappy moment about you, for you seemed to be enjoying yourself, and I was so glad. I knew he loved to see you bright. When you part from him at Georgetown, I know you'll have another trial.

My own darling child, be good and faithful to every duty. Say your prayers as you have been taught to do from your babyhood, and be assured of our own never failing love. . . . Read the little prayer for you I wrote in your album that last day. Do write me anything about your

Cousins Eva and Charlie and of your visit to them. I am so obliged to dear Mrs. Robb[11] for her sweetness to you, and glad she liked your playing. Do your best, always. Try to improve any opportunity.

I hope Eva will write me soon. I am glad the grayheaded gentleman was pleased with you. I am always pleased when elderly people are pleased with my children. Oh, what I would not give to hear the music you've enjoyed! But I would rather do without than have you miss it. Ah, isn't Central Park grand? And the flowers and music! Ah, how I wish I could enjoy them! Never mind, perhaps next summer. I had a long letter from Aunt Ellen[12] today. She sends you a great deal of love.

Papa says bless your heart! Hold up your head and be brave. Never mind being parted from your young friends. . . . I wish I could hold you to my heart this day, my sweet child, but I commit you to God. . . .

Your devoted Mother

1. Minnie Gresham, Sallie's cousin from Macon, and Mamie Soullard, her friend from Savannah, decided to go to school in Baltimore rather than at Georgetown.

2. In 1866 Charles C. Jones, Jr., moved to New York, where he practiced law until 1877 when he returned to Georgia and lived in Augusta, the home of his second wife, Eva Berrien Eve.

3. Lily Ford, sister of Ella Ford Clinch.

4. Jack Battle, eighteen, was listed in the 1860 census as a student in the household of W. J. Northen, along with twenty-two other young men, students in Northen's school at Mt. Zion. Northen was later governor of Georgia.

5. Malcolm Johnston, son of Richard Malcolm Johnston.

6. Samuel W. Wynn appears in the 1860 census of Wilkes County.

7. No Hollo is listed in the 1860 Georgia census.

8. Lucy Terrell Dawson was grieving for her mother, William Eliza Terrell, who died that year. Mrs. Terrell was named William for her father, William Rhodes, a wealthy North Carolina planter.

9. Mrs. James H. Burnet or her daughter-in-law, Mrs. William Burnet (Frances Soullard).

10. Uncle Leroy Wiley, prosperous businessman and planter, maintained headquarters in New York. He financed young Sallie's education at Georgetown. Wiley was the brother of Mary Wiley Baxter of Athens.

11. Not identified.

12. Sallie Bird's brother Thomas Baxter married Ellen Scott. They lived in Baltimore following the Civil War.

Sallie Bird to Sallie (Saida) Bird

Granite Farm, 16 September 1866

My precious child,

. . . For three nights I've had very little rest and my head is heavy and my eyes weary from loss of sleep. Dear darling Papa, whose poor body has been so severely shattered by pain for a year past, has had a new form of suffering. This time, however, it is not, we think, connected with his general health. It is a dreadful rising in his ear which has closed the orifice entirely and which has swelled his neck and cheek. But, oh! The pain! It makes my heart ache to see this prolonged torture. The swelling has not broken yet, so that I can't tell when the pain will subside.

George Holmes and Willie Hill came home with Wilson Friday and will be here until tomorrow (Monday). Louise and Terrell Dawson[1] came down on Friday morning and are still here, and Amy Johnston has been here for a week. The little folks were all to have gone home today, but it has been raining steadily all day and they cannot get off. Cousin Lizzie Harris and Jane Connell came down Thursday and staid till Saturday, so you see I've had a house full. . . . They both talked so long and so tenderly of you. . . .

I enclose you M. A. Rutherford's[2] picture which she enclosed for you in a letter to Walton. . . . Walton and Malcolm went to see Jule[3] this Friday and Saturday and were to have returned today, but I suppose, of course, the rain keeps them, as they were in an open buggy. . . . Bud goes on studying, only he has much more to do and is very busy, so busy that he has to study late at night which has inflamed his eyes, and we are trying to arrange the day as to prevent any night work. . . .

Oh, my beloved child, your pictures have come and so delighted us all! . . . The double picture is lovely. I think of both you and dear Mamie. I am so very glad you sent me one, for I think it a far better likeness than the larger one, or single one. Papa, however, likes the single one better. He says the other one is sweet, but this one looks nobler. You see, we praise you in our letters, if we don't to your face.

I dare not look forward to next summer, so sad and uncertain is life, but can only pray that we may all get on by the time your school closes and spend two happy months in travel and recruiting our health. I am far from well, yet am faithfully following the doctor's prescriptions and hope I shall improve. The anxiety about your Father wears me greatly. I pray God to grant him freedom from pain, after this sad pain is over.

I am rejoiced to hear all you wrote of darling Eva—of your trip up the glorious Hudson and of your going to the theatre. Who is the Mr. Ripley[4] from Macon? He must be a newcomer there as I never heard the name before. You speak of going to the theatre with him, and Papa is quite exercised lest you and he went alone. I think it highly improbable that you did so, and do tell him.

The evening in the Stewart box (you spell the name Stuart—he is the great sugar man. A.L.S. is *Stewart*)[5] must have been delightful, and I'm so glad you've had a chance to enjoy it. . . . I can imagine how glad you were to hear thro' Tom Hamilton[6] of all your dear Athens friends. You spoke of trying for another picture. I hope you did and succeeded finely. Don't forget Caro and M. Lou and Mrs. Whitehead. I like them small, I believe, better than large. As for Mrs. Robb's, it is simply lovely, and what a truly noble face she has. . . . I am glad they like your music. It makes me very glad to think you do anything well. Do improve every hour you can, both in study and practice.

Your Cousin Charlie sent Papa by express today a superb meerschaum pipe with a charming letter. You had just left his house the evening before. He proposes that you spend the winter with them and you and Eva employ masters and study French and Music, and then with his library, great improvement can be made. . . . Of course, it is out of the question for you to give up the school. It is for other things than the school room we wished you to be in Georgetown. . . . I am so glad your tooth is out! Now, take such care of the remainder that you'll never lose another. . . .

Cousin Jane brought a long letter from Mamie and Jule enclosing the poetry you and she wrote for Jule and Walton. The letter was commenced at Poughkeepsie and ends at Baltimore. They had decided to go to a Miss Kummer's, I think, or some such name, instead of to the

Pegram School. Mrs. Soullard[7] was to board at the Gilmer House and Lily to go on as a day scholar at some school with Mamie. . . . Do, Sallie, try to improve in your hand writing. . . . Take pains with your letters, all of them. Write as soon as you can to your dear Grandma. . . . She is so glad you have been with dear Eva and Mrs. Robb. She rarely hears from Sister.[8] . . . And now goodbye, my dear, dear daughter. . . .

Your own affectionate Mother,
S.C.B.

1. Lucy Terrell and Edgar Dawson had four children including Louise and William Terrell Dawson.

2. Mary Ann Rutherford of Athens, the daughter of Williams Rutherford and Laura Cobb, later married Frank Lipscomb. *Dictionary of Georgia Biography,* 2:863–64.

3. Jule Connell, daughter of Jane Baxter Connell of Cornucopia, Mt. Zion.

4. Lorenzo and Samuel Ripley are listed in the 1860 census in Bibb County.

5. Alexander T. Stewart (1803–1876), the great New York merchant, in 1862 opened the largest retail store in the world. After the Civil War he erected on Fifth Avenue what was considered the finest mansion in America. The firm of Robert and Alexander Stuart was a leading refiner of sugar. *Dictionary of American Biography,* 18:3–5; 176–77.

6. Thomas A. Hamilton, son of James S. Hamilton and Rebecca Crawford of Athens. Hull, *Annals of Athens,* 453, 487.

7. Mrs. Edward A. Soullard, Jr. (Cornelia Ann Smith) was staying at the Gilmore House in Baltimore.

8. Mary Gresham of Macon, Ga., who accompanied her daughter Minnie to Baltimore.

Sallie Bird to Sallie (Saida) Bird

Sparta, 28 September 1866

My precious child,

Your dear letter of Wednesday came yesterday. A thousand thanks for the permission given you. But, my darling, I just couldn't live without more than one letter from you during a week. I write from Lucy's[1] where we have spent two days and nights. The first night, your Father went on his first fox hunt. You can scarcely imagine how very glad I am that he is at last able to go out on horseback. They had a very pleasant time, and he is none the worse for it, altho' he was greatly fatigued by the ride. . . .

I write this often to comfort you, my dear darling, for it makes me very sad to think you are homesick. It is very natural, darling, very. How could a loving heart like yours help yearning for the loved ones at home? . . . Your sweet Cousin Lucy says she'll be on the last of October, and then she'll see you often. She will spend the winter in Baltimore and says if you are allowed to leave the convent, she'll come after you and take you to Baltimore to spend Sunday with them. Moreover, best of all, she says she'll take you to hear *Ristori!*[2] Only think of it! What a life-long recollection that will be to you.

I promise you this treat therefore, if you are brave and bright and get over your homesickness. Conquer it as soon and as entirely as possible, and while you must love us dearly and devotedly, you must also try to be happy. . . . Now, remember what a reward, hearing the greatest living tragedienne. In fact, the only woman who could and did successfully rival Rachel.[3] I enclose you a scrap of Emma Harris'[4] wedding cake. Mrs. H and Lucy say you are to dream on it. Emma had a superb outfit. Was married on the 25th and is in Augusta. Wedding very private. Don't fail to tell me all about yourself and your kind friends. I hope you'll love Hallie. It will be such a sweet comfort to me to hear that your heart has clung lovingly to one of your school mates. Do tell me every emotion you have. Your letters are not inspected, so write me all your heart.

I had a letter from the Pitzers today. They send warmest love to you. I write in a room full of talking. Lucy says she knows she is bothering me awfully. She goes the Bay route, and therefore does not pass through Washington, but will go over to see you as soon as she has rested and got settled. She says I am to tell you she is coming to dine with you and will do it. So please expect her. Papa sends a world of love. Bud is at home, of course. Has written to you. Will write again. I'll write very often. This letter is very hurried.

Zeph[5] is very ill; no better I'm sorry to say. Miss Laura sends her love and some verses to you, which I'll enclose in my next, as the cake may grease them. The Wileys, Johnstons, Connells, and Dawsons send a lot of love—and are so glad to hear from you. I staid with Mary Wiley[6] last night. . . . I do thank and love Sister Loretta[7] for her goodness to you. May heaven bless her and Sister Bernard for the bunch of flowers. That was sweet. I'll write a long letter next mail. Your devoted Mother, S.C.B.

1. Lucy Terrell Dawson.

2. Adelaide Ristori (1822–1906), Italian actress. She won acclaim in Paris in 1855 and paid the first of four visits to the U.S. in 1866 where she had great success with Giacomatti's *Elizabeth,* an Italian study of the English sovereign.

3. Rachel (1821–1858), French actress whose real name was Elizabeth Felix. She toured the United States in 1855.

4. Emma Harris was the daughter of Myles G. and Lucy Harris of Hancock County.

5. Zephemine, a servant at Granite Farm.

6. Mary Wiley was the wife of William Wiley.

7. Sister Loretto (not Loretta) entered the Convent of the Visitation in 1852, soon after being graduated there. She was directress of the Academy and was twice elected mother superior, filling the office of directress at the same time. She died in 1893. *A Story of Courage,* 332–33.

Edgeworth Bird to Sallie (Saida) Bird

Granite Farm, 30 September 1866

Another letter from you today, my darling child, and you've been so good about writing, never letting us be uneasy about not hearing from you, that it would indeed seem hard not to keep you abundantly supplied with news from home. You need never fear it, my daughter, while Mama wields so glib a pen and you shall not be neglected by Papa, tho' not quite so *au fait* at such matters as the Mother Bird. I believe she has also written today. You should see what a welcome your letters have. How Mama weeps and laughs together, weeps that you have been so sad and homesick and laughs that all that sort of thing is to so soon pass away and you are to be so happy and contented as you make acquaintances and select a few congenial friends to be admitted to the inner temple.

Of course you were depressed to be among all strangers and have a hundred or more strange eyes on you. One was almost enough to unman our beloved Davis, but in your case all that was to quickly subside and your good strong sense was to walk in and say, "I must shake off this sadness, Mamie and Minnie are 40 miles away, but then here's Hallie. We are beginning to love each other and I'll form other friendships and Papa was right about the advantages I'd have here. What mind would not brighten and mature under such culture as Sister Loretta gives, and such music and French advantages—and then I am to be so good, and then who knows but what I am to make Papa happy by looking at matters as he does. . . ."

I know you'll not stay there long, but I'm glad you find such competent teachers. I am assured of what you will accomplish, now that you have a chance. Are you alone in your studies and are all your recitations to Sister Loretta? Your letter makes that impression. I am really sorry that you do not have two years there. I am sure you do not longer wish you were at Baltimore, even to be with the girls. I assure you your advantages are manyfold better than they have. Are you not struck with the nice adjustment of one's time? Recreation and study are so well intermixed that one is not overburdened.

How was your Uncle Leroy pleased? But everything was so new mannered and strange to him. Don't fail to write him quite often and, daughter, don't delay too long writing your Grandpa. Send him a letter at intervals. Are there not some Capertons there? Daughters of Hugh Caperton[1] who married Miss Mosher; was at college awhile during my time. And have you learned whether Mr. Walter Cox[2] lives in Georgetown? A lawyer, I think. Is he married? Ask some of the town girls. I presume Joe Semmes' daughter has gone to the Convent of the Sacred Heart. His sister, Mrs. Eda Clark, was recommending it so highly to Eva. I prefer you where you are, tho' Eva and Charlie Jones are dear souls and we love them greatly for their interest in you. Always remember me with affection to Father Maguire, Curley, and my well remembered friends on College Hill. I know they will feel an interest in you.

I think Jeff Lane[3] will surely go to Georgetown in September next, and most probably Bud also, but we can't spare you both at once. Would it not have been better for you to have been in the regular course? How I do wish you could have been there two years. Well, avail yourself fully of this year's opportunity. Your uncle writes that at the end of your term of study he will give Minnie and yourself quite a holiday airing, and that he won't spare you home until frost. Can you imagine one of more genuine liberal kindness, and isn't he the dearest of uncles to yourself and Mama? Don't fail to make him understand that you appreciate all he does for you, by frequent and affectionate letters. I returned home yesterday from a visit of several days to the Wileys and town. Took one foxhunt. Enjoyed it, but was awfully broken down, but felt I have improved.

Have suffered much from a rising in the ear. Am now nearly well of it. There has been an elopement in town. Billy Martin[4] and Miss Nannie Reeves decamped to Hamburg, S.C. and were made one. She is younger than you. The affair furnished gossip for a day. I happened to be in town the morning they left. I shouldn't hold up the example for imitation. You don't say whether you got the prayer book, or did you find better use for your small change? Let us know if you have any pocket money and what you are to do with it. . . .

At present, your Mama is especially enthusiastic about Sisters Loretta and Blandine. Her unflinching attention is to haunt any of the sisters who don't treat you mighty well; please, for humanity's sake, put them on their guard. Mrs. Dawson, God bless her, proposes to spend the winter in Baltimore, for which I am very sorry, and expresses her resolve to run over to see you now and then, at which you are quite ecstatic. She designs to steal you for a few days, if Ristori should visit Baltimore, that you may hear the great Tragedienne, but I tell her that this is very doubtful, and rests entirely with Sister Bernard.

Mrs. D is your Mother's dearest friend, but Sister B is the present arbiter of your destiny. Jule Connell was confirmed the other day, rather a sudden affair, I take it, neither father or mother present, and travelling the wrong way, to be sure. Jule is a dear sweet girl, and I am so sorry she isn't with you. Walton promises to write you often. Grandma says there are big revival doings in Athens. Among others, Horace Blease has joined the Methodist Church. I hope the brethren won't object to his playing chess, for Horace handles a skillful lance in a joust of that sort.

Mama Bird and Grandpa all well and send on oceans of love. I am improving with the cool weather. Goodbye, my darling child, may God bless you. . . . Love to all who love you,

Very affectionately,
Your Father,
William E. Bird

1. Hugh Caperton, a native of Union, W. Va., took second honors in his class at Georgetown at 1841 commencement exercises. He subsequently studied law at the University of Virginia and was admitted to the bar of the District of Columbia 14 Jan. 1843. He married a daughter of "the late James Mosher." *Georgetown College Journal*, 6:18–19.

2. Walter Smith Cox, a judge of the Supreme Court of the District of Columbia, graduated from Georgetown College in 1843. He married Margaret Dunlop, who died young, leaving two children. *Georgetowner*, 14 Jan. 1971.

3. Jeff Lane and Wilson (Bud) Bird went to the University of Georgia.

4. Billy Martin was possibly William T. Martin, listed as first sergeant, Company E, 15th Georgia Volunteer Infantry, Hancock Volunteers. The 1860 census lists William Martin, a clerk, age seventeen, living in the household of I. T. Martin, blacksmith.

Sallie Bird to Sallie (Saida) Bird

Granite Farm, 9 October 1866

My darling,

Your letter to Bud is just received and read. It always cheers me immensely to get your affectionate loving words, and I am so happy to see that this letter had not one homesick word in it. Your going out to the gallery to steal a little cry was very natural, when you received mine and Bud's letters. I hope you've received Papa's long one and mine equally long, written since. Cousin Sam Barnett and your young friend and Cousin Sam are to spend tonight with us. This is Court Week in Sparta, and he will be out this evening. Young Sam comes over in the buggy for his Father, as he will be needed at home sooner on account of the installation of a new minister.

I've just received a letter from Mother in which she acknowledges your letter, and one from Minnie. Says she cannot write to either of you except by messages through Sister and myself. I had also a long letter from Sister. Josiah Casey has joined the Methodist Church, Charley DuBose[1] the Presbyterian. Ginny Lane had called very socially and friendly to see Mother, and she liked her for it. We have very earnest hopes that Richard will buy the Latimer place. If so, 'twill be a great accession to our happiness and social ranks here. Walton sent me one of her illegible notes today. If I have room, I'll enclose it. Are my letters to you opened? I enclosed $5 in my last to you. Shall enclose $5 in this. Get one of the Sisters to take care of it for you, till you need it.

I've heard of the Monteeros in Richmond in some way, but forget which. Bud is going to get a full account of the family of Roziers, etc. from his Grandpa on Saturday and write it, so that you and your Dulany friend may talk it over. Do they know the Daingerfield Lewis (he is of that family) who is to marry the pretty Nowal Caskin of Richmond, Mrs. Morris' niece? The lady who raised or brought up your grandfather was Miss Harriet Rozier who afterwards married Dr. Henry Daingerfield, so I heard your Grandpa say today. One of the Misses Rozier married a Dulaney. How familiar all these names seem!

How often and with what ineffable tenderness I've heard your Grandma dwell upon them, and Papa always said, "Aunt Daingerfield and Aunt DeCourcy" and so on, and Mrs. May (who has just lost her husband), he called Cousin Henrietta. She was Miss DeCourcy.[2] Don't you remember the pretty ivory miniatures that used to be on the parlor mantel piece in Sparta and the pictures of Miss Harriet Rozier and her sister that are still here?

How glad, how glad I shall be, if dear Eva does get to see you, only you are not to be homesick after she is gone. I'll write Sister Bernard by Lucy, or about that time, that you may go out with her when it does not interfere with your studies. Just here, Papa returned from a fox hunt, and it was nearly dark, so I sat by him as he lay on the couch, and listened to the adventures of the field. He was sent for last night by Mr. Dawson to join the hunt, and went up to town after tea—staid at Mrs. Dawson's and they had a glorious day. Caught a large, superb red fox—ran him in the ground, dug him out, and then brought him to town.

They now have him chained and locked up and, poor fellow, he is to be run again tomorrow morning. Only think, the Rockby boys are to have the benefit of it. The fox is to be let loose there. The "meet" takes place there at day break and the boys are to have holiday. They are wild with delight at the prospect, judging from Bud's delight.

Mr. Dawson is always so eager to get Wilson into such pleasures, that I really feel grateful to him. The hunting party came back to Mrs. Dawson's, took dinner, and Papa came home late this evening: quite tired and delighted, and no worse for his fatigue. On the contrary, says it does him good. I really trust it is so. At any rate, it gladdened my heart to see him mounted and able to ride once more. What do you think? I've actually written today to Emma Huger. I felt so drawn to her by hearing of her frequent letters to you, and then I knew her interest in Athens, so I wrote giving her the latest dots from Mother's letters. The Barnetts did not come tonight—were persuaded to go by Rockby and see the fun in the morning. They come here after it. . . .

Piney Thomas[3] and Mr. Adams were married by Mr. Burkhead assisted by Dr. Lipscomb. The papa-in-law sent as a bridal gift 137 volumes of poetry! I'd like to select what I fancy among them. It would be a treat. Caro, Mary Lou, and Ham, have all professed communion, and I suppose will all be Methodists. By the way, don't be too much taken with the "white veil" and chapel decorations, etc. I incline more and more, I think, to the pure, simple faith of my fathers.

And let me say here, my child, you must take more care with your direction, at least of your letters. Every word you write is so precious to me, and to us all, that they deserve to be enshrined more fittingly. . . . I'm sorry you write with pencil for we read and reread. . . . Do you ever kiss the nuns? If so, kiss Sister Loretta for me and tell her how I bless her for every kind word she utters to my darling. Beg her to write to me. Tell Sister Bernard I look eagerly for a reply to my letter, for I know I will have news of you. . . . Papa and Bud send hearts full of love to their absent darling. Your devoted Mother, S.C.B.

1. Charles DuBose was the son of Sparta attorney Charles Wilds DuBose and his wife Catharine Ann Richards.

2. Aunt DeCourcy was Eliza, daughter of Henry Notley Rozier of Notley Hall, Prince Georges County, Md. She married

William Henry DeCourcy, a planter who died in 1848 and who was the son of Captain Edward DeCourcy of the Revolutionary army. Cousin Henrietta was Eliza Rozier DeCourcy's daughter who married Henry May.

3. Paulina (Piney) Thomas married W. H. Adams. She was the daughter of Stevens Thomas and Isabella Hayes of Athens. Hull, *Annals of Athens*, 475.

Edgeworth Bird to Sallie (Saida) Bird

Granite Farm, 14 October 1866

Last night's mail brought a letter from you, my precious daughter, to gladden our hearts. Johnny Walton and Bud rode up about sundown and brought it down. . . . There was a bright, cheerful tone about this letter which did us all good. . . . Be frank and pleasant to all. This is due to all your school mates but your deep affections are your own to bestow—be very careful they are properly placed.

We had quite a morning's sport at Rockby a few days since, a captured fox was turned loose and a grand chase ensued. Several of the legal fraternity were present, Mr. Wingfield, Sam Barnett, and John Stephens.[1] The chase came off at sun up and lasted some 20 minutes. After that, some of the boys asked me to get them [a] holiday. I took the legal gents along and together we ran over Colonel Johnston, and so the boys had the whole day. The fox race was delightful. Present, Edgar Dawson, Jim Dawson of Augusta, Louis Ford, Jim Alfriend, Billy Wiley, Epps, Sykes, McMillan, George Davis, W. Dalton Bird, myself, and some few others.

I write these names to please your eye, being home names—but every rose has its thorn. The chase led through some of Mr. Henry Rodgers' fields, and some of his fences were left down. Woe to all of us! Vesuvius in full blast only equals the old gentleman's wrath. The next day he made over to Billy Wiley's and singed him all over. Mr. DeWitt has gone to town again and will go into business. I haven't seen any of the Connells in some time, but hear from them occasionally. Shall probably go there on this day week. Dr. C has sent word to Dawson and myself to come Sunday and arrange for the dogs to meet on his plantation. You see, I am improving as the hot weather goes. The hunts fatigue me awfully but, I think, are of decided benefit. The Fords are very pleasant people and a great acquisition. I like the doctor extremely. How could I forget to say Miss Walton Johnston was one of the mounted field and seemed to enjoy herself greatly under the guidance of one of the Rockby boys. . . .

I tried to add a note in Mama's letter where she warned you against being taken with the *bridal* veils, as she calls them, but the willful young woman wouldn't allow it. I am greatly pleased to find your letters becoming so cheerful. They are like yourself. It's true there isn't much ice cream to be had, and ice cream is a very good thing, but I have a good idea that could be found nearer home. I am sure that dear Sister Loretta will help you put numberless saucers of ice cream of knowledge in your head, and that doesn't melt away so soon.

When your Uncle Leroy comes to see you, can't you have him shown over the establishment? He seemed to think it strange that he was not. You know, while you are there, he is *in loco parentis*. Your Mother will tell you how kind he has been in sending a lot of good things. God bless him, say I. He's a trump of an uncle. Edgar D[2] goes to Columbus tomorrow and your Mother goes up to Mrs. Dawson to spend several days. When he comes back, they go on north, and you'll see Cousin Lucy. Be sure to practice hard to come out from that musical shadow you represent yourself as being in, but I know you do not need urging to avail yourself in every way of your present advantages. I know your Uncle L. thinks Minnie is at the best school. I know it's a grand mistake. You must let him see it. Write him cheerfully and take pains with your hand writing.

Mother was brought up in the family of Mrs. Harriet Rozier[3] at Notley Hall, opposite Alexandria on the Maryland side. She had many friends among the Dulaney family. When we visited the DeCourcys, we often dined at Mr. Daniel Dulaney's near Falls Church. In the fall of 1861 our Regiment was quartered one night in the family mansion, a large brick house. I knew it at once. I think it now owned by his son

Daniel, who, when a young man, was in the Navy. Goodbye, my darling child. All well. Your affectionate Father,

William E. Bird

1. John Stephens is listed in the 1860 census of Wilkes County, as is Samuel Barnett.

2. Edgar Dawson.

3. Mrs. Harriet Rozier was the wife of Henry Notley Rozier of Notley Hall. He was executor of the will of Dr. John Casey (Edgeworth Bird's grandfather). The 1790 Maryland census for Prince Georges County lists the household of Henry Rozer [*sic*] as two white males, five free white females, and 120 slaves.

Sallie Bird to Sallie (Saida) Bird

Granite Farm, 17 October 1866

My sweet child,

I expect you'll get a short and hurried letter this time. Your dear Cousin Lucy[1] has been with me all this week, and I have not been able to write you my "semi-weekly." . . . Lucy is quite unwell, so much so that she thinks she must go up home, so I hurriedly write a line to go by her. We are all in our usual health. I have been feeling badly from severe cold, but am better today. Lucy has Hill with her. She says she means to dress him up beautifully, when she goes to see you. I tell her, if the girls at the convent are like all other girls, they'll almost devour this beautiful boy. He is splendid.

Your last letter telling me of the beautiful outfit from New York was received. Oh! daughter, try to appreciate and thank our noble uncle for his generous kindness, and the best proof (and to him the most satisfying) is to take care of your beautiful clothes and don't call on him till spring for anything. Let us know if you need anything we can supply. I am so afraid he'll think you extravagant. . . .

Lucy Alexander is at home, or rather in Washington, Wilkes, as I wrote you. Will probably come by to see us. I am so sorry she did not come by Georgetown to see you. I know she would have done so, if she could have arranged it. . . . Oh, Sallie, you don't know how intensely I watch your career; how ardently I pray to God to make you all my fond heart craves. I saw Walton the other day and gave her your message. She sends much love and says she misses you more and more. . . . Jule C has written, I think. They both talk constantly of you. Be sure to mention the receipt of the various $5 bills I enclose. I've none now, but will try to get change, so as to enclose one in this. I must stop now. Lucy is ready to go. Papa sends a world of love. Dr. Ford and Mrs. Clinch came in sociably to dinner the other day. Willie Lee spent a day and night recently; Bob Pierce[2] last night.

Bud's question for debate is "Was Mary Stuart an accomplice in the murder of Darnley?" He says she was!!

God bless you, darling. A short, hurried letter is better than no letter at all. Mother always sends you her warm love. So did Cousin Sam Barnett.

Your devoted Mother

1. Lucy Terrell Dawson.

2. Bob Pierce was a student at Rockby.

Edgeworth Bird to Sallie (Saida) Bird

Granite Farm, 28 October 1866

My precious little daughter sent us no letter to reach us by today's mail, which caused quite a depression in the spirits market at the farm. . . . Mr. Soullard has returned. I did not see him, but hear he gives glowing accounts of the Baltimore school. I am so glad the girls are well situated, but I am glad you are not at Baltimore in the present threatening times, and I prefer you where you are at all times, and, my darling, I begin to believe from your letters that you are of that opinion. . . .

I'm powerfully exercised about the ice cream and oysters that you don't have, but, never mind, my Bunnie, some of these fine days you shall have them every semi-now and then. Hugh Caperton I remember as a very nice and smart fellow. He was much older than I, but I think I remember I was something of a pet of his. I knew very well the family into which he married. There was a son, Theodore Mosher,[1] in my class til he left college—is he still in Georgetown? We are so much obliged to Miss Nesbit for introducing you to Miss Caperton.[2] Do you hear of a Mr. Walter Cox? He was one of the nicest boys in college. I asked you before to quietly inquire of the day scholars.

I've been riding about a good deal of late and improving with the returning cool weather, but there's a screw loose in my head for a few days past. It's rather corky and inclined to let my heels usurp its place. Shall have to diet a little.

Edgar Dawson and I spent a night at Dr. Connell's recently. Saw Mrs. Eli and Miss Lizzie[3]—delivered your messages to Jule. Their present plan is to send Jule to Charlotte to school. The Connells will not go to Texas, at least for another year. Dr. C went hunting with us next morning. Was well up when the fox went away, and 'twas quite amusing to see his enthusiasm. He shouted gleefully and declared he felt like he was at a camp meeting, and, in fact, quite edified the party by his vivacious ardor. Jule promises to write you oftener. I haven't seen Walton for ten days past. I had three games at chess with Ned Campbell yesterday and was inhospitable enough to beat him.

Poor Zephemine[4] died a day or so since after a lingering illness. Our John and family, and Bill's Isaac and family set out for Liberia day after tomorrow.[5] They go in a ship which leaves Charleston early next month. You ask for all items of home news. I give them as they occur to me. Mama's garden is in splendid order. She has been receiving splendid bulbs and plants from Northern seedsmen and goes into ecstatics every day over anticipated spring blooming; has put out a splendid bed of strawberries, several very choice varieties which I am educated to believe are to grow as large as goose eggs.

And now, dearest daughter, won't you do what Papa wishes—give great care to your *handwrite* when you write to your Uncle Leroy. He thinks the *sentiment* of your letters most excellent and greatly desires an improvement in your handwrite. . . . He is so careful of your feelings, he won't mention it to you himself. . . .

Your loving father,
William E. Bird

1. Theodore Mosher (sometimes Moshier) entered Georgetown 1 May 1832 as a full boarder. He reentered 13 Sept. 1837 and left 15 Feb. 1841.

2. Miss Caperton was a daughter of Hugh Caperton.

3. Mrs. Eli Baxter of Hancock County and her unmarried daughter Elizabeth.

4. Zephemine, a former slave at Granite Farm, had been ill for some time.

5. Former slaves from Sparta, forty-six in number, were to sail for Liberia from Charleston on the *Golconda*, but were prevented from going by the sickness of the headman and the death of two of his children. *Annual Report, American Colonization Society,* vols. 44–53 (Washington, D.C., 1861–70), Fiftieth Annual Report, 10.

Sallie Bird to Sallie (Saida) Bird

Granite Farm, 11 November 1866

My darling,

. . . Willie Lee[1] has come over to see Papa, hearing he was not so well. He will remain during the day. Dr. Alfriend has come down to see Papa, too. They talk of various things while I write to you. We have not had a rain in some weeks, but today is a regular November drizzler. The leaves are falling fast and rustle mournfully. Your Father and I have been trying to imagine that they sound like a pretty piece, "Falling Leaves," and I feel each year more sadly the decay of nature. I used to love Autumn best of all the seasons, but now Spring and Early Summer are my favorites. I love to see nature revive and the early flowers, my sweet pets, come forth again.

We are all getting on as usual. No news at all. I enclosed you a note from Walton[2] recently. She leaves for Athens next Saturday. She and Annie Barnett go for a visit. Edge has just taken a little toddy and some crackers and drank to the health of his little daughter. Bud has just returned from town and brings your dear letter of today one week ago.

Sunday night—It was entirely impossible, my dear child, to write today, while there was such a busy chat around me. So I closed my portfolio and now take my pen again, by lamp light. I do not feel at all like writing, which is rather unusual for me, so I fear I'll send you a dull letter. Willie Lee enjoyed the reading of your letter, for nothing would do your *doting* Papa but that I should read it aloud immediately. . . .

I knew, my precious daughter, that you could take tickets for excellence in all your studies if you chose and I knew that you *chose* for I've felt satisfied of your desire ever since I've observed your faithful devotion to History, etc. Persevere, my darling, and you'll never repent one hour's study. . . .

Willie Lee goes down to Augusta this week to attend Ellen Stovall's[3] wedding. She is to marry Lula's brother and Lula is to be a bridesmaid, so he will meet his lady love. He spoke so gratefully and affectionately today of the happy days he spent at Granite Farm. Says he has never been won by any one as by your Father. . . . Sallie Hunt's[4] wedding finery creates quite a stir, Dr. Alfriend tells us. He says that her Father spent "two or three loads of Cotton" on it in Augusta. I confess it makes one sorry to hear of a girl assuming the cares and duties of a woman, as young as Sallie is. Neppie[5] has been very ill, but has recovered. The physicians report it from tight lacing, so I hear. I always liked Neppie and I really liked her Mother for her warm heart and good sense.

I had a note from Cousin Jane a day or two since. They can't sell Cornucopia, it seems. Cousin J wants to send Baxter to college, and yet wants to send Jule off, too. I am very sorry she can't do both. She says she can't, and thinks her preference should be given to Baxter. I only wish Jule could go to the Academy. It would be the very place for her in every way. Now don't you *breathe* the secret I tell you! Marion V proposed to Walton by letter. W declined. He was very polite and gentlemanly after it. Mr. J told Edge and me of it the other night, but enjoined silence, of course. He told it to bring in something else. Said he told V it was like a boyish attack of measles, would soon pass on. "A 16 year old!" said Mr. J with inimitable drollery of manner. . . .

Walton finds it very dull here now. In truth it is, and unusually so for the young people, I believe. There is great room for improvement in the young society here. Edge had a letter from Mr. Henry Hull today on business. He had one also from Richard who had reached home safely, or rather Athens, but was going on next day to his place where Mother and Kate were. He heard on the cars that Sallie Casey's wedding was a grand affair.[6] Dr. Alfriend told us today (Dr. Will) that he heard they had 400 yards of carpeting spread down between the carriages and the church. It was a capital idea, as it kept all their dresses in nice order, but it seems rather expensive. . . .

We are building a lot of castles in the air relative to Kate and Richard living near us—the pleasant days—the nice drives, etc., we are to have to see one another. Mr. Johnston is delighted and says it will be a great addition to you and Walton. Kate will be charmed, R says. . . .

Bud had a letter from Mrs. Whitehead begging him for a lot of rose cuttings, etc., that he was to send them up, attend to cutting and labelling, etc., and she'd give him the most interesting book she could find. Of course, he'll attend to it with pleasure. She seemed very glad to get your picture, but did not think it did you justice. Oh, how I love to look at mine! The one with Mamie is so pleasant. The single picture looks sad. You must not be thin and white. I insist on that. Take your iron regularly and bitters and eat cold bread as if it was a delicacy.

I am so glad you enjoyed the day and the dinner at Mrs. Caperton's. What did you wear? And you don't wear your little bows, etc.? Do you wear white collars and a breast pin? All the better if you dress plainly. What did you all do at Mrs. C's? And does she live in Georgetown or Washington? And did you see her husband?

I wrote you of the death of dear Sallie DuBose[7] and of poor Zeph. Death is so frequent. It shocks and then the shock is forgotten. I wonder at it, too, for people must feel the uncertainty of life—and yet we live on unmindful of the great eternity before us. Let us love God and keep his commandments and meet in a better world. Pray often and regularly and pray for us as we do for you. . . [close missing]

1. Willie Lee was a teacher at Rockby, Richard Malcolm Johnston's school for boys.

2. Walton Johnston.

3. Ellen was the daughter of Pleasant A. Stovall of Athens and Augusta. She

married James H. Whitner. Hull, *Annals of Athens*, 473.

4. Sallie Hunt was the daughter of William B. Hunt and Elizabeth Anne Alfriend of Hancock County. She married first a Mr. Adams and second John Treadwell. Smith, *History of Hancock County*, 2:91.

5. Neppie Hunt was the daughter of Judkins Hunt and Rebecca Lewis Alfriend. She was a local leader in the activities of the United Daughters of the Confederacy for much of her life.

6. Sarah Berrien Casey married Thomas Saunderson Morgan of Augusta. After her husband's death she became the first president of the Association for the Education of Georgia Mountaineers, honorary president of the trustees of Tallulah Falls Industrial School, and organizer and state regent of the Daughters of the American Revolution. Myers, *Children of Pride*, 1486.

7. Sallie DuBose, daughter of Robert Toombs and wife of Dudley McIver DuBose, died 27 Oct. 1866 in her hometown, Washington, Ga., while her father was in exile in France. Her husband continued to practice law in Washington until his death in 1883.

Edgeworth Bird to Sallie (Saida) Bird

Granite Farm, 15 November 1866

My darling child,

I am to fill Mama's place, especially today, at least to attempt to do so. So you won't have as long and nice a letter as usual. That blessed little woman has a wee briar in her finger, and as she shrinks from the extracting ordeal, it has inflamed and is quite sore, too much so for her to handle the goose quill.

Your friends Walton and Annie B. go to Athens in a day or so on a regular lark. . . . Walton and her father came over day before yesterday in the evening and spent the night. The former remained all day and Mama assisted her in the cunning fashioning of a new dress.

The winter months are just on us. A rain and strong wind today are stripping the Pride of India trees of their last golden leaves. How do you like the cold of the District? The sweeping northwester that rushes down on you from the Georgetown Heights is a rougher and more vigorous wooer than that icy blast that greets us as we pass the fair grounds and which we are accustomed to dread. You must be very careful of yourself in this change of climate and be sure to put on those flannel undershirts Mama wrote Sister Bernard about.

I have to tell you of several weddings we've had of late. First, Berrien Eve, which I presume has come off, then Sallie Casey, which is also *un fait accompli*. I hear there were four hundred yards of carpet spread from the carriages to the church to preserve the trails from soiling. Now we are asked to Edge Eve's[1] wedding—the Miss Lizzie you've heard of. Again our presence is desired to witness how becoming the orange bud will prove to the fair brow of Miss Gayle Lewis.[2]

I'm writing in a great hurry. It is nearly sun down and Bud is to ride Castle Man to town with the letter that it may start to you tomorrow morning, and then Mrs. Ford and mama are sitting by and a great chatting is going on. I suppose mama has already announced it, but I'll repeat that your Uncle Richard has purchased the John S. Latimer place and Kate is to be your near neighbour when you come back. Now isn't that real good news? We accomplished that much to be desired event on the first Tuesday in this month at public sale in Sparta.

You will have received your Grandpa's letter before this reaches you. You've had several disappointments about Mrs. Dawson, but she will certainly go soon and will come home again in February. Your Mother has told me of the last box from that best of our kind friends, Mr. Wiley. Mama sent your cards of merit to him. Daughter, always take great pains in writing him. You see what stress he puts on the handwrite. It is sun down and Bud is waiting. He goes to tea with Lewis Ford and will bring out the mail. Good bye, darling; all send love. Yours lovingly,

William E. Bird

1. Francis Edgeworth Eve married Mary Elizabeth Lamkin of Columbia County, near Augusta, on 20 Nov. 1866. The son of William Joseph Eve and Philoclea Edgeworth Casey, he settled on a plantation near Augusta after his marriage. He later practiced law with his brother-in-law Charles C. Jones, Jr., in Augusta. Myers, *Children of Pride*, 1516.

2. Gayle Lewis was Mary Gayle Lewis, daughter of James Gayle Lewis and Martha Ann Lewis of Hancock County. Smith, *History of Hancock County*, 2:102.

Sallie Bird to Sallie (Saida) Bird

Granite Farm, 30 November 1866

My precious child,

You must try to imagine me seated before the most exquisitely beautiful desk that I ever saw, and christening it by a letter to you. Yes, when Willie Lee presented me with this charming *chef d'oeuvre* three days ago, I resolved that I would send you the first letter penned upon the exquisite magenta lining. . . . My letter, neither in appearance or composition, will be worthy of the delicately lovely desk upon which it is written. Let me describe it. It is of finest rosewood, elaborately inlaid with pearl, lined with magenta velvet, and little apartments in it for every possible convenience. . . .

Now, am I not lucky? For of all things I did surely need just such an affair, only I never dreamed of one so elegant. Willie showed sincere regret at parting with us, and says the happiest hours he has known in Hancock were spent at dear Granite Farm. He said he hoped the desk would serve to keep him in our memories. He has gone to Mississippi to live, and, oh, am I not sorry! For he did bring Bud on so rapidly and the boys were all devoted to him. . . . Rockby closed its school doors yesterday, and Bud is free. He loves school, but evidently enjoys his holiday. . . .

Your Father, bless his heart! is, I think, rather better for ten days past, tho' as yet I see no decrease in the spleen. We are all in love with Hallie's eyes, as seen in the picture sent, for which I send thanks to you both. I do hope some day she will come to see you at home, if I do not meet her before. . . . You must, of course, be kind and polite to Miss M, but intimacy with her when her family is so common, is, of course, out of the question. It is very sad, when you speak in such warm terms of her, but *caste* is absolutely necessary in society.

Papa and Bud have just taken a notion to ride to town, and I am now in a great hurry to finish my letter, so it may prove, after all, shorter than I had intended. To our great surprise, not one of the Cornucopians have been to see sister,[1] nor have Aunt J and Cousin Lizzie[2] been to see me, altho' they named several days, but failed to come. The Wileys, Johnstons and Lucy D all invited her to their houses, and Mrs. Ford called. Lewis Ford gave another dance last night, rode down especially to invite Bud to go and to spend the night, but Bud could not go. Lilla Pardee[3] invited him to a sociable on her birthday, which he did not attend, as Edge and your Aunty and I were absent. He had the house to care for.

If I had another dining room, it would be fine, for my present one looks very library like, since Lucy gave me the library she used to have. It is full of books and looks very inviting. . . . I've made my dress (the Solferino spots), made it Parodi, ripped it all up and remade plain waist, trimmed with velvet and it really looks very stylish. I wish, darling, I could send you a bouquet from the pit. The salvias are superb and white camellias, fuchsias and heliotropes are in bloom, too, and I could send you a sweet cluster.

Papa is ready, so I kiss you my blessing, my own dear child, and commend you to our Father's care. God bless and guide you, sweet one, prays your devoted Mother.

1. Mary Wiley Gresham was visiting from Macon.

2. Cousin Lizzie was Mrs. James Harris, the former Elizabeth Wiley. Aunt J was Julia Richardson Baxter.

3. Lilla Pardee was the daughter of S. A. Pardee, a merchant. She was listed as age nine in the 1860 census.

Sallie Bird to Sallie (Saida) Bird

Granite Farm, 6 December 1866

My precious child,

. . . Cousin Lucy[1] leaves tomorrow for Baltimore. So this letter goes by her and oh, my darling, if I could only go with her and see you as she soon will! I think I could talk you out of that sad feeling which seems to have quite overcome you since Eva's visit. We went to town today to bid our dear friends, the Dawsons, good bye. I loaded them all with kisses for you, my darling. . . . I send one of your white waists and a thick pair of gloves for you.

I don't very highly appreciate Mrs. Maguire's talks to you on Catholicism. I fancy your Father and I are enough to talk to you on religious subjects. Cling to your Mother, no better safeguard in all the world for any child. And daughter, tho' the girls are not all nice, some are, and you can enjoy them. Meanwhile, you have plenty of outside friends and the sisters! You may talk as freely as you please to Lucy. I know her practical good sense ever balances her affection, and she will advise you worthily and well. I have invested her with full powers to talk anti-Catholic to you. . . .

I will write to Sister Bernard by Lucy and ask her to allow you to spend Christmas week with Lucy. . . . And then I'll ask her to allow you to go out to hear Ristori. Do, dear daughter, be sweet and good and return to your duties encouraged and not depressed by being with loved ones. . . . I've just received my cards from Caro's wedding.[2] It is to be very large, I hear, and there are to be three bridal parties. . . . They are to be married at the house, as you can see.

Never mind! When you come home, you and Mary Lou will enjoy yourselves fully and you shall have every pleasure that is proper and that we can afford—*that is*—provided you are my good, true, brave child and do your duty. . . . Think of the charming programme my good uncle has prepared for you next summer! And Sister says he means to give you and Minnie a watch! Now I didn't get that until I was married. And some good years after, in fact.

May God bless you, my daughter, and give you strength to do your duty in every relation of life. You have our happiness too much at heart, I am sure, to pass any time in idle repining after things that the Baltimore girls enjoy. . . . And don't speak against your school to them. . . . You have already assured me of your willingness, yes eagerness, to have Jule Connell go there, because of the excellent opportunities for education. . . .

If you need any pocket money [on the Christmas visit to Baltimore], get it from Mr. Dawson or Lucy. We'll pay them. . . . Edgar said today he would furnish you with as much money as we wished, say a hundred or two! Helas, that would be rather heavy for such poor people as we are now. Goodbye to money for this year. We've barely made the two ends meet. Papa still talks of doing great things next year, if his health improves. I only pray it may. How delightful it would be for us to come on next summer and travel with you! Or see you enjoy the first burst of society! . . .

Be discreet about everything in your visit to Baltimore. Offend no one by exclusiveness. Be as affectionate to Minnie as to Mamie and shew our appreciation of your sweet Cousin Lucy's kindness. . . . The children go as far as Whaley's[3] this P.M. Lucy and Mr. D go there in our carriage tomorrow. Dear sweet Lucy, how I shall miss her, I cannot tell. Papa is on the couch nearby and sends a myriad of kisses to his little one. Bud and Jeff Lane are off hunting. Sallie Hunt was married last night very privately. No one there but relatives and attendants—table (or contents) delicious etc. I've heard no more.

The weather is lovely and I've made great improvements in my grounds. Sister left yesterday. Mary Wiley spent two days with us this week. Goodbye, my darling. God abundantly bless you, prays your Mother.

1. Lucy Dawson.

2. Caro Yancey married Hugh Harris of Athens. Hull, *Annals of Athens*, 453.

3. Whaley's was an inn near Mayfield where the railroad to Augusta terminated until the connecting link to Milledgeville was completed. Hancock County passengers caught all trains at Mayfield. From there they could go to Augusta and make connections north, or they could go to Camak and transfer to a line to Atlanta.

Sallie Bird to Sallie (Saida) Bird

Granite Farm, 4 January 1867

I am going to commence this sheet to you, my dear daughter, but can't tell whether I shall finish it. The day is so dark and so gloomy that it will probably be dark 'ere I can get through. . . . The papers tell of a fearful snowstorm all the way North, and the Northern mails have been greatly interrupted. . . . I enclosed you a letter from my dear Mother . . . that you might see how good she is. The New Year's box of goodies came, and I assure you were very acceptable, inasmuch as we had had no sweet things whatever.

Just imagine how we all are situated, not a negro on the place, but Nina. She still continues faithful and will do all she can for me. I am perfectly quiet and hope to get servants, but can't tell. Things do not look promising as yet, as I wrote you in a former letter. We are all as quiet and peaceable as possible. A great many persons have no servants yet. I'm sorry we refused Isaac's wife (our old Isaac); we did not refuse her, but we spoke discouragingly, and therefore he retreated and hired her to O'Donnell. I hate to dwell so much on servants, and yet there is very little to talk of now, except that all pervading topic. The negroes are fools and stay off; won't make contracts; hoping for more and more.

I wish I could have a nice fire in the parlor tonight, and we could all go there and hear you play. I sigh for the sweet pleasure it will be to me to sit down and listen. I wrote you of the huge dinner at Rockby. No news since my last letter. The snow lies yet on the ground, and there hasn't been a ray of sunshine in a week. If it clears off cold, we are going to try to kill hogs, but where are the hands? . . . I wrote you, I think, that Dr. Ford examined Papa carefully today or the other day and decidedly pronounced him better. Says there is no perceptible diminution of the enlargement in his side. How grateful I am for this assurance.

The Lanes have no hands yet either, and they have several out looking for them. We've got two nice kittens now who amuse us very much by their frolics. . . . I hope you enjoyed your Christmas as much as you expected. . . . Goodbye and God's blessing on you.

Ever your own affectionate Mother,

S.C.B.

EIGHT

The Death of Edgeworth Bird

"Sallie told me, 'Jule, make the room sweet and white for my darling,' and dear Sallie Wiley and I did do it. We set the candles at the head and feet and trimmed them with the beautiful Funebris and laid garlands round them of evergreens, and in the dear hands I placed a bouquet . . ."

JULIA BURNET WHITEHEAD

In the cold snowy days of early January 1867 Edgeworth Bird set out to kill hogs and thus provide meat for his family for the coming months. The restless blacks, moving out of slavery, held back and would not sign contracts for the coming year. Edgeworth finally found white neighbors who helped him with his task. Long ill and weakened by war wounds, he was brought down by pneumonia as he supervised the slaughter in the bitter cold weather.

Soon he lay dying, asking that the priest be sent for. Richard Malcolm Johnston, his lifelong friend, sent one of his students at Rockby to Augusta to bring Father John Kirby to Granite Farm. Edgeworth Bird was dead before the priest arrived. His old friends and neighbors laid him out in his best black suit.

Julia Whitehead to Cornelia Soullard in Baltimore

Granite Farm, 12 January 1867

From this house of woe, dear Mrs. Soullard, I am writing you a few lines to beg you will, as tenderly as your Mother's heart can, break to my dear Saida the news of her Father's death! . . . There is so much sorrow and confusion here I can't collect myself. Mr. Whitehead wrote you of his extreme illness and begged you would go or write to the Sisters Bernard and Loretta to break the news to Saida and prepare her for worse.

He was taken with pneumonia on Monday night and died Friday evening at 1/2 past 7 o'clock. Conscious almost to the end and perfectly willing to go, he fell asleep in Jesus as calmly as an infant on its Mother's breast. Tell the poor child that her Mother seemed very thankful that I was permitted to be with her in this great sorrow, and I remained till her precious Mother[1] got to her. . . . We buried our dear, noble, generous, high hearted friend late yesterday evening[2] beside dear Leila.[3]

Mrs. Baxter and Mr. and Mrs. Richard Baxter are with my dear broken hearted *tearless* Sallie. Sallie Wiley and I were there till they got there. It is not decided what they will do about Saida's coming home. Sallie will leave it to her Mother and Uncle. . . . Sallie wishes you to go or write to her poor child and loves and thanks you for your goodness to her. She did not wish me to telegraph. Would save her as long as possible from the sorrowful news. . . . Love to you all from your friend, Julia C. W.

1. Sallie Bird's mother, Mary Baxter.

2. Some Southerners still speak of the afternoon as evening.

3. The Birds' child who died at age three in 1857.

Julia Whitehead to Sallie (Saida) Bird

Sparta, 24 January 1867

My precious child, my poor heart stricken child! How my heart yearns over yours in this first great sorrow of your young life! . . . I must write, because your heart is grieving for all the details of the past sorrowful two weeks! . . . He was the best husband I ever knew. I feel that if a woman was ever widowed on this earth, that woman is your broken-hearted Mother.

How I wish I could give you every word that fell from those loved lips. But I did not see him till the morning of that fatal Friday, and then his articulation was very indistinct and he could only speak a word at a time. Mama would kiss him and then ask for one for "daughter," and the poor, dying man would turn to Bud to kiss him, too. . . . When Mama asked, "Darling, in whom is your trust?" the answer came, clear and distinct, "Jesus." His lips responded to those kisses almost to the last and serenely, peacefully he fell asleep in Jesus.

Oh, my darling, if you could only have seen him after Mr. Johnston, Mr. DeWitt, Dr. Connel, Mr. Lane, Henry Culver, Sam Wiley and Mr. Hollo dressed him in a full suit of black and laid him on the mattress on Mama's little iron bedstead to the left of your room door, with his head to the west, so calm, so peaceful, so serene, so much handsomer than he has ever looked since he came back from the cruel war, which at last laid him in his grave. . . .

Sallie told me, "Jule, make the room sweet and white for my darling," and dear Sallie Wiley and I did do it. We set the candles at the head and feet and trimmed them with the beautiful Funebris and laid garlands round them of evergreens, and in the dear hands I placed a bouquet of the sweet verbena and geraniums from your pit with a few sweet violets I found. When Walton came, she made some beautiful cresses and we laid them about the dear frame, and Mrs. J sent the bouquet you laid in poor Lucie's hands to lie for a few hours on the dear breast.[1]

Frank[2] went to Augusta for the casket. It was the handsomest one I ever saw. Mrs. Campbell and I laid a wreath of laurel leaves all around the dear figure, after it was placed in the casket. Father Kirby[3] was sent for but did not get here till Saturday morning. He made a few remarks, and read the prayers for the dead and concluded all the services in your room.

At 3 o'clock Sunday the 13th we left Granite Farm, a long procession following the ambulance in which was conveyed the casket, and Frank sitting behind it to keep it steady. Loving hands, sorrowing hearts and streaming eyes, [we] laid him to rest in the end of Mama's yard nearest the street, leaving a space for her between him and Leila, by her desire. Monday morning Mr. Campbell and I went up to fix the yard nice, and covered the mound with earth and laid our gardenias above it. Mrs. C was sick. Sallie chose all the pallbearers, but Dr. Connel, Mr. Johnston, Mr. DeWitt and Will Burnet were sick and she chose others. I can't remember all. The two Wileys and Mr. Lane, H. Culver and Dr. Alfriend, Jack Smith. . . .

I forgot to tell you Fannie Johnston held your picture, the profile, a few hours before he died, and he murmured, "Dear daughter! isn't she pretty!" May God bless and comfort you is the daily prayer of

Your Aunt Jule

1. Lucie, who had recently died, was the daughter of Mr. and Mrs. Richard Malcolm Johnston.

2. Frank Burnet.

3. Father John F. Kirby, stationed in Augusta.

Sallie Bird to Sallie (Saida) Bird

Granite Farm, 29 January 1867

My precious, my beloved child, your dear, loving, heartbroken letters are received regularly. . . . Your grief hurts me to the very heart, and yet, oh yet, how could I fear for you not to grieve for so beloved, so precious a Father. If one evil feeling against mortal creature dwells in that pure heart, I, his wife, his beloved, trusted darling, did not know it. He abhorred sin, yet was so charitable to the sinner. Once when I said, "My precious, you judge everybody so kindly," he said, with that unaffected humility so deep a part of his nature, "Ah, dearest, I am too full of faults myself to dare to judge another."

He was too generous, willing to give of his substance not only to those he loved, but to the poor always. And, oh, daughter, there never lived a man more generous to his wife and children. You know, when he received money, what he did with it? Always handed it to me, sometimes saying playfully, "Give me a little sometimes, can't you, darling?"

Yes, Darling, God helping me I'll try to come to you soon. I shall send a telegram to that effect to Augusta to be sent you that it may comfort you. It will be very hard, but your Uncle John will go with me, he says, and I will see no one I know. And darling, if it will help you to do your precious Father's wish, I shall be repaid. Your blessed Grandma, who cares for me as if I were once again her baby, and without whom, it seems to me, I could not live, wants me to go to you, and helps me by saying she'll take care of your brother while I go. For dear Papa was very anxious for his education to be carried on vigorously, and if he stops, 'twould throw him back.

Don't hide your feelings too much. Weep them out on some dear bosom till I come to you, which I will do as soon as I am able and it is practicable. I try to be brave for your sake, dearest. You must keep well for mine. Your bereaved, sorrowing Mother.

EPILOGUE

OUT OF HER GRIEF and desolation, Sallie Bird eventually found the strength to build a new life for herself and her children. Saida graduated from the Academy of the Visitation in July 1867 and with her cousin Minnie Gresham toured the northern United States and Canada under the tutelage of their great-uncle Leroy Wiley.

Richard Baxter, Sallie's youngest brother, took up residence at Granite Farm with his wife and infant son. Money was a pressing problem for a time, and in the fall the newly widowed Sallie sought a loan from Cousin Jimmy Harris until her crops were sold. He was not able to oblige and suggested she get the money from her cotton broker in Augusta.

Early in 1868 Sallie and her children moved to Athens to the home of their mother and grandmother, Mary Baxter. Wilson (Bud), now called Edgeworth, began attending the University of Georgia. When the dogwoods bloomed that April, Mrs. Baxter was in Macon at the bedside of her dying brother, Leroy Wiley. His death 16 April left her the residual heir to what remained of his estate. John Gresham, tending the estate, went to New York to settle debts and make payments. Sallie wrote her friend Robert Toombs about some business matters she wanted him to check on in Europe.

A year after Leroy Wiley's death, in another Georgia spring, his sister Mary Wiley Baxter died. From her mother's estate, enlarged by bequests from Leroy Wiley, Sallie Bird was able to finance a new life away from painful memories in Georgia. Only weeks after her mother's death, she was at Pen Lucy, Richard Malcolm Johnston's school in Baltimore, visiting her friends the Johnstons, who had moved their school to that city.

Jane Connell had written Elizabeth Harris that the Johnston home was "almost palatial, so elegant, so convenient, with gas, waterworks, baths." Life in Baltimore would be easier than life at Granite Farm; the city was an attractive place for Southerners seeking to escape the rigors of Reconstruction. Sallie Bird established a home at Mt. Vernon Place that became a social and intellectual center. Her lifelong friend Lucy Terrell Dawson had moved to Baltimore from Sparta shortly after the end of the war, and she and her husband Edgar Dawson became well-known leaders there.

In 1871 Saida Bird married Victor Smith, an attorney, son of Confederate General Martin Luther Smith, and they lived at Mt. Vernon Place. Their son Victor Edgeworth Smith established the university newspaper when a student at Johns Hopkins and was active in real estate in New York for many years. Wilson Edgeworth Bird married Imogen Reid in 1877. A son, Andrew Reid Bird, prominent as a Presbyterian minister, was born in 1880. There are numerous descendants of Wilson Edgeworth Bird, but Saida Bird Smith had just the one son, Edgeworth Smith. His only son was Edgeworth Smith, Jr.

The year 1910 saw the deaths of Sallie Bird, her son Wilson Edgeworth, and Lucy Terrell Dawson. Sallie Bird was only thirty-nine when her beloved Edgeworth died. She never remarried. Victor Smith died in 1915 and Saida Bird Smith in 1922. The letters were preserved and handed down by Sallie Bird, then by Saida Bird Smith, then by Edgeworth Smith, Saida's son.

Edgeworth Bird and his infant daughter no longer lie in the Sparta Cemetery. Sallie Bird moved her husband and child to Oconee Hill Cemetery near the University of Georgia campus in Athens. Sallie's father and mother rest there too, among so many familiar names made known as friends and relatives to the reader of these letters. Sallie Bird, her son Edgeworth, her daughter, and her son-in-law Victor Smith are buried in Greenmount Cemetery in Baltimore. Lucy Terrell Dawson rests there, too, alongside her husband.

At the Shoals of the Ogeechee down in Georgia, the once busy spot is quiet. Colonel William Bird's mills are gone and the Aviary, the famous old home where the Georgia Birds were first nurtured, has been gone for almost a century. Colonel Bird is buried there, as is his widow, the spirited Catherine Dalton, who once knew the Washingtons back in Virginia. There, too, is Frances Pamela Casey, the undaunted young mistress of the early Georgia frontier who came to the Aviary as a bride and returned there in death. Granite Farm has vanished, but Frances Pamela's handsome town house in Sparta still stands. Beauty and sadness are there, despair and hope. For the sentient, two centuries of rich history lie everywhere at hand.

BIBLIOGRAPHY

Books and Articles

Andrews, Eliza Frances. *The War-Time Journal of a Georgia Girl.* Edited by Spencer B. King, Jr. Macon, Ga., 1960.

Annual Report, American Colonization Society. Vols. 44–53. Washington, D.C., 1861–70. Reprint 1969.

Augusta, Ga., *City Directory,* 1841, 1859.

Avary, Myrta Lockett, ed. *Recollections of Alexander H. Stephens.* New York, 1910.

Beers, Henry Putney. *Guide to the Archives of the Government of the Confederate States of America.* Washington, D.C., 1968.

Bleser, Carol, ed. *The Hammonds of Redcliffe.* New York and Oxford, 1981.

Boggs, Marion Alexander, ed. *The Alexander Letters, 1787–1900.* Athens, Ga., 1980.

Bonner, James C. "Genesis of Agricultural Reform in the Cotton Belt." *Journal of Southern History* 9 (1943): 475–500.

______. *A History of Georgia Agriculture, 1732–1860.* Athens, Ga., 1964.

______. *Milledgeville: Georgia's Antebellum Capital.* Athens, Ga., 1978.

______. "Profile of a Late Ante-bellum Community." *American Historical Review* 49 (1944): 663–80.

Bowen, Eliza A. *The Story of Wilkes County, Georgia.* Edited by Louise Hays. Marietta, Ga., 1950.

Bowman, John S., ed. *Civil War Almanac.* New York, 1982.

Bryan, T. Conn. *Confederate Georgia.* Athens, Ga., 1953.

Burnham, W. Dean. *Presidential Ballots, 1836–1892.* Baltimore, 1955.

Burt, Nathaniel. *The Perennial Philadelphians: The Anatomy of an American Aristocracy.* Boston, 1963.

Caperton, Hugh, obituary. *Georgetown College Journal* 6 (1877): 18–19.

Carroll, John M. *List of Staff Officers of the Confederate States Army.* Mattituck, N.Y., 1983.

Censer, Jane Turner. *North Carolina Planters and Their Children, 1800–1860.* Baton Rouge, La., 1984.

Chandler, J. A. C., et al., eds. *The South in the Building of the Nation.* 12 vols. Richmond, Va., 1909.

Coleman, Kenneth. *Confederate Athens.* Athens, Ga., 1967.

———. *Athens, 1861–1865, as Seen Through Letters in the University of Georgia Libraries.* Athens, Ga., 1969.

Coleman, Kenneth, and Charles Stephen Gurr, eds. *Dictionary of Georgia Biography.* 2 vols. Athens, Ga., 1983.

Coulter, E. Merton. *Old Petersburg and the Broad River Valley of Georgia: Their Rise and Decline.* Athens, Ga., 1965.

———. "Madison Springs, Georgia Watering Place." *Georgia Historical Quarterly* 47 (December 1963).

———. *College Life in the Old South.* 1928. Reprinted Athens, Ga., 1983.

Cox, Walter Smith, biographical sketch. *Georgetowner,* 14 Jan. 1871.

Daley, John M. *Georgetown University: Origin and Early Years.* Washington, D.C., 1957.

Davidson, Grace Gillam. "Colonel William Bird of the Shoals of Ogeechee." Atlanta *Journal,* 8 Nov. 1936.

———. *Early Records of Georgia.* 2 vols. Macon, Ga., 1932.

Davis, Burke. *The Long Surrender.* New York, 1985.

Dempsey, Elam Franklin. *Atticus Green Haygood.* Nashville, Tenn., 1939.

Dickson, David, and James M. Smith. *David Dickson's and James M. Smith's Farming.* Atlanta, 1910.

Donnelly, Edward C., obituary. *Georgetown College Journal,* January 1891.

DuBose, Dudley McIver. "Fifteenth Georgia at Gettysburg." *Southern Historical Society Papers* 19 (1891): 179–83.

DuBose, John Witherspoon. *The Life and Times of William Lowndes Yancey.* 2 vols. 1892. Reprinted New York, 1942.

Durkin, Joseph T. *Georgetown University: The Middle Years (1840–1900).* Washington, D.C., 1963.

Estes, Claud. *List of Field Officers, Regiments and Battalions in the Confederate States Army, 1861–65.* Macon, Ga., 1912.

Faust, Patricia L., ed. *Historical Times Illustrated Encyclopedia of the Civil War.* New York, 1986.

Ferslew, W. Eugene, comp. *The Second Annual Directory for the City of Richmond to Which Is Added a Business List for 1860.* Richmond, 1860.

Freeman, Douglas Southall. *Lee.* An abridgement by Richard Harwell of Freeman's four-volume *Robert E. Lee.* New York, 1961.

Friedman, Jean E. *The Enclosed Garden: Women and Community in the Evangelical South, 1830–1900*. Chapel Hill, N.C., 1985.

Georgia Historical Markers. Valdosta, Ga., 1973.

Gilmer, George R. *Sketches of Some of the First Settlers of Upper Georgia*. 1855. Reprinted Baltimore, 1965.

Harter, Eugene C. *The Lost Colony of the Confederacy*. Jackson, Miss., 1985.

Haynes, Draughton S. *The Field Diary of a Confederate Soldier*. Darien, Ga., 1963.

Henderson, Lillian, comp. *Roster of the Confederate Soldiers of Georgia, 1861–65*. 6 vols. Atlanta, 1955–62.

Hitchcock, Bert. *Richard Malcolm Johnston*. Boston, 1978.

Hull, Augustus Longstreet. *Annals of Athens, Georgia, 1801–1901*. Athens, Ga., 1906.

_____. *A Historical Sketch of the University of Georgia*. Athens, Ga., 1894.

Hynds, Ernest C. *Antebellum Athens and Clarke County, Georgia*, Athens, Ga., 1974.

Johnston, Richard Malcolm. *Autobiography of Richard Malcolm Johnston*. Washington, D.C., 1900.

_____. *Dukesborough Tales*. Baltimore, 1871.

Jones, Charles C. *Military Operations in Georgia During the War Between the States*. Augusta, Ga., 1893.

Jones, Charles Edgeworth. *Georgia in the War, 1861–65*. Augusta, Ga., 1909.

Jordan, Weymouth T., Jr., comp. *North Carolina Troops, 1861–1865: A Roster, Vol. IV Infantry*. Raleigh, N.C., 1973.

Ketchum, Richard M., ed. *The American Heritage Picture History of the Civil War*. New York, 1960.

King, Spencer B. *Sound of Drums*. Macon, Ga., 1984.

Lane, Mills, ed. *Marching Through Georgia: William T. Sherman's Personal Narrative of His March Through Georgia*. New York, 1978.

_____, ed. *The Architecture of Georgia*. Savannah, 1976.

Lathrop, George Parsons, and Rose Hawthorne Lathrop. *A Story of Courage: Annals of the Georgetown Convent of the Visitation of the Blessed Virgin Mary*. Boston and New York, 1894.

Leslie, Kent. "Amanda America Dickson." *Mind and Nature*, Jan. 1984, vol. 3, no. 1. Published by the Graduate School of Arts and Sciences, Emory University.

Linley, John. *Architecture of Middle Georgia: The Oconee Area*. Athens, Ga., 1972.

Long, E. B. and Barbara Long. *The Civil War Day by Day.* Garden City, N.Y., 1977.

Malone, Dumas, ed. *Dictionary of American Biography.* New York, 1936.

Mann, Harold W. *Atticus Greene Haygood: Methodist Bishop, Editor, and Educator.* Athens, Ga., 1965.

Marshall, Charlotte Thomas, ed. *Oconee Hill Cemetery.* Athens, Ga., 1971.

McCall, Mrs. Howard H., comp. *Roster of Revolutionary Soldiers in Georgia*. 4 vols. Baltimore, 1968.

Musgrave, Sir William, comp., and Sir George Armytage, ed. *Obituary Prior to 1800,* vol. 2. London, 1900.

Myers, Robert Manson, ed. *The Children of Pride: A True Story of Georgia and the Civil War.* New Haven and London, 1972.

National Society of Colonial Dames of America in the State of Georgia. *Early Georgia Portraits, 1715–1870*. Athens, Ga., 1975.

Naval History Division, Navy Department. *Civil War Naval Chronology, 1861–1865*. Washington, D.C., 1961.

Northen, William J. *Men of Mark in Georgia*. 2 vols. Atlanta, 1907–1912.

O'Connell, J. J. *Catholicity in the Carolinas and Georgia*. New York and Montreal, 1879.

Osborn, Thomas Ward. *The Fiery Trail: A Union Officer's Account of Sherman's Last Campaign*. Edited by Richard Harwell and Philip N. Racine. Knoxville, Tenn., 1986.

Owen, Thomas M. *History of Alabama and Dictionary of Alabama Biography.* 4 vols. Chicago, 1921.

Peterson, Owen. *A Divine Discontent: The Life of Nathan S. S. Beman*. Macon, Ga., 1986.

Phillips, Ulrich Bonnell. *The Life of Robert Toombs*. New York, 1913.

Pratt, W. S. *The New Encyclopedia of Music and Musicians*. New York, 1945.

Randall, J. G., and David Donald. *The Civil War and Reconstruction*. 2nd ed., revised. Lexington, Mass., 1969.

Rosengarten, Theodore. *Tombee: Portrait of a Cotton Planter.* New York, 1986.

Rozier, John. *Black Boss: Political Revolution in a Georgia County.* Athens, Ga., 1982.

———. "William Terrell: Forgotten Benefactor." *Georgia Historical Quarterly* 65 (Summer 1981).

Scharf, J. Thomas. *History of the Confederate States Navy.* Albany, N.Y., 1894.
Smith, Edgeworth, obituary. New York *Times*, 31 Oct. 1952.
Smith, Elizabeth Wiley. *The History of Hancock County, Ga.* 2 vols. Washington, Ga., 1974.
Smith, George G. *The Life and Times of George F. Pierce.* Sparta, Ga., 1888.
Sparks, W. H. *The Memories of Fifty Years.* Philadelphia and Macon, Ga., 1882.
Springs, Katherine Wooten. *The Squires of Springfield.* Charlotte, N.C., 1965.
Stacy, James. *A History of the Presbyterian Church in Georgia.* Atlanta, 1912.
Stegeman, John F. *These Men She Gave: Civil War Diary of Athens, Georgia.* Athens, Ga., 1964.
Stovall, Pleasant A. *Robert Toombs.* New York, 1892.
Stowe, Steven M. *Intimacy and Power in the Old South.* Baltimore, 1987.
Waddell, James D., ed. *Biographical Sketch of Linton Stephens.* Atlanta, 1877.
Wakelyn, Jon L., ed. *Biographical Dictionary of the Confederacy.* Westport, Conn., 1977.
Walker, Joseph E. *Hopewell Village: The Dynamics of a Nineteenth Century Iron-Making Community.* Philadelphia, 1966.
The War of the Rebellion: A Compilation of the Official Records of the Union and Confederate Armies. 128 vols. Washington, D.C., 1880–1901.
Warner, Ezra J. *Generals in Blue.* Baton Rouge, La., 1964.
_____. *Generals in Gray.* Baton Rouge, La., 1959.
Webb, Alfred. *Compendium of Irish Biography.* Dublin, 1878.
White, George. *Historical Collections of Georgia.* New York, 1854.
_____. *Statistics of the State of Georgia.* Savannah, 1849.
Wiley, Bell Irvin. *Embattled Confederates: An Illustrated History of Southerners at War.* New York, 1964.
_____. *Southern Negroes, 1861–65.* New Haven, 1938.
Wilhoit, Virginia Hill, "History of Warren County, Georgia." 6 vols. Typescript, Georgia State Archives, Atlanta, 1933.
Writers' Program, WPA. *Georgia: A Guide to Its Towns and Countryside.* Athens, Ga., 1940.

Manuscript Collections

Samuel L. Barnett Papers, Special Collections, Robert W. Woodruff Library, Emory University.

Baxter family genealogical folder, Georgia State Archives.

Sara Cobb Baxter Papers, Special Collections Department, University of Georgia Libraries.

Binion, John R., Civil War letters, Hancock County, Ga., Special Collections Department, University of Georgia Libraries.

Baxter-Bird-Smith Family Papers, Special Collections Department, University of Georgia Libraries.

Bird, W. Edgeworth, as a student. Georgetown University Archives.

Casey, Frances Pamela, diary. Baxter-Bird-Smith family papers, Special Collections Department, University of Georgia Libraries.

Dawson, Dr. William Terrell. Folder containing miscellaneous data on the Dawson and Terrell families. Special Collections Department, University of Georgia Libraries.

Ivy Duggan Papers, Special Collections, Robert W. Woodruff Library, Emory University.

R. G. Dun and Company Collection, Baker Library, Harvard University Graduate School of Business Administration.

Granite Farm description and a drawing from files of G. L. Dickens, Jr., Milledgeville, Ga. Material compiled by Miss Edith Guill.

John J. Gresham Papers, Special Collections Department, University of Georgia Libraries.

Harris family letters. Collection of Mrs. Ann Harris Marbury, Sparta, Ga.

The papers and diaries of Judge Franklin Lightfoot Little. Collection of Miss Sarah F. Little, Sparta, Ga.

Sparta, Ga., Presbyterian Church. Unpublished history in the files of the Historical Foundation of the Presbyterian and Reformed Churches, Inc., Montreat, N.C.

James Thomas Papers, Special Collections, Robert W. Woodruff Library, Emory University.

Lieutenant John M. Tilley letters. Microfilm Drawer 17, Box 78. Georgia State Archives.

James D. Waddell Papers, Special Collections, Robert W. Woodruff Library, Emory University.

Samuel H. Wiley Papers, Southern Historical Collection, Library of the University of North Carolina at Chapel Hill.

Benjamin C. Yancey Papers, Southern Historical Collection, Library of the University of North Carolina at Chapel Hill.

Government Documents

Bibb County, Ga., wills. On microfilm, Georgia State Archives. Will of Leroy Wiley probated 1868.

Bibb County, Ga., 1860 census.

Chatham County, Ga., 1860 census.

Clarke County, Ga., 1850 census, 1860 census.

Clarke County, Ga., wills. On microfilm, Georgia State Archives. Will of Mrs. Mary Baxter, 1869.

District of Columbia, 1850 census.

Hancock County, Ga., Tax Digest, 1856. Georgia State Archives, microfilm Drawer 55, Box 64.

Hancock County, Ga., 1850 census, 1860 census.

Jefferson County, Ga., 1860 census.

Mobile County, Ala., 1860 census.

Muscogee County, Ga., 1860 census.

Prince Georges County, Md., 1790 census.

Warren County, Ga., Wills 1813, B 15, microfilm, Georgia State Archives.

Wilkes County, Ga., 1860 census.

Newspapers

Atlanta *Journal*

Augusta *Chronicle and Sentinel*

Central Georgian, Sandersville, Ga.

Columbian Museum and Savannah Advertiser

Farmers Gazette, Sparta, Ga.

Hancock Advertiser, Mt. Zion, Ga.

Mirror of the Times, Augusta, Ga.

The Missionary, Mt. Zion, Ga.

New York *Times*

Savannah *Daily Georgian*

Southern Banner, Athens, Ga.

Southern Recorder, Milledgeville, Ga.

Southern Watchman, Athens, Ga.

Sparta, Ga., *Ishmaelite*

Times and Planter, Sparta, Ga.

INDEX